Kickstart Google Apps Script

Unleash End-to-End Automation, Boost Productivity, and Seamless Integration For Your Workspace with Google Apps Script

Dmitry Kostyuk

www.orangeava.com

First Published: July 2025

Published By: Orange Education Pvt Ltd, AVA®

Address: 9, Daryaganj, Delhi, 110002, India

275 New North Road Islington Suite 1314 London,
N1 7AA, United Kingdom

ISBN (PBK): 978-93-49888-52-4
ISBN (E-BOOK): 978-93-49888-47-0

Scan the QR code to explore our entire catalogue

www.orangeava.com

Dedicated To

My Wife Maria, Partner in Late-Night Coding, Whose Healthy Dinners Kept the Keyboard Clacking

The Worldwide Circle of Google Developer Experts, Apps Script Developers, My Blog Readers, and Every Client Who Grasped the Business Edge Inside a Few Lines of Code. You Asked the Tough Questions; You Celebrated Each Tiny Win. Powerful

Every Curious Mind Ready to Turn Imagination Into Scripts

About the Author

Dmitry Kostyuk is a recognized Google Developer Expert for both Google Workspace and Cloud technologies. He is the founder of Wurkspaces.dev OÜ, a consultancy specializing in transforming disorganized spreadsheets and scattered documents into efficient, code-driven workflows that teams depend upon.

Writing and instruction are central to Dmitry's expertise. His articles, such as notable pieces such as "*Steer Clear of These onEdit Traps in Google Apps Script: Top 3 Tips!*", "*Google Sheets Meets Game of Life: My Google Apps Script Adventure*", and "*Service Accounts & OAuth2 in Google Apps Script: Your A-Z Guide* 🛠", are widely read. These publications complement his popular FOSS project, Apps Script Engine – a comprehensive GitHub starter kit encompassing frameworks, developer tools, and CI/CD scaffolding, among other contributions.

Dmitry frequently speaks at various events—from major conferences such as Google Cloud Next to community-focused gatherings such as Google DevFests and Google Workspace Developer Summits—where he shares valuable, experience-based patterns that significantly reduce development time.

A frequent traveler, Dmitry engages with inspiring creators across numerous continents, exchanging insights on keyboard shortcuts, culinary recommendations, and innovative concepts in every time zone. His approach encourages connection, continuous learning, and collaborative building.

About the Technical Reviewer

Shivaji Bodkhe is a cloud transformation expert and automation specialist with over 9 years of experience across Google Workspace, Apps Script, AppSheet, and Microsoft 365. His expertise lies in modernizing enterprise IT environments through no-code/low-code solutions, secure SaaS adoption, and scalable automation practices.

Shivaji has delivered impactful technology solutions at organizations such as Okta, Airbus, GlobalFoundries, Genpact, and Searce (including projects for Flipkart, and Titan), where he led initiatives to decommission legacy systems, migrate to cloud platforms, and build intelligent bots and support tools. His work spans sectors including aerospace, pharma, semiconductors, and retail—empowering teams through secure collaboration and AI integration. With over 750 no-code/low-code solutions delivered, more than 1000+ legacy apps replaced, and 100+ security audits under his belt, Shivaji brings deep technical insight and practical problem-solving to every project.

He also shares his passion for automation and cloud transformation through his blog, helping professionals and businesses unlock the full power of Google technologies.

Acknowledgements

Writing a book is never a solo run.

The Google Workspace Developer Relations team created unforgettable events where ideas sparked over coffee and beer, those moments shaped entire chapters.

I also benefited immensely from mentors and peers encountered across the globe, whose shared code snippets, insightful experiences, and constructive feedback provided essential guidance and perspective.

Furthermore, I extend my sincere appreciation to the clients who entrusted me with automating their workflows, from spreadsheets to key performance indicators. Their real-world challenges became compelling case studies, offering practical lessons for us all.

Finally, I thank everyone who played a role in refining the initial drafts, pushing them towards the final, printed form. Their collective support and contributions have been instrumental in making this book a reality.

Preface

Automation is a fundamental principle, a driving force behind efficiency and innovation. The initial exploration into Apps Script stemmed from the need to transcend the limitations of manual spreadsheet operations. A concise, three-line script, executed with a single click, transformed hours of repetitive work into mere moments, a revelation that ignited a deep appreciation for the power of automation.

Over the subsequent decade, this foundational toolset has proven consistently invaluable, whether the task involves orchestrating complex prompt pipelines for Vertex AI or managing intricate shared drive structures. While the applications have evolved - with Sheets seamlessly integrating into BigQuery workflows and the nuances of OAuth operating in conjunction with service accounts - the core philosophy remains steadfast: prioritize rapid deployment, ensure robust data security, and cultivate a positive user experience.

Should these pages rest open before you, it is likely you embody at least one of three key roles: a proficient Workspace user seeking to implement a custom "*Do the boring part*" menu; a JavaScript or AI engineer exploring a lightweight, serverless execution environment; or a team leader tasked with maximizing the utility of your organization's existing technological investments. Regardless of your specific context, the insights within are designed to empower your automation endeavors.

This book is structured to provide a progressive learning journey, commencing with foundational concepts and culminating in advanced solution development, with each chapter thoughtfully building upon the knowledge established in the preceding ones. The exploration begins with the Foundations:

Chapter 1 introduces modern JavaScript within the online editor, offering a crucial starting point for both those new to scripting and those seeking to refresh their understanding.

Chapter 2 clarifies the essential distinction between bound and stand-alone scripts, enabling informed decisions regarding the most appropriate tool for any given automation task.

Chapter 3 delves into the capabilities of SpreadsheetApp for efficient data management.

Chapter 4 examines GmailApp, demonstrating effective techniques for automating email communication and inbox organization.

Chapter 5 guides you through DriveApp for streamlined file and folder management.

Chapter 6 introduces FormApp for the creation and processing of Google Forms.

Chapter 7 continues the automation journey with CalendarApp, unlocking the potential for efficient event management.

Chapter 8 explores SlidesApp, showcasing methods for dynamic presentation manipulation.

Chapter 9 covers DocumentApp, enabling the programmatic generation of dynamic content within Google Docs.

Chapter 10 unpacks the event-driven core of automation: triggers.

Chapter 11 guides you through the process of building custom user interfaces (UIs).

Chapter 12 explores the development of Web Apps using `doGet()` and other essential functions.

Chapter 13 bridges your scripts to the external digital world through the integration of external APIs using UrlFetchApp and the implementation of webhooks, expanding connectivity and integration possibilities.

Chapter 14 offers a comprehensive set of practical exercises and detailed solutions designed to solidify your understanding across all the key areas covered.

Embark on this exploration, and allow the power of scripting to streamline your workflows, freeing you to focus on more strategic and innovative endeavors.

Get a Free eBook

We hope you are enjoying your recently purchased book! Your feedback is incredibly valuable to us, and to all other readers looking for great books.

If you found this book helpful or enjoyable, we would truly appreciate it, if you could take a moment to leave a short review with a 5 star rating on Amazon. It helps us grow, and lets other readers discover our books.

As a thank you, we would love to send you a free digital copy of this book, and a **30%** discount code on your next cart value on our official websites:

www.orangeava.com

www.orangeava.in (For Indian Subcontinent)

☑ **Here's how:**

Leave a review for the book on Amazon.

Take a screenshot of your review, and send an email to **info@orangeava.com** (it can be just the confirmation screen).

Once, we receive your screenshot, we will send you the digital file, within 24 hours.

Thank you so much for your support – it means a lot to us!

Downloading the code bundles and colored images

Please follow the links or scan the QR codes to download the ***Code Bundles and Images*** of the book:

https://github.com/ava-orange-education/Kickstart-Google-Apps-Script

The code bundles and images of the book are also hosted on ***https://rebrand.ly/eeogjm9***

In case there's an update to the code, it will be updated on the existing GitHub repository.

Errata

We take immense pride in our work at **Orange Education Pvt Ltd,** and follow best practices to ensure the accuracy of our content to provide an indulging reading experience to our subscribers. Our readers are our mirrors, and we use their inputs to reflect and improve upon human errors, if any, that may have occurred during the publishing processes involved. To let us maintain the quality and help us reach out to any readers who might be having difficulties due to any unforeseen errors, please write to us at :

errata@orangeava.com

Your support, suggestions, and feedback are highly appreciated.

DID YOU KNOW

Did you know that Orange Education Pvt Ltd offers eBook versions of every book published, with PDF and ePub files available? You can upgrade to the eBook version at **www.orangeava.com** and as a print book customer, you are entitled to a discount on the eBook copy. Get in touch with us at: **info@orangeava.com** for more details.

At **www.orangeava.com**, you can also read a collection of free technical articles, sign up for a range of free newsletters, and receive exclusive discounts and offers on Print Books and eBooks.

PIRACY

If you come across any illegal copies of our works in any form on the internet, we would be grateful if you would provide us with the location address or website name. Please contact us at **info@orangeava.com** with a link to the material.

ARE YOU INTERESTED IN AUTHORING WITH US?

If there is a topic that you have expertise in, and you are interested in either writing or contributing to a book, please write to us at **business@orangeava.com**. We are on a journey to help developers and tech professionals to gain insights on the present technological advancements and innovations happening across the globe and build a community that believes Knowledge is best acquired by sharing and learning with others. Please reach out to us to learn what our audience demands and how you can be part of this educational reform. We also welcome ideas from tech experts and help them build learning and development content for their domains.

REVIEWS

Please leave a review. Once you have read and used this book, why not leave a review on the site that you purchased it from? Potential readers can then see and use your unbiased opinion to make purchase decisions. We at Orange Education would love to know what you think about our products, and our authors can learn from your feedback. Thank you!

For more information about Orange Education, please visit **www.orangeava.com**.

Table of Contents

Chapter 1
Introduction to Modern JavaScript in the Online Editor

Disclaimer

Diving into JavaScript is a complex endeavor. This chapter is here to provide a roadmap of its most essential parts.

If you are a seasoned JavaScript developer, feel free to skip this chapter entirely. If you've used JavaScript in the past, but your skills have become a little rusty, use this chapter as a refresher. For those of you who are new to JavaScript, use this chapter as a kick-start; however, the recommendation is to read a dedicated JavaScript book or complete a course before diving into the more advanced chapters in this book.

Introduction

Google Apps Script plays a crucial role in web-based applications. It provides developers with powerful tools to create dynamic integrations and enhance their work. *Chapter 1, Introduction to Modern JavaScript in the Online Editor*, takes you on an exciting journey through the history and evolution of JavaScript, a resilient and influential scripting language.

The chapter teaches you the basics of client-side JavaScript through a practical example. The Integrated Development Environment (IDE) of Google Apps Script is a key feature, and this chapter provides valuable insights into it. You will learn about the core concepts of JavaScript, including variables, arithmetic operations, objects, arrays, and more. From the simple "**`Hello World`**" program to advanced principles such as "**`Scope`**" and "**`Hoisting`**," this chapter serves as a guide for both new and experienced developers.

Get ready for an exciting adventure into the world of JavaScript!

Structure

In this chapter, we will cover the following topics:

- History of JavaScript
- Understanding Client-Side (Browser) JavaScript through a Simple Example
- Discovering Google Apps Script's Integrated Development Environment (IDE)
- Plunging into JavaScript Basics
  - The Classic "**`Hello World`**"
  - Understanding and Utilizing Comments
  - Unraveling the Mysteries of Variables
  - Arithmetic Operators in JavaScript
  - Incrementation and Decrementation in JavaScript
  - Comparison Operators
  - Conditions and Their Multifaceted Charm
  - Functions in JavaScript
  - Understanding Objects in JavaScript
  - Arrays: The Building Blocks of Data Handling
  - Complex Objects and Arrays
  - Scope in JavaScript
  - Hoisting in JavaScript

History of JavaScript

JavaScript was invented in 1995 as a scripting language for the Netscape Communicator browser. If JavaScript were a movie, its tagline might be, "*Born for the web, thriving everywhere!*" Its initial purpose was to make static websites more interactive. But with time, JavaScript evolved to run in other environments. Specifically, in 2009, Ryan Dahl created Node.js that allowed JavaScript to run on the server. In the same year, Google introduced Google Apps Script that allowed serverless execution of JavaScript in the environment of what was then called Google Apps for Work.

It is essential to make the following distinction:

- JavaScript is a programming language.
- This language can run in different environments, such as browsers, Google Apps Script, Node.js, and so on.

- Google Apps Script is one such environment that allows users to manipulate applications in Google Workspace, be it Google Sheets, Gmail, Google Drive, and beyond.

It is still important to know traditional browser JavaScript when working with Google Apps Script when building front-ends for the scripts and crafting stand-alone web apps.

Understanding Client-Side (Browser) JavaScript through a Simple Example

Websites and web apps are built in three different languages:

- Hypertext Markup Language (HTML) implements the structure.
- Cascading Style Sheets (CSS) style web pages with layouts, fonts, colors, and so on.
- JavaScript makes web pages interactive for the end user.

Let us look at a practical example to make things clear.

The Simple Name Greeting Example

Imagine a user is asked to enter their name into a text box and click a button. When they do it, they are greeted with a friendly "**`Hello {name}!`**" message. The possibility of taking and transforming user input into a different output is made possible by JavaScript.

Here is what this component may look like:

***Figure 1.1**: The Dynamic HTML we will build using HTML, CSS, and JavaScript*

Let us now look at the code that makes this happen:

```
<!DOCTYPE html>
<html lang="en">
  <head>
    <meta charset="UTF-8" />
    <meta name="viewport" content="width=device-width, initial
-scale=1.0" />
    <title>HTML/CSS/JS Example</title>
```

```
    <style>
      .button {
        background-color: #4caf50;
        border: none;
        color: white;
        padding: 15px 32px;
        text-align: center;
        text-decoration: none;
        display: inline-block;
        font-size: 16px;
        margin: 4px 2px;
        cursor: pointer;
      }
      .text-input {
        font-size: 16px;
        padding: 12px 20px;
        margin: 8px 0;
        border: 1px solid #ccc;
      }

      div#message {
        font-family: 'Segoe UI', Tahoma, Geneva, Verdana,
sans-serif;
        font-size: 18px;
      }
    </style>
  </head>
  <body>
    <input class="text-input" id="nameInput" type="text" place-
holder="Name" />
    <button class="button" onclick="sayHello()">Say Hello</button>
    <div id="message"></div>

    <script>
      const nameInput = document.getElementById('nameInput');
      const message = document.getElementById('message');

      function sayHello() {
        const name = nameInput.value;
        message.innerHTML = `Hello ${name}!`;
      }
    </script>
  </body>
</html>
```

Breaking Down the Code

- **HTML:** HTML provides the structure. The HTML code that is most important here is the following:

  ```
  <input class="text-input" id="nameInput" type="text" placeholder
  ="Name" />
  <button class="button" onclick="sayHello()">Say Hello</button>
  <div id="message"></div>
  ```

  The **`<input>`** element is the text box where the user enters their name. The **`<button>`** element is the button that the user clicks. The **`<div>`** element is where the greeting appears when the button has been clicked.

- **CSS:** Next, the CSS provides some style to our elements with fonts, colors, margins, borders, and so on. You will notice the **`<style>`** tags encompassing the CSS code. This makes our interface user-friendly. It is optional to have CSS for HTML to work, but it makes all the difference for the user experience!

- **JavaScript:** Last but not least, JavaScript makes our simple web page interactive. When the user clicks the button, it triggers a function named **`sayHello()`**. The function then reads the value the user entered into the text box, adds it to the greeting message, and then displays it in the following **`<div>`** element.

Each of these languages has a specific role to play, and by using all three, we can create dynamic, beautiful, and interactive user experiences on the web. In Google Apps Script, however, JavaScript can do much more than that: it can manipulate spreadsheets, documents, forms, emails, Google Drive files, and all other Google Workspace applications. Let us start diving into Google Apps Script now.

Discovering Google Apps Script's Integrated Development Environment (IDE)

Google Apps Script is relatively easy to get started with because you don't have to set up your machine with complex tools to start writing code. It comes with a free Integrated Development Environment (IDE). You can think of an IDE as a text editor for code packed with valuable tools. To get started, navigate to **`https://script.google.com`**, log in to your Google account if necessary, and click "New Project" to initiate a fresh endeavor.

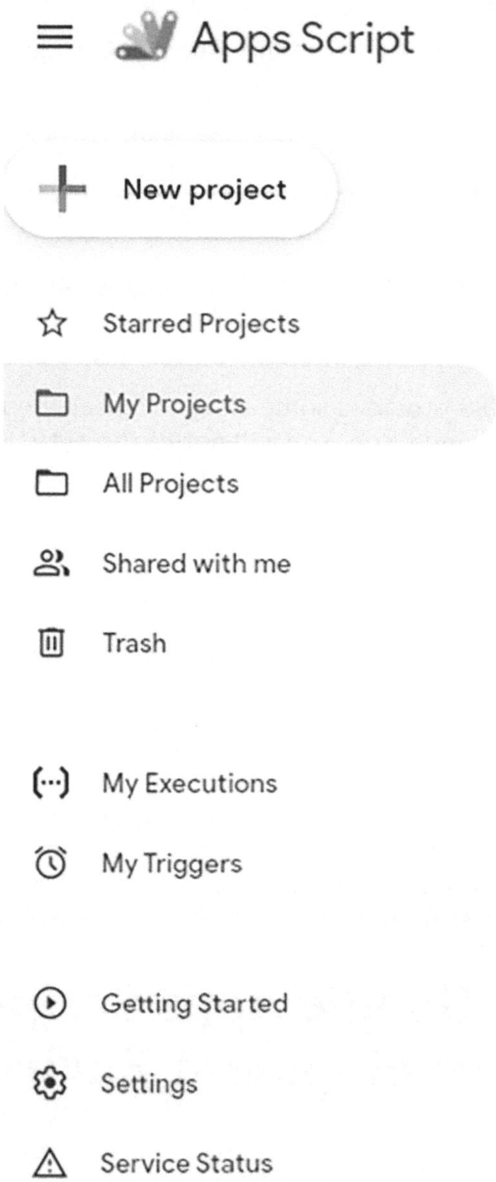

Figure 1.2: *Creating a New Google Apps Script Project*

You see the IDE for Google Apps Script with valuable features such as code highlighting, autocomplete, and a powerful search tool. It also comes with a debugger, access to libraries, event-driven triggers, an execution log, and customizable settings. We will learn to use these tools as we progress through the book.

Google Apps Script is best learned by doing, so let us start writing some code!

Plunging into JavaScript Basics

It is time for some action! Let us get our hands dirty by executing our first lines of Google Apps Script. When you start a new project, the IDE greets you with an empty function named **`myFunction`** – containing a pair of opening and closing curly braces. Hold that thought if you're wondering about the specifics of functions; we will delve deep into that topic later.

The Classic "`Hello World`"

For now, type out **`Logger.log('Hello world')`** between those braces mentioned earlier. Your code should look like this:

```
function myFunction() {
      Logger.log('Hello world');
}
```

Once you've done this, click "**`save`**" and "**`run`**."

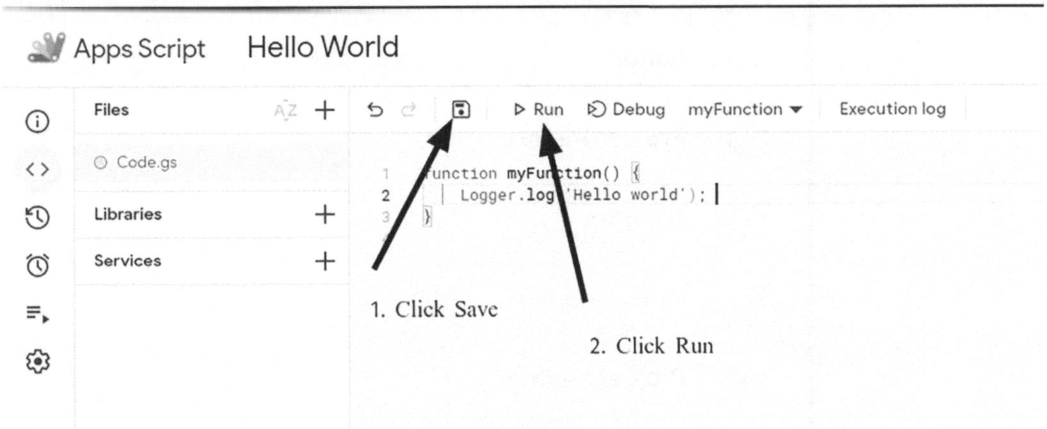

Figure 1.3: *Saving and Running Your Code in the Online Editor*

When you click **`run`**, the execution log will pop up from the bottom of the IDE with the following message:

***Figure 1.4**: The Execution Log of Our "Hello World" Example*

It allows us to see our output immediately. Quite handy. You can also see your previous executions by clicking "**`Executions`**" on the left sidebar. You can then return to the editor by clicking the link on the same sidebar.

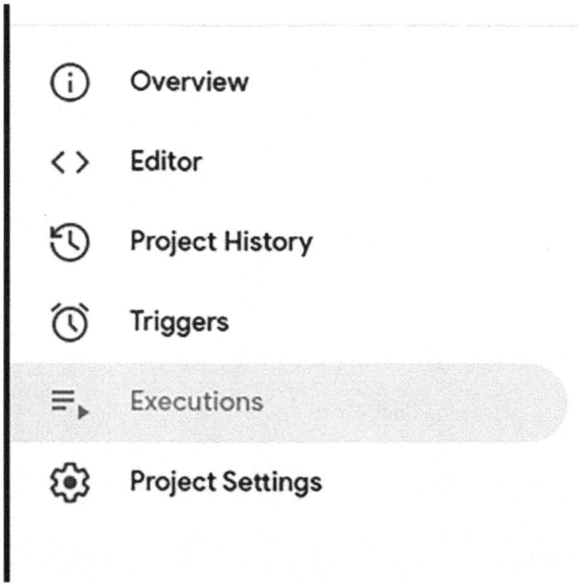

***Figure 1.5**: The Full Execution Log can be Found on the Left Sidebar*

Did you notice the semi-colon at the end of the statement on line two? In JavaScript, semi-colons are used to indicate the end of a statement. Although they are optional in most scenarios, it is essential to know how to use them and how they work – especially for those still journeying through the early stages of JavaScript; hence, the recommendation is to not skip them.

Now, for fun, try tweaking the message within the apostrophes to something unique: a personal greeting or your favorite quote. When you execute it again, the execution log will duly display your updated message.

Speaking of the execution log, let us shed some light on it. This nifty tool permits developers to print messages visible exclusively to them and remain hidden from the user's view. It acts as a trusty beacon, helping us monitor the state of our application, and ensuring we stay on the right path.

Understanding and Utilizing Comments

When you write your code, it is often a good idea to document what it does. Not only will this help other developers if you are working in a team, but it can also help you when you look through the code you wrote a few months ago and are having trouble piecing it all together. This is where comments come in. Comments are blocks of text within your code that are not executed but are purely descriptive annotations designed to provide clarity to human readers.

There are two primary forms of comments in JavaScript:

- Single-line comments, indicated with a double forward slash (`//`)
- Multi-line comments, which start with `/*` and end with `*/`

Let us look at the following example:

```
/*
Our debut function.
It cordially logs a greeting to the execution realm.
*/
function myFunction() {
  // Feel free to modify the message within the apostrophes
  Logger.log('Hello world');
}
```

When you re-run this function, despite the comments, you will see no difference in its behavior.

Unraveling the Mysteries of Variables

Variables in JavaScript are temporary containers that are used to store data. Every variable has to be given a name. We can then use their names to assign, read, or update data that they store.

Let us make a slight change to our function to include a variable:

```
function myFunction() {
  const greeting = 'Hello world';
  Logger.log(greeting);
}
```

Let us discuss how this variable works:

1. The keyword **`const`** is used to declare our variable.
2. Our choice of name, **`greeting`**, is arbitrary; you are the artist; paint it as you wish!
3. The = operator assigns our chosen value, **`'Hello world,'`** to our **`greeting`** variable.
4. The Logger prints the variable's value without needing apostrophes this time. Why? Because omitting apostrophes instructs JavaScript to fetch the variable's value instead of interpreting "**`greeting`**" as text.

Now, **`const`** is not the only way to declare a variable. There are actually three of them: **`const`**, **`let`**, and **`var`**. Each one functions differently from the other two:

- **`const`**: Represents constants whose values you cannot change once one has been assigned. As a guideline, you want to use this keyword about 80% of the time.
- **`let`**: More flexible; you can assign and reassign values to them. If you expect the value assigned to your variable to change, this is your choice.
- **`var`**: The deprecated old-timer of the bunch that you should not use for new projects. It behaves much like **`let`** but with differences in scope and hoisting. Though it is not recommended for use, it appears in legacy code and documentation; hence, you must still know about it.

Variables can hold different basic types of values, known as primitives:

Type	Description	Example
Boolean	Represents either **`true`** or **`false`**	`const a = false;`
Number	Holds integers or floating-point numbers	`const a = 2.34;`
String	A sequence of characters, or text	`const a = 'Hello world';`
Undefined	A value that's... well, not defined yet!	`let a;`
Null	Explicitly set to **`null`**	`let a = null;`
Symbol	Unique, anonymous symbols (a tale for another day)	`let a = Symbol();`

***Table 1.1**: Primitive Data Types in JavaScript*

When naming these variables, it is good to:

- Opt for descriptive names. For instance, **userAge** is clearer than just **a**.
- Employ camel case to separate words, for example, **const userFirstName = 'George';** the first word starts with a lower-case letter, and subsequent words start with a capital one. It is not a requirement, but it is a convention most JavaScript programmers use to make code more readable.

However, there are rules to this naming game:

- Names can include letters, numbers, _, and **$**.
- They must not start with a number.

Try out these principles in action:

```
function myFunction() {
  const userName = 'John'; // string
  Logger.log('My name is ' + userName);

  const userAge = 27;
  Logger.log(userAge);

  const isAdult = true;
  Logger.log(isAdult);

  let userOccupation;
  Logger.log(userOccupation);

  userOccupation = 'Google Apps Script Developer'; // Quite the occupation!
  Logger.log(userOccupation);

  userOccupation = null;
  Logger.log(userOccupation);
}
```

Running this snippet will display various values. Note the string concatenation using **+** on line 3; we use it to merge two pieces of text. Also, note how we reassigned the value of **userOccupation**: we only used the **let** keyword the first time we declared the variable, not the subsequent times we assigned new values to it.

Arithmetic Operators in Google Apps Script

In **Google Apps Script**, we can use the standard **arithmetic operators** to perform mathematical operations.

The Versatile + Operator

Adding numbers together is the most obvious use of the **+** operator. Here is a simple addition operation:

```
function myFunction() {
  const a = 3;
  const b = 2;
  const sum = 3 + 2;
  Logger.log(sum); // This will print 5
}
```

But as we saw earlier, we can also use it to concatenate strings. Let us delve into its dual functionality:

```
function myFunction() {
  const a = 3;
  const b = 2;
  const sum = 3 + 2;
  Logger.log('The sum of a and b is ' + sum);
  // Output: "The sum of a and b is 5"
}
```

Notice how we used the **+** operator twice: the first time to add `3 + 2`, and another time to concatenate the result to a string: `'The sum of a and b is ' + sum`. Let us look at how concatenation works in more detail.

Tricky Concatenation

You must be aware of the catch because we use the same operator for different use cases. When using the + operator with both numbers and strings, JavaScript's type coercion comes into play, potentially leading to unexpected results. Let us inspect further:

```
const a = 3;
const b = 2;

// The incorrect way:
Logger.log('The sum of a and b is ' + a + b); // Output: 32

// The correct way:
Logger.log('The sum of a and b is ' + (a + b)); // Output: 5
```

The issue in the first example arises because JavaScript processes the operators from left to right. Encountering a string and a number, JavaScript converts the number to a string and concatenates the resulting strings. This left-to-right processing leads to the value of b also being concatenated, resulting in `"32"` instead of "**5**." To ensure arithmetic takes precedence, enclose the addition operation in parentheses, guiding JavaScript to add before concatenating.

A Journey with Other Arithmetic Operators

Arithmetic isn't all addition and concatenation, right? Try out the following:

```
function arithmeticOperators() {
  // Addition
  Logger.log('3 + 2 = ' + (3 + 2)); // 3 + 2 = 5
  // Subtraction
  Logger.log('3 - 2 = ' + (3 - 2)); // 3 - 2 = 1
  // Multiplication
  Logger.log('3 * 2 = ' + 3 * 2); // 3 * 2 = 6
  // Division
  Logger.log('3 / 2 = ' + 3 / 2); // 3 / 2 = 1.5
  // Exponentiation
  Logger.log('3 ** 2 = ' + 3 ** 2); // 3 ** 2 = 9
  // Modulus division (returns the remainder)
  Logger.log('3 % 2 = ' + (3 % 2)); // 3 % 2 = 1,
}
```

Incrementation and Decrementation in JavaScript

Incrementation and decrementation operators are fundamental tools that allow developers to smoothly and efficiently manage variable values. As we plunge into this topic, remember that understanding these concepts is pivotal for scripting tasks ranging from simple loops to intricate algorithms.

Starting with the basics, let us observe the straightforward examples:

```
let a = 5;
let b = 11;

a = a + 1;
b = b - 1;

Logger.log(a); // output: 6
Logger.log(b); // output: 10
```

In this example, we use the **let** keyword because we anticipate that the values stored in our variables, **a** and **b**, will undergo a change. The **=** operator is used to assign values to our variables. But here is a fun fact! JavaScript evaluates the right-hand side of the assignment operator before executing the assignment itself. This means that in our first example, JavaScript evaluates **a + 1** (which translates to **5 + 1**), obtaining a value of **6**, and then assigns this resultant value to the variable **a**. The same logic applies to variable **b**, where we decrement its value by one.

Now, because programmers love to be efficient (or just downright lazy), JavaScript provides us with a shortcut:

```
let a = 5;
let b = 11;

a++;
b--;

Logger.log(a); // output: 6
Logger.log(b); // output: 10
```

The operators **++** and **--** are nifty tricks to increment and decrement by a value of 1, respectively. It is like giving your variable a gentle nudge up or down. But sometimes, a gentle nudge isn't enough. What if you want to give it a stronger push? Consider this example:

```
let a = 5;
let b = 11;

a += 3;
b -= 6;

Logger.log(a); // output: 8
Logger.log(b); // output: 5
```

In this case, the `+= <number>` and `-= <number>` operators come to the rescue. These operators increment or decrement the variable by the specified number, effectively streamlining our code. It is like ordering a double espresso instead of a single shot when you need that caffeine boost!

You can also use similar syntax with other arithmetic operators. Feel free to try them out by yourself:

Operator	Example	Same As
+=	x += y	x = x + y
-=	x -= y	x = x - y
*=	x *= y	x = x * y
/=	x /= y	x = x / y
%=	x %= y	x = x % y
**=	x **= y	x = x ** y

Table 1.2: *JavaScript's Arithmetic Operators*

Operators are pivotal tools in the scriptwriter's arsenal; you should get the hang of them early in your learning journey.

Comparison Operators

Comparison operators in JavaScript assess the relationship between two values and return a Boolean result: either true or false. Take the less-than `<` operator, for instance:

```
function myFunction() {
  const a = 67;
  const b = 234;
  const aIsLessThanB = a < b;
  Logger.log(aIsLessThanB); // true
}
```

In the preceding snippet, the expression `a < b` returns true because 67 is indeed less than 234. The outcome is stored in `aIsLessThanB`, which is subsequently printed. Let us look at the full list of operators:

Operator	**Description**
`<`	Less than
`>`	Greater than
`>=`	Greater than or equal to
`<=`	Less than or equal to
`==`	Equal to (compares value only)
`===`	Strictly equal to (compares value and type)
`!=`	Does not equal to (compares value only)
`!==`	Does not strictly equal to (compares value and type)

***Table 1.3**: JavaScript's Comparison Operators*

Notice the different equality and inequality operators, the strict and the regular ones. Let us now examine the difference between the two types:

```
const a = 77;
const b = '77';

Logger.log(a == b); // true
Logger.log(a === b); // false
```

The two variables in the preceding example contain the same value, 77. The difference is that **a** is a number and **b** is a string because of the encapsulating apostrophes.

The first comparison returns `true` because `==` only checks for value, not data type. By contrast, the `===` operator evaluates both value and data type, and it returns `false` because, even though the values match, the data types do not. And, if you've tried typing `a = b` instead of `a == b` and wondered why your script threw an error, here is why: it is because JavaScript thinks you're trying to reassign a "constant." The `=` is an assignment operator, and because **a** was declared with the **const** keyword, this operation is forbidden. This error is a good thing: it lets us know what went wrong; that is how the **const** keyword protects us from accidental bugs in our code.

If you are wondering which of the two types of operators to use, your default choice must always be the strict type, `===` and `!==`. They provide more robustness and avoid side effects that may be caused by implicit type conversion.

Mastering these operators in Google Apps Script paves the way for creating more robust and efficient scripts. As you continue your coding journey, being cautious with operators, especially in contexts like type coercion, can save you from unexpected debugging sessions. Keep practicing, and soon enough, these operators will be second nature.

Conditions and Their Multifaceted Charm

Every choice we make in life or programming depends on conditions. For instance, you could bring an umbrella if it looks like rain or wear sunglasses on a sunny day. In the world of Google Apps Script, conditions play a crucial role, too, albeit in a slightly less wet or shiny way!

Introduction to Conditions in JavaScript

Conditions allow developers to select a specific action based on the outcome returned by comparison operators. Think of it as the script's pondering, "*Should I go this way or that way*?" based on the data it encounters.

The most popular way to examine a condition in Google Apps Script is through the trusty if statement. Let us glance at a simplistic example:

```
function myFunction() {
  const budget = 100;
  const threshold = 200;
```

```
    if (budget < threshold) {
      Logger.log('The budget is below the threshold');
    }
  }
```

The script checks whether the **budget** is below the **threshold**. If this condition holds true, our script prints the respective message. No message will be printed if you change the values so that the budget meets or exceeds the threshold.

Multiple Choices with `else if` and `else`

Life isn't always black and white, and sometimes there are more than two choices. Scripts need to deal with multiple possible outcomes. We use the **else if** and **else** statements for such scenarios. Here is how:

```
function myFunction() {
  const budget = 100;
  const threshold = 200;

  if (budget < threshold) {
    Logger.log('The budget is below threshold');
  } else if (budget === threshold) {
    Logger.log('The budget is exactly at the threshold');
  } else {
    Logger.log('The budget is above threshold');
  }
}
```

The **else if** statement offers the script another chance. It is like saying, "*If the first condition isn't true, then let us see if this second one is.*" Should neither the **if** nor the **else if** conditions be satisfied, our script defaults to the **else** statement. In our given example, since we've already accounted for two possible budget scenarios, we can confidently conclude in the **else** statement that the budget is above the threshold without any explicit check.

Combining Conditions: The Power of Logical Operators

Sometimes, when we need to test for complex combinations of conditions, we use logical operators. Google Apps Script offers three primary logical operators: **&&** (AND), **||** (OR), and **!** (NOT).

- The **&&** operator checks if both conditions are true.
- The **||** operator evaluates if either of the conditions is true.
- The **!** operator negates a condition, converting true to false and false to true.

Let us expand our earlier budget example by introducing a new variable: **`department`**.

```
function myFunction() {
  const budget = 100;
  const threshold = 200;
  const department = 'sales';

  if (budget < threshold && department === 'sales') {
    Logger.log('The budget is below threshold');
  } else if (budget === threshold && department === 'sales') {
    Logger.log('The budget is exactly at the threshold');
  } else {
    Logger.log('The budget is above threshold or wrong
department');
  }
}
```

We're not just checking the budget against the threshold in the new code snippet. We are also verifying if the **`department`** is "**`sales`**." If both conditions - the budget being below the threshold and the department being "**`sales`**" - are met, then our script logs that the budget is below the threshold.

In essence, conditions and logical operators in Google Apps Script empower developers to create scripts that think, decide, and act based on the data they encounter. So the next time you're scripting, remember, you're not just coding; you're making choices!

Functions in JavaScript

A function is a reusable block of code containing instructions that can be followed multiple times. In JavaScript, these instructions are encapsulated within curly braces **`{}`**. If you've been diligently following along, you might recall that we've already danced with a function named **`myFunction`** in previous examples. Taking a closer look at its anatomy:

```
function myFunction() {
  // instructions
}
```

As you know, we use **`const`** or **`let`** when we declare variables. Similarly, we use the **`function`** keyword to usher a function into existence. These functions require names for identification, just like variables. The names are arbitrary, meaning you can choose almost any name, but they must abide by the same rules as variables.

You are not confined to a solitary function in a file. Just as a symphony has multiple instruments, you can have multiple functions in the same file, each playing its role.

Here is where the magic happens: functions can accept arguments, unlike variables. For instance:

```
function myFunction() {
  addNumbers(3, 6); // output 9
}

function addNumbers(a, b) {
  console.log(a + b);
}
```

Having sketched out two functions, it is worth noting a little process. After penning down your code and before you eagerly click "**Run**," ensure that **myFunction** is selected in this dropdown in the IDE:

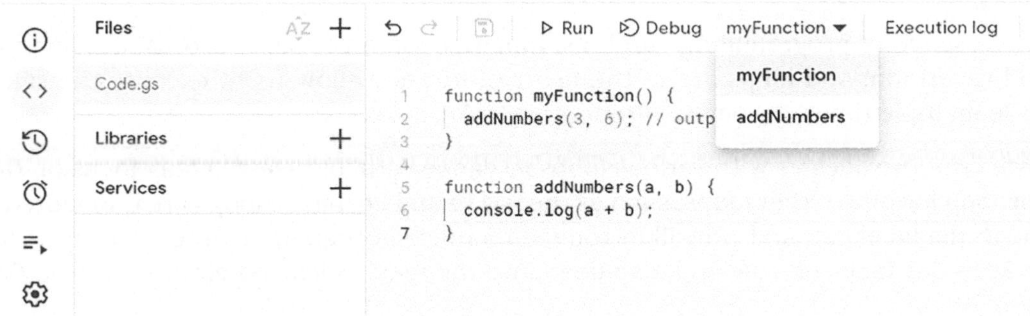

Figure 1.6: *Selecting the Function to Run in the Online IDE*

When you run **myFunction()**, it gracefully passes the baton to **addNumbers()**, furnishing it with two arguments: **3** and **6**. **addNumbers()**, then treats them like variables and outputs the result: 9.

Most of the time, you would prefer a function to return a value rather than print it out. Returning a value means that this value can be assigned to a variable and used elsewhere. Consider the following example:

```
function myFunction() {
  const a = 3;
  const b = 6;
  const result = addNumbers(a, b);
  Logger.log('a + b = ' + result);
}

function addNumbers(a, b) {
  const sum = a + b;
  return sum;
}
```

Here, we've neatly stored our values in the variables **a** and **b**. When we invoke **addNumbers()**, feeding it **a** and **b** as arguments, it gracefully adds them and returns the sum. True, we might have skipped the intermediate **sum** variable and written **return a + b;** directly. But sometimes, for clarity's sake, we use a descriptive variable. It is like adding a book title–it just clarifies things.

The value thus returned can be stashed away in the **result** variable inside **myFunction**, and we can then utilize it for a human-readable output.

You take a giant leap in your JavaScript/Google Apps Script journey by mastering functions. And remember, practice makes perfect, so don't hesitate to dive in and start scripting!

Repeating Instructions with for Loops

The essence of programming can be summarized in a couple of words: automation and repetition. And loops are at the heart of it! They allow us to execute the same code multiple times, automating repetitive tasks.

JavaScript provides us with various loops to dance with, but we will only focus on the **for** loop for now. Other loops, such as the **while** and **do while** loops are undoubtedly worth the limelight, and we will introduce them in subsequent chapters. For now, let us keep our focus narrow and dive deep into the mechanics and elegance of the **for** loop.

Why do we need the **for** loop, you ask? Simply put, to save time and reduce redundancy in our scripts. It enables us to execute the same piece of code a specified number of times, making our code shorter and our lives easier. Imagine having to write the same line of code ten times instead of looping it—that would be really tedious!

Consider the following example:

```
function myFunction() {
  for (let i = 0; i < 10; i++) {
    // i = i + 1
    Logger.log(i); // prints integers from 0 to 9
  }
}
```

The **for** loop looks slightly perplexing at first, but fear not, it is relatively straightforward once you understand its components. The loop takes three instructions:

1. **The Initialization: `let i = 0`** set the initial value; the variable can be named anything you like, but it is a common convention to use **i**, short for "*iteration*," inside of **for** loops.
2. **The Condition: `i < 10`** is a logical test determining whether the loop should

proceed. As long as this condition evaluates to true, our merry loop keeps dancing.

3. **The Increment:** `i++`, which is a shorthand for `i = i + 1`, defines how the loop's value (`i` in this case) changes after each iteration.

Thus, in this instance, the loop will start with `i` at 0 and keep running as long as `i` is less than 10, incrementing by 1 with every turn of the dance. And on every twirl, it logs the current value of `i`.

However, while counting numbers is undoubtedly entertaining, we can do so much more! Before we forge ahead, let us take a slight detour and introduce arrays. These data structures will illuminate the true potential of the `for` loop, making our coding journey both fun and functional. And speaking of fun, remember: while loops love to dance, they hate being stepped on—so always ensure they have a clear start and finish, or they might just dance forever!

Understanding Objects in JavaScript

Like arrays, objects are variables that store multiple entries. Unlike arrays, however, object values are retrieved by developer-defined keys rather than sequential indices.

In the vast realm of programming, objects stand as robust collections of data comprising properties and methods, the former being akin to variables and the latter to functions, but encompassed in their own structure with a slightly different syntax than standalone variables and functions.

A Peek into Object Structure

Consider this example:

```
function handleObjects() {
  // employee is an object
  const employee = {
    firstName: 'John',
    lastName: 'Doe',
    sayHello() {
      Logger.log('Hi there, my name is ' + this.firstName);
    },
  };

  Logger.log(employee.firstName); // John
  Logger.log(employee.lastName); // Doe
  employee.sayHello(); // Hi there, my name is John
}
```

From the preceding example, let us dissect the **`employee`** object:

1. It is introduced using the **`const`** keyword, similar to regular variables. The **`let`** keyword could also be employed here, but it is rare to need it; as long as you don't assign a new object to the variable that points to the object, you can add, remove, and update methods and properties of an object, even if it is stored in a variable declared with **`const`**.
2. The data contained within the object – its properties and methods – is encased in curly braces (**`{}`**).
3. The properties of the object, analogous to variables, are assigned values using the colon **`:`** operator.
4. Methods, reminiscent of functions but without the **`function`** keyword, are defined within the object.
5. The properties and methods are distinctly separated by commas rather than semicolons.
6. Within the object, the **`this`** keyword is employed to access its own properties and methods.

To interact with the properties and methods of an object, we resort to the dot notation. You are now very familiar with the **`Logger.log()`** syntax; it might pique your interest to know that it is an example of said dot notation. Indeed, **`Logger`** is an object (and **`log()`** is its method), as are all other Google Apps Script services we'll delve into in subsequent chapters.

Arrays: The Building Blocks of Data Handling

First and foremost, what exactly is an array? Think of an array as a special variable type that is not content with just one value. Declared with either **`const`** or **`let`**, an array is designed to hold a list of values. These values, known as elements, each have an assigned index starting from 0. In JavaScript, unlike some other programming languages, the elements within an array can be of different types. They can be strings, numbers, booleans, null values, undefined, symbols, and – adding a twist to our dance – they can even be other arrays or objects (hold out for objects in the next section)! It is this robust versatility that makes arrays so fundamental.

To illustrate, consider the following:

```
const array1 = [1, 2, 45, 32, 21, 88];
const array2 = ['Ross', 'Monica', 'Chandler', 'Phoebe', 'Joey',
'Rachel'];
```

The two variables in our example are arrays containing values within square brackets and separated by commas. To engage with a specific element, one would use the element's index:

```
function myFunction() {
  const array1 = [1, 2, 45, 32, 21, 88];
  const array2 = ['Ross', 'Monica', 'Chandler', 'Phoebe', 'Joey',
'Rachel'];

  Logger.log(array1[0]); // output: 1
  Logger.log(array2[2]); // output: 'Chandler'
}
```

Remember, the index of the first element is 0! So, **`array1[0]`** retrieves the value "**1**" and **`array2[2]`** gives us "Chandler."

Reading the first element of an array is straightforward, we use the **`0`** index. How do we read the last value, though? One property you should be aware of when dealing with arrays is **`length`**, as it gives us the number of elements contained in an array. Consider this example:

```
function myFunction() {
  const names = ['Alice', 'Bob', 'Carol', 'Dave', 'Eve'];
  Logger.log(names.length); // Output: 5
}
```

We can use this property to access the last element of an array. Keep in mind, though, that the number of elements and the last index of an array are offset by one because indices start at **`0`**:

```
function myFunction() {
  const names = ['Alice', 'Bob', 'Carol', 'Dave', 'Eve'];
  Logger.log(names[names.length - 1]); // names[4] => "Eve"
  Logger.log(names[names.length]); // names[5] => undefined
}
```

Our first **`Logger.log()`** statement prints out the last name in the array, "Eve ." The second one, however, prints **`undefined`**, one of the JavaScript primitives we saw earlier in the chapter; it lets us know that no value has been assigned to the element of index 5 in the array. However, if you were to set **`names[5] = "Frank";`** you would append a new entry to the array and increase its length by 1.

Because arrays have sequential keys, handling them with **`for`** loops is straightforward. Let us look at an example:

```
function loopThroughArray() {
  const names = ['Alice', 'Bob', 'Carol', 'Dave', 'Eve'];
  for (let i = 0; i < names.length; i++) {
```

```
        Logger.log(names[i]);
    }
}
```

The preceding snippet will print out all the names from the **names** array individually. It works by creating a **for** loop that iterates through values from 0 up to, but not including, **names.length**, incremented by 1 on every iteration. We can then use the value stored in **i** as an index for the **names** array and access each one of its elements.

Understanding how to proficiently add or remove elements from an array is also important. Let us dive into four pivotal methods that cater to these needs: **push()**, **pop()**, **shift()**, and **unshift()**. Each method has its own unique characteristics, and by the end of this section, you'll have a clear grasp of when and how to utilize them.

The push() Method: Adding to the End

The **push()** method is often the first choice for developers aiming to add one or more elements to the end of an array. It modifies the original array and returns the new length of the array. For instance:

```
const fruits = ['apple', 'banana'];
const newLength = fruits.push('cherry');
// fruits becomes ['apple', 'banana', 'cherry']
// newLength is 3
```

The pop() Method: Removing from the End

Conversely, if your goal is to remove the last element from an array, look no further than the **pop()** method. This method removes the last element and returns that element:

```
const fruits = ['apple', 'banana', 'cherry'];
const removedFruit = fruits.pop();
// fruits is now ['apple', 'banana']
// removedFruit is 'cherry'
```

The shift() Method: Removing from the Beginning

While **pop()** works its magic on the array's end, the **shift()** method focuses on the beginning. It removes the first element from an array and returns that removed element:

```
const fruits = ['apple', 'banana', 'cherry'];
const firstFruit = fruits.shift();
// fruits will be ['banana', 'cherry']
// firstFruit is 'apple'
```

The `unshift()` Method: Adding to the Beginning

Lastly, if your task is to prepend an array with new elements, the **`unshift()`** method is your ally. Like **`push()`**, it modifies the original array and returns the new length:

```
const fruits = ['banana', 'cherry'];
const newLength = fruits.unshift('apple');
// fruits is now ['apple', 'banana', 'cherry']
// newLength becomes 3
```

But the magic of arrays doesn't stop here. Arrays can encapsulate other arrays, leading to two-dimensional arrays. This is particularly vital as Google Sheets utilizes this format to store data. Let us dive deeper:

```
const spreadsheetData = [
      ['First Name', 'Last Name', 'Age'],
      ['John', 'Doe', 24],
      ['Jane', 'Doe', 19]
];

Logger.log(spreadsheetData[0][0]); // output: 'First Name'
Logger.log(spreadsheetData[1][2]); // output: 24
```

When you observe **`spreadsheetData[0][0]`,** the first index (**`[0]`**) directs us to the array **`['First Name', 'Last Name', 'Age']`**, and the subsequent index **`[0]`** hones in on the first element of that array, "First Name." Analogously, **`spreadsheetData[1][2]`** leads us to the age 24 of John Doe.

In the world of Google Apps Script, we often encounter situations where we need to manage multi-dimensional data. A two-dimensional array is one such data structure that allows us to organize data in rows and columns, similar to a spreadsheet. However, how do we efficiently loop through this kind of structure? Here is where the concept of nested loops comes into play.

Imagine for a moment: You are standing at the entrance of a large house with multiple rooms. Each room has its own set of objects. Your task is to list down every single object in the house. What would you do? Naturally, you'd enter each room individually and list the objects present therein. This is the approach we adopt when using nested loops to navigate a two-dimensional array.

Consider the following JavaScript code snippet:

```
function myFunction() {
  const spreadsheetData = [
    ['First Name', 'Last Name', 'Age'],
    ['John', 'Doe', 24],
    ['Jane', 'Doe', 19],
  ];
```

```
    for (let i = 0; i < spreadsheetData.length; i++) {
      for (let j = 0; j < spreadsheetData[i].length; j++) {
        Logger.log(spreadsheetData[i][j]);
      }
    }
}
```

Now, let us dissect this code to fathom its inner workings.

In the outer loop—visualize it as the rooms in our house analogy—the variable **i** represents each individual row in the **spreadsheetData** array. When **i** is 0, the inner loop—the equivalent of the objects inside a particular room—begins its journey. This inner loop, denoted by the variable **j**, then iterates over each column within the row pointed by **i**.

For each outer loop iteration (**i**), the inner loop (**j**) completes a full cycle, logging all the values in the current row. Once **j** has made its rounds, **i** advances to the next row, and the process begins anew. This tandem operation continues until every cell in our two-dimensional array has been explored and logged.

In simpler terms, for every room you enter (outer loop), you list all its objects (inner loop). Once done, you move on to the next room, and the cycle continues.

Grasping this concept is crucial for those venturing into Google Apps Script, especially when dealing with data in spreadsheets, which inherently mimics a two-dimensional structure. With this understanding, you're better equipped to manipulate and manage complex data structures, propelling your scripting skills to the next level. Happy coding!

Arrays are pivotal, versatile, and encompassing. As we've danced through their nuances, we find them at the heart of data representation in Google Apps Script. Let us now look at a new essential data structure in JavaScript: objects.

Complex Objects and Arrays

Objects and arrays are versatile structures capable of holding other objects and arrays within them. Observe:

```
const employee = {
  firstName: 'John',
  lastName: 'Doe',
  sayHello() {
    Logger.log('Hi there, my name is ' + this.firstName);
  },
  hobbies: ['skiing', 'chess', 'cooking'],
  address: {
    street: '123 Main Street',
```

```
      city: 'Anytown',
      state: 'CA',
      zipCode: '91234',
      country: 'USA',
    },
  };
```

Turn the tables, and you'll find that arrays can be hospitable hosts to objects as well:

```
function arrayOfObjects() {
  const ar = [
    {
      firstName: 'John',
      lastName: 'Doe',
    },
    {
      firstName: 'Jane',
      lastName: 'Doe',
    },
    {
      firstName: 'Peter',
      lastName: 'Parker',
    },
    {
      firstName: 'Mary',
      lastName: 'Jane Watson',
    },
    {
      firstName: 'Bruce',
      lastName: 'Wayne',
    },
  ];

  Logger.log(ar[3].firstName); // Mary
}
```

In such instances, accessing object properties requires a mix of array indices and dot notation. For example, **`ar[3].firstName`** references the fourth element in the **`ar`** array, which is an object, and then fetches that object's **`firstName`** property.

JavaScript objects are also at the root of the JSON file format, "**`JavaScript Object Notation.`**" This format makes storing and manipulating data easy with JavaScript's native syntax. It is useful to create and store files in this format, and it is the most popular standard for communicating with APIs and NoSQL databases. We will look into these use cases in the chapters to come.

Now let us look into another crucial JavaScript concept that remains to touch upon: scope.

Scope in JavaScript

In JavaScript, one concept that you will encounter time and again is "*scope*." Simply put, scope determines where in your script a variable is accessible. Let us delve deeper into this topic.

There are primarily three types of scope in JavaScript:

- **Global Scope:** Variables declared outside a function are accessible from everywhere.
- **Function Scope:** This pertains to variables declared within a function.
- **Block Scope:** A scope defined within curly braces, be it in conditional statements, loops, or other blocks.

To illustrate, consider this code snippet:

```
// Global Scope
const USER = 'Jane';

function printUserName() {
	Logger.log("The user's name is " + USER);
	// Output: The user's name is Jane
}

function greetUser() {
	Logger.log('Hello ' + USER + ', how are you today?');
	// Output: Hello Jane, how are you today?
}
```

Here, the constant **USER** is declared in the global scope, and thus, every function in our script has access to it. A keen observer might note that **USER** is in uppercase—a convention rather than a rule, designed to quickly distinguish global variables and enhance code readability.

Let us shuffle things up:

```
// Function Scope
function printUserName() {
  const user = 'Jane';
  Logger.log("The user's name is " + user);
  // Output: The user's name is Jane
}

function greetUser() {
  Logger.log('Hello ' + user + ', how are you today?');
  // Output: ReferenceError: user is not defined
}
```

Now, our variable **user** is tucked safely inside the **printUserName** function, making it inaccessible to **greetUser**, hence the error. A quirky note on strings: in **printUserName**, quotes surround the string to prevent confusion with the inner apostrophe. Alternatively, one could escape the apostrophe: **Logger.log('The user\'s name is ' + USER);** Whether you opt for quotes, apostrophes, or a hybrid, it boils down to style.

Next, let us uncover the mysteries of block scope:

```
// Block Scope
const AGE = 23;
const NAME = 'Jane';

function isAdult() {
  const response = "We don't know yet";
  if (AGE < 18) {
    const response = NAME + ' is not an adult';
    Logger.log(response);
  } else {
    const response = NAME + ' is an adult';
    Logger.log(response); // Jane is an adult
  }
  Logger.log(response); // We don't know yet
}
```

Block scope is the reign of code within curly braces—think of **if** statements, **for** loops, and more. In our example, despite multiple **response** declarations, their distinct block scopes ensure no clashes. Interestingly, while the **const** keyword prevents a variable's value from being overwritten, multiple block-scoped declarations are perfectly fine, given they're in separate blocks. Always remember, though: variables declared closer in proximity take precedence. Hence, the "We don't know yet" output at the end.

Now, a quick caveat regarding the **var** keyword. Recall our prior counsel against **var** in favor of **const** and **let**? Behold its peculiar scope behavior:

```
const AGE = 23;
const NAME = 'Jane';

function isAdult() {
  var response = "We don't know yet";
  if (AGE < 18) {
    var response = NAME + ' is not an adult';
    Logger.log(response);
  } else {
    var response = NAME + ' is an adult';
    Logger.log(response); // Jane is an adult
```

```
    }
    Logger.log(response); // Jane is an adult
}
```

Here, the function-scoped nature of **var**, even when declared within a nested block of code, leads to overwriting, an issue not encountered with **const** or **let**. Re-declaring with **var** does not yield errors, setting the stage for elusive bugs. While tempting to delve into the peculiarities of **var**, let us heed this advice instead: avoid it like avoiding pineapple on pizza (although some might enjoy that combination!). You will still encounter **var** in legacy code and documentation, so beware.

One last concept we need to look at before moving on to practical Google Apps Script is hoisting.

Hoisting in JavaScript

In JavaScript, understanding the intricacies can be the key to writing efficient and bug-free code. One such peculiarity is the concept of hoisting.

Hoisting can be likened to the behavior of a stage manager in a play who sets the stage by ensuring all props are in place before the curtain rises. In JavaScript's theater, this manager is the compiler. During the compilation phase, certain declarations (such as variables and functions) are moved to the top of their respective scopes, be it a function or the global scope. This mechanism is called hoisting.

When you declare a function using the **function** keyword, the entire function is hoisted to the top. This implies that you can invoke a function even before its declaration in the code.

Consider this:

```
greet();

function greet() {
  Logger.log('Hello!');
}
```

Even though the function invocation comes before the function's declaration, the code runs without errors. This is hoisting at work, with the function declaration being moved to the top during the compilation phase.

However, the waters get a bit murkier when we introduce **let** and **const**. Unlike variables declared with the **var** keyword, variables declared with **let** and **const** are not initialized with **undefined**. They are hoisted but remain in a "*Temporal Dead Zone*" (TDZ) until the code execution reaches their actual declarations. This means you'll get a **ReferenceError** if you try to access them before their declaration. This behavior underscores the importance of organizing your code logically and understanding the nuances of these declarations.

Let us come back to **var**. A relic from JavaScript's earlier days, **var** is indeed hoisted. However, only the declaration is hoisted, not the initialization. Hence, a variable declared with **var** will return **undefined** if accessed before its declaration.

```
console.log(message); // Outputs: undefined
var message = 'Hello!';
```

Historically, JavaScript was a much simpler language, and this hoisting mechanism with **var** was likely considered a feature, not a pitfall. It allowed for more flexibility in script organization. As the language matured and the demands grew more complex, this very behavior became a source of bugs and confusion. Given these complications, the modern consensus is to eschew **var** in favor of **let** and **const**, which offer block-level scoping and more predictable behavior.

In conclusion, hoisting is an essential concept to grasp for anyone delving into JavaScript and Google Apps Script. It harks back to some historical decisions in JavaScript's evolution, but understanding it paves the way for more structured and robust scripts.

Conclusion

As we journey through the annals of the evolution of JavaScript, it is clear to see its pivotal role in shaping the interactive and dynamic web experiences we cherish today. From its humble beginnings, JavaScript has become the bedrock upon which many modern web applications are built. The foray into Client-Side JavaScript offered a glimpse into its capabilities, acting as a curtain-raiser for the complex functionalities that await us. The Google Apps Script's Integrated Development Environment (IDE) further exemplifies the culmination of JavaScript's capabilities, providing developers with a robust platform to craft ingenious scripts.

Our exploration into the fundamental tenets of JavaScript unraveled an array of features. Starting with the rudimentary "**Hello World**," progressing into the nuances of variables and exploring arithmetic and comparison operators, we embarked on a deep dive into the mechanics of the language. Through conditions, functions, objects, and arrays, we unearthed the quintessential tools for robust data handling. Furthermore, JavaScript's intriguing facets of scope and hoisting punctuate its depth and versatility.

However, the foundational knowledge we've established in this chapter is merely the tip of the iceberg. As you stand at the threshold of understanding, prepare to delve deeper into the realm of Google Apps Script and discover its expansive capabilities.

In our next chapter, *Container-Bound versus Stand-Alone Scripts*, we will distinguish between these two types of scripts, shedding light on their unique attributes, advantages, and potential applications as Google Apps Script developers, distinguishing between these types of hands will be pivotal in harnessing the full potential of the platform.

Key Terms

- **JavaScript:** A dynamic, object-oriented programming language. It began as a means to make web pages interactive and has evolved into the backbone of modern web development, now extensively used on both the client and server side.
- **Client-Side JavaScript:** Refers to scripts that run within a user's browser. This contrasts with server-side scripts, which are executed on the server before the page is sent to the user.
- **Google Apps Script's IDE:** A cloud-based IDE developed by Google to script routine tasks in Google Workspace applications. It provides a straightforward way to automate workflows and extend the capabilities of various Google services.
- **Comments:** Non-executable text in code used to clarify or describe the purpose of a code segment. In JavaScript, single-line comments start with //, and multi-line comments are enclosed between /* and */.
- **Variables:** Containers for storing data values. In JavaScript, they can be declared using let, const, or the older var keyword.
- **Arithmetic Operators:** Symbols used to perform mathematical operations such as addition (+), subtraction (-), multiplication (*), division (/), and modulo (%).
- **Incrementation and Decrementation:** Refers to increasing or decreasing a value, respectively. In JavaScript, ++ is used to increment, and -- is used to decrement.
- **Comparison Operators:** Used to compare two values. Common operators include == (equal to), != (not equal to), === (strictly equal to), !== (strictly not equal to), < (less than), and > (greater than).
- **Conditions:** Help execute certain segments of code based on specified criteria. The if, else if, and else statements are fundamental constructs for managing conditions in JavaScript.
- **Functions:** Reusable blocks of code designed to perform a specific task. They can take inputs (parameters) and return a result.
- **Objects:** Collections of related data and functions. In JavaScript, objects can be created using curly braces **{}**.
- **Arrays:** Ordered collections of items. In JavaScript, arrays are zero-indexed,

and items can be retrieved or modified by referencing their index.

- **Scope:** Pertains to the accessibility of variables. Variables can have local or global scope.
- **Hoisting:** In JavaScript, declarations (not initializations) are moved to the top of their containing function or global code, which can lead to unexpected results if not understood.

CHAPTER 2
Container-Bound versus Stand-Alone Scripts

Introduction

As we dive deeper into the world of Google Apps Script, a versatile tool in our tech arsenal, we face choices that shape our workflow. Whether you are crafting your first script or you are a seasoned developer, understanding the fork in the road between bound and stand-alone scripts is paramount. It is the very first decision that will set the stage for your project. So, let us roll up our sleeves and delve into this pivotal topic.

Structure

In this chapter, we will cover the following topics:

- Container-Bound Scripts: Tightly Integrated and Context-Aware
    - Stand-Alone Scripts: Versatile and Independent
- Tailoring the User Experience with Bound Scripts
    - Container-Bound Script in Action: A Simple Example
- Exploring Stand-Alone Scripts: A World of Possibilities
    - A Real-World Example: The Stand-Alone Web App
    - Decoding the Sorcery Behind the Script

Container-Bound Scripts: Tightly Integrated and Context-Aware

Imagine bound scripts as the inseparable companions of their host applications. They are the Siamese twins of Google Workspace documents, whether that be a Google

Sheet, Doc, Slide, or Form. Bound scripts are cozy, living right within the document's ecosystem, and they have insider access to the document's data, making them incredibly efficient for tasks specific to that document.

Here is what makes bound scripts unique:

- **Intrinsic Connection**: They are intrinsically connected to a Google Workspace document. This relationship is deep-rooted and exclusive.
- **Out of Sight in Drive**: You will not find them loitering in Google Drive because they are snugly integrated into their container documents.
- **Customization Kings**: They wield the power to tailor the host file with custom menus, dialog boxes, or sidebars, adding a personal touch and enhanced functionality.
- **Copycats**: Like magic, when you duplicate the host document, the bound script duplicates with it. Voila!
- **Trigger Happy**: They excel at running specific triggers. Think of them as the behind-the-scenes maestro conducting the orchestra when a user edits a spreadsheet or opens a document.

Stand-Alone Scripts: Versatile and Independent

On the flip side, stand-alone scripts are the lone wolves of the scripting world. Remember the JavaScript exercises in the online IDE from chapter one? That is where we encountered these independent entities. They do not pledge allegiance to any particular document but instead exist freely, executing code from the comfort of https://script.google.com (https://script.google.com/home?pli=1).

Here is the rundown on stand-alone scripts:

- **Liberated Creation**: You are not confined to a single point of creation. From Google Drive, simply click **`New > More > Google Apps Script`**, or take the shortcut by typing **`script.new`** in your browser's bar. Freedom is their playground.
- **Google Drive Presence**: They play hide and seek in Google Drive, but you can always find them if you have the right permissions.
- **Permission Guardians**: Speaking of permissions, these scripts are like private journals. Only those you have entrusted with access can peek inside and make their mark.

Now, equipped with the essence of bound and stand-alone scripts, let us explore the practical scenarios where each shines. It is not just about what they do, but how they can make your Google Apps Script journey more intuitive and impactful. Stay tuned as we navigate through real-world use cases and examples, where your newfound knowledge will leap off the page into practical application.

Tailoring the User Experience with Container-Bound Scripts

Bound scripts truly shine when it comes to creating a custom-tailored experience within Google Workspace. They are intrinsically linked to a host document–be it a Sheet, Doc, Slide, or Form–allowing you to manipulate the document from the inside out. It is like having a personal assistant embedded in your document, ready to take on tasks immediately.

- **Direct Reference to Host**: Forget about juggling file IDs. With bound scripts, you are already inside the host document. Need to grab the current selection in a Google Doc or the active range in Sheets? It is a breeze.
- **User Interface Wizardry**: Want to add custom menus, dialog boxes, or even sidebars? Bound scripts are your go-to, transforming the vanilla Google interface into something that fits your workflow like a glove.
- **Custom Functions in Sheets**: Elevate your spreadsheets by defining custom functions that can be used just like native spreadsheet functions, making data analysis and manipulation intuitive and powerful.
- **Automate Like a Pro**: Formatting and processing data can be a chore. Bound scripts turn monotonous tasks into one-click wonders, saving you time and frustration.

Container-Bound Script in Action: A Simple Example

Imagine you want to greet every viewer of your spreadsheet with a friendly message. Let us walk through how to set that up:

1. Fire up a new Google Sheet and pop Hello world into the `A1` cell. It is a classic!

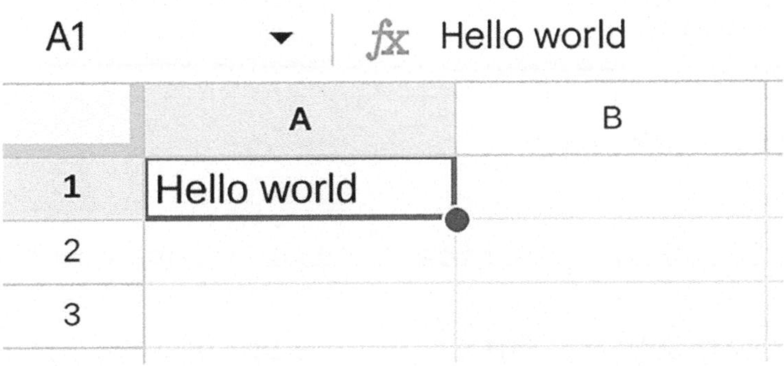

Figure 2.1: *New Spreadsheet with "Hello world" Greeting in Cell A1*

2. Time to bind a script. Click on **`Extensions`** and drag your cursor down to **`Apps Script`**.

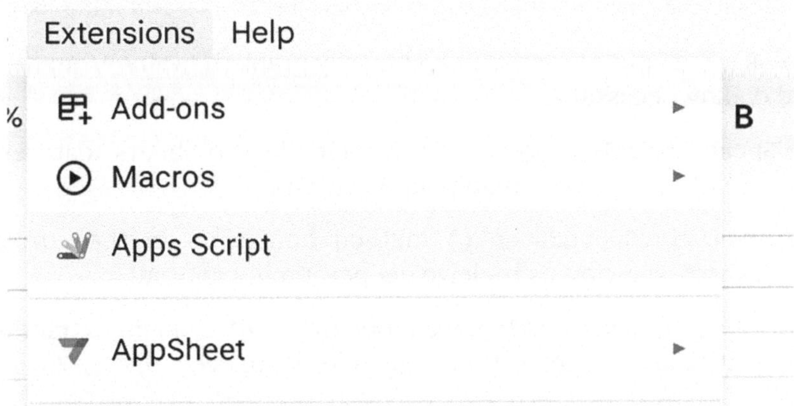

Figure 2.2: *Initiating a Bound Script from the "Extensions" Menu*

3. Voilà, you are now in the Apps Script IDE, your canvas for code. It is the same environment we introduced in the previous chapter, but it is directly tied to our open document this time.

4. Within the IDE, let us replace the placeholder content of **`myFunction`** with the following snippet:

```
function myFunction() {
  const a1 = SpreadsheetApp.getActiveSpreadsheet()
    .getActiveSheet()
    .getRange('A1')
    .getValue();
  Logger.log(a1);
}
```

5. Execute this function and check out the log. There is our **`Hello world`** message, just as expected.

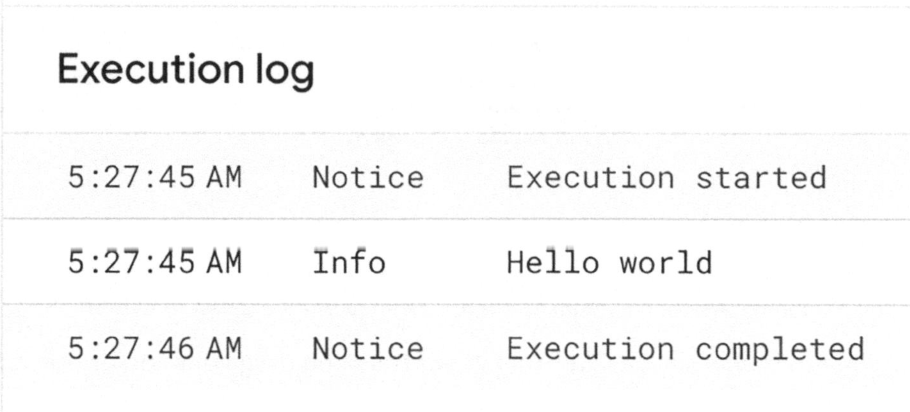

Figure 2.3: *The Execution Log Displaying Our "Hello world" Message*

a. Here is the magic: Our script dynamically grabs the value from the A1 cell—no hard coding necessary.

b. The **`SpreadsheetApp`** object is your golden key to Sheets' features, providing methods to navigate and manipulate the data.

c. The **`getActiveSpreadsheet()`** method homes in on the currently active spreadsheet, allowing us to delve deeper into its content.

d. By invoking **`getRange('A1')`**, we pinpoint the **`A1`** cell and extract its contents with **`getValue()`**, which is then logged for us to see.

e. Feel free to swap Hello world with anything else in the **`A1`** cell and rerun the function. It is dynamic and responsive—just what we need.

Bound scripts are also uniquely capable of responding to document-specific events, such as real-time edits in a spreadsheet. Plus, while they are cozy in their container, they are not confined to it. You can still reach out and interact with other Google Sheets if required, using **`openById(id)`**. That is flexibility with a capital 'F'!

A solid grasp of bound scripts paves the way for some serious automation and customization within your Google Workspace environment. But remember, this is just the tip of the iceberg. As we advance through this guide, we will uncover even more layers of potential bound scripts.

Now, with the prowess of bound scripts in our toolkit, let us shift gears and explore the realm of stand-alone scripts. They have a different set of strengths that are equally exciting.

Exploring Stand-Alone Scripts: A World of Possibilities

Stand-alone scripts are akin to Swiss Army knives in your scripting toolbox. They are independent entities, not tethered to any single document, thus offering a broader range of applications:

- **Utilities on Demand**: They jump into action as independent utilities, performing tasks across various Google Workspace documents without being launched from within a specific file.
- **Web Powerhouses**: Stand-alone scripts shine as web apps, webhooks, or the backbone for Google Workspace add-ons, leveraging Google's robust infrastructure.
- **Connectivity Maestros**: Despite their independence, these scripts can still interact with any document within Workspace. The catch? You will need to wield the power of document IDs or URLs with precision and intent.

A Real-World Example: The Stand-Alone Web App

Let us re-use the Google Sheet we created previously when we learned about bound scripts (or just create a new sheet and write "**`Hello world`**" in cell **`A1`**). That sheet, teeming with data, is about to play a central role in our stand-alone script scenario. Ready to harness its power? Let us roll up our sleeves and start:

1. Pluck the ID from your sheet's URL; it is nestled right after **`/d/`**: **`https://docs.google.com/spreadsheets/d/{id}/edit`**.
2. Chart a course to https://script.google.com/ (https://script.google.com/home) and conjure up a new script.
3. Write the following code into the IDE:

   ```
   function doGet() {
     const ssid = 'ENTER GOOGLE SHEET ID HERE';
     const a1 = SpreadsheetApp.openById(ssid)
       .getSheets()[0]
       .getRange('a1')
       .getValue();
     return HtmlService.createHtmlOutput('<h1>' + a1 + '</h1>');
   }
   ```

4. Replace **`ENTER GOOGLE SHEET ID HERE`** with the actual ID of your Google Sheet.

Before we unleash this script into the wild as a web app, let us march through the deployment ritual:

1. Click **`Deploy`**, then **`New Deployment`** in the top-right corner.

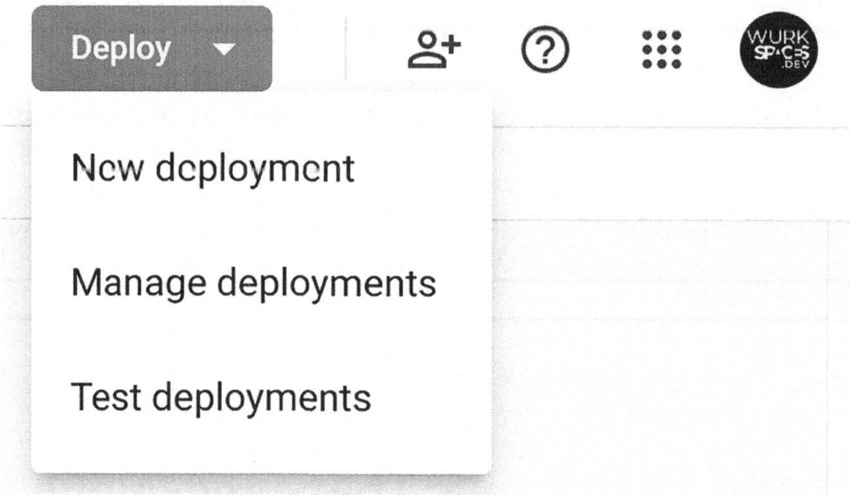

***Figure 2.4**: The Script Deployment Menu*

2. Click on the gear icon beside **`Select type`** and anoint it as a **`Web app`**.

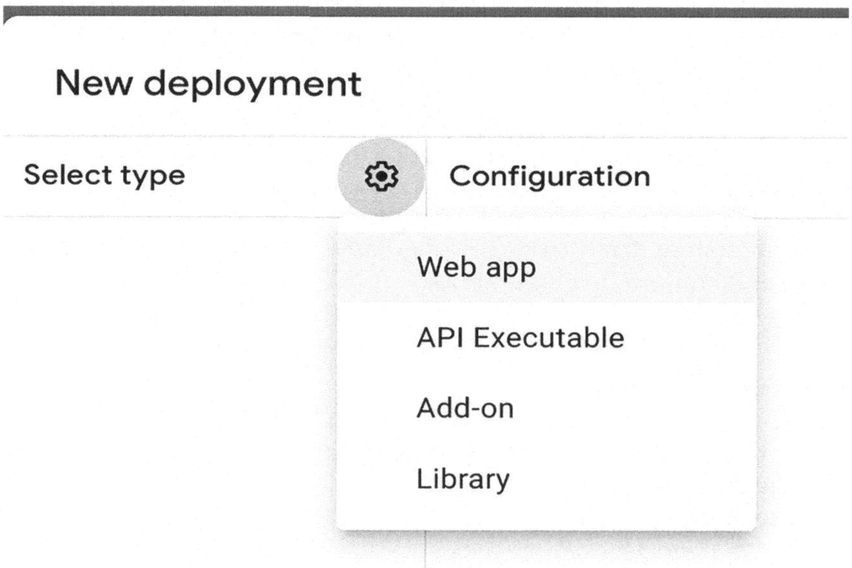

***Figure 2.5**: Selecting Script Deployment Type*

3. Ignore the other fields for now (we will circle back to them in future chapters) and simply click Deploy.

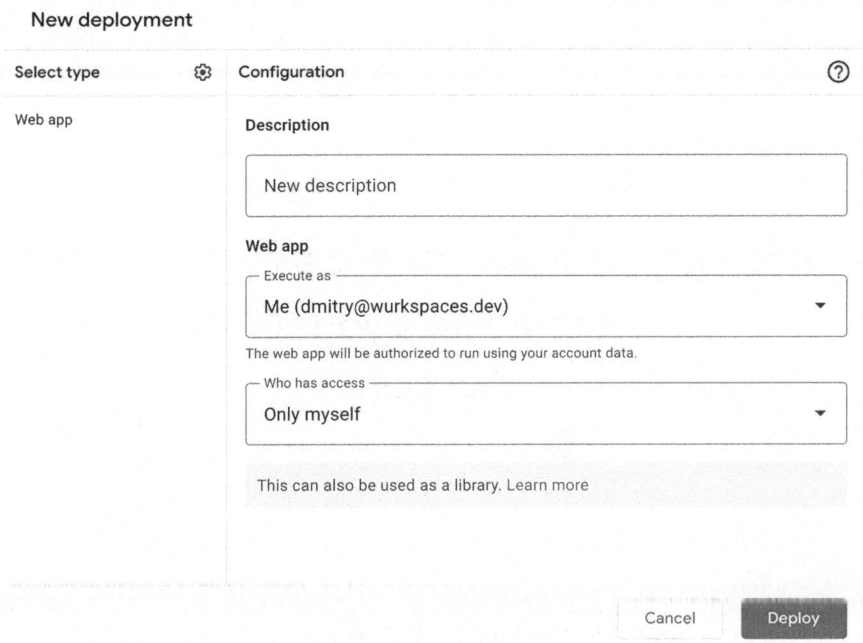

Figure 2.6: *Deploying a Script as a Web App*

4. Grant your script the keys to the kingdom by authorizing access.

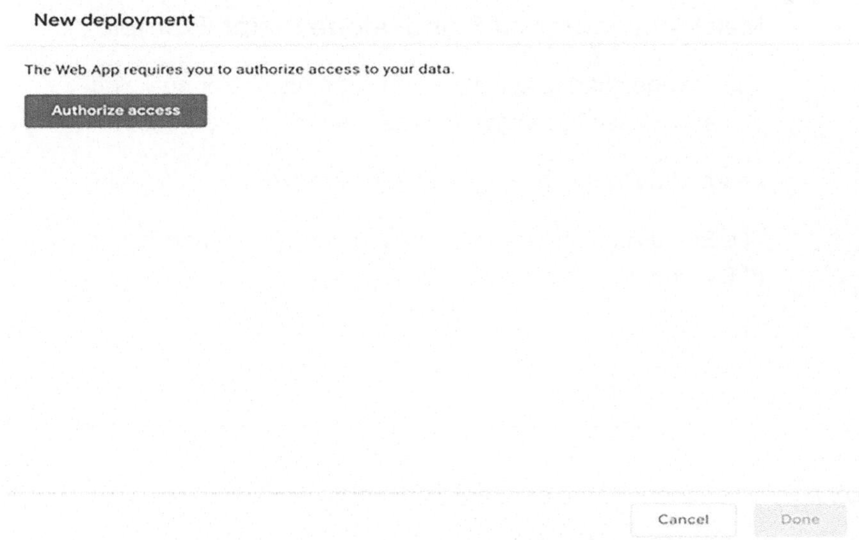

Figure 2.7: *Authorize the Script Before Deployment*

5. Choose your account and bestow the necessary permissions. Observe how Apps Script astutely anticipates that we are interfacing with Spreadsheets:

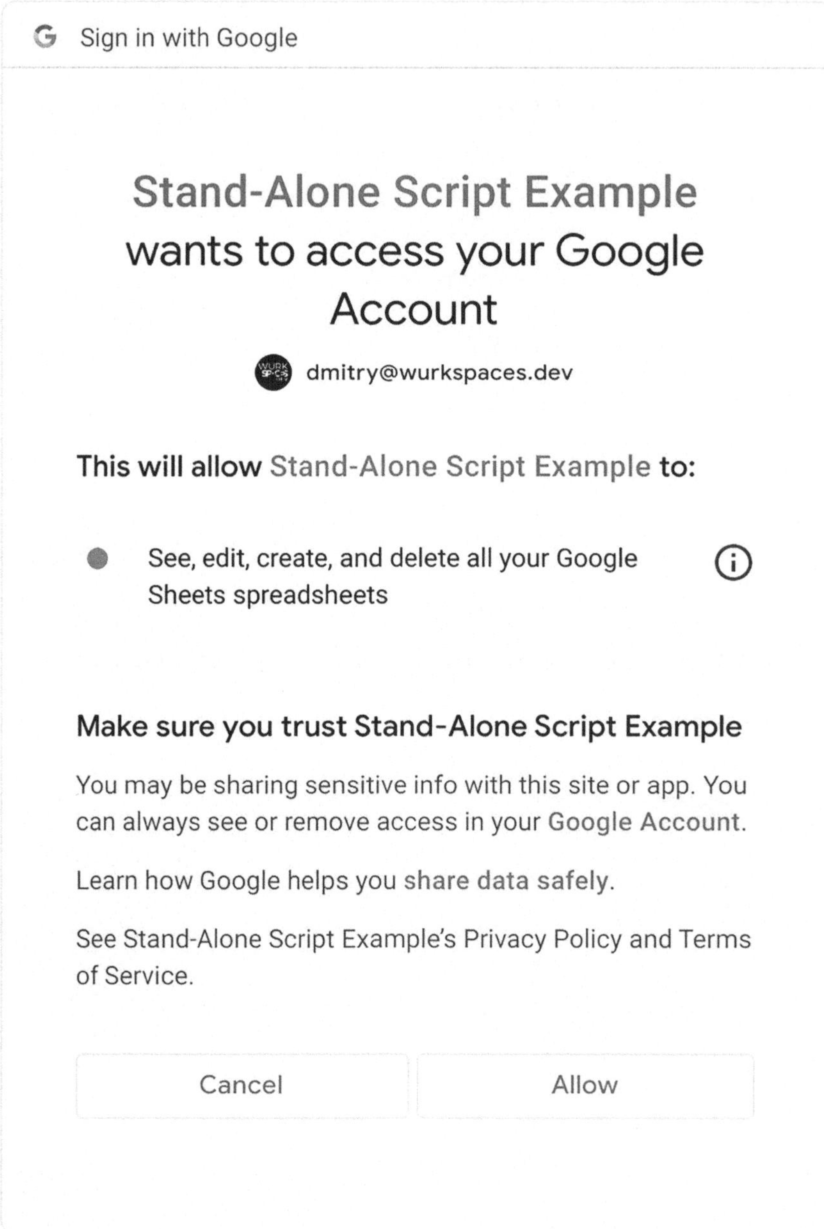

Figure 2.8: *Google Apps Script Permissions*

6. Post-authorization, you will be greeted with a URL unique to your web app. Click it and behold the magic.

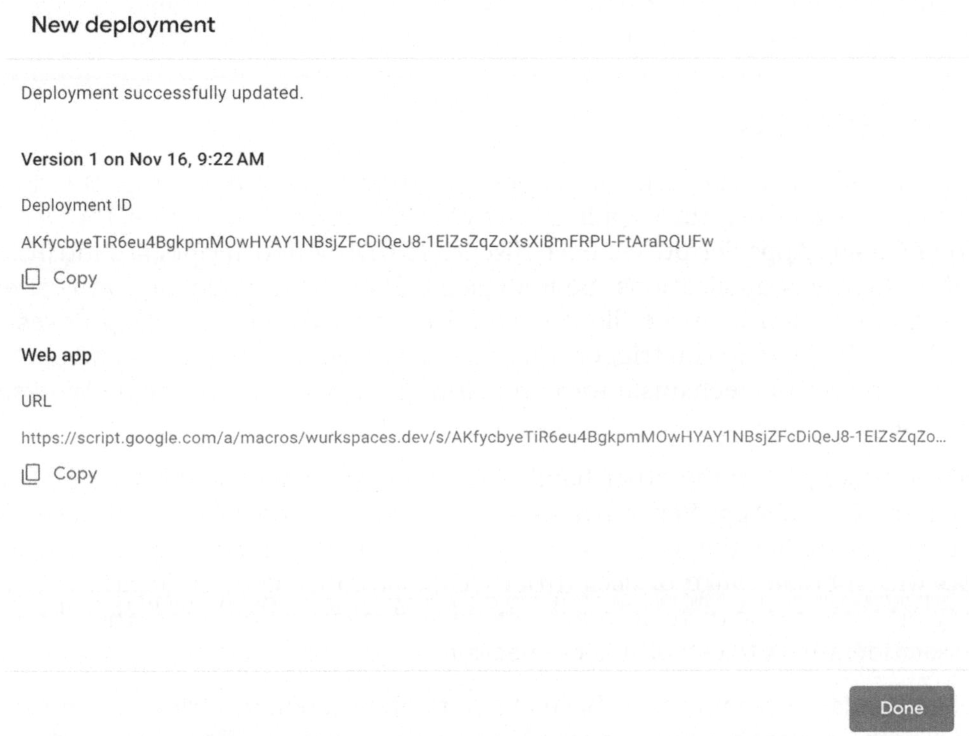

Figure 2.9: *Deployment Confirmation with URL*

Upon visiting your web app's URL, assuming Hello world resides in cell **`A1`** of your spreadsheet, you will be greeted by a page echoing that very message within a majestic **`<h1>`** tag.

A playful challenge for you: tweak the contents of cell **`A1`** and refresh the web page. Like magic, the title transmutes to reflect your changes.

Decoding the Sorcery Behind the Script

Let us unravel the enchantments within our script:

1. The **`doGet`** function is essentially our script's welcoming committee, responding to web requests with grace.
2. The **`ssid`** variable is our secret passcode to the spreadsheet's treasure trove of data.
3. The **`a1`** variable becomes the steward of our desired cell's content, meticulously extracted through a series of methodical calls.
4. Lastly, we craft an HTML response with our cell's value triumphantly displayed.

If you feel like your head is exploding, fret not. Our journey through Google Apps Script is just beginning. With each chapter, the fog of mystery will clear.

Conclusion

As we conclude this foundational chapter, we have traversed through the distinct characteristics and practical applications of each script type within the versatile world of Google Apps Script. We have discerned that bound scripts are intrinsically linked to their host applications—be it a Google Sheet, Doc, Slide, or Form—offering seamless integration with the file it customizes through menus, dialog boxes, and sidebars. Their ability to run triggers on document events such as edits and openings provides a powerful mechanism for automating tasks within the Google Workspace environment.

Stand-alone scripts, on the other hand, exhibit a more independent nature. Created through the Google Apps Script IDE or directly via the Google Drive interface, these scripts do not confine themselves to a single document. Instead, they serve as utility scripts with a broad range of uses—from web apps to Google Workspace add-ons—leveraging their capacity to interact with any document, provided they have the necessary identifiers to establish a connection.

Through hands-on examples, we have illustrated how a bound script can effortlessly interact with its container document to log a simple “Hello world” from a Google Sheet. In contrast, a stand-alone script showcased its prowess by turning a Google Sheet’s content into a dynamic web page title, demonstrating the power of Google Apps Script to build web applications.

The examples provided serve not only as a testament to the capabilities of Google Apps Script but also as a guide to spur your creativity in developing your own scripts. Whether it is a bound script that enriches the functionality of a Google Doc or a stand-alone script that transforms a spreadsheet’s data into a web app, the potential applications are vast and varied.

As we pivot to the next chapter, Exploring Core Services in Google Apps Script, we will delve deeper into the essential building blocks that empower these scripts. This upcoming chapter will unravel the intricacies of Google Apps Script services, which form the backbone of the automation and customization tasks that you will undoubtedly master. We will dissect the core services, explore their utilities, and learn how to harness their power to extend the functionality of your Google Workspace documents and beyond.

Embark on this journey with us as we continue to unfold the layers of Google Apps Script, ensuring that by the end of this guide, you will be equipped with the knowledge to craft both bound and stand-alone scripts that are functional and ingenious in their design and implementation. Prepare to expand your understanding and elevate your skills to the next level with Google Apps Script.

Key Terms

- **Container-Bound Scripts:** These scripts are intrinsically linked to a Google Workspace document, such as Google Sheets, Docs, Slides, or Forms. They are designed to interact directly with the content of their container document and cannot exist independently on Google Drive.
- **Stand-Alone Scripts:** Scripts created and operated independently of a Google Workspace document. They can be stored and managed in Google Drive and have the capability to interact with various Google services, although they need explicit identifiers to work with specific documents.
- **Google Workspace Document:** A file created with Google's productivity suite, which includes Google Docs, Sheets, Slides, and Forms. These documents live in the cloud on Google Drive and can be shared and collaborated on in real time.
- **Integrated Development Environment (IDE):** A software suite consolidating the basic tools developers need to write and test software. Google Apps Script's IDE is a web-based platform for developers to write, run, and debug scripts.
- **Container Document:** The specific Google Workspace document (Sheet, Doc, Slide, or Form) to which a bound script is attached.
- **Triggers:** Scripts that are set to run automatically in response to specific events or at specific times in Google Workspace documents, such as opening a document or editing a spreadsheet.
- **Google Drive:** A file storage and synchronization service created by Google. Users can store files in the cloud, synchronize files across devices, and share files.
- **Google Apps Script Project:** A project within Google Apps Script's IDE where scripts are written, stored, and managed. Each project can contain multiple scripts and associated files.
- **Deployment:** Publishing a script or application to be used in a production environment. In Google Apps Script, this typically involves setting up access permissions and possibly creating a web app URL.
- **A1 Notation:** A common way of referring to cells in spreadsheets where the column label is followed by the row number (for example, `"A1"` refers to the cell at the intersection of column A and row 1).
- **OAuth Authorization:** A protocol that allows applications to authenticate against Google services on behalf of the user. When deploying a script, users

are often prompted to authorize these permissions to allow the script to interact with Google services.

- **Google Workspace Add-Ons:** Custom extensions for Google Workspace applications that enhance their functionality. These can be stand-alone scripts that provide additional features within the Workspace environment.
- **Web Apps:** A type of stand-alone script deployment that allows scripts to serve web pages over the internet. This can be used to create interactive applications that integrate with Google Workspace data.

CHAPTER 3
SpreadsheetApp

Introduction

Let us now look at **SpreadsheetApp**, a cornerstone class in Google Apps Script, essential for accessing and manipulating spreadsheets. If you recall, we touched upon this class in our discussion about bound scripts in the previous chapter. But that was just a glimpse! **SpreadsheetApp** is a powerhouse of capabilities, and in this chapter, we will start unlocking its potential.

Before we dive into the specifics of **SpreadsheetApp**, it is essential to familiarize ourselves with the architecture of Google Sheets. Understanding this architecture is like learning the rules of a game—it is fundamental for writing effective and powerful scripts. So, let us roll up our sleeves and dive in, starting with the basics and gradually moving toward the more intricate aspects of **SpreadsheetApp**.

Structure

In this chapter, we will cover the following topics:

- The Google Sheets Architecture
- Navigating the Google Apps Script Documentation
- The **SpreadsheetApp** Class
- The **Spreadsheet** Class
- The **Sheet** Class
- The **Range** Class
- Building Graphic User Interfaces
- Builder Methods
- Other Noteworthy Classes

The Google Sheets Architecture

Let us delve into the architectural backbone of Google Sheets, which is essential for mastering **SpreadsheetApp**. Understanding this architecture is like learning the alphabet before writing a novel. In Google Sheets, everything revolves around key classes, each serving a distinct purpose. And remember, in our journey, we will often use the terms "`class`" and "`object`" interchangeably.

First and foremost, we have the **`SpreadsheetApp`** class. This is the grand gatekeeper of all things related to Google Sheets. It is our starting point for any script that intends to interact with spreadsheets.

Next in line is the **`Spreadsheet`** object. Think of it as your access card to a specific spreadsheet. Whenever you want to work on a particular spreadsheet, **`Spreadsheet`** is the object you will interact with.

Then we have the **`Sheet`** object. This is more granular than **`Spreadsheet`**. If a **`Spreadsheet`** object is akin to a book, a **`Sheet`** object is like a page in that book. It gives us access to a specific sheet (or tab) within a spreadsheet. This is where most of your sheet-specific operations will take place.

Last but not least is the **`Range`** object. This is where the precision work happens. A **`Range`** represents a single cell or a group of adjacent cells within a sheet. It is your go-to object for any operation that involves reading from or writing to specific cells in a spreadsheet.

Understanding these classes and their roles sets a strong foundation for your Google Sheets scripting adventure. Each class has its unique properties and methods, which we will explore in more detail. But for now, let us keep in mind that these are the building blocks we will be working with as we delve deeper into the functionalities of **`SpreadsheetApp`**.

Navigating the Google Apps Script Documentation

Before we dive into the intricacies of **`SpreadsheetApp`** and its related classes, let us equip ourselves with a fundamental skill: navigating the Google Apps Script documentation. Why is this important, you ask? Well, for a couple of critical reasons:

- **Quick Reference**: The realm of Google Apps Script is vast. You do not need to memorize everything, but you should be adept at finding information swiftly. The documentation is your encyclopedia, always there to provide answers.
- **Staying Updated**: Google Apps Script is a living, evolving entity. It is updated regularly with new features and improvements. Regularly consulting the documentation ensures you are always in sync with the latest advancements.

Ways to Navigate the Documentation

Let us start with **`SpreadsheetApp`**. When you visit the documentation page for **`SpreadsheetApp`** (https://developers.google.com/apps-script/reference/spreadsheet/spreadsheet-app), your journey into its depths begins. Here's what to do:

- **Explore the Methods**: The documentation lists various methods available under **`SpreadsheetApp`**. These methods are your tools, each performing a specific function.
- **Understand Return Types**: Notice what each method returns. Generally, they return other objects, leading you to further functionalities.
- **Discover Object Capabilities**: Once you know the objects returned by **`SpreadsheetApp`** methods, explore what you can do with these objects. It is like following a trail to uncover more possibilities.

The SpreadsheetApp Class

Now, back to our central focus: **`SpreadsheetApp`**. We have established that **`SpreadsheetApp`** is the key class that opens the door to all spreadsheet functionalities in Google Sheets. It is a global object, meaning it is readily available in your script environment. Just type **`SpreadsheetApp`**, and you're set to harness its power.

When you revisit the documentation, let us focus on some key operations:

- **Getting and Opening Spreadsheets**: Methods such as **`openById()`** and **`openByUrl()`** are crucial for accessing specific spreadsheets.
- **Creating New Spreadsheets**: You can create new sheets directly through **`SpreadsheetApp`** with methods like **`create()`**.
- **Accessing Active Elements**: Methods including **`getActiveSheet()`** or **`getActiveSpreadsheet()`** are handy for interacting with currently active sheets or the spreadsheet.

Understanding these operations is like learning the basic chords in music – once you know them, you can start creating your symphony in Google Sheets scripting. Let us turn the page and dive into the key objects and some specific examples that will illuminate the practical applications of these concepts.

Creating a New Spreadsheet

Creating a new spreadsheet is a breeze with Google Apps Script, and it is a great starting point for understanding how to manipulate Google Sheets programmatically. Let us walk through the process step-by-step.

To create a new spreadsheet, you use the **`SpreadsheetApp.create(name)`** method. If you need more control over the size of the spreadsheet, there is an overload of this method: **`SpreadsheetApp.create(name, numRows, numColumns)`**. This allows you to specify the number of rows and columns right off the bat.

When you invoke this method, it returns a **Spreadsheet** object. It is a common practice to store this object in a variable. Why? Because it lets you manipulate the spreadsheet further. Let us see this in action with an example: **SpreadsheetApp.create('Hello World').getUrl()**. This creates a new spreadsheet and gets its URL. Try logging this URL to the console to see the magic happen!

Here's a simple script to try out:

```
function createNewSpreadsheet() {
  const newSpreadsheet = SpreadsheetApp.create('Created with
Google Apps Script');
  const spreadsheetUrl = newSpreadsheet.getUrl();
  Logger.log(spreadsheetUrl);
}
```

Name your stand-alone script (Named "**Hello World**" in this case.) and enter the preceding code. When you run this script, Google Apps Script will prompt you to authorize it. This is a crucial security feature, as **SpreadsheetApp** can manipulate all spreadsheets you can access.

You will be greeted with a pop-up asking you to select your Google Account or to log in. Upon doing so, you will encounter a security alert:

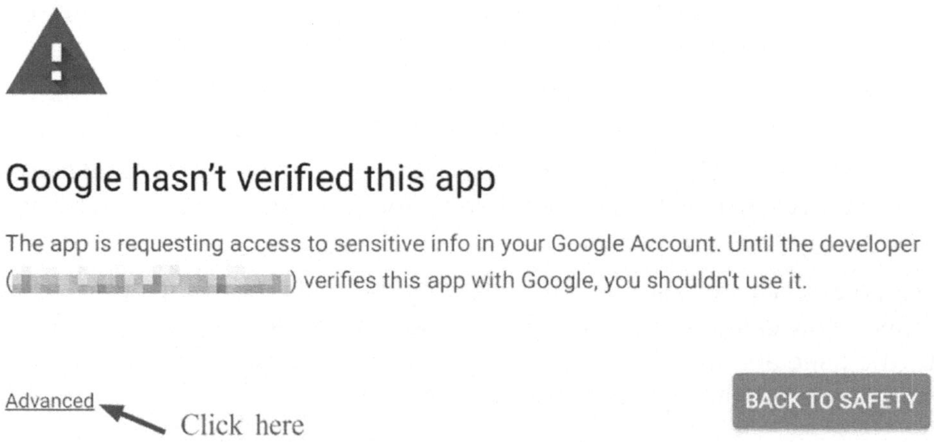

***Figure 3.1:** Security alert for Google Apps Script*

Do not worry, this is standard procedure. We know our script is safe, so click on **'Advanced'** and proceed to:

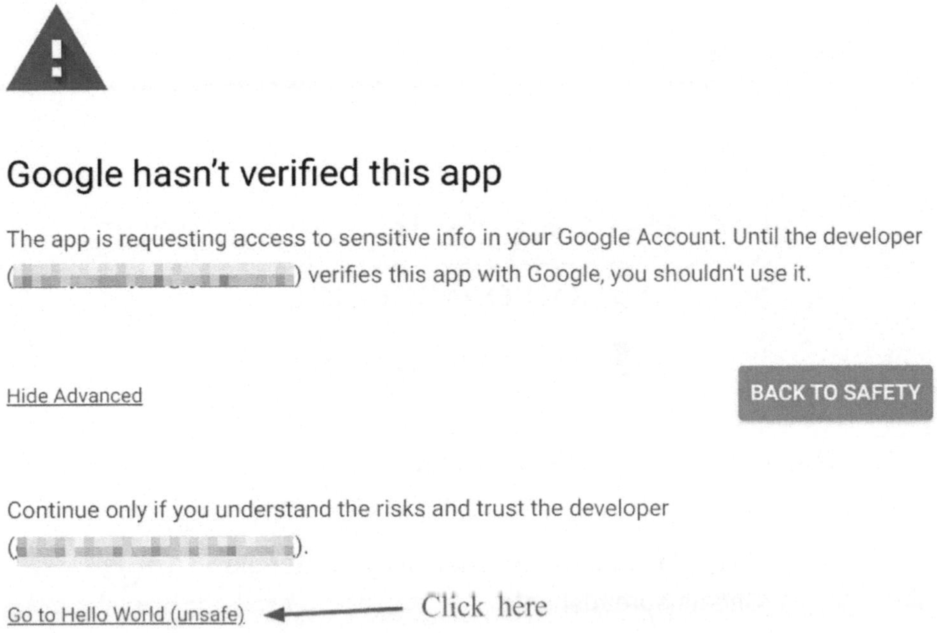

Figure 3.2: *Authorizing Google Apps Script Execution*

Next, you will see a summary of the access rights the script requires. In our case, it is permission to manipulate Google Spreadsheets:

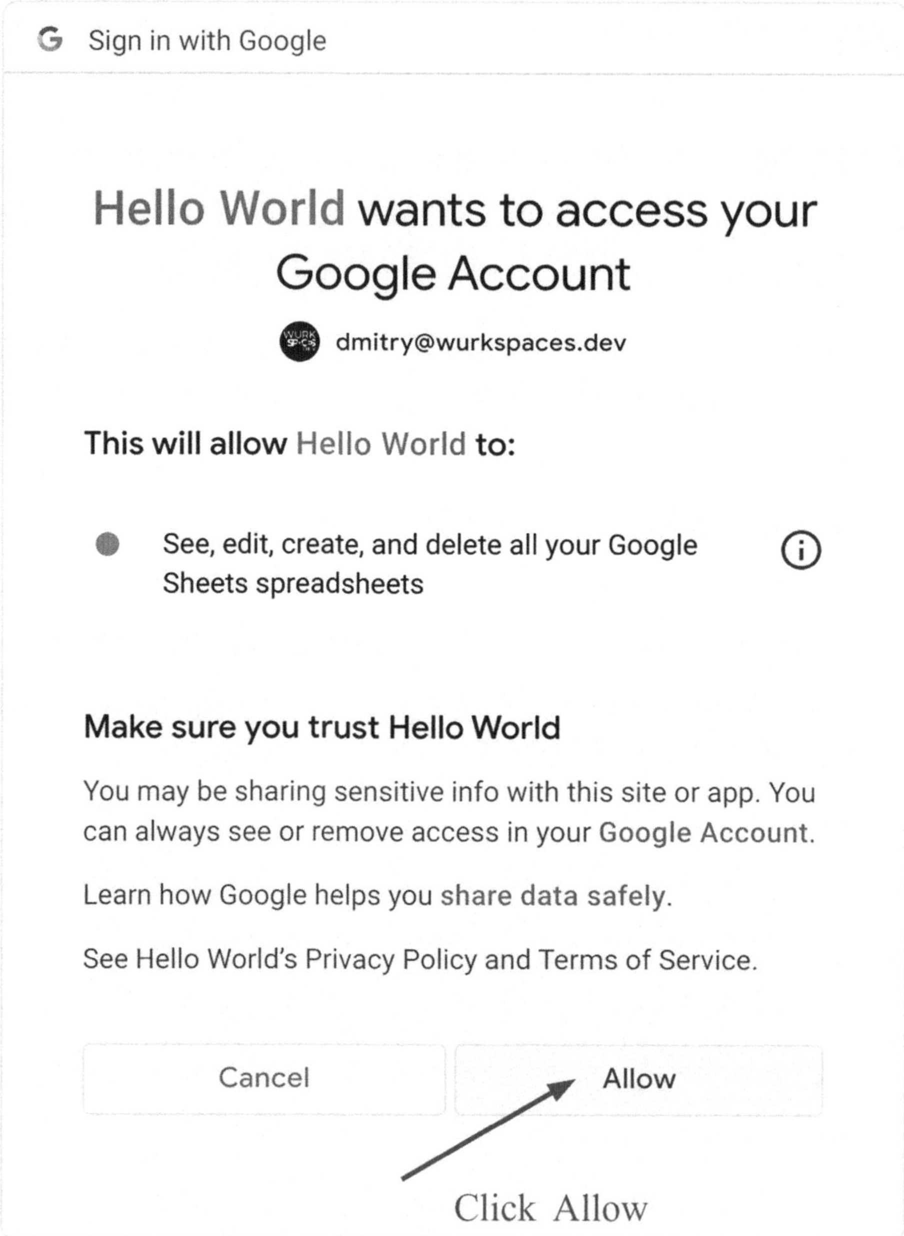

Figure 3.3: *Allowing Google Apps Script to run*

Click **`'Allow'`**, and your script is now authorized to run. This authorization is a one-time process, provided the script's scope does not change. However, if you later integrate it with, say, **`DocumentApp`** for Google Docs, you will need to go through the authorization process again.

If you have followed these steps, you should now see a URL in the execution log:

Figure 3.4: *Google Apps Script execution log*

Copy and paste this URL into a new browser tab, and voilà! You should see a brand-new spreadsheet titled "**`Created with Google Apps Script`**":

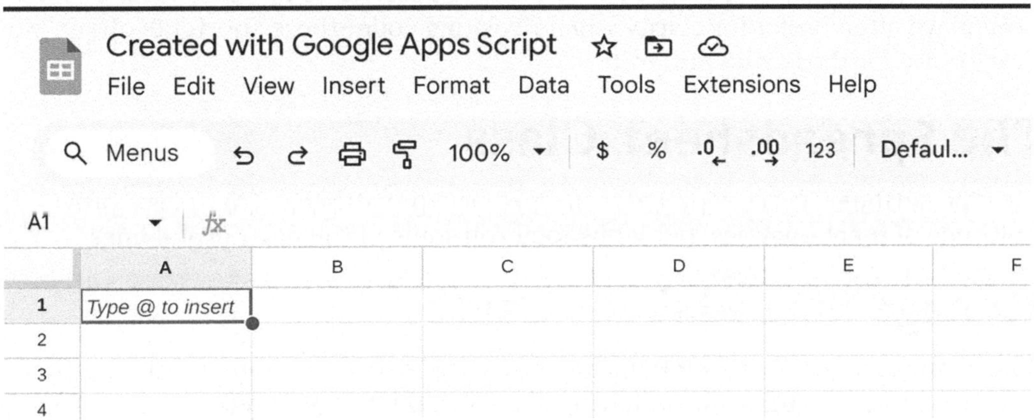

Figure 3.5: *A newly programmatically created Google Sheet*

Accessing an Existing Spreadsheet

Manipulating an existing spreadsheet is a common task in Google Apps Script. Depending on the type of script you are working with (container-bound or stand-alone), you have different options for accessing a spreadsheet.

For container-bound scripts directly attached to a Google Sheets file, use **`getActiveSpreadsheet()`** or the shorthand **`getActive()`**. These methods are convenient when working within the context of the spreadsheet hosting your script.

In contrast, for stand-alone scripts, you will use **`openById(spreadsheetId)`** or **`openByURL(spreadsheetUrl)`**. These methods are perfect when your script is separate from any specific spreadsheet and you need to access a sheet by its unique identifier or URL.

We have previously discussed the distinctions between container-bound and stand-alone scripts in depth. For those who need a refresher or want to experiment further, it is recommended to revisit our earlier discussions or exploring the Google Apps

Script documentation at https://developers.google.com/apps-script/reference/spreadsheet/spreadsheet-app.

Some Shortcuts

Despite the logical progression from app to spreadsheet, spreadsheet to sheet, and sheet to range, Google Apps Script offers shortcuts for bound scripts. These shortcuts are handy when you want to access something specific, like the active range of cells, without navigating through each level.

Methods such as **getActiveRange()**, **getSelection()**, and **getCurrentCell()** can be used directly from **SpreadsheetApp**. While it is possible to navigate level by level—a method we often prefer for clarity when revisiting code—these shortcuts offer a more direct route for those who prefer it.

The Spreadsheet Class

The **Spreadsheet** class represents a specific spreadsheet. This class provides a multitude of functionalities, but let us focus on some of the most useful ones.

Manage Spreadsheet Users

Google Apps Script allows you to manage view and edit access rights to a spreadsheet. Of course, this is contingent on having access rights to the spreadsheet in question. Here are some of the capabilities:

- **Retrieve the Spreadsheet Owner**:

  ```
  const sheet = SpreadsheetApp.getActiveSpreadsheet();
   const owner = sheet.getOwner(); // returns the User class
   Logger.log('This spreadsheet is owned by ' + owner.getEmail());
  ```

- **Add Viewers or Editors**:

  Methods such as **addEditor(emailAddress)**, **addEditors(emailAdresses)**, **addViewer(emailAddress)**, and **addViewers(emailAdresses)** allow you to add users with specific access rights. These methods accept either a single email or an array of emails.

  For example:

  ```
  const sheet = SpreadsheetApp.getActiveSpreadsheet();
  sheet
      .addViewer('john.doe@company.com')
      .addEditor('jane.doe@company.com');
  ```

  This code snippet adds a viewer and an editor to the spreadsheet. The ability to chain methods like **addViewer()** and **addEditor()** comes from the fact that these methods return the **Spreadsheet** class, allowing for subsequent calls to other class methods. This chaining is a powerful design pattern in Google Apps Script, and we will see more of it in the following chapters. It is a crucial concept to grasp for effective script writing.

Manage Spreadsheet Properties

When working with the **Spreadsheet** class in Google Apps Script, there is a plethora of operations you can perform to manage spreadsheet properties. Let us explore some of these functionalities:

- **Get and Rename Spreadsheet**

  You can easily fetch the current name of a spreadsheet or rename it. Here is how:

  ```
  const sheet = SpreadsheetApp.getActiveSpreadsheet();
  Logger.log(sheet.getName()); // prints the old name
  sheet.rename('New Sheet Name');
  Logger.log(sheet.getName()); // prints the new 'New Sheet Name'
  name
  ```

- **Get the Number of Sheets**

  Knowing the number of sheets in a spreadsheet can be particularly useful, especially if you need to loop over them:

  ```
  const sheet = SpreadsheetApp.getActiveSpreadsheet();
  const numSheets = sheet.getNumSheets();
  Logger.log(`This spreadsheet contains ${numSheets} sheets`);
  ```

  Notice the use of template literals here. It is a cleaner way to concatenate strings and variables compared to the traditional approach.

- **Get/Set Spreadsheet Locale**

  You can also retrieve or set the locale of a spreadsheet:

  ```
  const sheet = SpreadsheetApp.getActiveSpreadsheet();
  const locale = sheet.getSpreadsheetLocale();
  Logger.log(`This document's locale is ${locale}`);
  // prints: "This document's locale is hi_IN"
  ```

- **Get Spreadsheet Timezone**

  Retrieving the spreadsheet's timezone is just as straightforward:

  ```
  const sheet = SpreadsheetApp.getActiveSpreadsheet();
  const timeZone = sheet.getSpreadsheetTimeZone();
  Logger.log(`This document's time zone is ${timeZone}`);
  // prints: "This document's time zone is Asia/Calcutta"
  ```

- **Get Spreadsheet URL**

  To fetch the URL of the current spreadsheet, simply use:

  ```
  const url = SpreadsheetApp.getActiveSpreadsheet().getUrl();
  ```

More `Spreadsheet` Operations

There are numerous other operations you can perform with the **`Spreadsheet`** class. While we will not delve into all of them here, they are well-documented, and it is suggested to refer to the Google Apps Script Reference for more details. Here are a few highlights:

- **`copy(name)`**: This method copies the entire spreadsheet and returns the new one.
- **`createTextFinder(findText)`**: A powerful feature for finding and replacing text within the spreadsheet.
- **`getFormUrl()`**: If a Google Form is linked to the spreadsheet, you can retrieve its URL with this method.

We can also manipulate individual sheets (tabs) within a spreadsheet. This topic, however, is extensive enough to warrant its own section. So let us turn our attention to that next.

The `Sheet` Class

Exploring the **`Sheet`** class in Google Apps Script reveals a versatile set of capabilities for handling individual sheets within a spreadsheet. Let us use a practical example to illustrate these functionalities. We will be working with the following sample spreadsheet, and encourage you to create a similar one on your account to follow along:

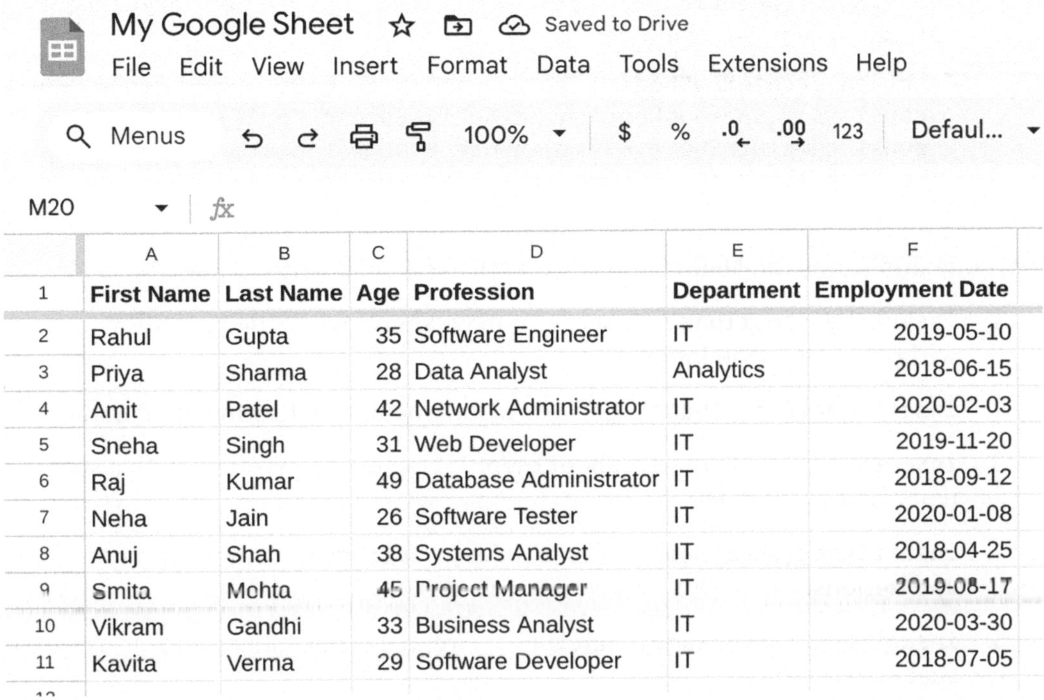

	A	B	C	D	E	F
1	First Name	Last Name	Age	Profession	Department	Employment Date
2	Rahul	Gupta	35	Software Engineer	IT	2019-05-10
3	Priya	Sharma	28	Data Analyst	Analytics	2018-06-15
4	Amit	Patel	42	Network Administrator	IT	2020-02-03
5	Sneha	Singh	31	Web Developer	IT	2019-11-20
6	Raj	Kumar	49	Database Administrator	IT	2018-09-12
7	Neha	Jain	26	Software Tester	IT	2020-01-08
8	Anuj	Shah	38	Systems Analyst	IT	2018-04-25
9	Smita	Mehta	45	Project Manager	IT	2019-08-17
10	Vikram	Gandhi	33	Business Analyst	IT	2020-03-30
11	Kavita	Verma	29	Software Developer	IT	2018-07-05

Figure 3.6: *A sample spreadsheet*

When dealing with **Sheet** objects, you generally have two paths: creating a new sheet or working with an existing one. Let us begin with how to create a new sheet.

`insertSheet()`

The primary method for creating a new sheet is **`insertSheet()`**. Like many in Google Apps Script, this method is overloaded, meaning it has multiple versions with different parameters. Here's a basic example:

```
function createNewSheet() {
  const spreadsheet = SpreadsheetApp.getActiveSpreadsheet();
  spreadsheet.insertSheet();
}
```

Executing this function adds a new sheet to your spreadsheet with a default name, such as **Sheet2**. But the flexibility of **`insertSheet()`** is evident in its various forms:

- **`insertSheet()`**: No arguments, adds a new sheet with a default name.
- **`insertSheet(sheetIndex)`**: Inserts the new sheet at the specified index (0-based).

- **insertSheet(sheetIndex, options)**: Similar to above, but also accepts an **options** object. For example:

```
function createNewSheet() {
  const ss = SpreadsheetApp.getActiveSpreadsheet();
  const templateSheet = ss.getSheetByName('Sheet1');
  ss.insertSheet(1, { template: templateSheet });
}
```

This code duplicates the **Sheet1** template at the second position (index 1).

1. **insertSheet(options)**: Inserts a new sheet with the specified options, without defining an index.
2. **insertSheet(sheetName)**: Creates a new sheet with the specified name.
3. **insertSheet(sheetName, sheetIndex)**: Creates a new sheet with a specified name at a given index.
4. **insertSheet(sheetName, sheetIndex, options)**: Combines name, index, and options.
5. **insertSheet(sheetName, options)**: Creates a new sheet with a name and specified options.

Method overloading is a common design pattern in Google Apps Script. Always refer to the documentation to explore the possibilities each method offers.

Accessing Existing Sheets

After covering sheet creation, let us shift our focus to working with existing sheets. Accessing an existing sheet is fundamental, especially when you want to read or manipulate data in a specific sheet. There are several ways to do this, which we will explore in the following section.

Retrieving Existing Sheets

In Google Apps Script, you can retrieve a sheet either by its name or by its index. Let us compare these two approaches with a practical example:

```
function getSheetByName(sheetName) {
  return SpreadsheetApp
    .getActiveSpreadsheet()
    .getSheetByName(sheetName);
}

function getSheetByIndex(sheetIndex) {
  return SpreadsheetApp
```

```
    .getActiveSpreadsheet()
    .getSheets()[sheetIndex];
}

function main() {
  // retrieves sheet named 'Sheet1' or null
  const sheet1 = getSheetByName('Sheet1');

  // retrieves sheet with index 0
  const sheet2 = getSheetByIndex(0);
}
```

Building upon the concept of method overloading, we can create our function that handles both retrieval by name and index. This is achieved by checking the type of the argument passed to the function:

```
function getSheet(indexOrName) {
  const spreadsheet = SpreadsheetApp.getActiveSpreadsheet();
  if ('string' === typeof indexOrName) return spreadsheet.
getSheetByName(indexOrName);
  if ('number' === typeof indexOrName) return spreadsheet.
getSheets()[indexOrName];
  return null;
}

function main() {
  // retrieves sheet named 'Sheet1' or null
  const sheet1 = getSheet('Sheet1');
  Logger.log(sheet1.getName());

  // retrieves sheet with index 0 or null
  const sheet2 = getSheet(0);
  Logger.log(sheet2.getName());
}
```

Executing the **main()** function should produce the following output in the execution log:

Figure 3.7: *Google Apps Script execution log*

Our **`getSheet(indexOrName)`** function is versatile, allowing us to pass either an index (number) or a name (string). This flexibility is achieved by using the **`typeof`** operator. The function then uses either **`getSheetByName(name)`** or **`getSheets()[index]`** based on the argument type. The function returns **`null`** if no matching sheet is found.

A couple of other coding techniques are used here:

a. **Omission of Curly Braces**: Notice the absence of curly braces after the **`if`** statements. This is a stylistic choice that can make the code cleaner and more readable, but it only works when the statement following the **`if`** fits on a single line and is not broken down by **`;`**.

b. **Skipping `else` Statements**: The use of **`return`** statements in the **`if`** blocks renders **`else`** or **`else if`** statements unnecessary. Once a return statement is executed, the function ends, so the subsequent conditions are only checked if the previous ones are false.

Here is an alternative version of the function with more syntax "**`noise`**":

```
// Avoid this version with else statements and unnecessary curly
braces
function getSheet(indexOrName) {
  const spreadsheet = SpreadsheetApp.getActiveSpreadsheet();
  if ('string' === typeof indexOrName) {
    return spreadsheet.getSheetByName(indexOrName);
  } else if ('number' === typeof indexOrName) {
    return spreadsheet.getSheets()[indexOrName];
  } else {
    return null;
  }
}
```

Although this version works identically, it is less streamlined and harder to read. Good code should be easily understandable by humans, not just machines.

After retrieving a sheet, a world of possibilities opens up for what we can do with it. Let us now explore some examples of how to work with the **Sheet** object.

Manipulating Rows and Columns

Working with rows and columns is fundamental to manipulating spreadsheets using Google Apps Script. Once you have retrieved a **Sheet** object, you can perform a variety of operations, including adding, updating, or deleting rows and columns. Let us explore these capabilities.

Determining the Number of Rows and Columns

First, it is useful to determine the existing number of rows and columns in a sheet. The following example demonstrates this:

```
function getLastRowAndColumn() {
  const sheet1 = SpreadsheetApp
    .getActiveSpreadsheet()
    .getSheetByName('Sheet1');

  const lastRow = sheet1.getLastRow();
  const lastColumn = sheet1.getLastColumn();

  Logger.log(`Sheet "${sheet1.getName()}" contains ${lastRow}
rows and ${lastColumn} columns`);
}
```

Executing this function will yield the number of rows and columns in the sheet:

Sheet "**Sheet1**" contains 11 rows and 6 columns

This is exactly what the spreadsheet contains:

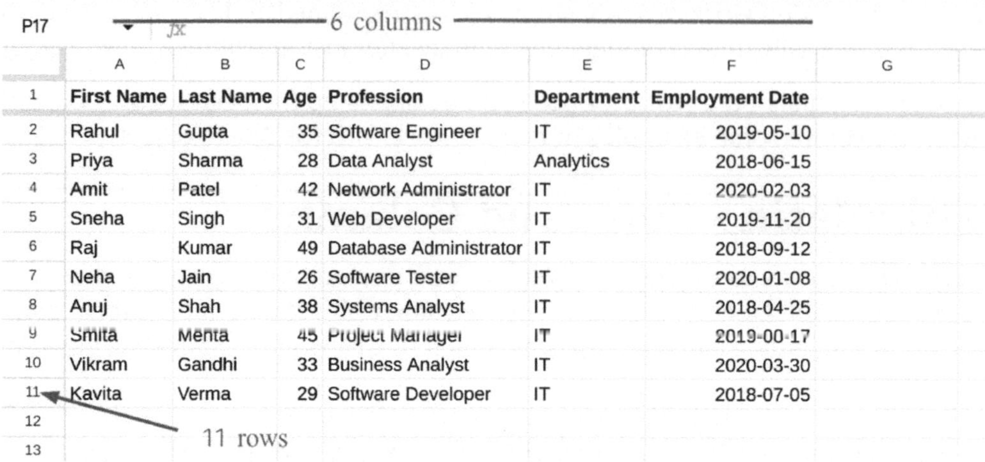

	A	B	C	D	E	F	G
1	**First Name**	**Last Name**	**Age**	**Profession**	**Department**	**Employment Date**	
2	Rahul	Gupta	35	Software Engineer	IT	2019-05-10	
3	Priya	Sharma	28	Data Analyst	Analytics	2018-06-15	
4	Amit	Patel	42	Network Administrator	IT	2020-02-03	
5	Sneha	Singh	31	Web Developer	IT	2019-11-20	
6	Raj	Kumar	49	Database Administrator	IT	2018-09-12	
7	Neha	Jain	26	Software Tester	IT	2020-01-08	
8	Anuj	Shah	38	Systems Analyst	IT	2018-04-25	
9	Smita	Mehta	45	Project Manager	IT	2019-00-17	
10	Vikram	Gandhi	33	Business Analyst	IT	2020-03-30	
11	Kavita	Verma	29	Software Developer	IT	2018-07-05	
12							
13							

Figure 3.8: *Rows and columns in a spreadsheet*

Note that **`getLastRow()`** and **`getLastColumn()`** return the *positions* of the last row and column, not their indices. This distinction is crucial, as the first position is "**`1`**", whereas the first index is "**`0`**".

Adding a New Row

Rows in a spreadsheet are represented as JavaScript arrays. The order of elements in the array should match the column order in your spreadsheet. Here's an example:

```
function getSheet(indexOrName) {
  const spreadsheet = SpreadsheetApp.getActiveSpreadsheet();
  if ('string' === typeof indexOrName) return spreadsheet.
getSheetByName(indexOrName);
  if ('number' === typeof indexOrName) return spreadsheet.
getSheets()[indexOrName];
  return null;
}

function addNewRow() {
  const row = [
    'Priya',
    'Aurora',
    43,
    'Scrum Master',
    'IT',
    '2024-01-08'
  ];
  const sheet = getSheet(0);
  sheet.appendRow(row)
}
```

Executing **`addNewRow()`** will insert a new row into the spreadsheet:

12:12 ▾ *fx* Priya

	A	B	C	D	E	F	G
1	**First Name**	**Last Name**	**Age**	**Profession**	**Department**	**Employment Date**	
2	Rahul	Gupta	35	Software Engineer	IT	2019-05-10	
3	Priya	Sharma	28	Data Analyst	Analytics	2018-06-15	
4	Amit	Patel	42	Network Administrator	IT	2020-02-03	
5	Sneha	Singh	31	Web Developer	IT	2019-11-20	
6	Raj	Kumar	49	Database Administrator	IT	2018-09-12	
7	Neha	Jain	26	Software Tester	IT	2020-01-08	
8	Anuj	Shah	38	Systems Analyst	IT	2018-04-25	
9	Smita	Mehta	45	Project Manager	IT	2019-08-17	
10	Vikram	Gandhi	33	Business Analyst	IT	2020-03-30	
11	Kavita	Verma	29	Software Developer	IT	2018-07-05	
12	Priya	Aurora	43	Scrum Master	IT	2024-01-08	
13							

***Figure 3.9**: Programmatically inserted new row*

Notice that we are re-using the **`addNewRow()`** function that we built before. This is in fact one of the main features of functions: they allow us to write small, manageable, and re-usable blocks of code, making them easy to maintain and to read.

If you now re-run **`getLastRowAndColumn()`**, it should now print:

Sheet "**`Sheet1`**" contains **12** rows and 6 columns

Deleting Rows

Suppose we want to delete all rows containing "**`Analyst`**" in a specific column. The following function demonstrates this:

```
function removeAnalysts() {
  const sheet = getSheet(0);
  const numRows = sheet.getLastRow();
  const professionColumn = 4;
  for (let i = 1; i <= numRows; i++) {
    const profession = sheet.getRange(i, professionColumn).
getValue();
    if (profession.includes('Analyst')) sheet.deleteRow(i);
  }
}
```

After running this function, the spreadsheet should have no rows containing "**Analyst**":

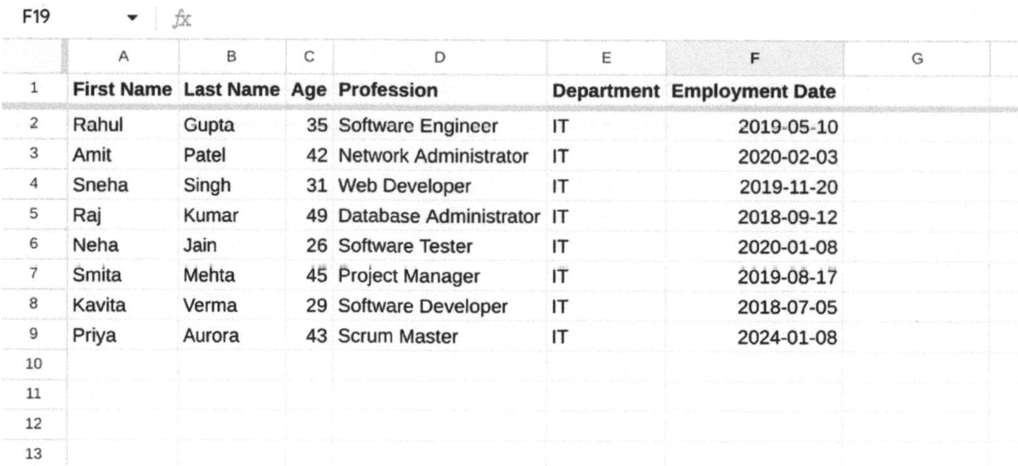

F19

	A	B	C	D	E	F	G
1	**First Name**	**Last Name**	**Age**	**Profession**	**Department**	**Employment Date**	
2	Rahul	Gupta	35	Software Engineer	IT	2019-05-10	
3	Amit	Patel	42	Network Administrator	IT	2020-02-03	
4	Sneha	Singh	31	Web Developer	IT	2019-11-20	
5	Raj	Kumar	49	Database Administrator	IT	2018-09-12	
6	Neha	Jain	26	Software Tester	IT	2020-01-08	
7	Smita	Mehta	45	Project Manager	IT	2019-08-17	
8	Kavita	Verma	29	Software Developer	IT	2018-07-05	
9	Priya	Aurora	43	Scrum Master	IT	2024-01-08	
10							
11							
12							
13							

Figure 3.10: *Rows containing analysts removed*

This function loops over every row and checks the profession that we know is in column D, which has position 4. We read the value in that column in every row and check whether it contains the word "**Analyst**" with the built-in JavaScript **String** method, **includes()**. If such is the case, we call **deleteRow()**.

Note: *The above method for deleting rows is not the most efficient, especially for larger spreadsheets. We will explore more efficient ways later.*

More Sheet Operations

The **Sheet** class in Google Apps Script offers a rich set of functionalities beyond what we have covered so far. While we will not delve into each one in detail, listed below are some additional operations that can significantly enhance your ability to manipulate and manage sheets. For a deeper understanding, you can refer to the documentation at https://developers.google.com/apps-script/reference/spreadsheet/spreadsheet and `https://developers.google.com/apps-script/reference/spreadsheet/sheet`.

- **Delete a Sheet**: You can delete a specific sheet or the currently active sheet using **deleteSheet(sheet)** or **deleteActiveSheet()**, respectively, from the **Spreadsheet** class.
- **Duplicate the Active Sheet**: Create a copy of the active sheet with **duplicateActiveSheet()** from the **Spreadsheet** class.
- **Move the Active Sheet**: Change the position of the active sheet within the

spreadsheet using **moveActiveSheet(pos)** from the **Spreadsheet** class.

- **Sort a Sheet**: Organize data in a sheet by a specific column using **sort(columnPosition, [ascending])** from the **Sheet** class.
- **Insert Images**: Add images to your sheet using **insertImage**, which has four overloads, from the **Sheet** class.
- **Delete Columns/Rows**: Remove specific columns or rows using **deleteColumn(columnPosition)**, **deleteColumns(columnPosition, howMany)**, **deleteRow(rowPosition)**, or **deleteRows(rowPosition, howMany)** from the **Sheet** class.
- **Manage Frozen Rows/Columns**: Control frozen rows and columns using **getFrozenColumns()**, **setFrozenColumns(columns)**, **getFrozenRows()**, or **setFrozenRows(rows)** from the **Sheet** class.
- **Hide/Unhide Columns and Rows**: Conceal or reveal columns and rows with **hideColumn(column)**, **unhideColumn(column)**, **hideRow(row)**, or **unhideRow(row)** from the **Sheet** class.
- **Identify Hidden Columns/Rows**: Determine if columns or rows are hidden by the user or by a filter using **isColumnHiddenByUser(columnPosition)** or **isRowHiddenByUser(rowPosition)** from the **Sheet** class.
- **Get User Selection**: Retrieve the current selection in the sheet with **getSelection()** from the **Sheet** class.
- **Get Images**: Access any images within the sheet using **getImages()** from the **Sheet** class.
- **Insert Rows**: Add rows at specific positions with **insertRowAfter (afterPosition)**, **insertRowBefore(beforePosition)**, **insertRowsAfter (afterPosition, howMany)**, or **insertRowsBefore(beforePosition, howMany)** from the **Sheet** class.

Each of these operations opens up new possibilities for automating and enhancing your work with Google Sheets. Up next, we will turn our focus to ranges. Ranges provide more granular control over spreadsheet data, allowing for precise manipulation and analysis of cell-based data. Let us dive into how ranges can elevate your scripting capabilities.

The Range Class

You will likely use the **Range** class at least 90% of the time when writing scripts for Google Sheets. It gives us granular control over the contents of a spreadsheet.

Retrieving Values, Formulas, and Formatting

We start by extracting values from a range. The **extractValues** function demonstrates this process:

```
function extractValues() {
  const sheet = getSheet(0); // Retrieve the first sheet
  const lastRow = sheet.getLastRow(); // Get the last row with
data
  const lastColumn = sheet.getLastColumn(); // Get the last
column with data
  const range = sheet.getRange(1, 1, lastRow, lastColumn);
// Define the range
  const values = range.getValues(); // Get all values from the
range
  Logger.log(JSON.stringify(values, null, 2)); // Log values in a
readable format
}
```

Executing this function yields a JSON output of a two-dimensional array:

```
[
  [
    "First Name",
    "Last Name",
    "Age",
    "Profession",
    "Department",
    "Employment Date"
  ],
  [
    "Rahul",
    "Gupta",
    35,
    "Software Engineer",
    "IT",
    "2019-05-09T18:30:00.000Z"
  ],
  [
    "Amit",
    "Patel",
    42,
    "Network Administrator",
    "IT",
    "2020-02-02T18:30:00.000Z"
```

```
  ],
  ...
]
```

The first sub-array contains the headers and the following ones contain actual data. This is an incredibly simple yet effective data structure that can be easily processed with naive JavaScript; we will look into this shortly.

To simplify the process, you can use **getDataRange()** to automatically identify the range:

```
function extractValues() {
  const sheet = getSheet(0); // Retrieve the first sheet
  const range = sheet.getDataRange(); // Automatically get the
data range
  const values = range.getValues(); // Get values from the range
  Logger.log(JSON.stringify(values, null, 2)); // Log values
}
```

getDataRange() determines the first and last columns and rows with data. To see the difference in the output format, let us use **getDisplayValues()**:

```
function extractValues() {
  const sheet = getSheet(0); // Retrieve the first sheet
  const range = sheet.getDataRange(); // Automatically get the
data range
  const values = range.getDisplayValues(); // Get display values
from the range
  Logger.log(range.getA1Notation()); // Log the A1 notation of
the range, e.g. 'A1:F9'
  Logger.log(JSON.stringify(values, null, 2)); // Log values
}
```

The JSON output is similar, but notice the difference in how certain data types are represented:

```
[
  [
    "First Name",
    "Last Name",
    "Age",
    "Profession",
    "Department",
    "Employment Date"
  ],
  [
    "Rahul",
    "Gupta",
    "35",
```

```
        "Software Engineer",
        "IT",
        "2019-05-10"
      ],
      [
        "Amit",
        "Patel",
        "42",
        "Network Administrator",
        "IT",
        "2020 02 03"
      ],
      ...
    ]
```

When working with data in Google Sheets using Google Apps Script, understanding the nuances of the **Range** class methods, such as **getValues()** and **getDisplayValues()**, is crucial. The **getValues()** method retrieves data from a range as **Number** and **Date** objects, corresponding to their native JavaScript types. This functionality is particularly powerful because it allows for direct manipulation of these data types using JavaScript, enabling complex calculations and data processing.

In contrast, **getDisplayValues()** extracts all values as strings, exactly how they appear in the Google Sheet. This includes any formatting applied to the data, such as date formats or number formatting. This method is particularly useful when you need to present or utilize the data in the same format as it appears visually in the sheet. The key difference between these two methods lies in the data types they return and their intended use cases.

Beyond these methods, the **Range** class provides several others that target different aspects of the data:

- **getFormulas()** extracts the actual formulas present in the cells, if any, instead of their calculated output. This is useful for analyzing or replicating the logic used in the spreadsheet.
- **getTextStyles()** returns the text styles (font size, color, and so on) for the cells in the range, allowing for a programmatic understanding of cell formatting.
- **getFontWeights()** provides the weight (normal, bold, and so on) of the font in the top-left corner of the range, which can be used for styling analysis or modifications.

Each of these methods has a singular counterpart such as **getValue()**, **getDisplayValue()**, **getFormula()**, and so on, which operate on the single cell at the top-left corner of the range, returning a single value instead of a 2D array.

Similarly, to write data back to the spreadsheet, methods such as **setValue(value)** and **setValues(values)** are used. While **setValue(value)** is used to write a single value to a cell, **setValues(values)** accepts a 2D array of values, matching the size of the range it is applied to. This distinction is important for correctly updating spreadsheet data, whether updating a single cell or a larger range.

For example, consider a scenario where you need to update a range of cells with new data, perhaps calculated or retrieved from an external source. In this case, **setValues(values)** would be the method of choice, allowing you to efficiently update multiple cells in a single operation efficiently, thus maintaining the integrity and structure of your data within the spreadsheet. The capability to read from and write to a range using these methods underpins much of the functionality of Google Apps Script, making it a versatile tool for spreadsheet automation and enhancement.

Writing Data with setValues()

To write data to a range, we use **setValues()**. The following example demonstrates this:

```
// A helper function that calculates the number of days between
two dates
function getDifferenceInDays(date1, date2) {
    date1 = (date1 instanceof Date) ? date1 : new Date(date1);
    date2 = (date2 instanceof Date) ? date2 : new Date(date2);

    const timeDiff = Math.abs(date2.getTime() - date1.getTime());
    const diffDays = Math.ceil(timeDiff / (1000 * 3600 * 24));
    return diffDays;
}

// Calculates number of days employees worked in the company
// and inserts them into the spreadsheet
function insertEmploymentDays() {

  // Initiate a new array that we will insert into the sheet
  // It will be a 2D array with one column and multiple rows
  const daysEmployed = [['Days Employed']];

  // Extract last row and column and the current values from the
sheet
  const sheet = getSheet(0);
  const lastRow = sheet.getLastRow();
  const lastColumn = sheet.getLastColumn();
  const range = sheet.getRange(1, 1, lastRow, lastColumn);
  const values = range.getValues();
```

```
  // Extract the current date
  const now = new Date();

  // The column index where the employment date is stored
  const employmentDateIndex = 5;

  // Iterate over the values, starting with index 1 as we want to
skip the headers
  for(let i = 1; i < values.length; i++) {
    // Extract the employment date for the current row
    const employmentDate = values[i][employmentDateIndex];

    // Calculate the number of days worked in the company using a
helper function
    const daysAtWork = getDifferenceInDays(employmentDate, now);

    // Push the calculated value into daysEmployed as an array
with a single value
    // Representing a single column
    daysEmployed.push([daysAtWork])
  }

  // Insert the values into a new column (lastColumn + 1)
  // The length property helps us make sure that the range is the
same size
  // as the array we are inserting
  sheet
    .getRange(1, lastColumn + 1, daysEmployed.length, day-
sEmployed[0].length)
    .setValues(daysEmployed);
}
```

This script calculates and inserts the number of days each employee has worked into the spreadsheet. In this script, we calculate and insert the number of days each employee has worked into the spreadsheet, showcasing the robust capabilities of the **`setValues()`** method in conjunction with a two-dimensional array structure. Central to this process is the **`getDifferenceInDays`** function, intricately designed to determine the tenure duration of each employee by calculating the difference in days between two dates.

The function adeptly manipulates the JavaScript **`Date`** object for handling and processing dates and times. It starts by ensuring that both inputs, **`date1`** and **`date2`**, are **`Date`** objects, converting them if necessary. This flexibility allows the function to handle various date formats seamlessly. The core of the calculation lies in using **`Date.prototype.getTime()`**, which fetches the time in milliseconds since the Unix Epoch, providing a reliable basis for time difference computation. To ensure a positive outcome irrespective of the dates' sequence, **Math.abs()** is employed, followed by dividing the millisecond difference by the number of milliseconds in a day (accounting for seconds, minutes, and hours in a day). Finally, **Math.ceil()** rounds up the result to the nearest whole number, ensuring that partial days are considered in the total count.

Complementing this calculation is the **Array.prototype.push** method, a fundamental tool in JavaScript for appending new elements to an array's end while updating its length. In our script, this method sequentially adds the calculated number of days each employee has worked into the **daysEmployed** array.

The structure of the **daysEmployed** array is a prime example of the effectiveness of two-dimensional arrays in organizing data. It is formatted such that each internal array represents a row in the Google Sheet. The first element is the header **['Days Employed']**, and each subsequent sub-array contains a single element – the computed days each employee has worked.

To accurately place this data into the Google Sheet, we use the **.getRange** method of the **Sheet** object. This method is adept at specifying particular ranges in the sheet for data manipulation. In our usage, the method's parameters – starting row index **1**, new column index **lastColumn + 1**, total number of rows **daysEmployed.length**, and number of columns **daysEmployed[0].length** – are meticulously set to ensure that the data from **daysEmployed** precisely fits into a newly created column in the spreadsheet, corresponding to the necessary rows and columns. This detailed and methodical approach guarantees that the data is inserted correctly, reflecting the calculated days of employment for each employee in the specified range.

Manipulating 2D Arrays

Two-dimensional arrays are integral to working with Google Sheets in Google Apps Script, as they effectively represent the data in a sheet. Understanding JavaScript arrays and their methods is key to successful scripting. Here's a deeper look into working with these arrays.

The `length` Property

Understanding the **length** property of arrays is fundamental. It indicates the number of elements in an array. For example, executing **Logger.log(['Banana', 'Apple', 'Orange'].length)** prints **3**. Remember that array indices start at **0**, so the index of the last element is **length - 1**.

Accessing the last element of an array can be done as follows:

```
const fruits = ['Banana', 'Apple', 'Orange'];
const lastFruit = fruits[fruits.length - 1]; // Orange
```

For two-dimensional arrays, understanding the length of both the outer and inner arrays is crucial:

```
function twoDimArrayLength() {
  const warehouseData = [
    ["Item ID", "Item Name", "Quantity"],
    ["101", "Screwdrivers", 150],
    ["102", "Hammers", 85],
    ["103", "Wrenches", 200]
  ];

  Logger.log(`Number of rows: ${warehouseData.length}`);
  Logger.log(`Number of columns: ${warehouseData[0].length}`);
}
```

The **warehouseData** array is structured as a two-dimensional array, meaning it is an array containing other arrays as its elements. Each of these inner arrays represents a row within our conceptual spreadsheet.

In our specific case, **warehouseData** comprises four such inner arrays. This is reflected in its **length** property, which is 4. This length signifies the number of rows in our data set. However, to understand the structure of each row, we need to examine the inner arrays. These inner arrays, or rows, each consist of three entries, which is evident when we inspect the length of any of these inner arrays. For instance, **warehouseData[0].length** yields a value of 3, indicating that there are three columns in our data.

An important characteristic of such two-dimensional arrays in Google Apps Script is the uniformity in the length of these inner arrays. Regardless of whether some cells in the spreadsheet are empty, they are represented as empty strings (**''**) in the array. This ensures that each inner array, or row, maintains a consistent length across the dataset. Therefore, the length of any inner array (such as **warehouseData[0].length**) reliably indicates the number of columns.

This consistency plays a significant role in scripting for Google Sheets. For example, when we need to ensure that a range within a sheet is the same size as our array, we can use the **.getRange()** method with parameters that reflect the dimensions of our array. In the **daysEmployed** array scenario, we used **.getRange(1, lastColumn + 1, daysEmployed.length, daysEmployed[0].length)** to accurately define the range. This approach ensures that our range in Google Sheets corresponds precisely to the size and shape of our two-dimensional array, allowing for seamless data manipulation and analysis.

Reading Values and Looping Over 2D Arrays

To access specific data in a 2D array or to loop through it, you will often use nested loops. For instance, to access the quantity sold of Paracetamol in the following array:

```
const pharmacySalesData = [
  ['Medicine', 'Quantity Sold', 'Revenue'],
  ['Aspirin', 100, 2000],
  ['Paracetamol', 150, 3000],
  ['Ibuprofen', 80, 1600]
];
```

You would use **pharmacySalesData[2][1]**.

To effectively iterate over each element in such an array, nested **for** loops are typically used. These loops allow you to access each row and column within the array.

Let us consider the **pharmacySalesData** array, which contains information about various medicines, their quantities sold, and the resulting revenue. To loop over this data, we employ two nested **for** loops: the outer loop iterates over each row (each medicine), and the inner loop iterates over the columns (the attributes of each medicine).

Here's an example function demonstrating this approach:

```
function loopOver2DArray() {
  const pharmacySalesData = [
    ['Medicine', 'Quantity Sold', 'Revenue'],
    ['Aspirin', 100, 2000],
    ['Paracetamol', 150, 3000],
    ['Ibuprofen', 80, 1600],
  ];

  const bestSellers = [['Medicine', 'Quantity Sold']];

  for (let i = 0; i < pharmacySalesData.length; i++) {
    for (let j = 0; j < pharmacySalesData[i].length; j++) {
      Logger.log(pharmacySalesData[i][j]); // Logs every element
in the array
    }
  }

  Logger.log(bestSellers);
}
```

In this function, every element of the **pharmacySalesData** array is logged, providing a row-by-row and column-by-column breakdown of the data.

Looping over this array to extract specific data can be done as follows:

```
function loopOver2DArray() {
  const pharmacySalesData = [
    ['Medicine', 'Quantity Sold', 'Revenue'],
    ['Aspirin', 100, 2000],
    ['Paracetamol', 150, 3000],
    ['Ibuprofen', 80, 1600],
  ];

  const bestSellers = [['Medicine', 'Quantity Sold']];

  for (let i = 1; i < pharmacySalesData.length; i++) { // Start
at 1 to skip headers
    if (pharmacySalesData[i][1] >= 100) { // Check if quantity
sold is >= 100
      bestSellers.push([pharmacySalesData[i][0], pharmacySales-
Data[i][1]]);
    }
  }

  Logger.log(bestSellers);
}
```

This function creates a new array, **bestSellers**, containing only those medicines that have sold 100 or more units. The loop skips the header row by starting at index 1, and only items meeting the sales criteria are added to **bestSellers**.

Understanding and effectively utilizing 2D arrays is a vital skill in Google Apps Script. It allows for more advanced data manipulation and analysis directly within your scripts, facilitating robust and dynamic interactions with your Google Sheets data.

Code Quest

This exercise is an excellent way to apply your understanding of JavaScript arrays and Google Apps Script:

1. **Create a Spreadsheet**: Enter the sales data from the **pharmacySalesData** array into a new Google Sheet.
2. **Create a Bound Script**: In the spreadsheet, create a script that includes the **loopOver2DArray()** function.
3. **Modify the Function**: Adapt **loopOver2DArray()** to read data directly from the spreadsheet, determine bestsellers, create a new sheet, and insert the bestscllcr data into it.

push(), pop(), shift(), unshift()

These methods modify arrays at their start or end:

a. **push()**: Adds one or more elements to the end of an array and returns the new length.

b. **pop()**: Removes the last element from an array and returns that element.

c. **shift()**: Removes the first element from an array and returns that element.

d. **unshift()**: Adds one or more elements to the beginning of an array and returns the new length.

Here's a combined example using a 2D array:

```
const inventory = [['Item', 'Quantity'], ['Screws', 100],
['Nails', 200]];
inventory.push(['Bolts', 300]); // Add to the end
inventory.unshift(['Item ID', '0001']); // Add to the start
inventory.pop(); // Remove 'Bolts'
inventory.shift(); // Remove 'Item ID'
Logger.log(inventory);
```

slice(), splice(), delete()

These methods offer more complex operations:

a. **slice()**: Returns a shallow copy of a portion of an array.

b. **splice()**: Changes the contents of an array by removing or replacing existing elements and/or adding new elements in place.

c. **delete()**: Deletes an element from an array (leaves an **'undefined'** hole).

Example demonstrating their differences:

```
const inventory = [['Item', 'Quantity'], ['Screws', 100],
['Nails', 200]];
const sliced = inventory.slice(1, 3); // Copies part of the array
inventory.splice(1, 1, ['Bolts', 300]); // Replaces 'Screws' with
'Bolts'
delete inventory[2]; // Deletes 'Nails'
Logger.log(sliced);
Logger.log(inventory);
```

`toString()`, `join()`, `JSON.stringify()`, `JSON.parse()`

These methods are used to convert arrays into strings or JSON and vice versa:

- **`toString()`**: Converts an array into a string with commas between elements.
- **`join()`**: Joins all elements of an array into a string and can accept a separator.
- **`JSON.stringify()`**: Converts an array into a JSON string.
- **`JSON.parse()`**: Parses a JSON string, constructing the JavaScript value or object described by the string.

Example:

```
const inventory = [['Item', 'Quantity'], ['Screws', 100],
['Nails', 200]];
const stringified = JSON.stringify(inventory);
const joined = inventory.join('; ');
const parsed = JSON.parse(stringified);
Logger.log(stringified);
Logger.log(joined);
Logger.log(parsed);
```

These examples and explanations offer a fundamental understanding of array manipulation in JavaScript, crucial for effective Google Apps Script programming, especially when dealing with data in Google Sheets.

Advanced Array Methods in JavaScript

In the realm of Google Apps Script and JavaScript, mastering advanced array methods can significantly enhance your ability to manipulate and process data. These methods often involve the concept of callback functions, a fundamental aspect of JavaScript that allows for functional programming approaches. A callback function is a function passed into another function as an argument and then executed inside the outer function.

Let us now look at the most useful array methods.

`forEach()`

The **`forEach()`** method is a straightforward yet powerful tool. It executes a provided function once for each element in an array. This method is particularly useful for iterating over array elements to perform operations such as logging data or applying a function to each element. In the following example, **`forEach()`** is used to log each row of sheet data, effectively iterating over the array and performing an action for each row:

```
const sheetData = [['Product', 'Price'], ['Pen', 1.2],
['Notebook', 2.5]];

function logEachRow(row, index) {
  if (index > 0) Logger.log(`Row ${index}: ${row[0]},
${row[1]}`);
}

function iterateSheetData() {
  sheetData.forEach(logEachRow);
}
```

map()

The **map()** method is used to transform elements in an array. It creates a new array by calling a provided function on every element in the calling array. This method is ideal for scenarios where you need to apply a transformation to an array's elements and create a new array with the transformed values. For instance, in the following example, **map()** is used to calculate and add tax to the prices of products:

```
const sheetData = [['Product', 'Price'], ['Pen', 1.2],
['Notebook', 2.5]];

function priceWithTax(row, index) {
  return index === 0 ? row : [row[0], row[1] * 1.1];
}

function applyTaxToPrices() {
  const updatedSheetData = sheetData.map(priceWithTax);
  Logger.log(updatedSheetData);
}
```

filter()

filter() creates a new array with all elements that pass a test implemented by a provided function. It is particularly useful when you need to select a subset of elements from an array based on certain criteria. In the following example, **filter()** is used to extract items from a dataset that have a price greater than a specified amount:

```
const sheetData = [['Product', 'Price'], ['Pen', 1.2],
['Notebook', 2.5]];

function filterExpensiveItems(row) {
  return row[1] > 2;
```

```
}

function getExpensiveItems() {
  const expensiveItems = sheetData.filter(filterExpensiveItems);
  Logger.log(expensiveItems);
}
```

reduce()

Finally, the **reduce()** method executes a reducer function on each element of the array, resulting in a single output value or in a format transformation, like an object. This method is extremely versatile and can be used for tasks such as summing values, compiling data into a single structure, or even constructing new objects. In the following example, **reduce()** is employed to calculate the total price of items in a sheet:

```
const sheetData = [['Product', 'Price'], ['Pen', 1.2],
['Notebook', 2.5]];

function calculateTotalPrice(accumulator, row) {
  return typeof row[1] === 'number' ? accumulator + row[1] :
accumulator;
}

function getTotalPrice() {
  const totalPrice = sheetData.reduce(calculateTotalPrice, 0);
  console.log(`Total Price: ${totalPrice}`);
}
```

In this case, **reduce()** starts with an accumulator value of **0** and adds up the prices of each product, skipping the header row. The final result is a single value representing the total price.

Understanding and utilizing these advanced array methods can significantly streamline your Google Apps Script code, allowing for more concise, readable, and efficient scripting. Each method offers unique benefits and capabilities, making them indispensable tools in the JavaScript programmer's toolkit.

Other Key Operations

Going beyond the basic manipulation of the **Range** class, let us look at some other operations that can be useful.

Range Class Methods

The **Range** class in Google Apps Script offers numerous methods to interact with spreadsheet data. Here are a few notable ones:

- **canEdit()**: Determines whether the user has permission to edit every cell in the range. Useful for scripts that need to check edit permissions before attempting to modify a range.
- **clear()**, **clearFormat()**, **clearNote()**: These methods clear content, formats, and notes from a range, respectively. They are handy for resetting or cleaning up data in specific ranges.
- **copyTo()**: Copies data from one range to another. This method is crucial for data manipulation tasks such as copying a set of values to another part of the sheet.
- **createPivotTable()**: Creates an empty pivot table from the range. Pivot tables are powerful tools for data analysis, and this method simplifies their creation.
- **createFilter()**: Applies a filter to the specified range, allowing for the sorting and filtering of data within the range.
- **merge()**: Merges the cells in the range together into a single block. This method is often used for formatting purposes.
- **randomize()**: Randomizes the order of the rows in the range. It can be used for tasks including shuffling data or creating random samples.
- **check()**, **uncheck()**: Changes the state of checkboxes in the range to "**checked**" or "**unchecked**," respectively. These methods are useful for managing checklists or forms within a sheet.

RangeList Object

A **RangeList** object represents a collection of non-adjacent ranges within a Google Sheet. It is especially useful for performing operations on multiple, discrete ranges simultaneously.

- **Key Differences Between Range and RangeList:**
  - **Range**: Represents a contiguous block of cells.
  - **RangeList**: Represents multiple, non-contiguous cell ranges.
- Example of Using RangeList:

```
function highlightSpecificTasks() {
   const sheet = SpreadsheetApp.getActiveSpreadsheet().get
ActiveSheet();
   const ranges = ["A2:F2", "A5:F5", "A8:F8", "A11:F11"]; //
```

```
Non-contiguous rows

    const rangeList = sheet.getRangeList(ranges);
    rangeList.setBackground("yellow"); // Highlights specified
tasks
  }
```

SpreadsheetApp.flush()

SpreadsheetApp.flush() is a crucial method for ensuring that all pending changes to the spreadsheet are applied immediately. This can be particularly important in scripts where the timing and order of operations are critical.

Here are some usage scenarios where this method is useful:

- **Data Synchronization**: Ensures that a certain set of changes is completed before the next set begins.
- **Sequential Operations**: Critical in complex scripts where one operation's output affects the input of another.
- **User Interaction**: Updates the spreadsheet with results before continuing with user interactions.

Example:

```
 function updateBudgetSheet() {
    const sheet = SpreadsheetApp.getActiveSpreadsheet().get
SheetByName("Budget");
    sheet.getRange("B2:B10").setValues(newExpenses); // Update
expenses
    SpreadsheetApp.flush(); // Apply changes immediately

    const totalExpenses = calculateTotalExpenses();
    sheet.getRange("B11").setValue(totalExpenses); // Calculate
total after updates
  }

  function calculateTotalExpenses() {
    // Function to calculate total expenses
    // ...
  }
```

Building Graphic User Interfaces

Creating graphical user interfaces (GUIs) like custom menus, add-on menus, sidebars, and dialog windows enhances the user experience. These interfaces allow users to execute script functions in a more intuitive way, without needing to access the script editor.

Benefits

The benefits of GUIs are as follows:

- **User-friendly**: Makes script functions accessible through familiar GUI elements.
- **Efficiency**: Users can execute complex script functions with just a few clicks.

We will delve deeper into building GUIs in a future chapter, focusing on the specifics of designing and implementing these interfaces in Google Apps Script. If you are eager to start building GUIs, feel free to explore ahead to those sections.

Builder Methods

In programming, particularly in JavaScript, the Builder pattern is a design pattern used to construct complex objects step by step. It separates the construction of an object from its representation, allowing the same construction process to create various representations. This pattern is often used in Google Apps Script and you can often recognize them as they are called directly from the `SpreadsheetApp` class and start with `new`.

Here's an example that creates a conditional format rule with `newConditionalFormatRule()`:

```
// Retrieve the active sheet from the current spreadsheet.
const sheet = SpreadsheetApp.getActive().getActiveSheet();

// Define the range within the sheet to apply the conditional
formatting.
const range = sheet.getRange('A1:B3');

// Create a new conditional format rule using the Builder pat-
tern.
const rule = SpreadsheetApp.newConditionalFormatRule()
    .whenNumberBetween(1, 10) // Set the condition: cell value
between 1 and 10.
    .setBackground("#FF0000") // Define the background color to
set when the condition is met.
    .setRanges([range])       // Apply the rule to the previously
defined range.
    .build();                 // Finalize the rule creation.
```

```
// Retrieve existing conditional format rules from the sheet.
let rules = sheet.getConditionalFormatRules();

// Add the new rule to the array of existing rules.
rules.push(rule);

// Update the sheet with the new set of conditional format rules.
sheet.setConditionalFormatRules(rules);
```

In this example, the Builder pattern is initiated with **`SpreadsheetApp.newConditionalFormatRule()`** Each subsequent method adds a specific detail to the rule, culminating in the **`.build()`** method which finalizes and returns the complete **`ConditionalFormatRule`** object. Using **`const`** and **`let`** for variable declarations enhances scope management and code readability.

Other Noteworthy Classes

Beyond the classes and methods already discussed, Google Apps Script offers additional classes that can further enhance your work with Google Sheets:

- **`NamedRange`**: Enables the creation, access, and modification of named ranges in a spreadsheet. Named ranges are useful for referencing specific cell ranges by a custom name rather than cell addresses.
- **`DeveloperMetaData`**: This class allows access and modification of developer metadata, providing a way to store custom information within a spreadsheet that can be programmatically accessed and manipulated.
- **`Filter`**: Modify existing filters in a sheet. Useful for automating data sorting and filtering processes.
- **`CellImage`** and **`CellImageBuilder`**: These classes allow you to build and add images directly into cells, providing a way to visually enhance your spreadsheet data.
- **`Embedded`** Charts: Various classes exist for creating and manipulating different types of embedded charts, enhancing the data visualization capabilities within your sheets.
- **`Slicer`**: Slicers are visual filters for pivot tables. They allow users to quickly filter the data in the pivot table, making it easier to segment and analyze subsets of data.
- **`PivotTable`**: This class represents pivot tables within a sheet. Pivot tables are powerful tools for summarizing and analyzing large datasets, allowing you to dynamically rearrange and group data.

- **`Protection`**: Provides methods to protect and unprotect ranges and sheets. This is crucial for controlling user access and editing permissions, ensuring data integrity and security.

Each of these classes offers unique functionalities that can significantly elevate the capabilities of your Google Sheets projects. Whether it is enhancing data visualization, managing data access, or creating more dynamic and interactive spreadsheets, these classes are valuable tools in the Google Apps Script environment.

Conclusion

As we wrap up this chapter, it is clear that Google Apps Script is a powerful tool for enhancing and automating Google Sheets. We have embarked on a journey through the intricate landscape of Google Sheets programming, exploring a variety of classes and methods that form the backbone of this scripting environment.

From the foundational **`SpreadsheetApp`** class to the versatile **`Range`** and **`Sheet`** objects, we have uncovered the essentials of spreadsheet manipulation. We delved into the world of two-dimensional arrays, learning how to harness their power for sophisticated data handling. The exploration of builder methods, particularly in the context of the Builder Pattern, highlighted the elegance and efficiency of constructing complex objects like conditional format rules.

Moreover, we ventured beyond the basics to explore advanced features such as **`NamedRange`**, **`DeveloperMetaData`**, **`Filter`**, **`CellImage`**, embedded charts, **`Slicer`**, **`PivotTable`**, and **`Protection`**. These tools open up a world of possibilities, from enhancing data visualization to ensuring spreadsheet security and data integrity.

This chapter serves as your gateway into the rich capabilities of Google Apps Script in Google Sheets. Whether you're automating repetitive tasks, analyzing complex datasets, or building interactive tools, the knowledge you have gained here will be invaluable. Remember, the power of Google Apps Script lies not only in its functionality but also in its ability to make your work with Google Sheets more efficient, dynamic, and impactful.

As you move forward, it is suggested to experiment with these concepts and tools. The real strength of a developer lies in applying knowledge to solve real-world problems creatively. So, take these learnings, apply them to your projects, and watch as your spreadsheets transform into more powerful, automated, and interactive tools.

In the next chapter, we are going to look at **`GmailApp`**, another very useful class that allows manipulating emails in Gmail accounts.

Happy scripting, and may your journey through Google Apps Script lead to many successful and innovative solutions!

Key Terms

- **`SpreadsheetApp` Class:** This is the primary class in Google Apps Script for accessing and manipulating spreadsheets. It provides a range of methods to interact with Google Sheets, including opening, creating, and editing spreadsheets.
- **`Range` Class:** Represents a cell or a group of cells in a Google Sheet. The **`Range`** class is crucial for reading and writing data, applying formats, and implementing various spreadsheet functions at the cell level.
- **`Sheet` Class:** Corresponds to a single sheet (or tab) within a Google Spreadsheet. The **`Sheet`** class provides functionalities for manipulating and accessing data within a specific sheet, such as adding rows, modifying cells, and managing sheet properties.
- **Builder Pattern:** A software design pattern used for constructing complex objects step by step. It separates the creation of an object from its representation, allowing for different representations to be created using the same construction process.
- **RangeList Object:** Represents a collection of multiple, possibly non-contiguous ranges within a Google Sheet. It is useful for executing operations on several distinct cell ranges simultaneously, especially when they are not adjacent to each other.
- **`ConditionalFormatRule`:** A rule in Google Sheets that applies specific formatting to cells based on defined conditions. These rules can be created and manipulated using Google Apps Script to dynamically format data in a spreadsheet.
- **`NamedRange`:** A feature in Google Sheets that allows naming a particular range of cells. **`NamedRange`** in Google Apps Script provides methods to create, access, and modify these named ranges programmatically.
- **`DeveloperMetaData`:** Refers to custom metadata that can be attached to various elements in a Google Sheet, like ranges or sheets. This metadata is accessible and modifiable through Google Apps Script, providing a way to store and manage custom information within a spreadsheet.
- **`Filter` Class:** Used to create and modify filters in a Google Sheet. Filters are tools for sorting and organizing data, and the **`Filter`** class allows scripts to automate and control these data filtering processes.

- **`PivotTable` Class:** Represents a pivot table in a Google Sheet, a powerful tool for summarizing, analyzing, and presenting large datasets. The **`PivotTable`** class in Google Apps Script allows for the creation and manipulation of pivot tables within a script.
- **`Protection` Class:** Provides methods to protect and unprotect ranges and sheets within a Google Spreadsheet. It is crucial for managing user access and editing permissions, thus safeguarding data integrity and security.

Chapter 4
GmailApp

Introduction

The **GmailApp** opens up all kinds of doors in Gmail for you, just like **SpreadsheetApp** does for Google Sheets. You can create new email drafts, send emails, sort through your emails, organize them with labels, and even search for specific messages. Plus, it lets you do neat things such as marking emails as read or unread, putting them in the archive, or highlighting important ones with a star.

Before we dive into all the cool stuff you can do, let us take a moment to understand how **GmailApp** works. Imagine it as a big toolbox that Google Apps Script gives you to work with your Gmail. This toolbox is designed to be user-friendly, so even if you are not a tech wizard, you can start automating your email tasks and making your email life a lot easier.

Understanding **GmailApp** is the first step to doing amazing things with your emails. It is not just about knowing what each tool does, but also about seeing how you can use them together to make your email management smarter and more efficient. So, let us get ready to explore all the fantastic things **GmailApp** can do for you, turning your Gmail into a powerhouse of productivity with Google Apps Script.

Structure

In this chapter, we will cover:

- Exploring the Gmail Architecture
- Getting Started with **GmailApp**
- Mastering **GmailDraft**
- Navigating through **GmailThread** and **GmailMessage**
- Automating Email Invitations with Google Apps Script

Exploring the Gmail Messaging Architecture

In the world of Gmail and Google Apps Script, understanding the structure of your emails is like knowing the layout of your house. It makes navigating and organizing a breeze. Let us break down this structure into its basic components: messages, drafts, labels, and threads.

First off, there are two main types of messages you will deal with: **`GmailMessage`** and **`GmailDraft`**. A **`GmailMessage`** is like a sent letter; once it is sent, you cannot change it. You can read it, move it around, or even throw it away, but you cannot alter the words inside. On the other hand, a **`GmailDraft`** is more like a letter you are still writing. You can change it as much as you want until you decide to send it. Once you send a draft, it transforms into a **`GmailMessage`**. It is like magic – the draft disappears and a new message is born!

Now, let us talk about labels, or **`GmailLabel`**. Think of labels as folders or tags you put on your emails to keep them organized. Every email can have multiple labels attached to it. There are two kinds of labels: system labels and user labels. System labels are the ones Gmail gives you by default, such as **INBOX**, **TRASH**, and **SPAM**. You cannot change these; they are part of Gmail's furniture. But user labels? Those are yours to play with. You can create them, change them, or delete them, either manually or with Google Apps Script. They are like customizable shelves for your emails.

Finally, we have threads, grouped by the **`GmailThread`** class. A thread is a series of related messages, like a conversation. When you reply to an email and someone replies back, all those emails are linked together in a thread. It is a way to keep the conversation organized and easy to follow.

By understanding these basic elements—messages, drafts, labels, and threads—you are well on your way to becoming a Gmail organization expert. With Google Apps Script, you can automate tasks around these elements, making your email management not just smarter, but also more efficient and tailored to your needs.

Getting Started with `GmailApp`

Kicking off with **`GmailApp`** is straightforward and does not require navigating complex settings. Since Gmail does not allow scripts to run directly within its environment, we are going to use stand-alone scripts or scripts that are bound to other Google apps such as Sheets.

Let us try a new way of creating a stand-alone script for a change. Simply type **`script.new`** into your browser's address bar. This shortcut swiftly opens a new blank script project for you to start coding (you will be asked to log in with your

Google account if that is not already the case). It is an effortless way to dive right into scripting, as shown in the neat trick here:

Figure 4.1: *Typing* ***script.new*** *in your browser's address bar creates a new stand-alone Google Apps Script project*

One of the basics you will likely use in **GmailApp** is the **sendEmail()** function. It is pretty simple and requires just three things: the email address of the person you are sending it to, your email's subject, and the message body. Here is a small example to illustrate:

```
const recipient = 'hello@example.com'; // Change this to the email you're sending to
const subject = 'Hello world!';
const body = 'Sent with GmailApp.';
GmailApp.sendEmail(recipient, subject, body);
```

This function is handy, but it does not give you a message object to work with afterward. If you want to further interact with your sent email, such as starring it or getting its ID, there is a workaround:

```
const sentMessage = GmailApp
    .createDraft(recipient, subject, body) // First, it creates a draft
    .send() // Then, it sends the draft, turning it into a message
    .star(); // Finally, it stars the sent message
```

By creating a draft and then sending it, you get a message back that you can interact with, like adding a star. This method provides flexibility and shows how **GmailApp** can be user-friendly.

Sending an email to yourself using this approach should result in a starred message appearing in your inbox, just like in the following figure:

Figure 4.2: *A starred email to ourselves sent with Google Apps Script*

Depending on your needs, you can choose either method to send emails. Both offer unique advantages for email management and automation through **GmailApp**.

Next up, we will take a closer look at how to effectively use drafts and messages, enhancing our ability to manage emails with **GmailApp**.

Mastering `GmailDraft`: From Creation to Customization

Let us delve into creating, reading, and updating Gmail drafts.

Creating Drafts

Starting with drafts in **`GmailApp`** is as simple as deciding not to send an email right away. Whether you are preparing a message that you will send later or just want to save some thoughts for future refinement, creating a draft is the first step. Here is how you can create one:

```
GmailApp.createDraft('hello@example.com', '🖂 New Draft',
'Created with GmailApp');
```

When you run this line of code, you are essentially telling **`GmailApp`** to save a new draft message. This draft appears in your Gmail Drafts folder, ready for whenever you decide to return to it, as depicted in *Figure* 4.3.

***Figure 4.3:** A draft message generated with Google Apps Script*

Reading Drafts

Now that you have a draft saved, you might wonder how to find and interact with it, or any other drafts you have saved. **`GmailApp`** provides a method called **`getDrafts()`**, which returns an array of **`GmailDraft`** objects. This array allows you to access each draft and do things such as read their subjects or contents. Here is an example of how you might list the subjects of all your drafts:

```
function listDrafts() {
  const drafts = GmailApp.getDrafts();
  drafts.forEach(draft => Logger.log(draft.getMessage().
getSubject()));
  // You could also call getBody() to see the content
}
```

This function iterates over each draft, logging its subject to the console. The choice between using an arrow function or an anonymous function depends on your preference; both achieve the same result.

Updating Drafts

What if you want to change a draft? **GmailApp** makes it easy with the **update()** method. You can modify a draft's recipients, subject, or body. For instance, if you want to rename the subject of drafts created with **GmailApp** and add new recipients, here is how you could do it:

```
function updateDrafts() {
  const re = /Created with GmailApp/i;
  const newRecipients = ['john@example.com', 'jane@example.com'];
  GmailApp.getDrafts().forEach(draft => {
    const message = draft.getMessage();
    const body = message.getBody();
    if (!re.test(body)) return;
    const to = message.getTo();
    const subject = message.getSubject();
    const newSubject = `${subject} renamed by Apps Script`;
    const newTo = `${to},${newRecipients.join(',')}`;
    draft.update(newTo, newSubject, body);
    Logger.log(`Successfully renamed "${subject}" to
"${newSubject}" and added the following recipients: ${newRecipi-
ents.join(', ')}`);
  })
}
```

Let us break down the preceding code.

First, we construct a regular expression to scrutinize the content of the drafts. If you are not yet familiar with regular expressions, it is highly recommended to dedicate some time to learn them; they are incredibly powerful. We iterate over each draft, retrieving the **GmailMessage** instance for every draft in the process. Upon obtaining the message, we examine the body's content against our regular expression. If the content does not match, we use **return** to exit the current iteration and proceed to the next message. This step is crucial for efficiency—it is important to terminate your functions early to prevent unnecessary code execution and reduce delay for the user. Make it a practice to ensure that only necessary code runs. Upon finding a match, we extract the recipient and subject to formulate a new subject line. Then, we invoke **update()**, wherein the body remains unchanged, but the subject and recipients are updated. It is worth noting how we employ **join()** to amalgamate email addresses; this is because specifying multiple recipients requires a string of comma-separated emails. For convenience, we also log the outcome.

When you execute this function, and provided that you had created the draft with "**`Created with GmailApp`**" in the body, you should see the following in the execution log:

```
Successfully renamed "🖂 New Draft" to "🖂 New Draft renamed by Apps Script" and added the following recipients: john@example.com, jane@example.com
```

You should also see that the draft has been updated in your Gmail with a new subject and recipients:

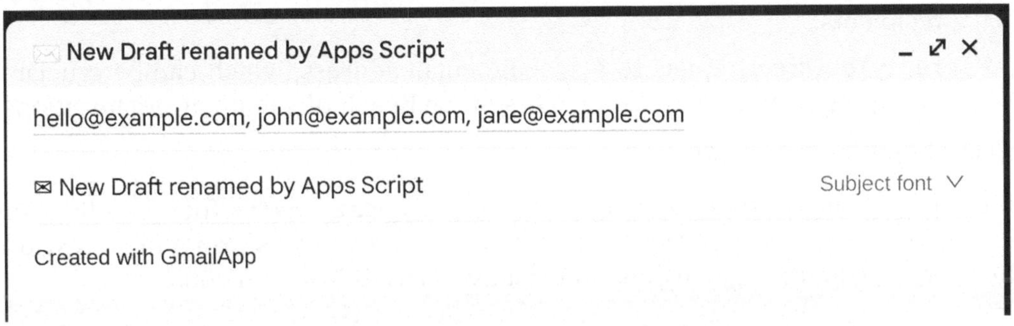

Figure 4.4: *A draft message generated with Google Apps Script*

Warning:

`Please limit yourself to using single-character emojis with` **`GmailApp`**`. The management of two-character emojis exceeds the scope of this book.`

Enhancing Your Emails with the `options` Parameter

When you have gotten the hang of creating and updating drafts in **`GmailApp`** with basic elements such as the recipient, subject, and body, you might find yourself wanting more. This is where the `options` parameter comes into play, significantly expanding what you can do with your emails. Whether it is adding attachments, using HTML for rich text formatting, or managing your recipients in more sophisticated ways, `options` opens up a world of possibilities.

What Can You Add with `options`?

The **`options`** parameter is incredibly versatile, allowing you to include:

- **`attachments`:** Attach files to your emails for comprehensive communication.
- **`bcc`:** Add blind carbon copy recipients to keep some recipients hidden from others.
- **`cc`:** Use carbon copy to include other recipients openly.

- **from:** Choose from your Gmail aliases for sending emails, enhancing your flexibility and control over your sender identity.
- **htmlBody:** Elevate your email's appearance with HTML formatting. For emails that need to stand out or convey information more vividly, adding colors, bold text, or images can make a big difference.
- **inlineImages:** Embed images directly within your email's HTML body, perfect for newsletters or detailed reports.
- **name:** Specify the sender's name to personalize how your email appears to recipients.
- **replyTo:** Direct replies to a specific email address, which can be crucial for managing responses or for emails sent on behalf of a team or organization.

Practical Application of options

Let us apply some of these enhancements to our **updateDrafts** function. By adding CC recipients and incorporating an HTML body, we can transform a plain text draft into something more engaging and informative. Here is how you could do it:

```
function updateDrafts() {
  const re = /Created with GmailApp/i;
  const newRecipients = ['john@example.com', 'jane@example.com'];

  // ADDED: carbon copy recipients;
  const carbonCopy = ['alex@example.com', 'murphy@example.com']

  GmailApp.getDrafts().forEach(draft => {
    const message = draft.getMessage();
    const body = message.getBody();
    if (!re.test(body)) return;
    const to = message.getTo();
    const subject = message.getSubject();
    const newSubject = `${subject} renamed by Apps Script`;
    const newTo = `${to},${newRecipients.join(',')}`;

    // ADDED: HTML body
    const htmlBody = '<p><span style="color: red;">Created with</
span> <b>GmailApp</b></p>';

    // ADDED: the options parameter
    draft.update(newTo, newSubject, body, {
      htmlBody,
      cc: carbonCopy.join(','),
    });
  });
}
```

By executing this updated function, your drafts gain a layer of sophistication with visually appealing HTML content and a broader reach through Cc recipients, as showcased in *Figure 4.5*.

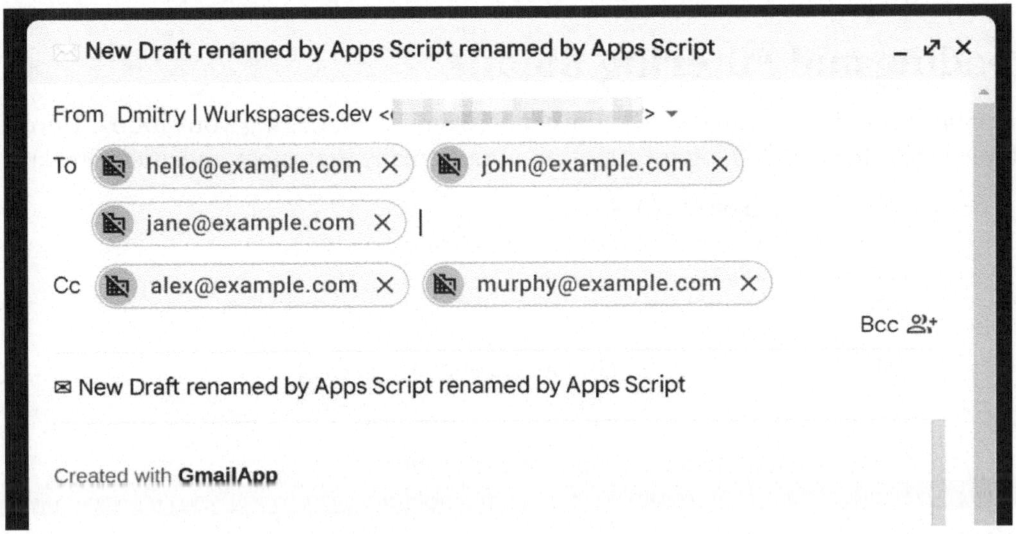

Figure 4.5: *A draft message updated with carbon copy recipients and HTML body*

This example illustrates just a fraction of what is possible with the **`options`** parameter. As you become more familiar with these capabilities, you will find new ways to enhance your emails, making them more effective and aligned with your communication goals. Whether you are sending out a simple update, a detailed newsletter, or anything in between, **`GmailApp`** provides the tools you need to do it with style and precision.

Navigating Through `GmailThread` and `GmailMessage`

In Gmail, every email you send or receive is part of a conversation, or what we call a **`GmailThread`**. Each **`GmailThread`** can contain one or more **`GmailMessage`** items, which are the individual emails within the thread. These classes allow us to interact with and manipulatc cmails and threads programmatically using **`GmailApp`**.

Working with Messages

Once an email is sent, it becomes a **`GmailMessage`**, and while you cannot change its content, you can still interact with it in various ways. You can:

- Retrieve details such as the recipients, body, and subject using **`getTo()`**, **`getBody()`**, and **`getSubject()`**.

- Mark the message as read or unread with **markRead()** and **markUnread()**.
- Check if it is in the inbox or trash using **isInInbox()** and **isInTrash()**.
- Reply to the message or move it to trash with **reply()** and **moveToTrash()**.

Reading and Filtering Emails

Filtering through your emails efficiently is crucial for managing your inbox. Here is a simple script to read and log information about emails that meet specific criteria:

```
function readEmails() {
  const threads = GmailApp.getInboxThreads();
  let threadsRead = 0;
  const maxThreads = 5;

  for (let i = 0; i < threads.length; i++) {
   // For the sake of this example, we won't dive into more than
5 threads
    if (threadsRead >= maxThreads) break;

   // Gets the thread and message count
    const thread = threads[i];
    const numMessages = thread.getMessageCount();

    // For the sake of this example, let's skip threads that are
too small or too big
    if (numMessages < 3 || numMessages > 5) continue;

    // Gets the subject of the first message
    const subject = thread.getFirstMessageSubject();
    Logger.log(`Found thread "${subject}" with ${numMessages}
messages`);

   // Loops through the messages of the thread
   // and prints some basic information
    const messages = thread.getMessages();
    messages.forEach((message, i) =>
      Logger.log(`Message ${i + 1} ${message.getFrom()} to
${message.getTo()}`)
    );
    threadsRead++;
  }
}
```

Utilizing Gmail's Search Functionality

For more targeted searches, you can leverage Gmail's search functionality, using the same syntax as in the Gmail app. This is especially useful for finding specific types of emails quickly:

```
function findEmails() {
  const searchQuery = 'in:inbox from:tldr is:unread';
  const threads = GmailApp.search(searchQuery);

  threads.forEach(thread => {
    const subject = thread.getFirstMessageSubject();
    Logger.log(subject);
  });
}
```

The search query is a string that specifies that we are looking for threads in the inbox, from TLDR, which is a newsletter I receive, and I am only interested in unread emails. Executing this function produced the following result for me:

```
12:57:45   Infos   ChatGPT security flaws 🔓, Discord's HQ live streaming 🎥, Pokemon GO on GCP
```

`12:57:45   Infos   GPT-4.5 leak 🧠, conversational robots 🤖, what are design engineers 👨` Feel free to adapt your search query and try it out on your account. You can learn more about Gmail search at this URL: https://support.google.com/mail/answer/6593

Labeling Threads

Organizing emails with labels can help keep your inbox tidy. Here is how to apply labels to specific threads programmatically:

```
function findEmails() {
  const searchQuery = 'in:inbox from:tldr is:unread';
  const threads = GmailApp.search(searchQuery);
  threads.forEach(thread => {
    const subject = thread.getFirstMessageSubject();
    Logger.log(subject);
    // Adds a label
    thread.addLabel(getLabel('TLDR'));
  });
}

// Retrieves a label if it exists, otherwise creates a new one
function getLabel(text) {
  const label = GmailApp.getUserLabelByName(text);
  if (label) return label;
  return GmailApp.createLabel(text);
}
```

Let's first look at the **getLabel()** function. It first calls **GmailApp.getUserLabelByName(name)**. This method will either return an instance of **GmailLabel** or **null** if one does not exist. If it finds the label, it returns it, otherwise it creates one and then returns it. We can then use its return value to add the label to our threads in **findEmails** but passing it to **thread.addLabel(label)**.

By running these scripts, you can automate tasks such as organizing newsletters into their own labeled category in your inbox, as shown in *Figure 4.6*.

Figure 4.6: *TLDR newsletters with their own label*

Through these examples, you have seen how to manage and interact with your emails using **GmailThread** and **GmailMessage**. These tools open up numerous possibilities for email automation and organization, setting the stage for more complex projects, including combining **SpreadsheetApp** and **GmailApp** for tasks such as mail merges.

Mini Project: Sending Personalized Event Invitations with GmailApp

In this mini project, we are harnessing the power of **GmailApp** to send out personalized invitations for an event. By integrating Google Sheets to manage recipient data and track which messages have been sent, we can streamline the entire process. This approach not only saves time but also adds a personal touch to each invitation.

Preparing Your Database

First, we have a Google Sheet that serves as our database for invitation recipients. Following is an example of what the database might look like:

1	Recipient Name	Email Address	Event Name	Event Date	Location	RSVP Link	Invitation Sent (Y/N)
2	Samantha	samantha@funnydomain.com	Birthday Bash	2024-07-15	Mumbai	https://forms.gle/12345	
3	Aryan	aryan@funnydomain.com	Wedding Reception	2024-09-05	Delhi	https://forms.gle/12345	
4	Riya	riya@funnydomain.com	Housewarming Party	2024-08-25	Kolkata	https://forms.gle/12345	
5	Vikram	vikram@funnydomain.com	Baby Shower	2024-07-10	Chennai	https://forms.gle/12345	
6	Neha	neha@funnydomain.com	Farewell Party	2024-08-20	Bangalore	https://forms.gle/12345	
7	Rohan	rohan@funnydomain	Prom Night	2024-07-05	Hyderabad	https://forms.gle/12345	
8	Anjali	anjali@funnydomain.com	Graduation Ceremony	2024-09-15	Pune	https://forms.gle/12345	
9	Raj	raj@funnydomain.com	House Party	2024-08-10	Jaipur	https://forms.gle/12345	
10	Kavya	kavyafunnydomain.com	Bachelor Party	2024-07-20	Ahmedabad	https://forms.gle/12345	
11	Rahul	rahul@funnydomain.com	Office Retreat	2024-09-10	Lucknow	https://forms.gle/12345	

Figure 4.7: *Database of invitation recipients in Google Sheets*

It is worth noting that email addresses for Rohan and Kavya are not in the correct format. This is intentional, allowing us to explore error handling within our script.

Crafting the Email Template

Next, we have an email template designed to be personalized for each recipient. This template incorporates merge fields denoted by double curly braces (for example, **`{{field}}`**). These fields correspond to the columns in our spreadsheet, enabling us to tailor each email to its recipient.

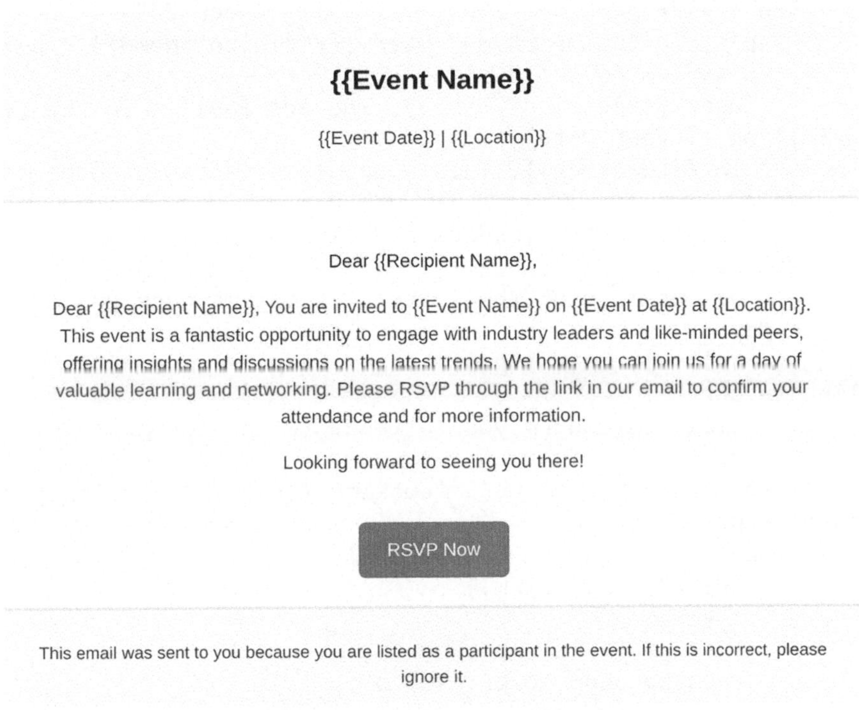

Figure 4.8: *Email template preview*

Here is the HTML source code for the template:

```
<table
  width="100%"
  cellspacing="0"
  cellpadding="0"
  style="max-width: 600px; margin: auto; border-collapse:
collapse"
>
  <tr>
    <td
      style="
        background-color: #f8f8f8;
        padding: 20px;
        text-align: center;
        border-bottom: 2px solid #ddd;
```

```
      "
    >
      <h2 style="color: #333">{{Event Name}}</h2>
      <p style="color: #555">{{Event Date}} | {{Location}}</p>
    </td>
  </tr>
  <tr>
    <td style="padding: 20px; text-align: center">
      <p style="color: #333">Dear {{Recipient Name}},</p>
      <p style="color: #555">
        Dear {{Recipient Name}}, You are invited to the {{Event
Name}} on {{Event Date}}
        in {{Location}}. This event is a fantastic opportunity to
engage
        with industry leaders and like-minded peers, offering
insights and
        discussions on the latest trends. We hope you can join us
for a day of
        valuable learning and networking. Please RSVP through the
link in our
        email to confirm your attendance and for more information.
      </p>
      <p style="color: #555">Looking forward to seeing you
there!</p>
      <a
        href="{{RSVP Link}}"
        style="
          display: inline-block;
          background-color: #007bff;
          color: white;
          padding: 10px 20px;
          text-decoration: none;
          border-radius: 5px;
          margin-top: 20px;
        "
        >RSVP Now</a
      >
    </td>
  </tr>
  <tr>
    <td
      style="
        background-color: #f8f8f8;
        padding: 10px 20px;
        text-align: center;
        border-top: 2px solid #ddd;
      "
```

```
      >
        <p style="color: #555; font-size: 12px">
          This email was sent to you because you are listed as a
participant in
          the event. If this is incorrect, please ignore it.
        </p>
      </td>
    </tr>
  </table>
```

To incorporate this template into your Apps Script project, create a new HTML file. Here is how:

1. Open the script bound to your spreadsheet.
2. Click on the plus (+) sign next to "**`Files`**" and select "**`HTML`**".

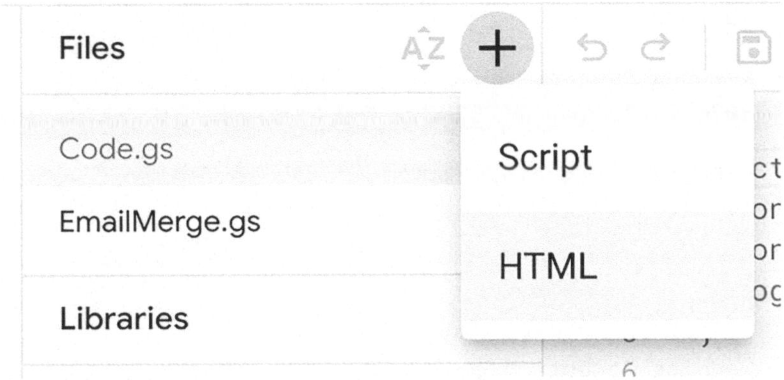

Figure 4.9: *Creating an HTML file in a Google Apps Script project*

3. Name your file something like "**`EmailTemplate`**" and paste the provided HTML code into it. Make sure to save your changes.

Automating Email Invitations with Google Apps Script

In this section, we delve into the practical aspects of automating email invitations using **`GmailApp`** and data stored in Google Sheets. Our goal is to send personalized event invitations and track the sending status directly within our spreadsheet.

Transforming Data for Ease of Use

First, it is essential to structure our data in a format that simplifies manipulation and access. By converting a two-dimensional array (a typical format for sheet data) into an array of objects, we make our data more readable and easier to work with. This transformation allows us to refer to each piece of data by its column name, akin to working with named fields in a database.

Let us transform this:

```
[
  [
    'Recipient Name',
    'Email Address',
    'Event Name',
    'Event Date',
    'Location',
    'RSVP Link',
    'Invitation Sent (Y/N)',
  ],
  [
    'Samantha',
    'samantha@funnydomain.com',
    'Birthday Bash',
    '2024-07-15',
    'Mumbai',
    'https://forms.gle/12345',
    '',
  ],
  [
    'Aryan',
    'aryan@funnydomain.com',
    'Wedding Reception',
    '2024-09-05',
    'Delhi',
    'https://forms.gle/12345',
    '',
  ],
];
```

into this:

```
[
  {
    'Recipient Name': 'Samantha',
    'Email Address': 'samantha@funnydomain.com',
    'Event Name': 'Birthday Bash',
    'Event Date': '2024-07-15',
    Location: 'Mumbai',
    'RSVP Link': 'https://forms.gle/12345',
    'Invitation Sent (Y/N)': '',
  },
  {
```

```
    'Recipient Name': 'Aryan',
    'Email Address': 'aryan@funnydomain.com',
    'Event Name': 'Wedding Reception',
    'Event Date': '2024-09-05',
    Location: 'Delhi',
    'RSVP Link': 'https://forms.gle/12345',
    'Invitation Sent (Y/N)': '',
  },
];
```

Here is a class designed to encapsulate this transformation process:

```
class Records {
  constructor(sheetName) {
    this.spreadsheet = SpreadsheetApp.getActive();
    this.sheetName = sheetName;
    this.worksheet = this.spreadsheet.getSheetByName
(this.sheetName);
    if (null === this.worksheet)
      throw `Worksheet ${this.sheetName} does not exist`;
    this.data = this.worksheet.getDataRange().getDisplayValues();
    this.headers = this.data.shift();
    this.records = this.data.map(row =>
      row.reduce(
        (record, value, i) => ({ ...record, [this.headers[i]]:
value }),
        {}
      )
    );
  }
}
```

This `Records` class efficiently processes our Google Sheets data, separating headers, and converting rows into an easily accessible array of objects. The outer `map` method creates a copy of the array and replaces the inner arrays with objects transformed by the **`reduce()`** method. If you are still not comfortable with array methods such as `map` or **`reduce`**, it is quite important to catch up; it is one of the best time investments you can make.

Preparing Email Settings

To ensure our script is versatile and maintainable, we define settings related to our email-sending process in a separate object:

```
const EMAIL_SETTINGS = {
  subject: '{{Recipient Name}}, you are invited to the {{Event
Name}}',
```

```
  toField: 'Email Address',
  resultsField: 'Invitation Sent (Y/N)',
};

Object.freeze(EMAIL_SETTINGS);
```

This approach keeps our script organized and makes it easier to adjust settings without digging through the actual logic of our code.

Crafting and Sending Emails

With our data structured and settings in place, we proceed to the core function responsible for creating and sending the emails:

```
function createEmails() {
  // Extracts the contents of our HTML template
  const htmlTemplate =
    HtmlService.createHtmlOutputFromFile('EmailTemplate').get
Content();

  // Creates an instance of records in the Invitees sheet
  const rec = new Records('Invitees');

  // Stores the outcome of the email merge for each record
  const results = [];

  // Transforms records into emails and stores the result;
  rec.records.forEach(record => {
    let htmlBody = htmlTemplate;
    let subject = EMAIL_SETTINGS.subject;
    const to = record[EMAIL_SETTINGS.toField];

    // Replaces the merge fields with their respective values
    Object.entries(record).forEach(([key, value]) => {
      htmlBody = htmlBody.replace(new RegExp(`{{${key}}}`, 'g'),
value);
      subject = subject.replace(new RegExp(`{{${key}}}`, 'g'),
value);
    });

    // Tries to create the emails. The try-catch block allows
    // to record any failures without interrupting the whole app
    try {
      GmailApp.createDraft(to, subject, '', { htmlBody });
      results.push('Y');
    } catch (err) {
      Logger.log(`ERROR trying to send to ${to}: ${err}`);
```

```
      results.push('N');
    }
  });
  Logger.log(results);
  return { rec, results };
}
```

This function demonstrates the seamless integration of our HTML email template with the personalized data from our Google Sheet. By leveraging regular expressions, we replace template placeholders with actual data from our records, tailoring each email to its recipient. The use of a **`try-catch`** block ensures our script gracefully handles errors, such as invalid email addresses, by logging them, adding "**`N`**" to the **`results`** array, and continuing with the next record.

Through these steps, we have established a robust system for sending personalized event invitations. This process not only demonstrates the power of combining **`GmailApp`** with **`SpreadsheetApp`** but also highlights best practices in data manipulation and error handling within Google Apps Script.

Wrapping Up the Email Merge Mini Project

In wrapping up our mini project, we reach a crucial phase where the script returns an object that includes both the **`Records`** instance and the results array. This setup paves the way for the final step: updating our Google Sheet with the outcomes of our email merge operation.

Here is the function that achieves just that:

```
// Accepts the object containing a Records instance and the re-
sults array
function updateResultsInSheet({ rec, results }) {

  // Finds the index of the column that stores the results in the
spreadsheet
  const colIndex = rec.headers.findIndex(
    header => EMAIL_SETTINGS.resultsField === header
  );

  // Throws an error if such column was not found.
  if (-1 === colIndex)
    throw `Could not find column "${EMAIL_SETTINGS.resultsField}"
in sheet ${rec.sheetName}`;

 // Inserts the results into the sheet
  const range = rec.worksheet
```

```
        .getRange(2, colIndex + 1, results.length, 1)
        .setValues(results.map(result => [result]));
}
```

This piece of code meticulously updates our spreadsheet with the results of each attempted email send, providing a clear record of our project's success.

Next, we introduce a function that orchestrates this entire process:

```
function merge() {
  const mergeResults = createEmails();
  updateResultsInSheet(mergeResults);
}
```

Executing **merge()** initiates the flow from creating emails (or drafts) to logging the results in our Google Sheet, showcasing the seamless integration of **GmailApp** and **SpreadsheetApp**.

Upon running our script, we observe the logs, revealing both successes and areas needing attention–specifically, errors related to invalid email formats for Rohan and Kavya.

```
Info  ERROR trying to send to rohan@funnydomain: Exception:
Invalid argument: : Invalid To header
Info  ERROR trying to send to kavyafunnydomain.com: Exception:
Invalid email: kavyafunnydomain.com
Info  [Y, Y, Y, Y, Y, N, Y, Y, N, Y]
```

The "**Invitation Sent (Y/N)**" column in our spreadsheet now accurately reflects these outcomes, marking each invitation as sent or indicating failures where applicable.

1	Recipient Name	Email Address	Event Name	Event Date	Location	RSVP Link	Invitation Sent (Y/N)
2	Samantha	samantha@funnydomain.com	Birthday Bash	2024-07-15	Mumbai	https://forms.gle/12345	Y
3	Aryan	aryan@funnydomain.com	Wedding Reception	2024-09-05	Delhi	https://forms.gle/12345	Y
4	Riya	riya@funnydomain.com	Housewarming Party	2024-08-25	Kolkata	https://forms.gle/12345	Y
5	Vikram	vikram@funnydomain.com	Baby Shower	2024-07-10	Chennai	https://forms.gle/12345	Y
6	Neha	neha@funnydomain.com	Farewell Party	2024-08-20	Bangalore	https://forms.gle/12345	Y
7	Rohan	rohan@funnydomain	Prom Night	2024-07-05	Hyderabad	https://forms.gle/12345	N
8	Anjali	anjali@funnydomain.com	Graduation Ceremony	2024-09-15	Pune	https://forms.gle/12345	Y
9	Raj	raj@funnydomain.com	House Party	2024-08-10	Jaipur	https://forms.gle/12345	Y
10	Kavya	kavyafunnydomain.com	Bachelor Party	2024-07-20	Ahmedabad	https://forms.gle/12345	N
11	Rahul	rahul@funnydomain.com	Office Retreat	2024-09-10	Lucknow	https://forms.gle/12345	Y

Figure 4.10: *The results of the email merge*

Furthermore, a review of the drafts created during this process reveals the success of our personalized email templates:

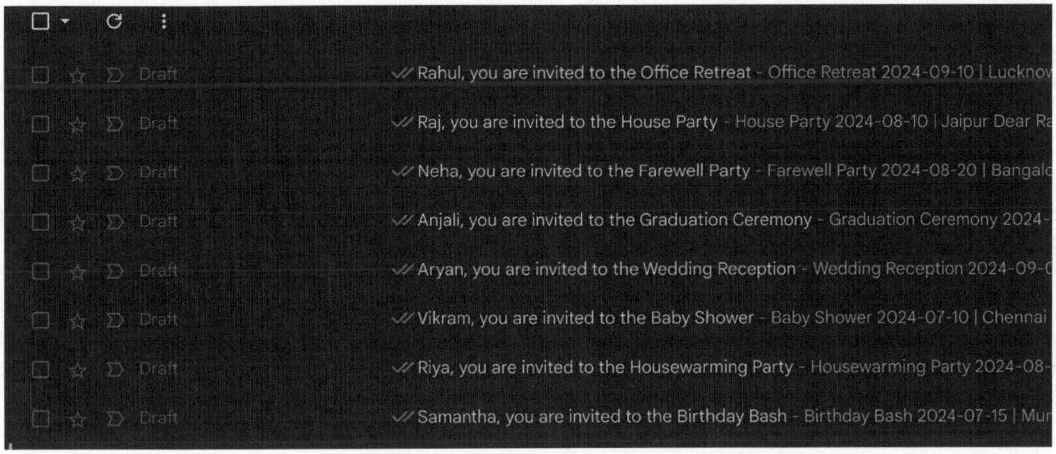

***Figure 4.11:** The created drafts*

Opening one of these drafts confirms the effectiveness of our placeholders and the overall personalization strategy:

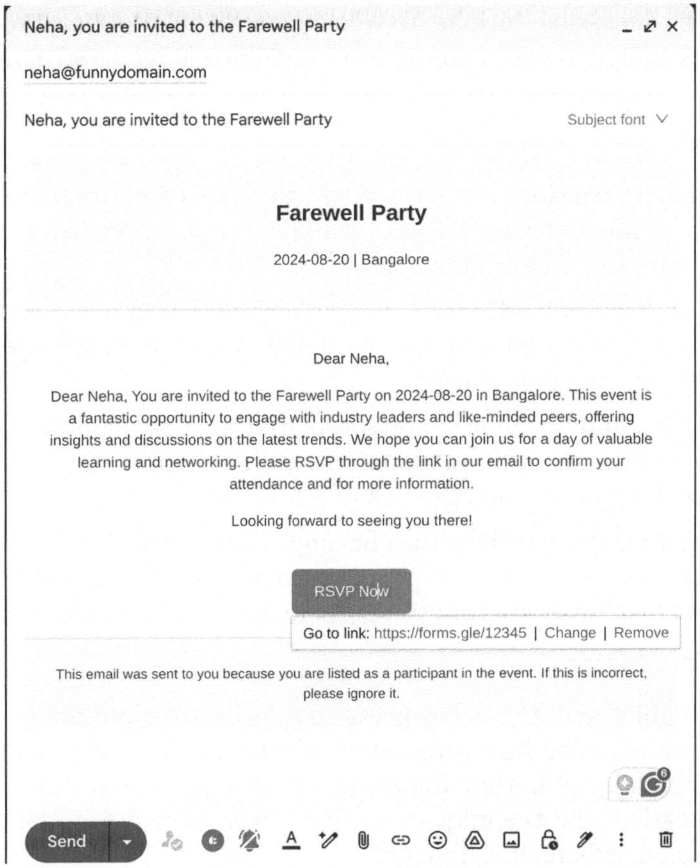

***Figure 4.12:** Personalized email*

Each draft is tailored to its recipient, featuring personalized content and correctly formatted RSVP links.

For testing purposes, we opted to create drafts rather than send the emails outright. This approach allows for review and adjustment before final send-off. To transition from drafting to sending, a simple replacement of **`GmailApp.createDraft(to, subject, '', { htmlBody })`** with **`GmailApp.sendEmail(to, subject, '', { htmlBody })`** is all that's needed, showcasing the flexibility of our script.

This mini project not only demonstrates the practical application of Google Apps Script for automating personalized communications but also highlights the importance of thorough testing and validation in ensuring the accuracy and effectiveness of our automated processes.

Conclusion

We have journeyed through the realms of **`GmailApp`** and Google Sheets, unlocking the secrets to automating personalized email invitations. From transforming raw data into structured, easily accessible formats to weaving personal touches into each message, this chapter has equipped you with the tools and knowledge to streamline your email tasks efficiently.

Key Takeaways

- **Data Transformation:** We learned the importance of organizing data in a way that makes it easy to work with, turning a simple spreadsheet into a powerful database for our email campaigns.
- **Template Personalization:** By using placeholders in our email templates, we discovered how to inject personal details into each message, making every recipient feel uniquely valued.
- **Automation and Efficiency:** We automated the entire process of creating and sending emails (or drafts) through scripting, demonstrating how technology can save time and reduce the risk of human error.
- **Error Handling:** We tackled the challenge of error handling, ensuring our script can gracefully manage unexpected issues, such as invalid email addresses, without crashing or stopping.

The Power of Integration

This chapter highlighted the synergistic potential of combining **`GmailApp`** with Google Sheets, showcasing how integrated solutions can address complex problems with elegant simplicity. Whether for event invitations, newsletters, or any form of mass communication, the techniques outlined here offer a foundation for creating impactful, personalized email campaigns.

Moving Forward

As you continue to explore and experiment with Google Apps Script, remember that the possibilities are as vast as your creativity allows. The skills you have developed here are just the beginning. With practice and exploration, you will find new ways to leverage these tools, automating tasks, enhancing productivity, and, perhaps most importantly, crafting messages that connect and resonate with people in meaningful ways.

Key Terms

- **Google Apps Script:** A cloud-based scripting language for automating tasks across Google products and third-party services.
- **`GmailApp`:** A class in Google Apps Script that provides methods to automate actions within Gmail, such as sending emails or managing drafts.
- **Google Sheets:** A web-based spreadsheet program, part of Google Drive, used for creating and managing data in tabular form.
- **Template:** A pre-designed layout or format for an email or document, often with placeholders for inserting specific data.
- **Placeholder:** A marker or symbol in a template that is replaced with actual data when the template is used.
- **Array:** A data structure used to store multiple values in a single variable, accessible by an index.
- **Object:** In programming, a collection of properties, where each property is defined as a key-value pair.
- **HyperText Markup Language (HTML):** The standard markup language used for creating web pages and web applications.
- **Personalization:** The process of tailoring content or messages to individual users' preferences or characteristics.
- **Error Handling:** The method of responding to and managing errors or exceptions that occur during the execution of a program.
- **Regular Expression:** A sequence of characters that define a search pattern, often used for string searching and manipulation.
- **`try-catch` Block:** A construct in many programming languages used to handle exceptions, allowing the program to continue running even if an error occurs.
- **Data Transformation:** The process of converting data from one format or structure into another.

- **Automation:** The technique of making a system operate automatically, reducing human intervention in processes.
- **Integration:** The process of linking together different computing systems and software applications physically or functionally, to act as a coordinated whole.

Chapter 5
DriveApp

Introduction

Google Apps Script's **DriveApp** is a powerful tool that allows us to manage files and folders on Google Drive with great ease and flexibility. Through **DriveApp**, you can create, read, update, and delete (often referred to as CRUD operations) files and folders. Additionally, it provides functionalities to list, search, and convert files to various formats. One of the standout features of **DriveApp** is its integration with other Google services; for example, it can attach files directly to Gmail messages using **GmailApp**. This integration enhances the capabilities of your scripts and allows for seamless interactions between different Google services.

By the end of this chapter, you should be proficient in managing and automating tasks in Google Drive using **DriveApp**, enhancing your scripts' functionality and your overall productivity. Let us get into it!

Structure

In this chapter, we will delve deep into the functionalities provided by **DriveApp** and how it interacts with Google Drive's architecture. The topics covered will include:

- Getting Started with **DriveApp**
- CRUD Operations
- Listing Files and Folders Recursively
- Converting Files to PDF
- File Search
- Attaching Files to Gmail

Overview of DriveApp's Key Classes

Google Apps Script's **DriveApp** provides a comprehensive set of classes that allow for robust management of files and folders in Google Drive. These classes equip you with the tools necessary to perform a wide array of operations, from basic file handling to complex permissions management. Here, we will explore these key classes and their functionalities to help you effectively manipulate and interact with the contents of Google Drive.

`DriveApp`

The **`DriveApp`** class serves as the entry point for all script interactions with Google Drive. It offers methods to perform CRUD (Create, Read, Update, Delete) operations on files and folders. Additionally, you can access special folders such as the root of the user's drive, retrieve information about storage limits and usage, manage trashed files and folders, and conduct searches within Google Drive.

`File` and `Folder`

`File` and **`Folder`** are two pivotal classes in **`DriveApp`** that share many methods but also have some specific functions.

Common Features

- **Users**: These classes handle various user roles, such as owners, editors, viewers, and commenters.
- **Blob Data**: You can retrieve the file data as a blob, a binary large object that holds data in a single entity, similar to a file.
- **Metadata**: Attributes such as the creation date, URL, description, ID, last updated timestamp, and MIME type are accessible.
- **Access Rights**: Methods are available to get, set, and retrieve access rights for the file or folder.
- **Manipulation**: Functions include making copies, moving, and setting new content.
- **Organization**: You can star or trash files or folders to organize them according to your needs.

Specific to `Folder`

- **File and Folder Creation**: In addition to the capabilities of the **`File`** class, the **`Folder`** class allows you to create new files or subfolders within it.

`FileIterator` and `FolderIterator`

These iterator classes are essential when dealing with large collections of files or folders. They provide a way to loop through collections of files or folders one by one using the **`next()`** method. The **`hasNext()`** method checks if there are more items to process. **`getContinuationToken()`** is particularly useful for handling large sets of files or folders by saving the state of the iteration, which can be resumed later.

User

The **User** class represents anyone with access rights to a file or folder. It offers methods to retrieve information about the user, such as their domain, email, name, and photo URL. This is particularly useful for scripts that need to manage or report on file access and permissions.

Now that we have the basics down let us start coding!

Getting Started with DriveApp

Google Apps Script offers powerful tools for interacting with Google Drive, one of which is the **DriveApp** class. Let us explore a practical example that demonstrates retrieving and managing file information using Google Apps Script.

Basic File Listing Example

Following is a JavaScript function that lists files from your Google Drive:

```
function listFiles() {
  const files = DriveApp.getFiles();
  const fileNames = [];
  const MAX_FILES = 10;
  let fileCount = 0;
  while (files.hasNext() && fileCount < MAX_FILES) {
    fileNames.push(files.next().getName());
    fileCount++;
  }
  Logger.log(fileNames);
}
```

This script begins with calling **DriveApp.getFiles()**, which retrieves a **FileIterator**. This object allows for efficient iteration over files and is crucial for managing large datasets without encountering performance issues. The **hasNext()** method is used to check if there are more files to process, and the **next()** method retrieves the next file. This ensures the loop does not exceed the limit set by **MAX_FILES**. Executing this script in your Apps Script project will log the names of up to 10 files from your Google Drive, demonstrating basic file interaction.

Extending Functionality to Google Sheets

The following changes adapt the function to list files directly in a Google Sheet:

```
function listFiles() {
  const files = DriveApp.getFiles();
- const fileNames = [];
```

```
+ const fileNamesTypes = [['File Name', 'Mime Type']];
  const MAX_FILES = 10;
  let fileCount = 0;
  while(files.hasNext() && fileCount < MAX_FILES) {
+   const file = files.next();
-   fileNames.push(files.next().getName());
+   fileNamesTypes.push([file.getName(), file.getMimeType()]);
    fileCount++;
  }
- Logger.log(fileNames)
+ SpreadsheetApp
+   .getActiveSheet()
+   .getRange(1, 1, fileNamesTypes.length, fileNamesTypes[0].
length)
+   .setValues(fileNamesTypes)
}
```

These modifications include storing the file names and MIME types, retrieved with **`getMimeType()`**, in a two-dimensional array, **`fileNamesTypes`**, to facilitate insertion into a Google Sheet. The loop now collects each file's name and MIME type, and upon completion, the data is inserted into the active sheet using **`setValues()`**.

Enhancing Interaction with a Google Sheet

You can assign a script to an image within your Google Sheet to further enhance user interaction. Here is how to set it up:

1. Insert an image over cells in your Google Sheet, as shown here:

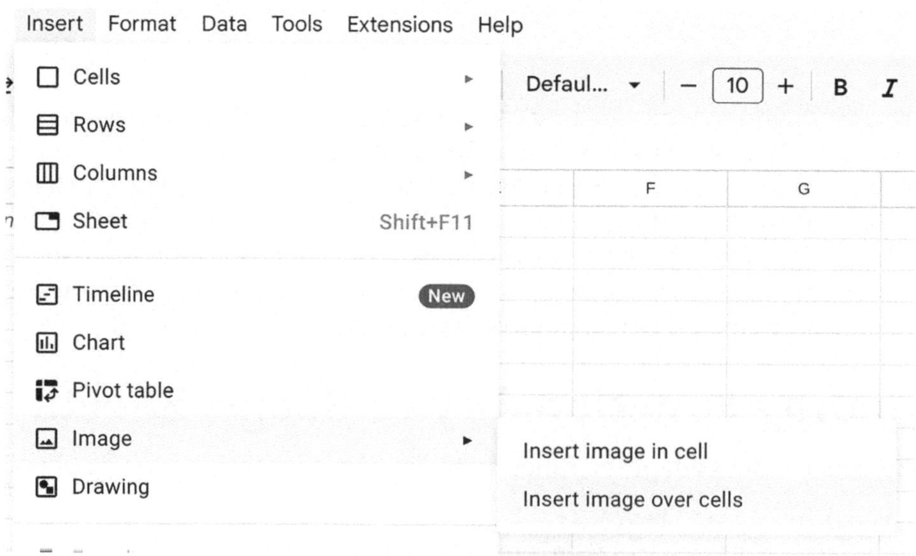

Figure 5.1: *Inserting an image over cells*

2. Select the image, click on the three dots in the top right corner, and select "**Assign script**":

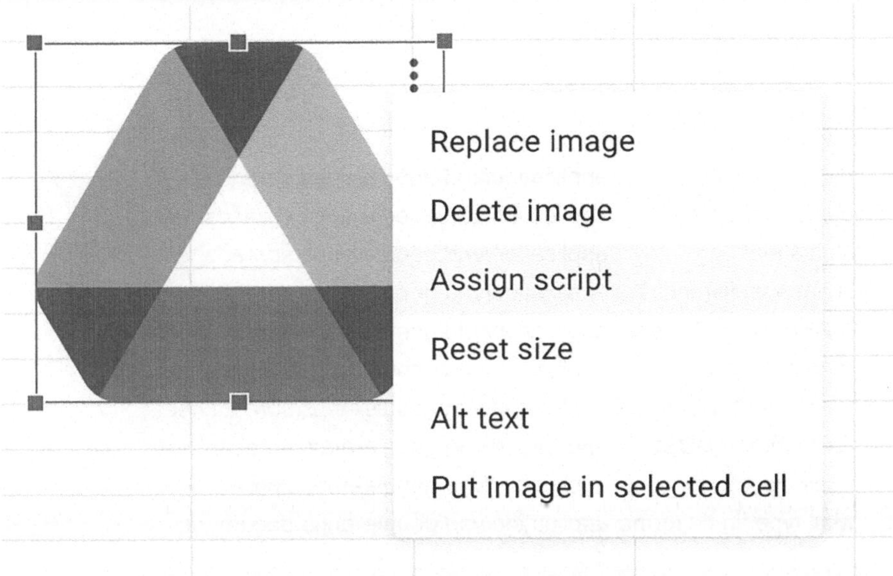

Figure 5.2: *Assigning a script to an image*

3. Enter **'listFiles'** (without the parentheses) in the prompt and confirm by clicking **OK**:

Figure 5.3: *Entering the script name to assign*

Now, when you click the image, it will execute the **`listFiles()`** function and list up to 10 files in your Google Drive directly in the spreadsheet:

F15 fx

	A	B	C
1	File Name	Mime Type	
2	My Google Sheet	application/vnd.google-apps.spreadsheet	
3	talent-pool-cockpit	application/vnd.google-apps.spreadsheet	
4	Worksheet Log	application/vnd.google-apps.spreadsheet	
5	Client Assessment Foı	application/vnd.google-apps.spreadsheet	
6	2023 à date - Tableau	application/vnd.google-apps.spreadsheet	
7	Invoice Tracker	application/vnd.google-apps.spreadsheet	
8	** comment only ** Ge	application/vnd.google-apps.spreadsheet	
9	[for mentors] GDSC 2(	application/vnd.google-apps.spreadsheet	
10	Invoices	application/vnd.google-apps.spreadsheet	
11	Mail type fin de forma	application/vnd.google-apps.document	
12			

Figure 5.4: *The output of the script*

Now that you have a basic idea of how **`DriveApp`** files work, let us examine file and folder operations.

Retrieving Files with DriveApp

When working with files in Google Drive using Google Apps Script, having granular access to files is often more useful than retrieving a large collection all at once. Similar to how you can open a specific spreadsheet by its ID, you can access files directly in Google Drive:

```
DriveApp.getFileById(id)
```

Retrieving Specific Collections of Files

Sometimes, you need to manage specific files within Drive. **`DriveApp`** provides several methods to retrieve collections of files based on different criteria:

Method	**Description**
`getFilesByName(name)`	Returns a collection of files in the user's Drive with the given name

`getFilesByType(mimeType)`	Returns a collection of files in the user's Drive of the given MIME type
`searchFiles(params)`	Returns a collection of files that match the search criteria
`getTrashedFiles()`	Returns a collection of files that have been trashed

Table 5.1: *Methods that retrieve collections of files*

Understanding MIME Types

A MIME type is a label used to indicate the nature and format of a document, file, or assortment of bytes. It is important when you are dealing with files across different formats and applications, especially in a diverse ecosystem such as Google Drive. The current list of MIME types for Google Workspace and Google Drive can be found here: https://developers.google.com/drive/api/guides/mime-types. Here's a snapshot of some common MIME types you might encounter:

MIME Type	Description
`application/vnd.google-apps.audio`	Audio file
`application/vnd.google-apps.document`	Google Docs
`application/vnd.google-apps.drive-sdk`	Third-party shortcut
`application/vnd.google-apps.drawing`	Google Drawings
`application/vnd.google-apps.file`	Google Drive file
`application/vnd.google-apps.folder`	Google Drive folder
`application/vnd.google-apps.form`	Google Forms
`application/vnd.google-apps.fusiontable`	Google Fusion Tables
`application/vnd.google-apps.jam`	Google Jamboard
`application/vnd.google-apps.mail-layout`	Email layout
`application/vnd.google-apps.map`	Google My Maps
`application/vnd.google-apps.photo`	Google Photos
`application/vnd.google-apps.presentation`	Google Slides
`application/vnd.google-apps.script`	Google Apps Script
`application/vnd.google-apps.shortcut`	Shortcut
`application/vnd.google-apps.site`	Google Sites
`application/vnd.google-apps.spreadsheet`	Google Sheets

`application/vnd.google-apps.unknown`	Unknown file type
`application/vnd.google-apps.video`	Video file

***Table 5.2:** MIME Types in Google Workspace and Google Drive*

Enhancing the Google Sheets Interface

To make our **`listFiles()`** function more interactive, let us add a dropdown menu in Google Sheets to allow users to select MIME types, enhancing file management capabilities:

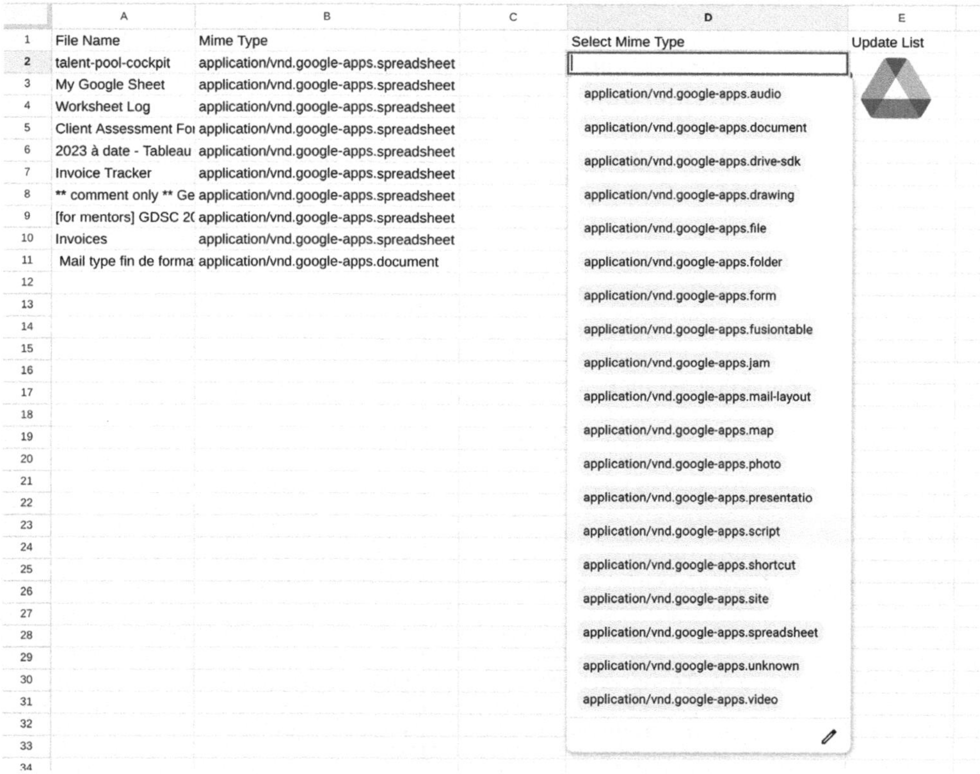

***Figure 5.5:** A drop-down with MIME types*

Now, modify the **`listFiles()`** function to list files by MIME type based on user selection:

```
function listFiles() {
+ const ws = SpreadsheetApp.getActiveSheet();
+ const mimeType = ws.getRange('D2').getValue();
- const files = DriveApp.getFiles();
+ const files = !!mimeType
+    ? DriveApp.getFilesByType(mimeType)
```

```
+    : DriveApp.getFiles();
  const fileNamesTypes = [['File Name', 'Mime Type']];
  const MAX_FILES = 10;
  let fileCount = 0;
  while (files.hasNext() && fileCount < MAX_FILES) {
    const file = files.next();
    fileNamesTypes.push([file.getName(), file.getMimeType()]);
    fileCount++;
  }
- SpreadsheetApp
-    .getActiveSheet()
-    .getRange(1, 1, fileNamesTypes.length, fileNamesTypes[0].
length)
-    .setValues(fileNamesTypes)
+ ws.getRange(1, 1, fileNamesTypes.length, fileNamesTypes[0].
length).setValues(
+    fileNamesTypes
+ );
}
```

Key changes to note:

- The **mimeType** variable retrieves the user-selected MIME type from cell 'D2'.
- The files are fetched based on the selected MIME type, using the ternary operator to determine which method to call.
- The double negation operator (!!) is used to convert the string value to a boolean, indicating whether a MIME type has been specified.

Selecting a specific MIME type, such as **application/vnd.google-apps.script** for Google Apps Script files, and running the script will produce a list specific to the chosen type:

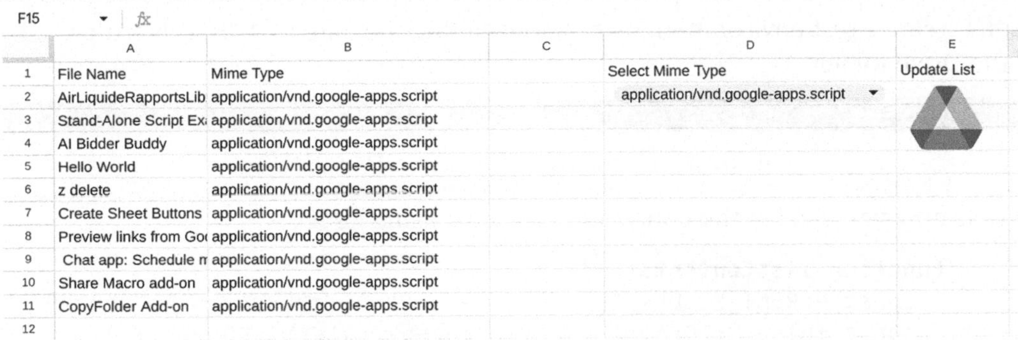

Figure 5.6: *Listing files by selected MIME type*

This example demonstrates how to integrate Google Drive file management with a Google Sheets interface, providing a more dynamic and user-friendly approach to handling files in Google Apps Script.

Now let us look into working with folders in **`DriveApp`**.

Working with Folders in `DriveApp`

Working with folders in Google Apps Script's **`DriveApp`** provides a versatile set of operations that allow you to manage and manipulate folders and their contents effectively. This section covers essential techniques for managing folders, including retrieving, creating, and organizing folder structures.

Basics of Folder Management

Let us look at how we can manage folders and their contents.

- **Getting a List of Folders**: **`DriveApp`** offers several methods to handle folders effectively. You can retrieve all folders in the root or specific folders by their IDs or names.
- **Retrieving Files and Sub-Folders from a Folder**: You can access files and sub-folders within a folder either by their ID or by querying for them by name. This allows you to work specifically with files nested within particular directories.
- **Creating Folders and Folders**: You can create folders at the root level or as sub-folders within existing directories. This includes the ability to work with files within these folders, such as moving files between folders or checking a file's parent folders.

Example: Managing Folder Contents

Let us create a test environment by first identifying the folder ID directly from the URL of the Drive folder:

Figure 5.7: *Identifying a file/folder ID in the URL*

Here is how you can list the contents of a folder using its ID:

```
function listContents() {
  const PARENT_FOLDER_ID = '1AjJP4obPXfAQmcVLUPpxholPn75be_kk';
  const folder = DriveApp.getFolderById(PARENT_FOLDER_ID);
  const subfolders = iteratorToArray(folder.getFolders());
  const files = iteratorToArray(folder.getFiles());
  Logger.log(subfolders);
  Logger.log(files);
```

```
}

function iteratorToArray(iterator) {
  const array = [];
  while (iterator.hasNext()) {
    const item = iterator.next();
    const data = {
      id: item.getId(),
      name: item.getName(),
    };
    if (item.getMimeType) {  // Check if getMimeType method ex-
ists
      data.mimeType = item.getMimeType();
    }
    array.push(data);
  }
  return array;
}
```

If executed correctly, the script logs the files and folders found within the specified Drive folder. Here is how it operates:

1. The script utilizes the unique folder ID to access the specific **`Folder`** instance through **`DriveApp`**.
2. It employs the **`getFiles()`** and **`getFolders()`** methods from the **`Folder`** class to retrieve the contents within that folder.
3. The **`iteratorToArray(iterator)`** function is a crucial component of this script. It transforms the iterators returned by **`getFiles()`** and **`getFolders()`** into more manageable arrays. This conversion is important for subsequent operations that require array manipulation.
4. Importantly, the script checks for the presence of the **`getMimeType()`** method, which is not available on **`Folder`** objects. This method is only invoked if the current object in the iteration is a file, thereby ensuring that the script does not attempt to call **`getMimeType()`** on a folder.

A word of caution: navigating through extensive folder structures can significantly prolong execution times, potentially leading to exceeding Google Apps Script's execution time limits. To manage large datasets without hitting these limits, you could utilize the **`getContinuationToken()`** method, which allows the script to pause and resume without starting over. This method of managing execution runtime is a more advanced topic that will be addressed in further detail in subsequent volumes.

Creating Files in Folders

To create new files within a folder, you can use the **createFile()** method provided by the **Folder** class:

```
function createFileInFolder() {
  const PARENT_FOLDER_ID = '1AjJP4obPXfAQmcVLUPpxholPn75be_kk';
  const folder = DriveApp.getFolderById(PARENT_FOLDER_ID);
  folder.createFile('MyText.txt', 'Hello world!', MimeType.PLAIN_
TEXT);
}
```

This function creates a plain text file within the designated folder. For native Google Workspace file types such as Google Sheets, the process involves creating the file first and then moving it to the desired folder:

```
function createSpreadsheetInFolder() {
  const PARENT_FOLDER_ID = '1AjJP4obPXfAQmcVLUPpxholPn75be_kk';
  const folder = DriveApp.getFolderById(PARENT_FOLDER_ID);
  const ss = SpreadsheetApp.create('My Spreadsheet');
  const file = DriveApp.getFileById(ss.getId());
  file.moveTo(folder);
}
```

Here is how the script functions when creating and manipulating a Google Spreadsheet through Google Apps Script:

1. The **SpreadsheetApp.create(name)** function is used to create a new spreadsheet. This action automatically places the spreadsheet file in the root folder of your Google Drive.

2. After creation, the script retrieves the file using **DriveApp** and then employs the **moveTo(Folder)** method to relocate it to a designated folder. This is a crucial step for organizing your files within Google Drive as you prefer.

3. One advantageous side effect of this method is that you immediately have access to the **Spreadsheet** instance. This means you can begin manipulating the spreadsheet right away, adding sheets, formatting cells, or populating it with data as required.

Managing file lifecycle is also straightforward. To delete the spreadsheet, you would call **setTrashed(true)** on the **File** instance, effectively moving it to the Google Drive trash. Conversely, you would call **setTrashed(false)** to restore the file from the trash.

Additionally, to explore the hierarchy or parental structure of the file, you can use the **getParents()** method. This returns a **FolderIterator**, allowing you to navigate through the file's folder ancestry within Drive.

Advanced: Recursion in Folder Management

Recursion is a powerful programming concept where a function calls itself to solve a problem that can be broken down into smaller, similar problems. This technique is particularly useful in cases where tasks are naturally hierarchical or nested, such as navigating file systems, processing nested data structures, or implementing algorithms such as quicksort and tree traversals.

A practical use case for recursion in Google Apps Script is to traverse a folder structure within Google Drive. By defining a recursive function, we can efficiently explore a folder and all its sub-folders, regardless of how deeply they are nested. The function starts by reading the contents of one folder, then recursively calls itself on each sub-folder it encounters. This process repeats, descending through the folder hierarchy, until there are no more sub-folders to explore. This method is ideal for tasks such as generating a comprehensive list of all files and directories within a specific directory, applying operations to files based on specific criteria, or organizing and categorizing data based on folder structures. Recursion simplifies the coding of such operations, making the code easier to write and maintain, especially when dealing with complex folder trees.

Let us traverse our folder:

```
function run() {
  const PARENT_FOLDER_ID = '1AjJP4obPXfAQmcVLUPpxholPn75be_kk';
  const fileTree = tree(PARENT_FOLDER_ID);
  Logger.log(JSON.stringify(fileTree, null, 2));
}

function tree(parentFolderId) {
  const recurse = ({ id, name }) => {
    const folder = DriveApp.getFolderById(id);
    const node = {
      id,
      name: name || folder.getName(),
      folders: iteratorToArray(folder.getFolders()),
      files: iteratorToArray(folder.getFiles()),
    };
    node.folders.forEach((folder, i) => {
      node.folders[i] = recurse(folder);
    });
    return node;
  };
  return recurse({ id: parentFolderId });
}
```

Running the **run()** function will provide a JSON representation of the folder structure, allowing you to visualize the entire hierarchy of folders and files:

```
{
  "id": "1AjJP4obPXfAQmcVLUPpxholPn75be_kk",
  "name": "TEST",
  "folders": [
    {
      "id": "1yFJQ5gA4TaV6318NaIvoGjY4JwpN3sA_",
      "name": "subfolder 3",
      "folders": [],
      "files": [
        {
          "id": "16K4orqoM1jfEW8VwRB2y83hWaPbSrFAzCUghE4jhDeziR-
VYtV6tJf1gr",
          "name": "zz Test move to shared drive",
          "mimeType": "application/vnd.google-apps.script"
        },
        {
          "id": "1NRLt5BaPJGtjUaJwgkbYPS7rmoCyM4UK",
          "name": "acc2.jpg",
          "mimeType": "image/jpeg"
        }
        // ...
    }
      // ...
  ],
  "files": [
    {
      "id": "1IEXKmrQom9Eljou3Yd_Yj2UbQYaxYS8Xt0_k9qgOHmc",
      "name": "My Spreadsheet",
      "mimeType": "application/vnd.google-apps.spreadsheet"
    },
    {
      "id": "1TLxFgmAuqEhxqyYQkb4rYUDFlcmN1U5X",
      "name": "MyText.txt",
      "mimeType": "text/plain"
    }
    //...
  ]
}
```

The **tree** function is designed to map out the structure of a folder in Google Drive by taking the parent folder as its argument. Within this function, a nested function named **recurse** is critical for its operation. The **recurse** function begins by constructing an object for each folder, encapsulating its ID, name, and its contents–both files and sub-folders. As it accesses each folder, it recursively calls itself on every sub-folder, thereby traversing deeper into the folder hierarchy and updating the object structure with data from each level.

Visual Representation Using Recursion

Further, you can use recursion to create a visual representation of the folder structure:

```
function drawTree(parentFolderId) {
  let str = '';
  const recurse = (node, depth = 0) => {
    str += `${' '.repeat(depth)}├─ 🗁 ${node.name}\n`;
    depth += 4;
    node.folders.forEach(folder => {
      recurse(folder, depth, str);
    });
    node.files.forEach(file => {
      str += `${' '.repeat(depth)}├─ 🗎 ${file.name}\n`;
    });
  };
  recurse(tree(parentFolderId));
  console.log(str);
}
```

This transformation uses recursion once again, not to traverse the folders themselves this time, but to navigate through the tree object created from the initial folder traversal. This method allows for a graphical representation of the folder structure, showing how folders and files are nested within one another, thus providing a clear, hierarchical view of the directory contents:

```
├─ 🗁 TEST
    ├─ 🗁 subfolder 3
        ├─ 🗎 zz Test move to shared drive
        ├─ 🗎 acc2.jpg
        ├─ 🗎 acc2.jpg
        ├─ 🗎 acc1.jpg
        ├─ 🗎 acc1.jpg
        ├─ 🗎 acc1.jpg
    ├─ 🗁 subfolder 2
        ├─ 🗁 folder  1
            ├─ 🗁 folder 1.1
                ├─ 🗎 test form
            ├─ 🗎 test pres
        ├─ 🗁 folder 2
            ├─ 🗁 folder 2.1
                ├─ 🗎 form 1
                ├─ 🗎 slides 1
```

```
    ├── 🗎 Hi there
    ├── 🗎 test
├── 🗀 subfolder 1
    ├── 🗀 folder  1
        ├── 🗀 folder 1.1
            ├── 🗎 test form
        ├── 🗎 test pres
    ├── 🗀 folder 2
        ├── 🗀 folder 2.1
            ├── 🗎 slides 1
            └── 🗎 form 1
    ├── 🗎 test
    ├── 🗎 Hi there
├── 🗎 My Spreadsheet
├── 🗎 MyText.txt
├── 🗎 MyText.txt
├── 🗎 test g doc
```

Next, we will explore how to manage access rights to files and folders, ensuring proper security and accessibility within your Google Drive environment.

Managing Access to Files and Folders

Managing permissions on files and folders within Google Drive via Google Apps Script is a straightforward process. These operations generally fall into three main categories: getting, adding, and removing access rights by role. Although these actions are relatively simple and we will thus not do a deep dive here, exploring them through the **DriveApp** documentation and experimenting with various permissions in your projects can be very insightful.

Getting Access Rights by Role

Understanding who has access to your files and folders is crucial for maintaining security and collaboration. The following methods allow you to retrieve access rights based on different roles:

Method	Return Value	Description
getAccess(email)	Permission	Returns permissions on the file/folder for the user identified by the email
getViewers()	User[]	Returns a list of viewers for the file/folder
getEditors()	User[]	Returns a list of editors for the file/folder
getOwner()	User	Returns the owner of the file/folder

Table 5.3: *Methods to get access rights for a file or folder by role*

Adding Access Rights by Role

Adding permissions is a key functionality that enhances collaborative efforts on documents and folders. Here are the methods used to add permissions by role:

Method	Return Value	Description
`addViewer(email)`	**`Folder`** or **`File`** for chaining	Adds a new viewer
`addViewers(emails)`	**`Folder`** or **`File`** for chaining	Adds multiple viewers
`addEditor(email)`	**`Folder`** or **`File`** for chaining	Adds a new editor
`addEditors(emails)`	**`Folder`** or **`File`** for chaining	Adds multiple editors
`addCommenter(email)`	**`File`** for **chaining**	Adds a new commenter; only works on files
`addCommenters(emails)`	**`File`** for **chaining**	Adds multiple commenters; only works on files

Table 5.4: *Methods to add access rights to a file or folder by role*

Removing Access Rights by Role

Similarly, there may be situations where removing access is necessary, whether to limit visibility or revise participant roles. The following methods facilitate the removal of access:

Method	Return Value	Description
`removeViewer(email)`	**`Folder`** or **`File`** for chaining	Removes a viewer
`removeViewers(emails)`	**`Folder`** or **`File`** for chaining	Removes multiple viewers
`removeEditor(email)`	**`Folder`** or **`File`** for chaining	Removes an editor
`removeEditors(emails)`	**`Folder`** or **`File`** for chaining	Removes multiple editors
`removeCommenter(email)`	**`File`** for **chaining**	Removes a commenter; only works on files
`removeCommenters(emails)`	**`File`** for **chaining**	Removes multiple commenters; only works on files
`revokePermission(email)`	**`Folder`** or **`File`** for chaining	Revokes all permissions for a user

`revokePermissions(emails)`	**`Folder`** or **`File`** for chaining	Revokes all permissions for multiple users

Table 5.5: *Methods to remove access rights for a file or folder by role*

With these methods, you can manage who has access to your files and folders in Google Drive, ensuring the right people have the right access at the right time.

Next, we will explore how to convert files to PDF format, a common requirement for sharing documents in a universally accessible format.

Converting Files to PDF

Converting documents to PDF is a common requirement in many workflows, particularly when sharing files across different platforms and devices. Google Apps Script offers built-in functionality to convert documents such as Google Docs into PDFs seamlessly.

Example: Converting a Google Doc to PDF

Let us look at how you can take a Google Doc and convert it to a PDF using Google Apps Script:

```
function convertToPdf() {
  // Get the file and convert it to a PDF blob with getAs()
  const fileId = '1490NJkgdJWkM7Lits2FLztKB24bdxxFqEf5xZs691QI';
  const file = DriveApp.getFileById(fileId); // a Google Doc ID
  const blob = file.getAs('application/pdf');

  // Use the blob to create a file in your target folder
  const folderId = '1AjJP4obPXfAQmcVLUPpxholPn75be_kk';
  const folder = DriveApp.getFolderById(folderId);
  const newFile = folder.createFile(blob);

  // Log out the URL for easy reference
  Logger.log(newFile.getUrl());
  return newFile;
}
```

In this script:

1. We start by retrieving the Google Doc using its unique file ID.
2. The document is then converted into a PDF using the **`getAs('application/pdf')`** method, which generates a binary large object, or blob, representing the PDF.

3. This blob is then used to create a new file in a specified folder within Google Drive.
4. Finally, the URL of the new PDF file is logged, providing a direct link to the newly created document.

Use Cases for Blobs

A blob is essentially a binary data type that can handle various kinds of content, not limited to text or images. In this context, the blob is used to store the PDF version of a Google Doc, which can then be manipulated further. For instance, this blob could be:

- Saved in a new format, as demonstrated.
- Attached to an email, enhancing the capabilities of your scripts to interact with other services such as Gmail.

In the following section, we will explore how to attach this newly created PDF file to an email, illustrating another practical application of blobs within Google Apps Script projects. This demonstrates not only the versatility of blobs but also how seamlessly Google Apps Script integrates with other Google services.

Gmail Attachments

Integrating Google Apps Script with Gmail allows you to automate the process of sending emails, including attaching files directly from Google Drive as PDFs. Let us examine how you can utilize a blob created from a Google Doc to draft an email with an attachment.

Creating a Gmail Draft with a PDF Attachment

In the previous section, we converted a Google Doc to a PDF. Now, we will use this PDF blob to create an email draft in Gmail. Here is how you can accomplish this:

```
function createGmailDraftWithAttachment() {
  // Get the file and convert it to a PDF blob with getAs()
  const fileId = '1490NJkgdJWkM7Lits2FLztKB24bdxxFqEf5xZs691QI';
  const file = DriveApp.getFileById(fileId); // a Google Doc ID
  const blob = file.getAs('application/pdf');

  // Create a draft email with the blob as attachment
  const draft = GmailApp.createDraft(
    'john@example.com',
    'An email with attachment',
    'Check the attachment',
```

```
    {
      attachments: [blob],
    }
  );
}
```

In this script:

1. We start by fetching the Google Doc using its ID and converting it directly to a PDF blob.
2. Using the **`GmailApp.createDraft()`** method, we set up a new email draft. The recipient's email address, the subject line, and the body text are specified straightforwardly.
3. Importantly, the **`attachments`** field in the **`options`** object of the draft includes our PDF blob. This allows the attachment to be added directly to the email.

Result: A Gmail Draft with an Attachment

After running the script, you should see a new draft in your Gmail with the PDF file attached:

Figure 5.8: *A Gmail draft with an attachment generated by Apps Script*

Advantages of Direct Blob Usage

One of the key benefits of this approach is efficiency. There is no need to store the blob as a file on Google Drive unless necessary. This direct method saves storage space and simplifies the workflow, as the PDF blob is sent directly in an email draft without intermediate steps. This showcases the power of Google Apps Script in creating seamless integrations across different Google services, enhancing both productivity and automation capabilities.

Things that we will Cover in Volume 2

Working with Google Drive through Google Apps Script offers a wide range of possibilities and functionalities. While we have explored many aspects of this topic in this volume, the vast scope of what can be accomplished encourages ongoing exploration. It is highly recommended to delve into the official documentation to uncover even more capabilities.

Upcoming Topics in the Next Volume

In the next volume, we will expand on our current foundation by covering more specialized and advanced topics, including:

- **Google File Picker API**: This is a graphical user interface (GUI) that allows users to select files and folders within Apps Script projects and beyond. It simplifies the process of file selection, making it more user-friendly, especially for applications that require user interaction.
- **Google Drive Activity API**: Monitoring changes in Google Drive is crucial for applications that need to track modifications or updates in real-time. The Drive Activity API provides the tools necessary to detect and respond to changes, offering insights into who changed what and when.
- **Drive Labels API**: Managing labels in Google Drive can help organize and classify files more efficiently. This API allows for the programmatic creation, modification, and deletion of labels, enhancing the ability to manage documents systematically.
- **Continuation Tokens**: When dealing with very large collections of files and folders, it is essential to handle data efficiently without exceeding script execution limits. Continuation tokens enable scripts to pause and resume iterating over large datasets, making it possible to process extensive amounts of data in manageable segments.

Each of these topics will provide deeper insights and additional techniques to enhance your ability to integrate and automate Google Drive functionalities in your applications. Stay tuned for these advanced topics that will further expand your scripting capabilities and improve your understanding of Google Apps Script's powerful features.

Conclusion

In this chapter, we have explored the extensive capabilities of Google Apps Script's DriveApp, delving into the management of files and folders on Google Drive. From basic operations such as creating, reading, updating, and deleting files, to more advanced techniques such as converting files to PDFs and managing email attachments with Gmail, this chapter has aimed to equip you with the knowledge to effectively harness the power of Google Apps Script in your projects.

We have covered how to:

- Interact with the file system using CRUD operations.
- List files recursively and interact with folders in a structured manner.
- Convert and manage file types, particularly focusing on PDF conversions.
- Use blobs for advanced file manipulation, including attaching files to emails.
- Manage access rights efficiently, ensuring the security and proper accessibility of files.

While we have covered a significant amount of functionality, the world of Google Drive and Google Apps Script is vast and continuously evolving. There are always more features and tricks to learn, and with each new API and improvement, your ability to create sophisticated scripts and applications will expand.

As you continue to build and refine your applications, it is suggested to experiment with the concepts and code examples provided in this chapter. Explore the Google Apps Script documentation for further details and updates, and prepare for the upcoming topics in the next volume, which will delve into more advanced APIs and techniques.

By mastering these tools, you will enhance your ability to create dynamic, efficient, and powerful applications that can leverage the full potential of Google Drive alongside other Google services. Whether you are automating routine tasks, managing documents on a large scale, or building complex systems, the knowledge you have gained here will serve as a solid foundation for your continued development journey.

Key Terms

- **Blob:** A Binary Large OBject that can store data of various types, including multimedia files.
- **CRUD Operations:** An acronym for Create, Read, Update, and Delete; fundamental operations for managing data.

- **Continuation Token:** A method in Google Apps Script that allows a script to save its progress and continue from the same point when restarted.
- **DriveApp:** A Google Apps Script service that provides methods to access and manipulate files stored in Google Drive.
- **`FileIterator`:** An object that allows for the sequential processing of a collection of files without loading all of them into memory at once.
- **`FolderIterator`:** Similar to FileIterator but for folders, allowing sequential access to a collection of folders.
- **Google File Picker API:** An interface that enables users to select files or folders from Google Drive via a graphical user interface.
- **Google Drive Activity API:** An API that tracks and reports changes made to files and folders in Google Drive.
- **Drive Labels API:** An API used for creating, modifying, and deleting labels in Google Drive, helping with the organization and classification of files.
- **`MimeType`:** A label used to identify the type of data contained in a file, helping systems understand how to process different file types.
- **Permission:** An object or setting that defines the access rights to a file or folder, such as viewing, editing, or ownership privileges.
- **Recursion:** A programming technique where a function calls itself in order to solve a problem that can be broken into smaller, similar problems.

CHAPTER 6
FormApp

Introduction

Google Forms are a convenient way to collect information from users for various purposes, such as surveys, quizzes, feedback, or registrations. They are versatile, easy to create, and can be shared widely with minimal effort. However, the true power of Google Forms is unlocked when combined with Google Apps Script.

In Google Apps Script, the **`FormApp`** class is a central piece for managing Google Forms. It allows developers to programmatically build, access, and submit forms, as well as process responses and react to submitted answers. Whether you are creating a form from scratch, customizing an existing one, or automating responses, **`FormApp`** provides the necessary methods and properties.

Let us get into it! We will start by understanding the basics of the **`FormApp`** class and then move on to practical applications. By the end of this chapter, you will have a solid foundation to build and manage your Google Forms programmatically using Apps Script.

Structure

In this chapter, we will cover the following topics:

- A High-level Overview of **`FormApp`**'s Classes
- Getting Started with **`FormApp`**
- Building a Modular Employee Engagement Survey with Built-in Score Calculation
- Managing Access to Forms
- A Quick Description of the **`onSubmit`** Trigger

Overview of `FormApp`'s Key Classes

Before diving into writing code, it is essential to understand the architecture and possibilities of the **`FormApp`** class. This knowledge will provide a solid foundation for leveraging the class effectively. For comprehensive details, always refer to the full documentation at https://developers.google.com/apps-script/reference/forms.

Form Metadata

The **`Form`** metadata encompasses data relevant to the form as a whole rather than its responses or individual components. This includes attributes such as URLs, name, description, whether it is a quiz, and if it collects emails. These properties are accessed via methods in the **`Form`** class, such as **`getPublishedUrl()`**, which retrieves the form's URL for collecting responses.

FormItem

Form items are the building blocks of a form, representing the various widgets that compose it. These items include text fields, multiple-choice fields, checkboxes, and lists. Following is a non-exhaustive list of items that can be used to compose a form:

Class	Description
`CheckboxItem`	Adds a checkbox
`CheckboxGridItem`	A matrix with multiple choices per row
`DateItem`	Allows selection of a date
`DateTimeItem`	Allows selection of a date and a time
`ImageItem`	Adds an image to the form
`ListItem`	A drop-down list
`ParagraphTextItem`	Allows entry of a block of text
`SectionHeaderItem`	Indicates a new section

Table 6.1: *Key form items*

FormResponse

The **`FormResponse`** object contains all the data related to a form response. With a form response, you can:

- Read its data
- Submit a new response programmatically
- Generate a URL with prefilled fields (not covered here, but well documented)

Reading Responses

Here are some key methods for reading responses:

Method	Description
`getItemResponses()`	Returns an array of **`ItemResponse`** objects (covered later)
`getRespondentEmail()`	Retrieves the respondent's email if email collection is enabled
`getResponseForItem(item)`	Gets the response for a specific item
`getTimestamp()`	Returns the timestamp when the response was submitted

Table 6.2: *Key form response methods*

Submitting a Response Programmatically

Creating a form response programmatically involves the following steps:

1. Call **`createResponse()`** on the **`Form`** instance to start a new response.
2. Create individual item responses.
3. Inject all item responses into the **`FormResponse`** instance.
4. When ready, call **`submit()`** on the **`FormResponse`**.

An example source code will be provided in the *Getting Started* section below.

Validation Classes

Validation classes ensure that the user submits data in the required format. If the data does not meet the criteria, the user will receive a warning, and submission will not be possible. Different item types have their own validation classes. Some examples include:

- **`CheckboxValidation`**
- **`TextValidation`**
- **`GridValidation`**

Understanding these classes and their methods will help you build robust forms that enforce data integrity and enhance user experience.

Getting Started with `FormApp`

To begin using **`FormApp`**, you need to create a Google Form and then access its bound script. Follow these steps:

1. Open your Google Form.
2. Click the three dots menu in the top-right corner.
3. Select "**`Script Editor`**" from the dropdown menu.

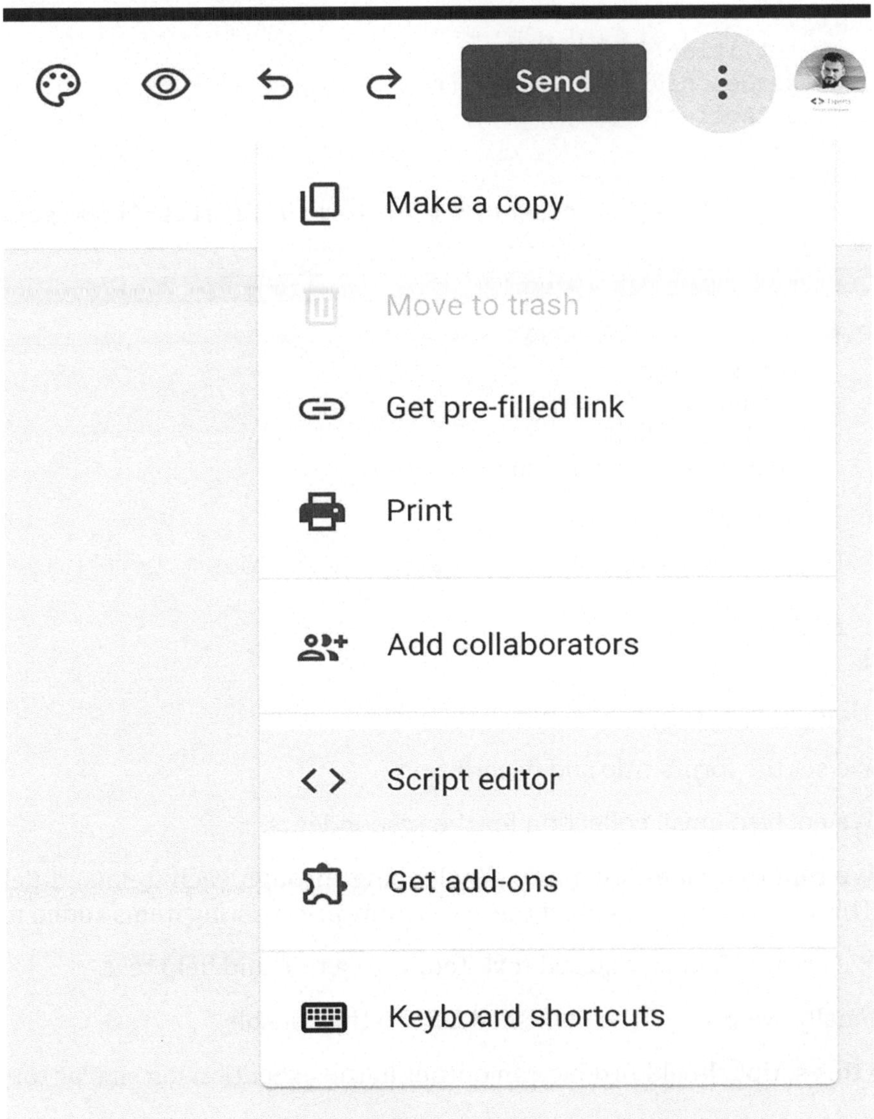

Figure 6.1: *Opening the script editor from within a Google Form*

Setting Up the Form Programmatically

Once you are inside the container-bound script for your form, you can start setting up the form programmatically. Enter the following code in the script editor:

```
function setUpForm() {
  // This is a bound script, so we can get the active form
  const form = FormApp.getActiveForm();

  // Set form's metadata
  form
    .setTitle('Test Form')
    .setDescription('This form is managed by Apps Script')
    .setCollectEmail(true);

  // Remove all current items
  form.getItems().forEach(item => form.deleteItem(item.getIn-
dex()));

  // Add a new name item
  form
    .addTextItem()
    .setRequired(true)
    .setTitle('Name')
    .setHelpText('Your first name');

  // The published URL allows submitting responses
  Logger.log(`Published URL: ${form.getPublishedUrl()}`);

  return form;
}
```

Explanation:

1. We set the form's title and description.
2. We enabled email collection for the respondents.
3. We removed all existing items by looping through each item and deleting it. This ensures a clean slate if there were any pre-existing items added manually.
4. We created a new required text item with a title and help text.
5. Finally, we printed the published URL to the console.

Running this script should produce an output in the execution log similar to:

```
Published URL: https://docs.google.com/forms/d/e/1FAIpQLSc.../
viewform
```

The actual form will now look like this:

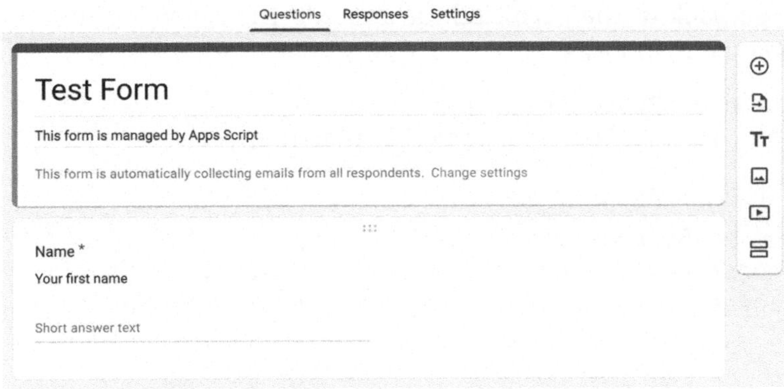

Figure 6.2: *A programmatically created Google Form*

Notice how the form's metadata and input correspond to the settings we defined in the script. Next, we will look at how to submit a form response and read the results.

Accessing Form Responses

Once you have set up your form programmatically, it is time to collect and access the responses. Follow these steps to see how it is done:

1. Grab the published URL generated in the previous section and paste it into a new browser tab. You should see the following:

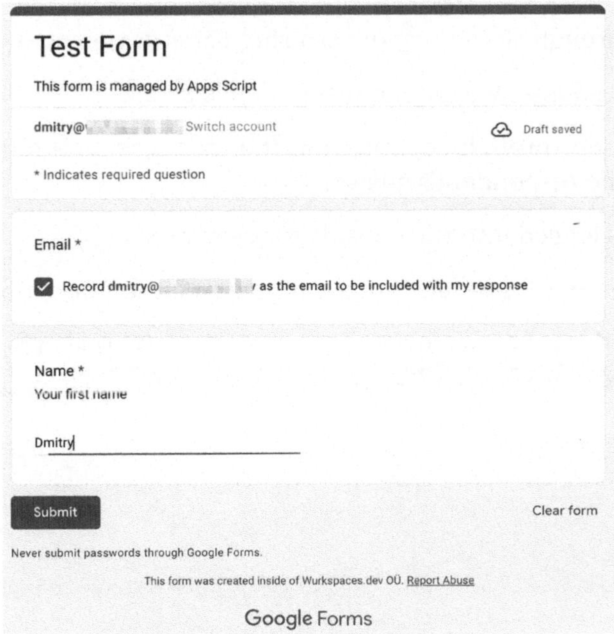

Figure 6.3: *The published Google Form*

2. Submit a response to the form.
3. Now, go back to the script editor and add the following function to retrieve and log the responses:

```
function getResponses() {
  const form = FormApp.getActiveForm();

  // Loop through all the responses
  form.getResponses().forEach(response => {
    const respondent = response.getRespondentEmail();
    Logger.log(`We have a response from ${respondent}`);

    // Loop through all the response items
    response.getItemResponses().forEach(item => {

      // Extract response data
      const title = item.getItem().getTitle();
      const response = item.getResponse();
      Logger.log(`* They answered {response} to {title}`);
    });
  });
}
```

Explanation:

1. We get the active form using **FormApp.getActiveForm()**.
2. We loop through all the responses using **form.getResponses()**.
3. For each response, we log the respondent's email.
4. We then loop through each item in the response, extracting the title of the item and the respondent's answer.
5. The data is logged into the console for easy viewing.

Running this function will produce output in the execution log similar to:

```
9:45:08 AM  Info  We have a response from dmitry@...
9:45:08 AM  Info  * They answered Dmitry to Name
```

This information should be identical to what you see in the **`Responses`** tab of the Google Form:

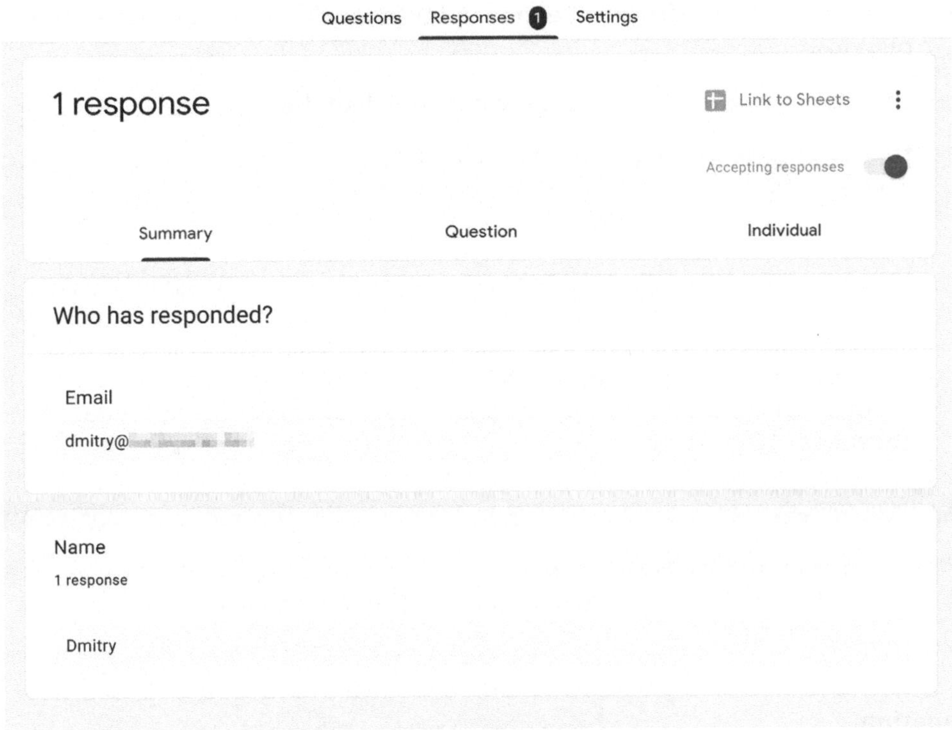

Figure 6.4: *Google Forms Responses*

This method provides a programmatic way to access and process form responses, which can be incredibly useful for automating workflows and integrating form data with other systems.

Next, we will explore how to submit form responses programmatically.

Submitting Form Responses Programmatically

Submitting form responses programmatically involves a few key steps. By following these steps, you can automate the process of filling out and submitting a Google Form. Here is how to do it:

1. **Create a `FormResponse` instance**: This is the container for your programmatic response.
2. **Create `ItemResponses` for all necessary items in the form**: These represent individual answers to form questions.

3. **Inject each `ItemResponse` into the `FormResponse` instance**: This step adds the answers to the response container.
4. **Call `submit()` on the `FormResponse` instance**: This finalizes and submits the response.

In the context of our form, the process would look like this:

```
function submitProgrammaticResponse() {
  const form = FormApp.getActiveForm();

  // Create a form response
  const programmaticFormResponse = form.createResponse();

  // Get an item and create an item response
  const item = form.getItems()[0];
  const programmaticItemResponse = item.asTextItem().create
Response('Sunil');

  // Inject the item response into the form response and submit
it
  programmaticFormResponse
    .withItemResponse(programmaticItemResponse)
    .submit();
}
```

Explanation:

1. **Creating the `FormResponse` instance**: We start by getting the active form and creating a new response object.
2. **Creating `ItemResponse`**: We retrieve the first item in the form using **`form.getItems()[0]`**. Since this returns a generic Item interface, we cast it to a TextItem using **`item.asTextItem()`**, then create a response for it with the desired answer ('Sunil' in this case).
3. **Injecting and Submitting:** We add the item response to our form response with programmatic **`FormResponse.withItemResponse(programmaticItemResponse)`** and submit it using **`submit()`**.

Key points:

- **`asTextItem()` Method:** This method is necessary because **`getItems()[0]`** returns a generic **`Item`** interface. Casting it to **`TextItem`** allows us to call createResponse on it.
- **Dynamic Type Checking:** If you prefer not to hard-code the item type, you can dynamically check the type using **`item.getType()`**.

Now that we have covered the basics and you have gotten some hands-on experience, let us take on a more complex, real-world project. Next, we will build an employee engagement survey (EES), demonstrating how to use **FormApp** to create a sophisticated form with built-in score calculation. This project will serve as a proof-of-concept for more advanced form management techniques.

Building and Analyzing an Employee Engagement Survey

An employee engagement survey (EES) is a practical, real-life use case that can benefit from being implemented programmatically. By making the survey modular, it can be adapted to different teams with ease. Our solution will allow you to pre-define various sections and choose which sections to include in the form. Additionally, you can insert page breaks between sections for a cleaner user experience. Finally, we will process the results and calculate average scores that can be programmatically inserted into different reports in Sheets, Docs, or Slides.

Building the EES

We will start by creating a reset function for our form, with a small twist. We will add a boolean parameter **hardReset** to indicate whether we want to delete previous answers. Additionally, we will separate the creation of form items into distinct functions for each section.

```
function resetAsEesForm(hardReset = false) {
  // This is a bound script, so we can get the active form
  const form = FormApp.getActiveForm();

  // Conditionally delete all existing responses
  if (hardReset) form.deleteAllResponses();

  // Set form's metadata
  form
    .setTitle('Employee Engagement Survey')
    .setDescription('This form is managed by Apps Script')
    .setCollectEmail(false); // The form is anonymous, so we will
not be collecting email data

  // Remove all current items
  form.getItems().forEach(item => form.deleteItem
(item.getIndex()));

  return form;
}
```

For this example, we will build two sections: Overall Satisfaction and Engagement.

Satisfaction Section

The Satisfaction section begins by adding a section header with a title and help text to guide the respondents. This is followed by a scale item that allows respondents to rate their satisfaction on a scale from 1 to 5, where 1 represents "**Very Dissatisfied**" and 5 represents "**Very Satisfied**." This scale item is set as a required field to ensure that all respondents provide an answer. Additionally, the section includes a multiple-choice item to rate the work environment. The choices for this item include "**Excellent**," "**Good**," "**Average**," "**Poor**," and "**Very Poor**," and it is also marked as a required field. Finally, an optional text item is added to collect any suggestions for improvements to the work environment.

Notice the **setChoices()** method; it expects to receive an array of **createChoice(choice)** calls, we use the array **map** method to make it a little more concise:

```
function SatisfactionSection(form = FormApp.getActiveForm()) {
  form
    .addSectionHeaderItem()
    .setTitle('Overall Satisfaction and Work Environment')
    .setHelpText('This section aims to understand your overall
satisfaction with the company and gather feedback on your work
environment.');

  form
    .addScaleItem()
    .setTitle('On a scale of 1 to 5, how satisfied are you with
your overall experience working at our company?')
    .setHelpText('Scale: 1 - Very Dissatisfied to 5 - Very
Satisfied')
    .setBounds(1, 5)
    .setRequired(true);

  const env = form
    .addMultipleChoiceItem()
    .setTitle('How would you rate your work environment?')
    .setHelpText('Include physical workspace, tools, and
resources')
    .setRequired(true);

  env.setChoices(
    ['Excellent', 'Good', 'Average', 'Poor', 'Very Poor'].
map(choice =>
      env.createChoice(choice)
```

```
    )
  );

  form
    .addTextItem()
    .setTitle('What improvements, if any, would you suggest for
your work environment?')
    .setHelpText('Free text')
    .setRequired(false);
}
```

Engagement Section

The Engagement section also starts with a section header that includes a title and help text. It features a scale item that asks respondents to rate their engagement with their work and the company on a scale from 1 to 5, with 1 meaning "**`Not Engaged at All`**" and 5 meaning "**`Highly Engaged`**." This item is mandatory for all respondents. The section then includes a multiple-choice item asking if the respondent would recommend the company as a great place to work, offering "**`Yes`**" and "**`No`**" as options, and this is also a required field. Additionally, the section contains a text item asking respondents to elaborate on their engagement with the company, requiring a minimum response length of 100 characters. This item uses the **`setValidation()`** method with **`FormApp.createTextValidation()`** to enforce the character limit and is marked as required.

Notice we used **`setChoiceValues()`** instead of **`setChoices()`**. It is a little simpler. The latter has other functionality that you can look up in the documentation, but if you do not need it, you can stick with the former.

```
function EngagementSection(form = FormApp.getActiveForm()) {
  form
    .addSectionHeaderItem()
    .setTitle('Engagement and Company Culture')
    .setHelpText('This section evaluates your engagement with the
company and your perspective on the overall company culture.');

  form
    .addScaleItem()
    .setBounds(1, 5)
    .setTitle('How engaged do you feel with your work and the
company?')
    .setHelpText('Scale: 1 - Not Engaged at All to 5 - Highly
Engaged')
    .setRequired(true);
```

```
  form
    .addMultipleChoiceItem()
    .setTitle('Would you recommend our company as a great place
to work?')
    .setChoiceValues(['Yes', 'No'])
    .setRequired(true);

  form
    .addTextItem()
    .setTitle('How engaged do you feel with your work and the
company?')
    .setHelpText('Minimum length: 100 characters')
    .setValidation(
      FormApp.createTextValidation()
        .requireTextLengthGreaterThanOrEqualTo(100)
        .build()
    )
    .setRequired(true);
}
```

Building the Main Function

Now, let us put these sections into a **`main()`** function:

```
function main() {
  const form = resetAsEesForm(true);
  SatisfactionSection(form);
  EngagementSection(form);
}
```

Running this function will produce the following result:

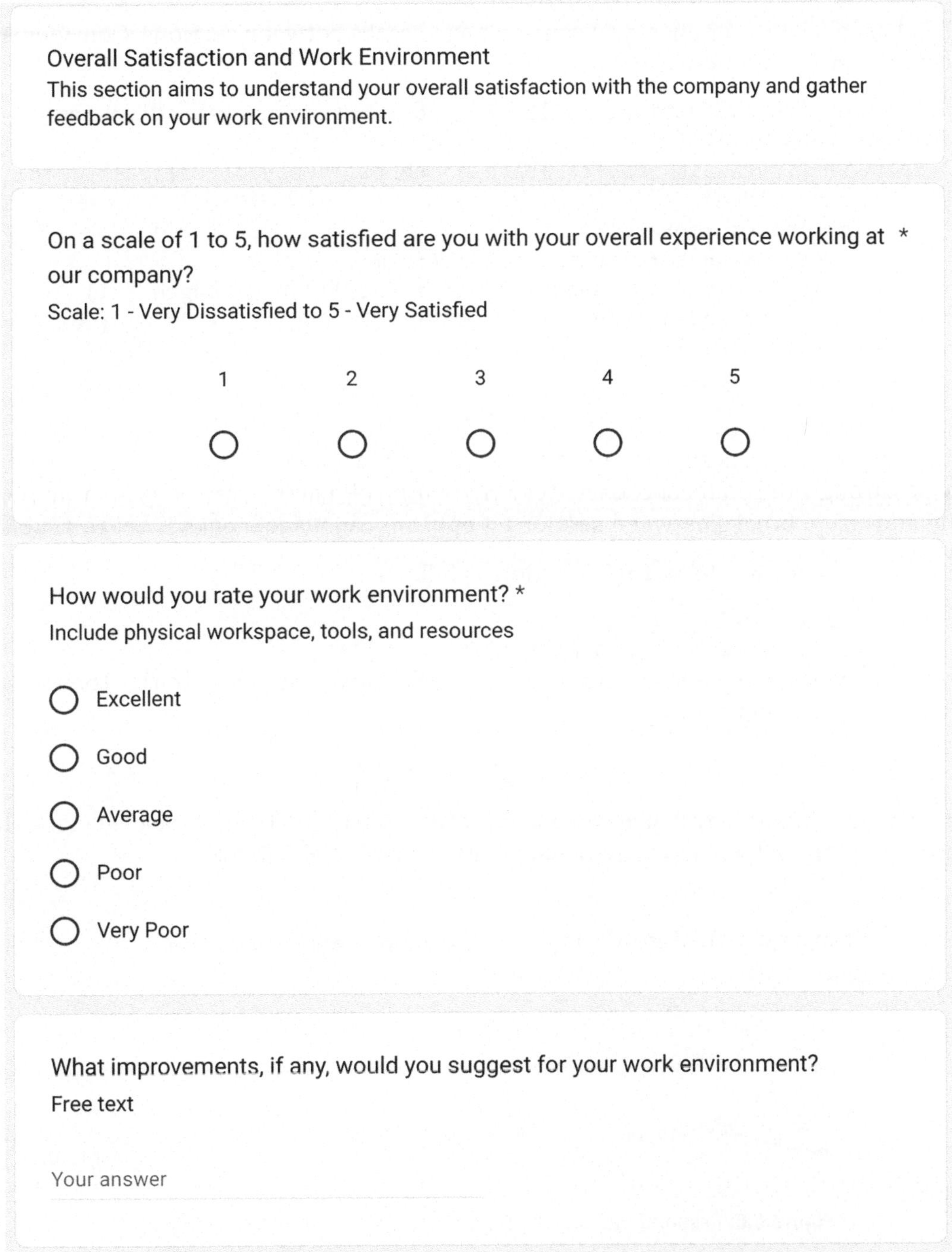

Figure 6.5: *The Satisfaction section generated with Apps Script*

Adding Page Breaks

To enhance user experience, you can add page breaks between sections. Consider the **addSections()** function as follows:

```
function addSections(callbacks, form = FormApp.getActiveForm(),
options = {}) {
  if (!Array.isArray(callbacks)) throw 'Array of callbacks was
not provided';
  callbacks.forEach((cb, i) => {
    cb instanceof Function && cb(form);
    if (options.addPageBreaks && i < callbacks.length - 1)
      form.addPageBreakItem().setTitle(`Page {i + 2} of {call-
backs.length}`);
  });
}
```

This function expects an array of callbacks, a **Form** instance, and an options object. It loops through the callbacks, executes them with the **Form** instance as a parameter, and adds page breaks between sections if **options.addPageBreaks** is set to **true**.

You can then update the **main()** function as follows:

```
function main() {
  const form = resetAsEesForm(true);
  addSections([SatisfactionSection, EngagementSection], form, {
    addPageBreaks: true,
  });
}
```

Running this function will give you a form with two pages. The first page will look the same as before but will now have a **Next** button instead of Submit:

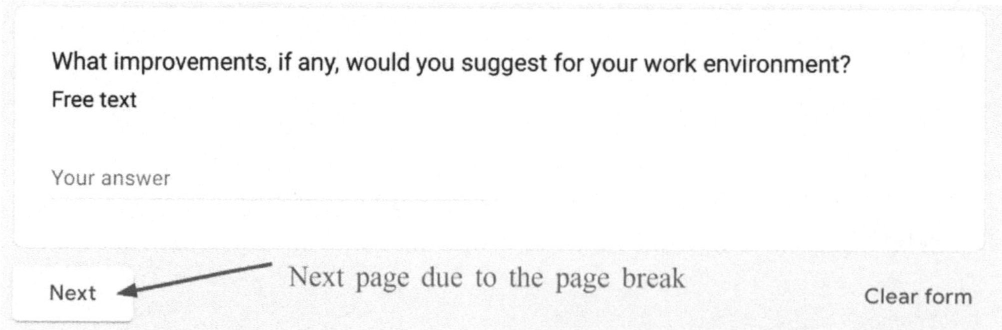

***Figure 6.6:** Respondents use the Next button to navigate between pages*

The second page will contain the Engagement section, and our **`TextValidation`** object will enforce the 100-character minimum length:

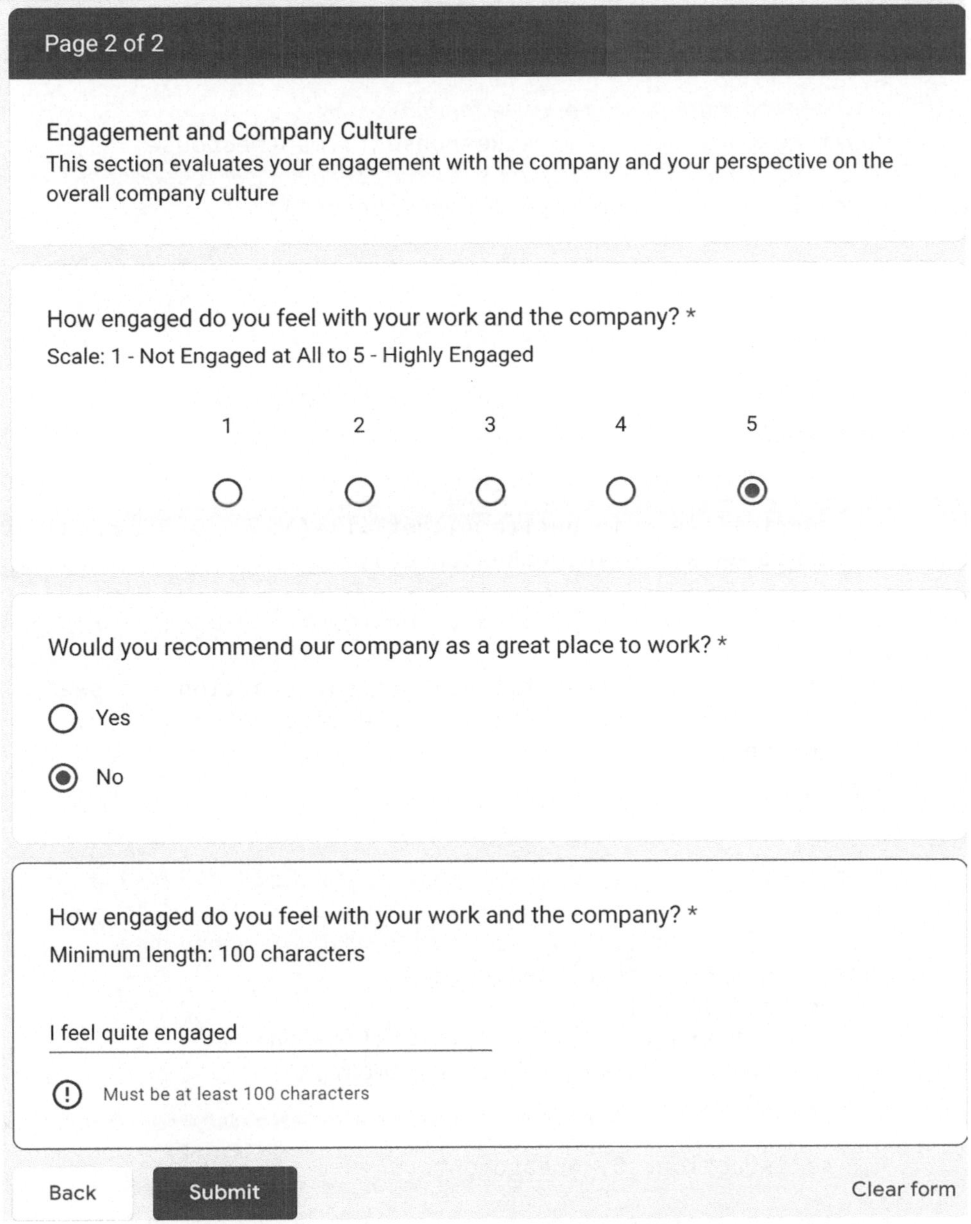

Figure 6.7: *The Engagement section generated with Apps Script*

Analyzing Results

Before proceeding, make sure your form has a sufficient number of responses so that we have some data to analyze. With data in hand, we can implement the following function to extract and calculate the average satisfaction and engagement scores:

```
function getScores() {
  const form = FormApp.getActiveForm();

  // Loop through the form responses
  const responses = form.getResponses().map(response => {
    // For every form response extract the item responses
    const irs = response.getItemResponses();

    // For every item response only extract satisfaction and
engagement scores
    return irs.reduce((acc, ir) => {
      // Exit quickly if item is not of type Scale
      if (ir.getItem().getType() !== FormApp.ItemType.SCALE)
return acc;

      // Extract item's title and answer
      const title = ir.getItem().getTitle();
      const answer = ir.getResponse();

      // Add the corresponding values to the accumulator object
and return it
      if (/satisfied/.test(title)) acc.satisfaction = answer;
      if (/engaged/.test(title)) acc.engagement = answer;
      return acc;
    }, {});
  });

  // Calculate the averages by first calculating the sums of both
indicators
  // Then dividing the sums by the number of responses
  const averages = responses.reduce(
    (sum, resp) => {
      sum.satisfaction += +resp.satisfaction;
      sum.engagement += +resp.engagement;
      return sum;
    },
    { satisfaction: 0, engagement: 0 }
  );
  averages.satisfaction /= responses.length;
  averages.engagement /= responses.length;

  console.log(averages);
  return averages;
}
```

Explanation:

This function processes the form responses to calculate the average satisfaction and engagement scores. Here is how it works:

1. **Looping through Responses**: The function begins by looping through all form responses and extracting the item responses for each form response.
2. **Filtering and Extracting Scores**: Within each response, it filters out item responses that are not of type **`SCALE`**. It then uses regular expressions to identify and extract the satisfaction and engagement scores based on the item titles.
3. **Calculating Averages**: The function sums up all the satisfaction and engagement scores and divides the sums by the number of responses to calculate the averages.
4. **Logging and Returning Averages**: The calculated averages are logged to the console and returned by the function.

When you run this function, the execution log will produce a result similar to:

```
{ satisfaction: 3.5, engagement: 3.6 }
```

Having a function that can calculate these averages opens up various possibilities for integrating these results into different workflows. For example, you could update a spreadsheet with the calculated scores, send them by email, or insert them into reports in Google Docs or Google Slides. This enables you to automate the process of collecting and analyzing survey data, making it easier to monitor employee engagement and satisfaction over time.

Managing Access to Forms

Managing access to Google Forms is quite similar to managing access in other Google Workspace apps such as Google Sheets. For editor access, you can manage editors using methods provided by the **`FormApp`** class. The following screenshot shows how autocomplete in the script editor can help you find and use these methods:

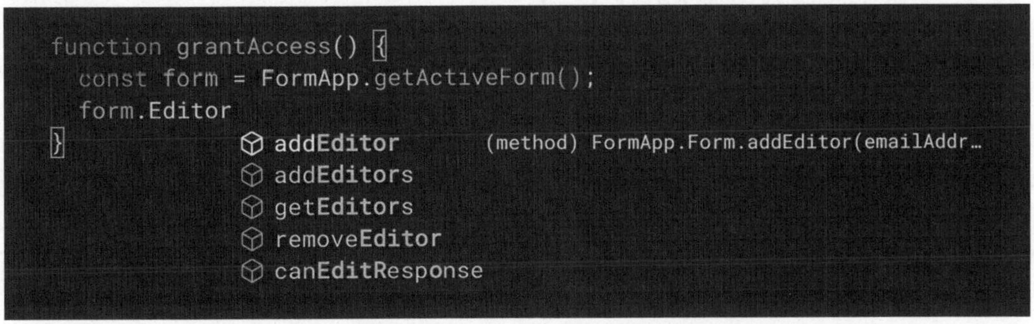

Figure 6.8: *Autocomplete helps to manage Google Form's editors*

To add or remove editors for a Google Form, you can use methods such as **`addEditor(emailAddress)`**, **`removeEditor(emailAddress)`**, and **`getEditors()`**. These methods allow you to programmatically manage who has editing privileges for the form, making it easy to control who can make changes to the form's structure and settings.

Managing access for respondents involves configuring various settings that control how users can interact with the form. Here are some key methods for managing respondent access:

1. **Accepting Responses**: You can start or stop accepting responses using **`form.setAcceptingResponses(true | false)`**.
2. **Allow Response Edits**: Allow or disallow respondents to edit their responses after submission using **`form.setAllowResponseEdits(true | false)`**.
3. **Collect Email Addresses**: Enable or disable email collection using **`form.setCollectEmail(true | false)`**.
4. **Require Login**: Require respondents to be logged into a Google account to fill out the form using **`form.setRequireLogin(true | false)`**.

Example Code

Here is how you can use these methods to manage respondent access:

```
function configureRespondentAccess() {
  const form = FormApp.getActiveForm();

  // Set form to accept responses
  form.setAcceptingResponses(true);

  // Allow respondents to edit their responses after submission
  form.setAllowResponseEdits(true);

  // Enable email collection from respondents
  form.setCollectEmail(true);

  // Require respondents to be logged into a Google account
  form.setRequireLogin(true);
}
```

By configuring these settings, you can control various aspects of how respondents interact with your form. For instance, enabling email collection can help you track responses back to specific users while requiring login ensures that only authenticated users can fill out the form.

Managing both editor and respondent access programmatically provides a flexible way to handle form permissions, making it easier to maintain control over your form and ensure that it meets your specific requirements.

A Note About the `onSubmit` Trigger

The **`onSubmit`** trigger is a powerful feature in Google Apps Script that allows your code to react to form submissions. When a form is submitted, the trigger can execute a specified function, giving you access to all the submitted data and enabling you to process it in various ways. For instance, you could compile the data into a document, send an email to a list of recipients, store the data in a database, or perform any other action your imagination can come up with.

However, we will not be delving into the details of triggers today. Triggers, including **`onSubmit`**, will be covered in a later chapter that will discuss triggers for all Google services, such as Sheets, Docs, and more. The reason for postponing this discussion is that it is much easier to leverage the full potential of triggers once you have a comprehensive understanding of all the core services in Google Apps Script.

In the meantime, focus on getting comfortable with the basics of using **`FormApp`** to create and manage forms. When you are ready, the chapter on triggers will provide you with the knowledge and tools to automate and enhance your workflows significantly.

Conclusion

In this chapter, we have explored the power and versatility of the **`FormApp`** class in Google Apps Script. Starting from the basics of setting up a Google Form programmatically, we delved into creating and managing form items, accessing and analyzing form responses, and managing access to forms. By learning to harness these capabilities, you can automate the creation and maintenance of forms, making them more dynamic and tailored to your specific needs.

We began by understanding the structure and key classes of **`FormApp`**, followed by a step-by-step guide on setting up forms and adding various items. We then demonstrated how to access and process form responses, including calculating average scores for an employee engagement survey. Additionally, we covered how to manage access for both editors and respondents, ensuring your forms are secure and appropriately accessible.

Although we touched briefly on the **`onSubmit`** trigger, we reserved a detailed discussion for a later chapter, where we will explore triggers in depth across all Google services. This will enable you to create sophisticated automation workflows that can react to form submissions and other events.

With the knowledge gained in this chapter, you are now equipped to create, manage, and analyze Google Forms programmatically. This sets a strong foundation for further exploration into more advanced topics in Google Apps Script, allowing you to build robust and efficient solutions for your organizational needs.

Keep experimenting with **`FormApp`**, and look forward to the upcoming chapters where we will unlock even more potential with triggers and other powerful features in Google Apps Script. Happy scripting!

Key Terms

- **`FormApp`:** A Google Apps Script class used to create, access, and manage Google Forms programmatically.
- **`Form`:** The primary object representing a Google Form, allowing manipulation of its metadata and items.
- **`FormItem`:** An element within a Google Form, such as text fields, multiple choice fields, checkboxes, or lists.
- **`FormResponse`:** An object containing all the data related to a response to a Google Form, including methods to read and submit responses.
- **`ItemResponse`:** Represents an individual's answer to a specific item in a form, used within **`FormResponse`**.
- **`ScaleItem`:** A type of form item that allows respondents to rate something on a numerical scale.
- **`MultipleChoiceItem`:** A form item that lets respondents choose one option from a set of predefined choices.
- **`TextItem`:** A form item that allows respondents to enter free text.
- **`Validation`:** Rules applied to form items to ensure the data submitted meets specific criteria.
- **`onSubmit` Trigger:** A trigger in Google Apps Script that executes a function when a form is submitted, allowing real-time processing of responses.

CHAPTER 7
CalendarApp

Introduction

Google Calendar is a cornerstone of productivity and is one of the most widely used Google Workspace apps. It offers robust features for managing personal and professional schedules, coordinating events, and collaborating with others. However, the true potential of Google Calendar can be unlocked when it is accessed and manipulated programmatically. You can automate and enhance your calendar management by leveraging Google Apps Script, leading to significant productivity gains.

Imagine automating the creation and management of multiple calendars, scheduling events with precise recurrence rules, adding and managing guests, and even customizing event details such as colors and visibility. With Google Apps Script, all of this and more is possible, allowing you to tailor Google Calendar to meet your specific needs.

By the end of this chapter, you will have a comprehensive understanding of how to harness the power of Google Calendar through Google Apps Script. Whether you need to automate event creation, manage guest lists, or send daily agenda emails, the `CalendarApp` service provides robust tools to streamline and enhance your calendar management tasks. Let us begin this journey to becoming a more productive and efficient Google Calendar user!

Structure

In this chapter, we will cover:

- Overviewing `CalendarApp`'s Classes
- Getting Started with `CalendarApp`
- Building a Daily Agenda Emailer
- Managing Access to Calendar Events

Overviewing `CalendarApp`'s Key Classes

The key classes for **`CalendarApp`** are:

- **`Calendar`**
- **`CalendarEvent`**
- **`EventGuest`**

There are others, and we will discuss them when they come up in later sections of this chapter, but we will focus on the ones above in this one.

Calendar

The **`Calendar`** class represents a user's calendar, whether it is one they own, have subscribed to, or have been shared with. Each user has a default calendar, but you can access and create or delete existing calendars. Additionally, you can work with a calendar's metadata, such as its name, timezone, description, and visibility.

`CalendarEvent`

Calendar events are the whole reason calendars exist. All events have a name and a date. Some have a start and end date-time, while others are whole-day events. Events can be one-off or recurring. You can manage the guests of an event, send reminders, read, create, and delete events. Furthermore, you can manage an event's visibility and set tags for events as metadata that will only be accessible through the script.

`EventGuest`

Events will likely have one or several guests if you are more than just time-boxing your tasks. With the **`EventGuest`** class, you can read, add, or remove guests from an event. You can also allow or disallow guests to invite others, modify the event, or see other guests.

Now that we have an understanding of **`CalendarApp`**'s structure let us get started with coding.

Getting Started with `CalendarApp`

Let us first look at our calendars:

```
function getAllCalendars() {
  const cals = CalendarApp.getAllCalendars().map(cal => ({
    ID: cal.getId(),
    NAME: cal.getName(),
```

```
    TIME_ZONE: cal.getTimeZone()
  }));
  Logger.log(JSON.stringify(cals, null, 2));
}
```

The **getAllCalendars()** function retrieves the list of calendars for the user's account and maps them to an array of objects containing the calendar ID, name, and time zone. It then logs out the result using **JSON.stringify()** for easier reading.

When you run this function, your output should be similar to the following:

```
[
  {
    "ID": "e_2_fr#weeknum@group.v.calendar.google.com",
    "NAME": "Week numbers",
    "TIME_ZONE": "Europe/Paris"
  },
  {
    "ID": "fr.french#holiday@group.v.calendar.google.com",
    "NAME": "Holidays in France",
    "TIME_ZONE": "Europe/Paris"
  },
  {
    "ID": "dmitry@...",
    "NAME": "dmitry@...",
    "TIME_ZONE": "Europe/Paris"
  },
  {
    "ID": "dmitry.kostyuk@...",
    "NAME": "dmitry.kostyuk@...",
    "TIME_ZONE": "Europe/Paris"
  },
  {
    "ID": "addressbook#contacts@group.v.calendar.google.com",
    "NAME": "Birthdays",
    "TIME_ZONE": "Europe/Paris"
  }
]
```

Notice that user's personal calendars have user's emails as names and IDs, whereas others, users are subscribed to, have explicit names and unique IDs in the **group.v.calendar.google.com** domain.

Let us now create a few events and invite some guests.

```
function createEventsInNewCalendar() {
  const calendarName = 'My Apps Script Calendar';
  const calendar =
```

```
    CalendarApp.getCalendarsByName(calendarName)?.[0] ||
    CalendarApp.createCalendar(calendarName).setColor
(CalendarApp.Color.RED_ORANGE);

  const events = [
    {
      title: 'Event 1',
      startTime: new Date(2024, 08, 01, 11, 00),
      endTime: new Date(2024, 08, 01, 12, 00),
    },
    {
      title: 'Event 2',
      startTime: new Date(2024, 08, 01, 13, 30),
      endTime: new Date(2024, 08, 01, 14, 30),
    },
    {
      title: 'Event 3',
      startTime: new Date(2024, 08, 01, 15, 00),
      endTime: new Date(2024, 08, 01, 17, 15),
    },
  ]

  events.forEach(e => calendar.createEvent(e.title, e.startTime,
e.endTime));
}
```

The function **createEventsInNewCalendar()** creates three different events in the calendar named "**My Apps Script Calendar**." If the calendar with this name does not exist, one is created. Notice the conditional **?.[0]**, which ensures we read the first item in the array returned by **getCalendarsByName()**, as we are not expecting any calendars with duplicate names.

When you run this function, you should see the new calendar appear in Google Calendar:

Figure 7.1: *A list of calendars*

You will also see the three events in the month of September:

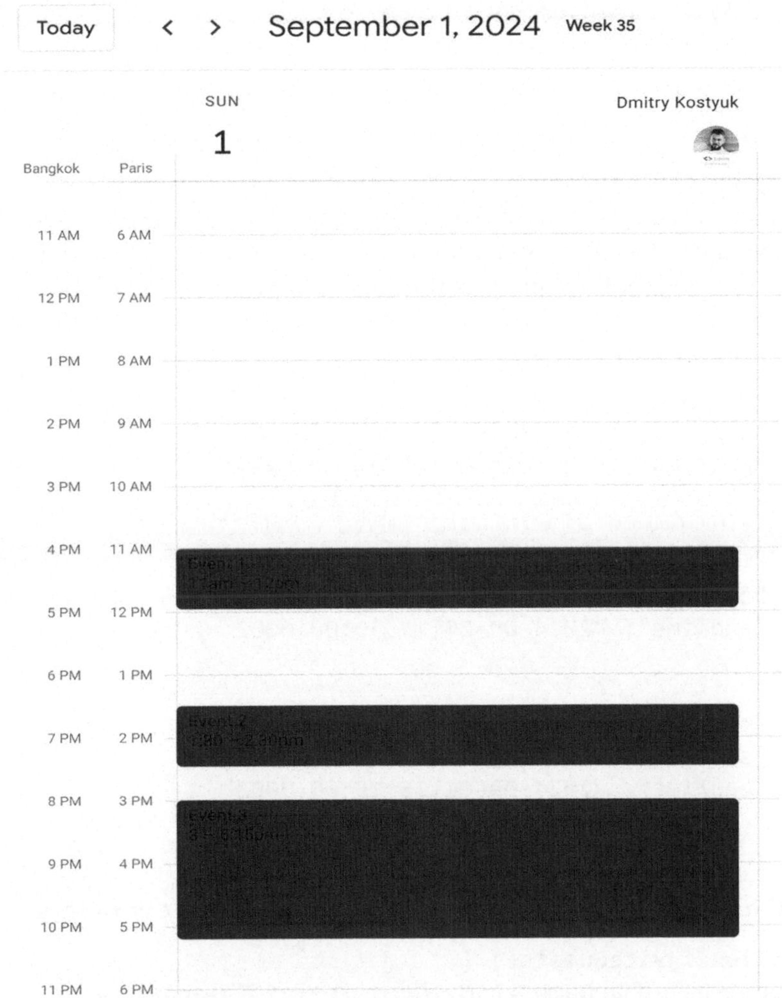

Figure 7.2: *Events created with Apps Script*

Let us now retrieve these events:

```
function getEvents() {
  const calendarName = 'My Apps Script Calendar';
  const calendar = CalendarApp.getCalendarsByName(calendarName)?.
[0];
  const date = new Date(2024, 08, 01);
  const events = calendar.getEventsForDay(date);
  Logger.log(
    JSON.stringify(
      events.map(e => ({
        title: e.getTitle(),
```

```
          startTime: e.getStartTime(),
          endTime: e.getEndTime(),
        })),
        null,
        2
      )
    );
  }
```

This function retrieves the events for the 1st of September 2024 using **getEventsForDay(Date)**. We then map them to an array of objects and pretty-print it with **JSON.stringify()**. Running this function will produce the following result:

```
[
  {
    "title": "Event 1",
    "startTime": "2024-09-01T09:00:00.000Z",
    "endTime": "2024-09-01T10:00:00.000Z"
  },
  {
    "title": "Event 2",
    "startTime": "2024-09-01T11:30:00.000Z",
    "endTime": "2024-09-01T12:30:00.000Z"
  },
  {
    "title": "Event 3",
    "startTime": "2024-09-01T13:00:00.000Z",
    "endTime": "2024-09-01T15:15:00.000Z"
  }
]
```

As a final exercise for this section, let us add some guests to our events:

```
function inviteGuests() {
  const calendarName = 'My Apps Script Calendar';
  const calendar = CalendarApp.getCalendarsByName(calendarName)?.
[0];
  const date = new Date(2024, 8, 1);
  const guests = [
    {
      eventName: 'Event 1',
      guestEmails: ['dmitry+test1@...'],
    },
    {
      eventName: 'Event 2',
      guestEmails: ['dmitry+test2@...'],
    },
    {
```

```
      eventName: 'Event 3',
      guestEmails: ['dmitry+test3@...'],
    },
  ];
  calendar.getEventsForDay(date).forEach(event => {
    const guestList = guests.find(
      guestList => guestList.eventName === event.getTitle()
    );
    if (undefined === guestList) return;
    guestList.guestEmails.forEach(email => event.addGuest(e-
mail));
  });
}
```

In this example, we have an array of guests' emails that we want to invite to each event. As before, we loop over all the events for September 1st, 2024, and see if their names match those we want to invite guests to. If so, we loop over the guest emails and call **`addGuest()`** one by one.

When you run this function, you should see that guests have been added accordingly:

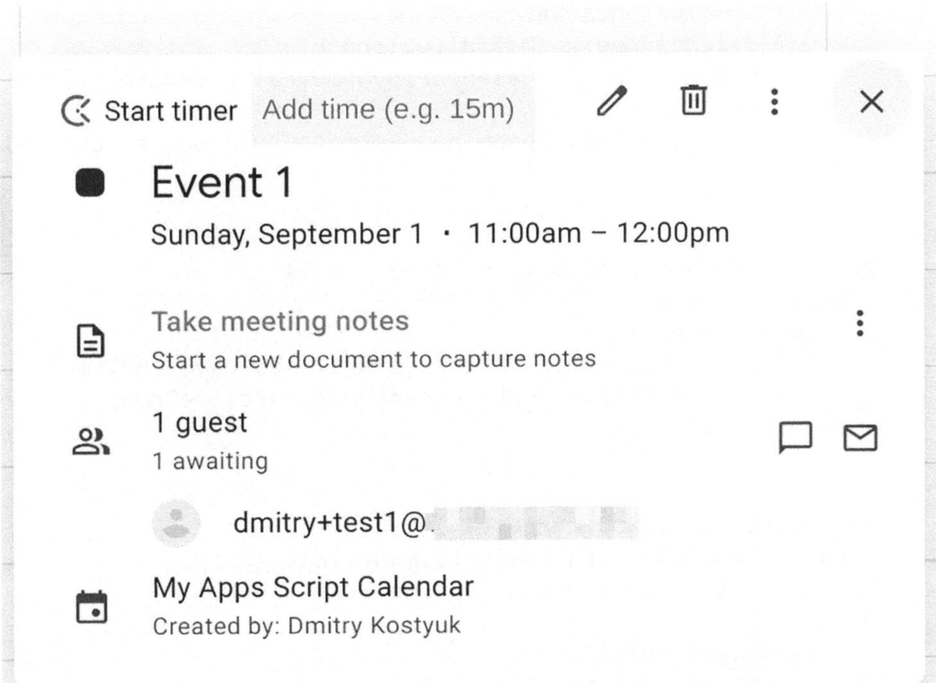

Figure 7.3: *Guests added to an event with Apps Script*

It is up to you as homework to check the documentation for ways to remove guests, delete events, and other useful functions.

Now let us build a small productivity-enhancement project: a script that will email us the agenda for the day or days ahead.

Building a Daily Agenda Emailer

The emailer's idea is to send us a summary for the next day in table format. It should work on a set-and-forget basis: we write the code once, and it executes once a day. In this project, we will use JavaScript's class syntax so that we can become familiar with some of the design patterns that are used in Google Apps Script's classes.

Extracting Events From the Calendar

Our first class will extract the events for a day or a specified period of time and output a two-dimensional array.

```
class AgendaExtractor {
  constructor(calendarName = null) {
    this.calendarName = calendarName;
    this.calendar =
      null === calendarName
        ? CalendarApp.getDefaultCalendar()
        : CalendarApp.getCalendarsByName(calendarName)?.[0];

    if (!this.calendar) throw new Error('Could not access calen-
dar');
  }

  getEvents(startTimeOrDay, endTime = null) {
    this.events =
      null !== endTime
        ? this.calendar.getEvents(startTimeOrDay, endTime)
        : this.calendar.getEventsForDay(startTimeOrDay);
    return this;
  }

  extractFieldsAsTwoDimArray() {
    const twoDimAr = this.events.map(event => [
      Utilities.formatDate(event.getStartTime(), 'GMT',
'HH:mm:ss'),
      event.getTitle(),
      event.getGuestList().length,
    ]);
    return [['Start Time', 'Title', 'Number of Guests'],
...twoDimAr];
  }
}
```

The constructor takes in the optional **calendarName** parameter and defaults to the default calendar if none is provided. The **getEvents()** method retrieves the events for the day if only one argument is provided or for a time interval if two arguments are provided. Notice that it returns **this**, the class instance; this is convenient for chaining, which we will put to use later. Finally, **extractFieldsAsTwoDimArray** returns the two-dimensional array with event data.

Notice we are making use of the built-in **formatDate()** method of the **Utilities** class to extract the time portion of the events (without the dates). You can find the full documentation here: https://developers.google.com/apps-script/reference/utilities/utilities#formatDate(Date,String,String).

Converting Events to HTML

Let us first create an HTML file in our Google Apps Script Project. When you click the "**+**" sign in the left sidebar next to "**Files**," you will be prompted to select the file type: Script or HTML; choose HTML. Name the file "**AgendaTemplate**."

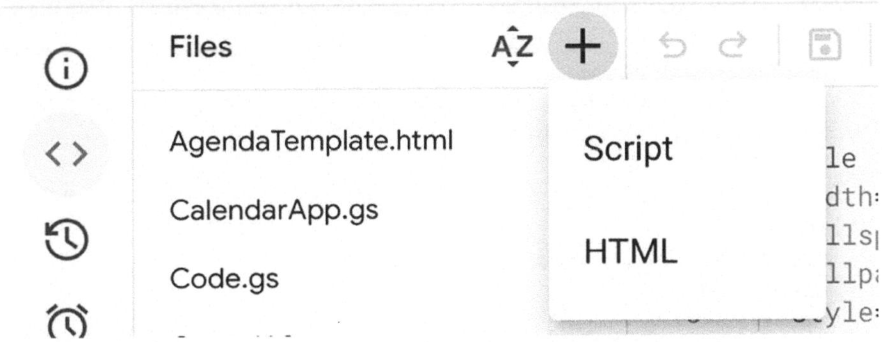

Figure 7.4: *Adding an HTML file to an Apps Script project*

Then insert the following HTML code:

```
<html>

<head>
  <title>Today's Events</title>
</head>

<body style="font-family: Arial, sans-serif; margin: 0; padding:
0; background-color: #f6f6f6;">
  <div
    style="width: 100%; max-width: 600px; margin: 0 auto;
background-color: #ffffff; padding: 20px; box-shadow: 0 0 10px
rgba(0, 0, 0, 0.1);">
    <div style="text-align: center; padding-bottom: 20px;">
      <h2>Today's Events</h2>
```

```
    </div>
    {{TABLE}}
    <div style="text-align: center; padding-top: 20px; font-size:
12px; color: #aaaaaa;">
      <p>&copy; 2024 Your Company. All rights reserved.</p>
    </div>
  </div>
</body>

</html>
```

Notice the **{{TABLE}}** merge field in the code. We will later replace it with an actual HTML table containing calendar events data. Now let us build the class that will do the conversion from our two-dimensional array to HTML:

```
class TemplateMerger {
  constructor(templateName) {
    this.templateName = templateName;
  }

  toHtmlTable(twoDimAr) {
    const thStyle =
      'style="padding: 10px; text-align: left; border-bottom: 1px
solid #dddddd; background-color: #f2f2f2;"';
    const tdStyle =
      'style="padding: 10px; text-align: left; border-bottom: 1px
solid #dddddd;"';
    const headers = twoDimAr.shift();
    const th =
      '<tr>' +
      headers.map(header => `<th {thStyle}>{header}</th>`).
join('') +
      '</tr>';
    const td = twoDimAr
      .map(
        row =>
          '<tr>' +
          row.map(cell => `<td {tdStyle}>{cell}</td>`).join('') +
          '</tr>'
      )
      .join('');
    this.table = `<table style="width: 100%; border-collapse:
collapse;"><thead>{th}</thead><tbody>{td}</tbody></table>`;
    return this;
  }

  mergeTemplate(mergeField) {
```

```
    return HtmlService.createHtmlOutputFromFile
(this.templateName)
      .getContent()
      .replace(new RegExp(`{{${mergeField}}}`), this.table);
  }
}
```

The constructor takes the **templateName** argument, which is the HTML file name (in our case, "**AgendaTemplate**"). The **toHtmlTable(twoDimAr)** method takes a two-dimensional array as an argument and converts it to an HTML table. Finally, **mergeTemplate** retrieves the HTML code from the HTML file using **HtmlService** and replaces the merge field (in our case, **{{TABLE}}**) with the actual table.

Sending the Email

Now that we are ready to build the full HTML content, let us create our final class that will send an HTML email:

```
class Emailer {
  constructor(recipients = []) {
    this.recipients = recipients;
  }
  setSubject(subject) {
    this.subject = subject;
    return this;
  }
  setContent(html) {
    this.content = html;
    return this;
  }
  send() {
    GmailApp.sendEmail(this.recipients.join(','), this.subject,
'', {
      htmlBody: this.content,
    });
  }
}
```

The constructor takes an array of recipients. The **setSubject** method records the email subject, and the **setContent** method records the HTML content. The **send** method sends an email with the data provided.

Launching the Full Workflow

All we need is a function that stitches the whole workflow together with the correct parameters:

```
function sendAgenda() {
  const date = new Date();
  const day = Utilities.formatDate(new Date(),
'GMT', 'yyyy-MM-dd');
  const calendarName = 'My Apps Script Calendar';

  const agenda = new AgendaExtractor(calendarName)
    .getEvents(date)
    .extractFieldsAsTwoDimArray();

  const html = new TemplateMerger('AgendaTemplate')
    .toHtmlTable(agenda)
    .mergeTemplate('TABLE');

  new Emailer(['dmitry+gasbook@wurkspaces.dev'])
    .setSubject(`Agenda for ${day}`)
    .setContent(html)
    .send();
}
```

Notice how the output of the **AgendaExtractor** becomes the input of the **TemplateMerger** class, and in return, its output becomes the input for the **Emailer** class. Also, notice how we are able to chain different methods together when they return **this**. It is a convenient pattern and built-in Google Apps Script classes often make use of it as well.

When you launch this function, you will receive an email with input similar to this:

Figure 7.5: *An email with today's events from the Google Calendar*

Great, our function is working as expected, but it would be inconvenient if we had to run it manually every time we needed an update. Luckily, there is a way to set up a trigger. Let us see how.

Setting a Manual Trigger

Triggers in Apps Script can be set manually or programmatically. We will cover them in detail in a future chapter. However, let us see how we can set a simple time trigger manually in the editor.

In the left sidebar, locate the Triggers button with the clock icon:

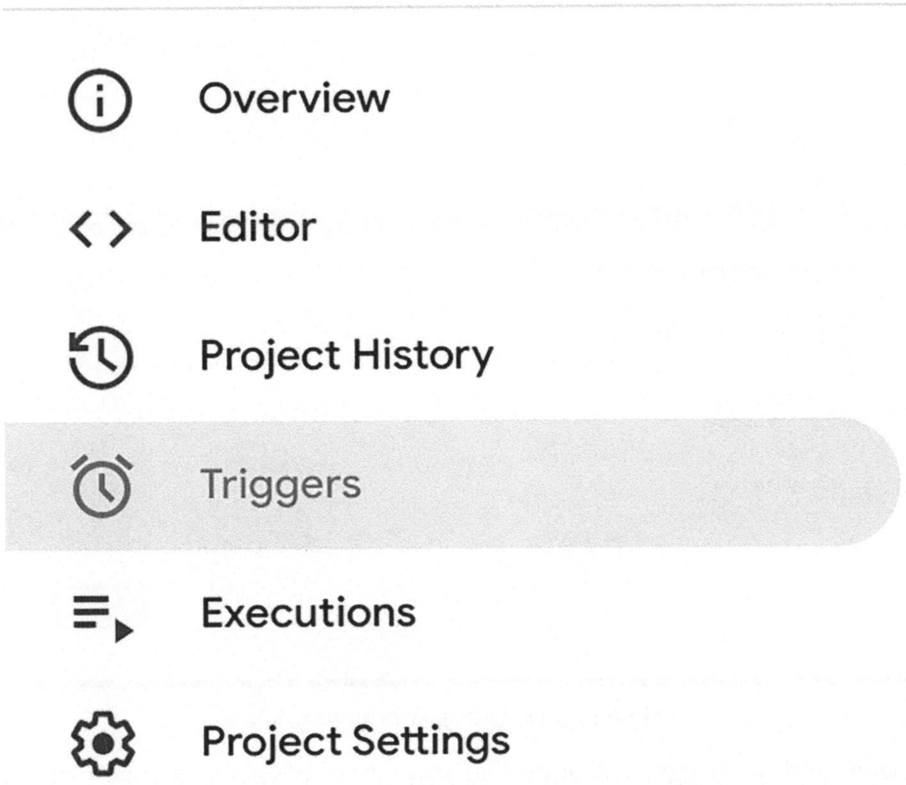

Figure 7.6: *Locating the triggers in a Google Apps Script project*

Click "**`Add Trigger`**." Then choose **`sendAgenda`** as the function to run, "**`Time-driven`**" as the source, "**`Day timer`**" as the type, and the time of day you want to trigger the function, as shown here:

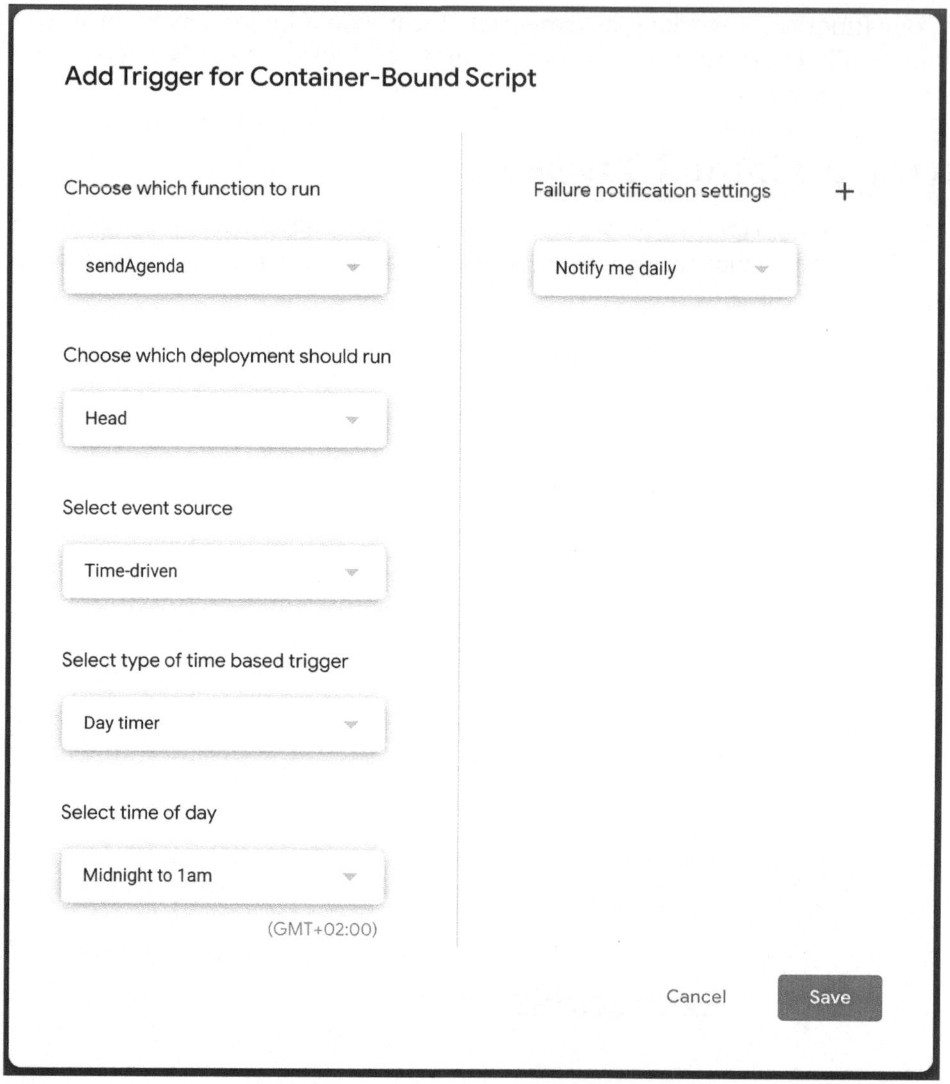

Figure 7.7: *Daily trigger configuration*

Click "**Save**," and the trigger will appear in your list of triggers. Now you will get your daily agenda by email automatically!

One last topic we need to cover is managing access to calendar events.

Managing Access to Calendar Events

In the previous sections, we explored how to add guests to events using the **`addGuest()`** method. Managing access to calendar events is a critical aspect of calendar management, especially when coordinating with multiple participants. Google Apps

Script provides various methods to control guest permissions and event visibility, allowing you to tailor the access settings according to your needs.

Here is a rundown of the key methods for managing access to calendar events:

- **`addGuest(email)`**: Adds a guest to an event. We have already seen how this method is used to invite participants to an event.
- **`removeGuest(email)`**: Removes a guest from an event. This method allows you to revoke access for specific guests.

You can also control guest permissions using the following methods:

- **`setAnyoneCanAddSelf(canAddSelf)`**: This method sets whether guests can add themselves to the event. Pass **`true`** to allow this or **`false`** to prevent it.
- **`setGuestsCanInviteOthers(canInvite)`**: Determines whether guests can invite others to the event. Use **`true`** to enable this or **`false`** to disable it.
- **`setGuestsCanModify(canModify)`**: Specifies whether guests can modify the event. Set to **`true`** to allow modifications or **`false`** to restrict them.
- **`setGuestsCanSeeGuests(canSeeGuests)`**: Controls whether guests can see the list of other guests. Use **`true`** to allow visibility or **`false`** to hide the guest list.
- **`setVisibility(visibility)`**: Manages the visibility of the event. You can set the visibility to **`CalendarApp.Visibility.DEFAULT`**, **`CalendarApp.Visibility.PRIVATE`**, or **`CalendarApp.Visibility.PUBLIC`** based on your requirements.

Here is an example demonstrating how to use these methods:

```
function manageEventAccess() {
  const calendarName = 'My Apps Script Calendar';
  const calendar = CalendarApp.getCalendarsByName(calendarName)?.
[0];
  const event = calendar.getEventsForDay(new Date(2024, 8, 1))
[0];

  // Add a guest to the event
  event.addGuest('guest1@example.com');

  // Remove a guest from the event
  event.removeGuest('guest2@example.com');

  // Set guest permissions
  event.setAnyoneCanAddSelf(true);
    .setGuestsCanInviteOthers(true);
    .setGuestsCanModify(false);
    .setGuestsCanSeeGuests(true);
```

```
    // Set event visibility
    event.setVisibility(CalendarApp.Visibility.PRIVATE);

    Logger.log('Access settings updated for event: ' + event.get
  Title());
  }
```

In this example, the **manageEventAccess()** function updates various access settings for an event on a specified date. It adds one guest, removes another, and sets guest permissions for adding themselves, inviting others, modifying the event, and seeing other guests. Finally, it sets the event visibility to private.

By using these methods, you can effectively manage who can access your events and what level of control they have, ensuring your calendar events are handled exactly as you need.

Conclusion

In this chapter, we have explored the powerful capabilities of the **CalendarApp** service within Google Apps Script. We started with a high-level overview of the key classes—**Calendar**, **CalendarEvent**, and **EventGuest**—which form the foundation for managing calendars and events programmatically.

We then delved into the practical aspects of getting started with **CalendarApp**, including how to retrieve and log calendar details, create new events, and invite guests. This foundational knowledge set the stage for building a more advanced project: a daily agenda emailer. Through this project, we saw how to extract event data, convert it into an HTML table, and send it via email, demonstrating the power of automating routine tasks to enhance productivity.

Finally, we examined how to manage access to calendar events, using various methods to control guest permissions and event visibility. This ensures that your calendar events can be shared and managed according to your specific needs and preferences.

By the end of this chapter, you should have a solid understanding of how to harness the power of Google Calendar through Google Apps Script. Whether you need to automate event creation, manage guest lists, or send daily agenda emails, the **CalendarApp** service provides a robust set of tools to streamline and enhance your calendar management tasks.

As you continue to explore Google Apps Script, remember that the concepts and techniques learned here can be applied and expanded upon in many other areas of Google Workspace automation. Keep experimenting, keep coding, and unlock new levels of productivity!

Key Terms

- **`CalendarApp`:** A Google Apps Script service that allows for programmatic interaction with Google Calendar.
- **Calendar:** Represents a user's calendar, which can be owned, subscribed to, or shared with the user.
- **`CalendarEvent`:** An object representing an event in a calendar, including its title, start and end times, and other details.
- **`EventGuest`:** Represents a guest invited to a calendar event, with methods to manage guest details and permissions.
- **Guest Permissions:** Settings that control whether guests can add themselves, invite others, modify the event, or see other guests.
- **Event Visibility:** Settings that determine whether a calendar event is public, private, or follows the default visibility.
- **HTML Template:** A structured HTML file used to format and present calendar event data in emails.
- **Two-Dimensional Array:** A data structure used to store and manipulate event details for conversion to an HTML table.
- **Trigger:** A time-driven or event-driven mechanism that automatically executes a script at specified intervals.

CHAPTER 8
SlidesApp

Introduction

This chapter will guide you through the powerful features of the **`SlidesApp`** class, providing you with the tools to programmatically create, modify, and manage Google Slides presentations.

Google Slides is a versatile tool that allows you to create professional presentations for various purposes, from business reports and educational lectures to creative portfolios and team collaboration. While its user interface is intuitive and easy to use, the true power of Google Slides is unlocked when you use Google Apps Script to automate and customize your slides beyond the standard functionalities.

In this chapter, we will cover everything you need to get started with scripting Google Slides, from understanding the basic architecture of slides and elements, such as masters, layouts, shapes, and images, to more advanced features such as dynamically embedding charts from Google Sheets and managing access permissions. You will learn how to use Google Apps Script to perform tasks that would be time-consuming or difficult through the standard interface alone.

By the end of this chapter, you will have a solid foundation in using the **`SlidesApp`** class to automate your presentations, making them more dynamic, interactive, and perfectly tailored to your needs. Whether you are a seasoned developer or a beginner looking to expand your skills, this chapter will provide you with the knowledge and practical examples to become a Google Slides automation pro. Let us dive in!

Structure

In this chapter, we will cover:

- Understanding Google Slides Architecture
- **`Presentation`** Class
- **`Slides`** Class
- **`Master`** and **`Layout`** Classes
- **`PageElement`** Class

- `Shape` Element
- `Image` Element
- `SheetsChart` Element
- `Table` Element
- `Group` Element
- `Video` Element
- `Line` Element
- Managing Access to Presentations

By the end of this chapter, you will have a comprehensive understanding of how to automate and enhance Google Slides presentations using Google Apps Script.

Understanding Google Slides Architecture

At first glance, Google Slides seems straightforward. You open a presentation, click to add a few slides, insert some text and images, and perhaps change some colors or themes. However, beneath this simple user interface lies a more intricate architecture that governs how presentations are structured and styled. Understanding this architecture is crucial for effectively using Google Slides, especially when automating tasks with Google Apps Script.

The Master Slide and Layouts

Every Google Slides presentation is built upon a foundation known as the "*master slide*," or "*theme*." This master slide acts as a blueprint that defines the default styles for the entire presentation. It includes elements such as font styles, background colors, and placeholder text formats. Essentially, the master slide sets the tone for the presentation's overall appearance.

Within the master slide, there are one or more "*layouts*" that determine the structure of individual slides. For example, you might have a layout designed for a title slide, another for a slide featuring a chart, and yet another for a timeline slide. These layouts provide a structured way to organize content across different types of slides. While each master slide comes with a set of predefined layouts, you also have the flexibility to create custom layouts to suit your specific needs.

The Relationship Between Masters, Layouts, and Slides

When you create a new slide in Google Slides, it adheres to the rules set by both the master slide and a selected layout. The master slide imposes a consistent style across all slides, ensuring uniformity in elements such as fonts and background colors. Meanwhile, the chosen layout defines the specific arrangement of placeholders and elements on that slide.

An important aspect of this architecture is that changes made to the master slide are automatically reflected across the entire presentation. For example, if you update the font style on the master slide, every slide that uses this master will adopt the new font style. Similarly, modifications to a specific layout will affect all slides that implement that layout. This cascading effect ensures consistency throughout the presentation and saves time when making global changes.

However, not all elements on a slide are bound by the master or layout rules. Elements that are not inherited from a master slide or layout, such as unique text boxes or specific images, can be updated independently on each slide. This allows for customization while maintaining overall consistency.

Types of Elements in Google Slides

Within each slide, various types of elements can be added. These elements range from basic shapes (often used as text boxes) to images, videos, tables, and more. Each element type has its own properties and behaviors, which can be manipulated through the Google Slides API and Apps Script to create dynamic and interactive presentations.

Getting Hands-On with Google Slides

If you are not already familiar with Google Slides, it is highly recommended that you take a moment to explore and practice building presentations manually. This hands-on experience will provide you with a better understanding of how master slides, layouts, and individual elements work together to form a cohesive presentation. Familiarity with these basics will make it much easier to grasp the more advanced concepts and techniques discussed later in this chapter.

Presentation Class

The `Presentation` class in Google Apps Script allows you to interact with Google Slides presentations programmatically. Similar to other Google Workspace documents such as Google Docs or Sheets, you can access a presentation by its unique ID or retrieve the active presentation if your script is container-bound (meaning it is directly tied to a specific Google Slides presentation).

To see how this works, let us try executing the following function. Be sure to replace **<YOUR_PRESENTATION_ID>** with the actual ID of your Google Slides presentation:

```
function getPresentation() {
  const p1 = SlidesApp.getActivePresentation();
  // TODO insert your presentation ID
  const p2 = SlidesApp.openById('<YOUR_PRESENTATION_ID>');
  Logger.log(p1.getName());
  Logger.log(p2.getName());
}
```

Running this function in the Google Apps Script online IDE will access the same presentation in two different ways:

- **SlidesApp.getActivePresentation()** retrieves the currently active presentation that the script is bound to.
- **SlidesApp.openById('<YOUR_PRESENTATION_ID>')** opens a presentation by its unique ID, which you need to provide.

The results logged in the console will look something like this:

```
1:18:37 PM   Info   My Apps Script Powered Google Slides
Presentation
1:18:37 PM   Info   My Apps Script Powered Google Slides
Presentation
```

Both log entries should show the name of the same presentation, demonstrating that we have accessed it using two different methods.

Creating a New Presentation

In addition to accessing existing presentations, you can also create new ones programmatically using the **create(presentationName)** method of the **SlidesApp** class. Here is a simple example:

```
function createPresentation() {
  const p = SlidesApp.create('Created with Apps Script');
  const url = p.getUrl();
  Logger.log(url);
}
```

When you run this function, it will create a new Google Slides presentation named "**Created with Apps Script**" and log its URL to the console:

```
1:26:25 PM   Info   https://docs.google.com/open?id=
<PRESENTATION_ID>
```

By copying and pasting this URL into a browser, you will see a new blank presentation has been created with the specified name.

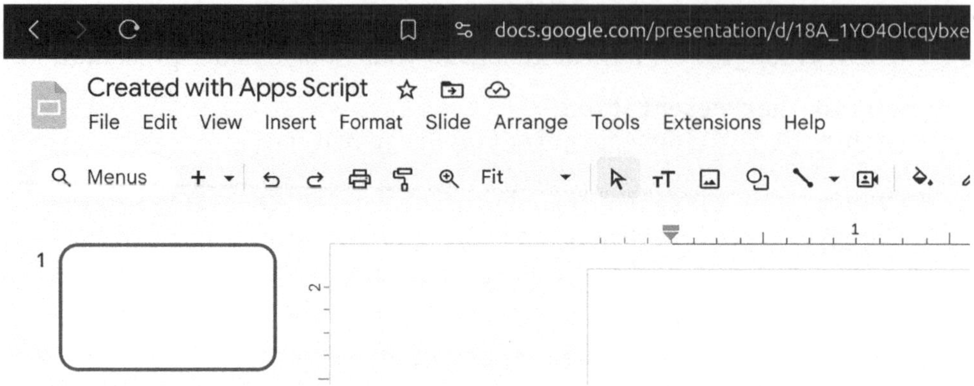

***Figure 8.1**: A blank presentation created with Apps Script*

Feel free to delete this presentation after verifying it, as we will not be using it further in this guide.

Now that you understand how to access and create presentations, let us move on to manipulating slides within a container-bound script to dynamically update content in your Google Slides presentations.

Slides Class

The **Slides** class provides a set of methods to interact with the slides within a Google Slides presentation. Let us explore some of the essential methods.

Listing Slides in a Presentation

To start, let us list some helpful information about the slides in our active presentation. The following function retrieves the active presentation, iterates through its slides, and logs their index, ID, and page type:

```
function listSlides() {
  const p = SlidesApp.getActivePresentation();
  const slides = p.getSlides();
  const list = slides
    .reduce(
      (acc, slide, i) =>
        acc +
        `Index: ${i}, ID: ${slide.getObjectId()}, Page Type:
${slide.getPageType()}\n`,
      ''
    )
    .trim();
  Logger.log(list);
}
```

This function extracts the index and ID of each slide, along with the page type. When you run this code, you will see output similar to the following in the logs:

```
Index: 0, ID: gd9c453428_0_16, Page Type: SLIDE
Index: 1, ID: ge9090756a_1_58, Page Type: SLIDE
Index: 2, ID: gd91e1f37e_0_0, Page Type: SLIDE
Index: 3, ID: ge9090756a_1_78, Page Type: SLIDE
Index: 4, ID: ge9090756a_1_232, Page Type: SLIDE
Index: 5, ID: ge9090756a_1_267, Page Type: SLIDE
Index: 6, ID: ge9090756a_2_12, Page Type: SLIDE
Index: 7, ID: ge9090756a_1_300, Page Type: SLIDE
Index: 8, ID: gd933c8c4a_0_32, Page Type: SLIDE
Index: 9, ID: gd5b09a965_5_0, Page Type: SLIDE
```

The index represents the order in which the slides appear in the presentation. Note that the page type is **SLIDE**. This is different from **LAYOUT**, which we will look into shortly. Each slide also has its own unique ID. You can spot the slide ID in the URL, like so:

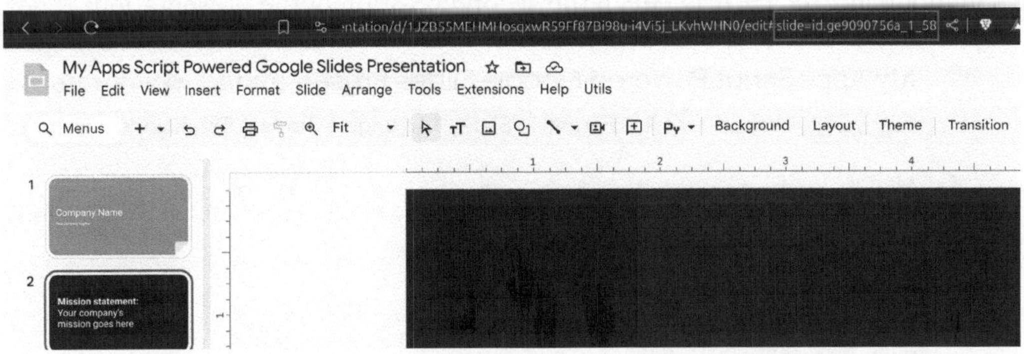

***Figure 8.2**: Spotting the slide ID in the browser URL*

Notice that the second slide's ID in the screenshot corresponds to the ID we logged out under index 1.

Duplicating a Slide

To duplicate a slide, you can use the **duplicate()** method. You can retrieve the slide either by its index or by its ID, as shown in the following examples:

```
function duplicateSlideByIndex() {
  const p = SlidesApp.getActivePresentation();
  p.getSlides()[1].duplicate();
}
```

```
function duplicateSlideById() {
  const p = SlidesApp.getActivePresentation();
  p.getSlideById('ge9090756a_1_58').duplicate();
}
```

Both functions will produce the same result: they create an exact copy of the second slide in the presentation.

Inserting a New Slide

You can insert a new blank slide at a specific position using the **`insertSlide()`** method:

```
function insertSlide() {
  const p = SlidesApp.getActivePresentation();
  p.insertSlide(1);
}
```

This function inserts a blank slide in the second position of the presentation:

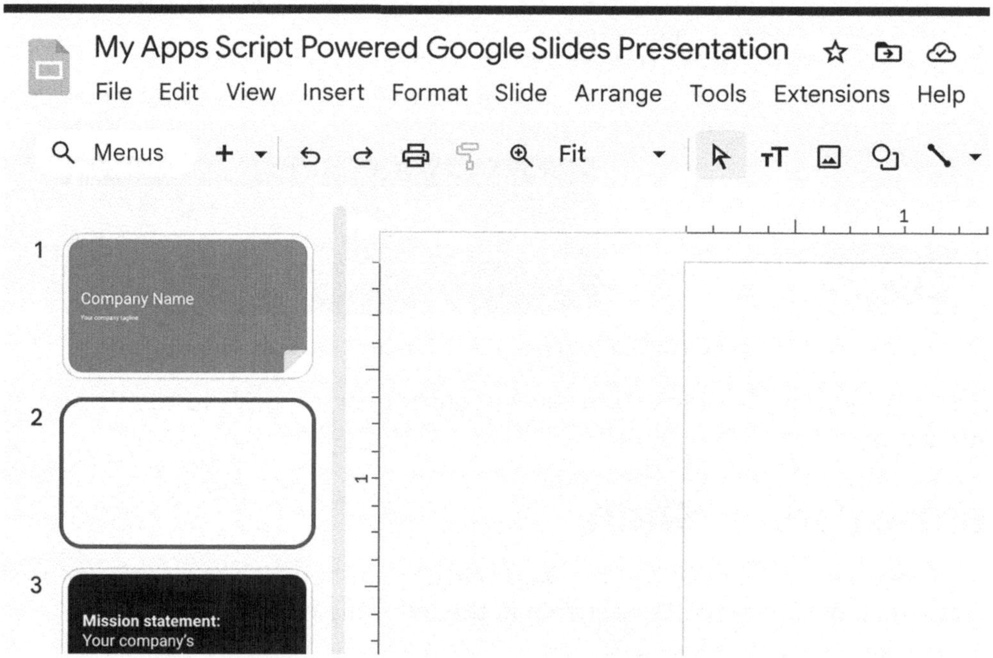

***Figure 8.3**: Inserting a blank slide into with Google Apps Script*

While inserting a blank slide is straightforward, it might not be visually appealing. The Google Slides user interface allows you to apply a layout to a slide, as demonstrated here:

Figure 8.4: *Every slide follows a layout*

Applying a layout can transform a slide into something more useful. If you want to delete this slide, you can do so manually or call the **`remove()`** method on the slide instance in your script.

Alternatively, if you want to use a specific layout when inserting a slide, you can provide a second argument to the **`insertSlide()`** method. For instance, using one of Google Slides' predefined (or system) layouts can be done with the **`PredefinedLayout`** enum:

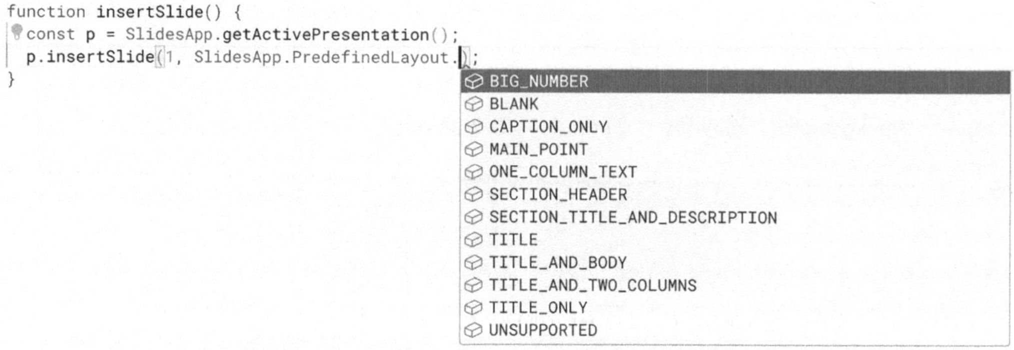

Figure 8.5: *Predefined layouts in Apps Script's autocomplete*

Let us try running this code:

```
function insertSlide() {
  const p = SlidesApp.getActivePresentation();
  p.insertSlide(1, SlidesApp.PredefinedLayout.TITLE_AND_TWO_
COLUMNS);
}
```

With this, the slide immediately looks more interesting:

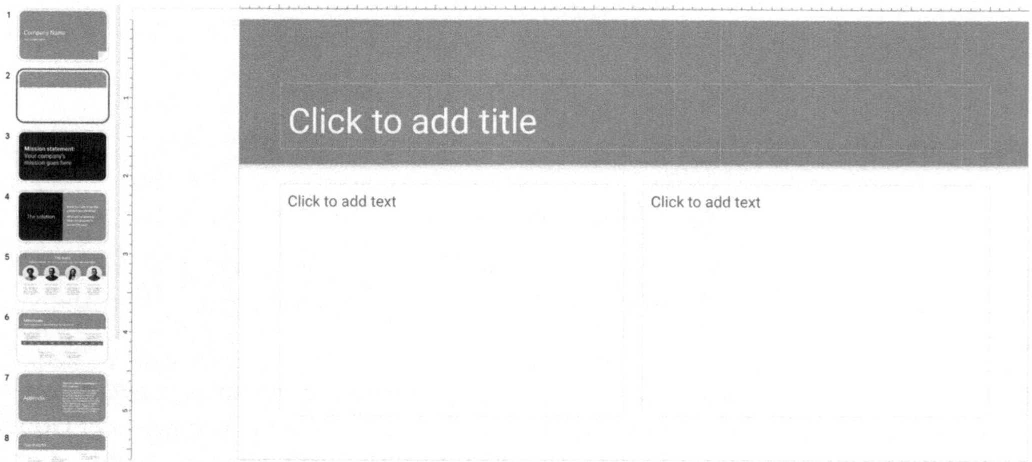

Figure 8.6: *Inserting a slide with a predefined layout*

If you have created a custom layout, you will not be able to define a new enum, but you can reference it by index:

```
function insertSlideWithCustomLayout() {
  const p = SlidesApp.getActivePresentation();
  p.insertSlide(1, p.getLayouts()[12]);
}
```

Make sure to use the correct layout index. Note that predefined layouts can also be selected using an index. Additionally, you can call **`appendSlide()`**, which inserts a slide at the end of the presentation–convenient when you do not want to calculate the index of the last slide.

Replacing Text Across Slides

Another useful trick is replacing a specific text string with a new one across all slides in the presentation. This can be achieved using the **`replaceAllText()`** method:

```
function replaceText() {
  const p = SlidesApp.getActivePresentation();
  p.replaceAllText('Powerpoint', 'Google Slides');
}
```

Now that we have covered some key functions for manipulating slides and briefly touched on layouts, let us dive deeper into layouts and master slides in the next section.

Master and Layout Classes

In Google Slides, layouts and masters play a crucial role in defining the visual and structural consistency of your presentations. Understanding how these components work together allows you to create more polished and professional-looking presentations with ease.

Understanding Layouts and Masters

As we discussed in the previous section, layouts in Google Slides function like slide templates. A slide that implements a layout inherits its structure, colors, fonts, and other styles from the layout. This ensures that all slides following the same layout maintain a consistent look and feel.

Above layouts, there is another level called the "**`master`**" or "**`theme`**." In the Google Slides user interface, a master is referred to as a theme. To see the relationship between a master and its layouts, navigate to your presentation, click on "**`Slide`**," and then select "**`Edit theme`**." You will see the master slide (theme slide) along with its child layouts, as shown here:

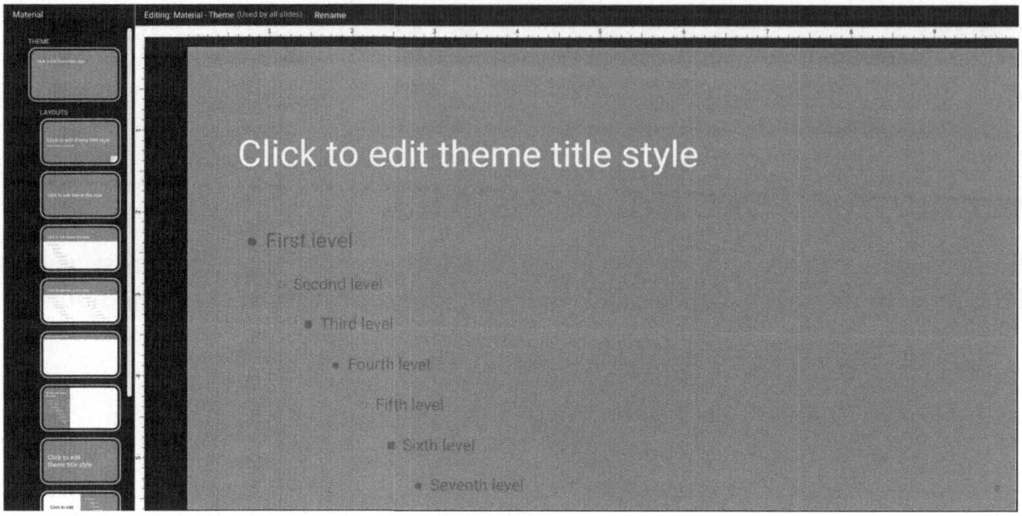

***Figure 8.7**: Theme and layouts in Google Slides*

If you change a style on the master slide, such as the color of a heading to red, all headings in the layouts will automatically change to red, and consequently, the headings on the actual slides that use these layouts will also turn red. This cascading effect allows you to maintain visual consistency across all slides efficiently.

By default, a Google Slides presentation starts with a single theme. However, a presentation can have multiple themes. This situation often arises when you import a slide from another presentation that uses a different theme. In such cases, you can access layouts by referencing their master like this:

```
SlidesApp.getActivePresentation().getMasters()[0].getLayouts();
```

Listing Layouts in a Presentation

To list all layouts available in a presentation, you can use a method similar to what we used for listing slides:

```
function listLayouts() {
  const p = SlidesApp.getActivePresentation();
  const layouts = p.getLayouts();
  const list = layouts
    .reduce(
      (acc, layout, i) =>
        acc +
        `Index: ${i}, ID: ${layout.getObjectId()}, Page Type:
${layout.getPageType()}\n`,
      ''
```

```
    )
    .trim();
  Logger.log(list);
}
```

When you run this code, it will produce an output similar to the following, showing the index, ID, and page type for each layout:

```
Index: 0, ID: ge9090756a_1_4, Page Type: LAYOUT
Index: 1, ID: ge9090756a_1_10, Page Type: LAYOUT
Index: 2, ID: ge9090756a_1_13, Page Type: LAYOUT
Index: 3, ID: ge9090756a_1_19, Page Type: LAYOUT
Index: 4, ID: ge9090756a_1_26, Page Type: LAYOUT
Index: 5, ID: ge9090756a_1_31, Page Type: LAYOUT
Index: 6, ID: ge9090756a_1_37, Page Type: LAYOUT
Index: 7, ID: ge9090756a_1_40, Page Type: LAYOUT
Index: 8, ID: ge9090756a_1_47, Page Type: LAYOUT
Index: 9, ID: ge9090756a_1_52, Page Type: LAYOUT
Index: 10, ID: ge9090756a_1_56, Page Type: LAYOUT
```

Replacing a Theme by Importing a Slide

There is a useful trick to change the theme of a presentation by importing a slide from another presentation that uses a different theme. Doing so will append a new master to the current presentation. If you delete the original master (at index 0), the new master's styles will be applied to the entire presentation. Here is how you can implement this:

```
function importTheme() {
  const p = SlidesApp.getActivePresentation();
  const templateSlide = SlidesApp.openById(
    '<PRESENTATION_ID>'
  ).getSlides()[0];
  const importedSlide = p.appendSlide(templateSlide);
  p.getMasters()[0].remove();
  importedSlide.remove();
}
```

This function accesses two presentations: the container-bound presentation (the one the script is attached to) and another presentation with a different theme. It appends a slide from the latter to the former, which also imports the new master slide (theme). By removing the old master and the appended slide, you effectively convert the theme of the entire presentation.

Shared Characteristics of `Master`, `Layout`, and `Slide` Classes

It is important to note that the **`Master`**, **`Layout`**, and **`Slide`** classes are all children of the **`Page`** class in Google Slides. Because of this, they share many methods and properties, although there are some differences based on their specific roles. One significant similarity among these page types is how you manipulate their elements. This consistency allows for a more unified approach when scripting interactions with different parts of a presentation.

As we move forward, let us dive deeper into manipulating page elements across slides, layouts, and master slides to make the most out of the Google Slides API.

`PageElement` Class

In Google Slides, a **page element** is essentially anything that you can place on a slide. The **`PageElement`** class provides a common set of methods and properties that all elements on a slide inherit, whether they are images, lines, shapes, tables, videos, or even groups of elements. Understanding this class and its common interface is key to effectively manipulating slide content using Google Apps Script.

Common Interface for All Page Elements

To explore the capabilities of the **`PageElement`** class, you can refer to the official documentation here: https://developers.google.com/apps-script/reference/slides/page-element. The documentation lists a comprehensive set of methods that apply to all page elements, regardless of their specific type. These methods allow you to perform actions such as moving elements up or down in the stack, resizing them, or setting their positions.

Following is a list of some of the most useful methods that are common across all page elements:

Method	**Return Type**	**Description**
`bringForward()` or `bringToFront()`	**`PageElement`** for chaining	Moves the element one level up or places it above all other elements.
`sendBackward()` or `sendToBack()`	**`PageElement`**	Moves the element one level down or places it underneath all other elements.
`getObjectId()`	**`String`**	Returns the unique identifier (UID) of the element.

`getPageElementType()`	**`PageElementType`**	Returns the type of the page element.
`select()`	**`void`**	Selects the element.
`setLeft()`, `setTop()`	**`PageElement`**	Sets the position of the element on the slide.
`setWidth()`, `setHeight()`, `scaleHeight()`, `scaleWidth()`	**`PageElement`**	Sets the dimensions of the element.
`setTitle()`	**`PageElement`**	Sets the alternate text (title) for the element.

Table 8.1: *Common methods for page elements*

Many of these methods return the **`PageElement`** itself, which allows method chaining. This feature can make your code more concise and readable, especially when configuring multiple properties of an element.

Getting the IDs of Page Elements

Unlike slides, where you can easily determine their order or IDs, identifying page elements on a slide is not as straightforward. To simplify this process, you can use a custom function to log the details of the selected elements:

```
function getElementData() {
  const p = SlidesApp.getActivePresentation();
  const els = p
    .getSelection()
    .getPageElementRange()
    .getPageElements()
    .map(el => `${el.getObjectId()} => ${el.getPage
ElementType()}`);

  Logger.log(els.join('\n'));
}
```

When you select one or more elements in a presentation and run this function, it will log information about each selected element, including its ID and type. Here is an example of the output you might see:

```
1:53:39 PM   Info   ge9090756a_1_81 => IMAGE
                   ge9090756a_1_82 => SHAPE
                   ge9090756a_1_83 => SHAPE
```

This function can be particularly useful for debugging or when you want to manipulate specific elements programmatically.

Casting Page Elements to Specific Types

The **`PageElement`** class also provides a set of methods that start with the keyword "**`as`**," such as **`asShape()`**, **`asImage()`**, or **`asSheetsChart()`**. These methods are used to cast a generic **`PageElement`** to its specific type. This casting is essential when you need to access methods or properties that are unique to a particular element type, such as manipulating the content of a text box or adjusting the properties of a chart.

However, it is important to first check the element type using **`getPageElementType()`** before casting to ensure you are working with the correct element type. Incorrect casting can lead to errors in your script.

Now that we have covered the basics of the **`PageElement`** class and its common methods, let us dive deeper into the specific types of elements—such as shapes, images, and tables—and see how we can work with them more effectively in the next sections.

Shape Element

Shapes in Google Slides are essentially text boxes with a specific shape around them, such as rectangles, cubes, hexagons, stars, and more. These shapes can be manipulated using the **`Shape`** class, which provides various methods to control their properties, such as size, position, text, and fill color. Let us explore how to work with shapes using Google Apps Script.

Inserting a Shape

Consider the following example, which demonstrates how to insert a shape into a new slide:

```
function insertSlideWithShape() {
  const p = SlidesApp.getActivePresentation();
  const newSlide = p.appendSlide(SlidesApp.PredefinedLayout.TITLE_
ONLY);
  const shape = newSlide
    .insertShape(SlidesApp.ShapeType.CHEVRON)
    .setTop(100)
    .setLeft(20)
    .setWidth(300);

  shape.getText().insertText(0, 'Hello World');
  shape.getFill().setSolidFill(SlidesApp.ThemeColorType.LIGHT1);
}
```

This function performs the following steps:

1. **Creates a new slide** with a **`TITLE_ONLY`** layout.
2. **Inserts a `CHEVRON` shape** onto the slide and sets its position (**`top`** and **`left`**) and width.
3. **Adds text** ("**`Hello World`**") inside the shape.
4. **Sets the fill color** of the shape to a light theme color.

Notice that to manipulate the text and fill properties of the shape, you need to use the **`getText()`** and **`getFill()`** methods to access the **`TextRange`** and **`Fill`** classes, respectively.

Also, pay attention to the enums **`ShapeType`** and **`ThemeColorType`**, which define the types of shapes and colors you can use. For more details, refer to the Google Slides API documentation (https://developers.google.com/apps-script/reference/slides/shape-type) for **`ShapeType`** and **`ThemeColorType`**.

The output should look something like this:

Figure 8.8: *A chevron shape created with Apps Script*

Working with Text Boxes

One of the values in the **`ShapeType`** enum is **`TEXT_BOX`**, which creates a shape without a visible border, making it essentially a plain text box. Since text boxes are commonly used, there is a shortcut method called **`insertTextBox`** that allows you to create text boxes with a simpler syntax.

Accessing Shapes on a Slide

Once you have added shapes to a slide, you might want to access and manipulate them. Here is a function that retrieves all shapes on the last slide of the presentation:

```
function getShapes() {
  const p = SlidesApp.getActivePresentation();
  const slides = p.getSlides();
  const lastSlide = slides[slides.length - 1];
  const els = lastSlide
    .getShapes()
    .map(
      shape =>
        `${shape.getObjectId()} | ${shape.getPageElementType()} |
${
          shape.getText().asString().trim() || '<NO TEXT>'
        }`
    );
  Logger.log(els.join('\n'));
}
```

Running this function will log details about each shape on the slide, such as its ID, type, and text content:

```
SLIDES_API606271053_1 | SHAPE | <NO TEXT>
SLIDES_API606271053_4 | SHAPE | Hello World
```

Handling Different Page Elements

Sometimes, you might need to loop over all page elements on a slide. It is essential to check the element type before performing operations specific to that type. For example, calling **`getText()`** on an image would throw an error. Consider the following slide:

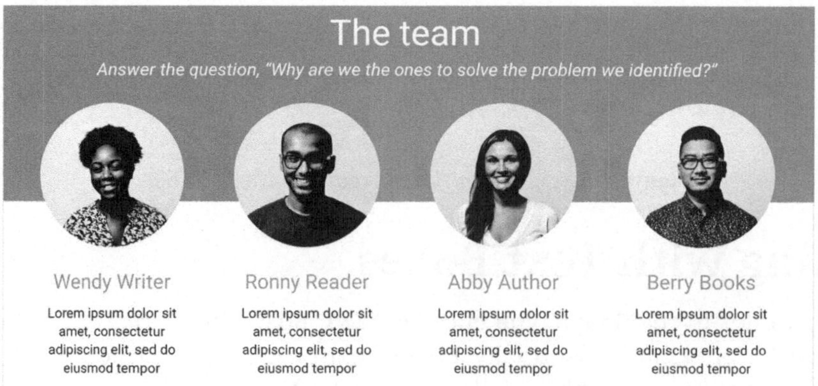

***Figure 8.9**: A slide with different kinds of page elements*

This slide contains both images and shapes. Let us say you want to extract the text content from shapes and the content URL from images. You can modify the function as follows:

```
function getShapesAndImages() {
  const p = SlidesApp.getActivePresentation();
  const slide = p.getSlides()[3];
  const els = slide.getPageElements().map(el => {
    const type = el.getPageElementType().toString();
    if ('SHAPE' === type)
      return `${el.getObjectId()} | ${el.getPageElementType()} | ${
        el.asShape().getText().asString().trim() || '<NO TEXT>'
      }`;
    if ('IMAGE' === type)
      return `${el.getObjectId()} | ${el.getPageElementType()} | ${
        el.asImage().getDescription() || '<NO URL>'
      }`;
  });
  Logger.log(els.join('\n'));
}
```

In this function:

1. **`getPageElements()`** retrieves all elements on the slide.
2. We then check each element's type using **`getPageElementType()`**.
3. Depending on the type, we cast the element to a shape (**`asShape()`**) or an image (**`asImage()`**) to access type-specific methods.

The output from running this function will be something like:

```
ge9090756a_1_85 | SHAPE | Ronny Reader
                   ge9090756a_1_88 | SHAPE | Abby Author
                   gd933c8c4a_0_21 | SHAPE | Lorem ipsum dolor
sit amet, consectetur adipiscing elit, sed do eiusmod tempor
                   gd933c8c4a_0_22 | SHAPE | Lorem ipsum dolor
sit amet, consectetur adipiscing elit, sed do eiusmod tempor
                   ge9090756a_1_90 | IMAGE | Corporate headshot
of a man
                   ge9090756a_1_91 | SHAPE | Berry Books
                   gd933c8c4a_0_23 | SHAPE | Lorem ipsum dolor
sit amet, consectetur adipiscing elit, sed do eiusmod tempo
```

By effectively utilizing the **`Shape`** class and these methods, you can manipulate text boxes and other shapes dynamically within your Google Slides presentations.

Now that we have touched on images in this section, let us explore how to work with them in more detail in the next section.

Image Element

Images are a fundamental part of creating visually appealing presentations. In Google Slides, the **Image** class provides several methods to insert and manipulate images within your slides. Let us explore how to insert images using different methods and how to manipulate them with Google Apps Script.

Inserting an Image

To insert an image into a new slide, you can use two different approaches: inserting an image from a URL or inserting an image from a blob, such as a file stored on Google Drive.

Inserting an Image from a URL

The following example demonstrates how to insert an image using a URL:

```
function insertImageFromUrl() {
  const p = SlidesApp.getActivePresentation();
  const newSlide = p.appendSlide(SlidesApp.PredefinedLayout.TITLE_
ONLY);
  newSlide
    .insertImage('https://picsum.photos/400/300')
    .alignOnPage(SlidesApp.AlignmentPosition.CENTER)
    .getBorder()
    .setWeight(2)
    .getLineFill()
    .setSolidFill(0, 200, 150);
}
```

This function creates a new slide with a **TITLE_ONLY** layout, inserts an image from a specified URL, centers it on the slide, and adds a border with a specified color.

After running this function, you should see an output similar to the following:

Figure 8.10: *An image inserted with Google Apps Script*

In this example:

1. The image is centered using the **`AlignmentPosition`** enum.
2. A border is added with a custom weight and color.
3. The ability to chain methods like this makes Google Apps Script a powerful tool for customizing slide elements efficiently.

Inserting an Image from Google Drive

To insert an image from Google Drive, you need to retrieve the image as a blob using the **`DriveApp`** service and then use that blob to insert the image:

```
function insertImageFromGoogleDrive() {
  const p = SlidesApp.getActivePresentation();
  const newSlide = p.appendSlide(SlidesApp.PredefinedLayout.TITLE_
ONLY);
  const blob = DriveApp.getFileById('1KXSQvFUmruwyiHJbKf00_gfYXN-
m23WsQ').getBlob();
  newSlide
    .insertImage(blob)
    .alignOnPage(SlidesApp.AlignmentPosition.CENTER)
    .getBorder()
    .setWeight(2)
    .getLineFill()
    .setSolidFill(0, 200, 150);
}
```

In this modified function, the only difference is the use of **`DriveApp.getFileById()`** to get the image file from Google Drive as a blob, which is then passed to **`insertImage()`**.

Depending on the image ID you use, you should see a similar result:

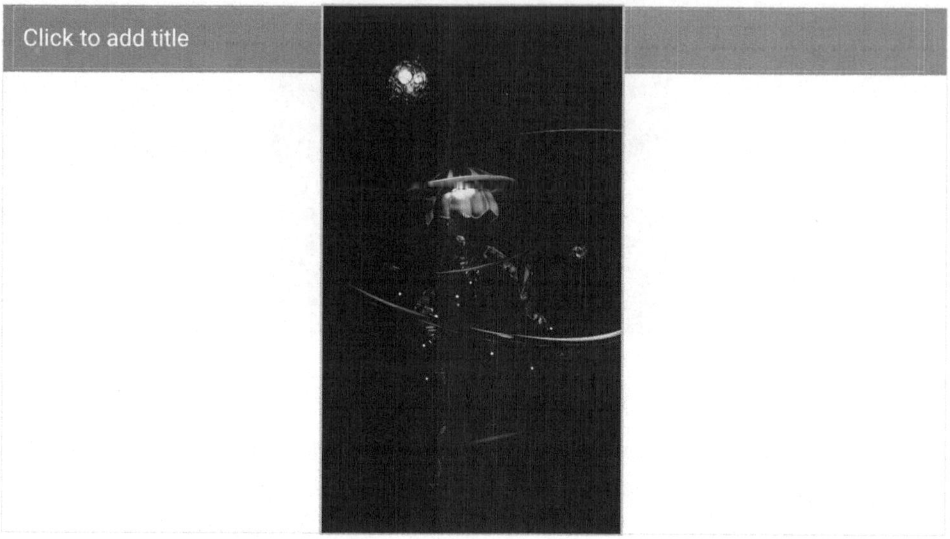

***Figure 8.11**: An image inserted as blob with Google Apps Script*

Retrieving Image URLs

Once you have images inserted into your slides, you may want to retrieve their content and source URLs. The following function shows how to do this:

```
function listImageUrls() {
  const p = SlidesApp.getActivePresentation();
  const slides = p.getSlides();
  const len = slides.length;
  const images = slides.slice(len - 2, len).map((slide, i) =>
    slide.getImages().map(image => ({
      contentUrl: image.getContentUrl() || '<NO CONTENT URL>',
      sourceUrl: image.getSourceUrl() || '<NO SOURCE URL>',
    }))
  ).flat();
  console.log(JSON.stringify(images, null, 2));
}
```

This function:

1. Retrieves the last two slides that were created.
2. Extracts the images from these slides.

3. For each image, it gets both the **contentUrl** and **sourceUrl**. If either URL is not available, a placeholder (**'<NO CONTENT URL>'** or **'<NO SOURCE URL>'**) is returned instead.

When you run this function, it will output something like the following:

```
[
  {
    "contentUrl": "https://lh7-rt.googleusercontent.com/slidesz/
AGV_vUd3NvJCnVtgQ8nkMcggl9Qqu91ERmhHNvRcwhN0L80_5i0T5m-H8MPQDg0s
30QDWZyDQBwAyXPH0uC6Q8eroQQCuHjBEjCUkizLHY5ov95Jb3h_LYUoIRHFQK_
5JxUER9QtWb8L6Gt1dalE43_lKxtv-X9m1g=s2048?key=Nbn6OPI_KGvq8AYS-
rUUUNw",
    "sourceUrl": "https://picsum.photos/400/300"
  },
  {
    "contentUrl": "https://lh7-rt.googleusercontent.com/slidesz/
AGV_vUdQxBw4jKOvVj4rSbbtzPb4cbrwFMN0ZCKFzDP0JowDsAVxzyFhHoDEtuh-
88DCb_jBD9uzYTTOxc5c5tS-lLcVM6J5nMuRIkYvL7jDCojjFThouZwhMkkwld-
Vrk0xpvHGI7-5_luMUZEZdhwQgGdWQNNQCTuQ=s2048?key=Nbn6OPI_KGvq8AYS-
rUUUNw",
    "sourceUrl": "<NO SOURCE URL>"
  }
]
```

In the output:

- **Content URLs** are temporary URLs that provide access to the image content stored in Google Slides.
- **Source URLs** are the original URLs from which images were fetched. This field will only be populated for images inserted via URL, not blobs.

Replacing an Image

You can also replace an existing image on a slide with a new one using the **replace()** method:

```
function replaceImage() {
  const p = SlidesApp.getActivePresentation();
  const slides = p.getSlides();
  const lastSlide = slides[slides.length - 1];
  lastSlide
    .getImages()[0]
    .replace(
       DriveApp
```

```
                .getFileById('<PRESENTATION_ID>')
                .getBlob()
        );
    }
```

When you run this function, the image on the last slide will be replaced with the new one from Google Drive. The new image will inherit the positioning, size, and border of the previous image, making it a seamless replacement.

By utilizing the **Image** class and its methods, you can dynamically add, retrieve, and replace images in your Google Slides presentations, enhancing both the visual appeal and functionality of your slides.

Next, let us explore the element that links Google Slides to Google Sheets: the **SheetsChart** element.

SheetsChart Element

The **SheetsChart** element in Google Slides allows you to seamlessly integrate and manipulate charts directly from Google Sheets. This feature is incredibly useful for presentations that rely on dynamic data, such as reports or dashboards. By linking a chart from Google Sheets, any updates made to the data in the sheet can be reflected in your presentation, saving time and reducing the likelihood of manual errors.

Inserting a Google Sheets Chart into Google Slides

To demonstrate how to work with **SheetsChart** elements, let us consider a Google Sheets document that contains statistical data and a chart:

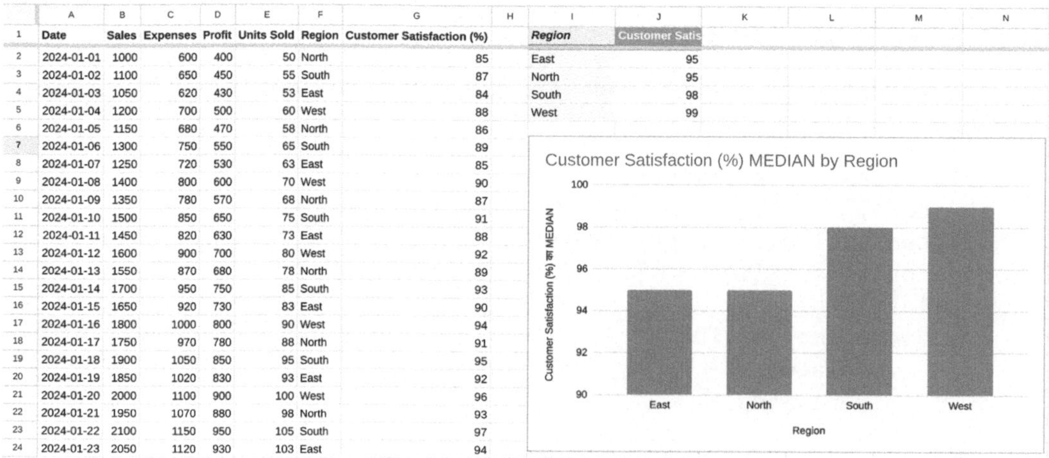

Date	Sales	Expenses	Profit	Units Sold	Region	Customer Satisfaction (%)
2024-01-01	1000	600	400	50	North	85
2024-01-02	1100	650	450	55	South	87
2024-01-03	1050	620	430	53	East	84
2024-01-04	1200	700	500	60	West	88
2024-01-05	1150	680	470	58	North	86
2024-01-06	1300	750	550	65	South	89
2024-01-07	1250	720	530	63	East	85
2024-01-08	1400	800	600	70	West	90
2024-01-09	1350	780	570	68	North	87
2024-01-10	1500	850	650	75	South	91
2024-01-11	1450	820	630	73	East	88
2024-01-12	1600	900	700	80	West	92
2024-01-13	1550	870	680	78	North	89
2024-01-14	1700	950	750	85	South	93
2024-01-15	1650	920	730	83	East	90
2024-01-16	1800	1000	800	90	West	94
2024-01-17	1750	970	780	88	North	91
2024-01-18	1900	1050	850	95	South	95
2024-01-19	1850	1020	830	93	East	92
2024-01-20	2000	1100	900	100	West	96
2024-01-21	1950	1070	880	98	North	93
2024-01-22	2100	1150	950	105	South	97
2024-01-23	2050	1120	930	103	East	94

Region	Customer Satis
East	95
North	95
South	98
West	99

Figure 8.12: A Google Sheets Chart

Here is how you can import this chart into a Google Slides presentation:

```
function insertChart() {
  const SS_ID = '<PRESENTATION_ID>';
  const chart = SpreadsheetApp.openById(SS_ID)
    .getSheetByName('Stats')
    .getCharts()[0];

  const p = SlidesApp.getActivePresentation();
  const newSlide = p.appendSlide(SlidesApp.PredefinedLayout.
BLANK);
  newSlide
    .insertSheetsChart(chart)
    .alignOnPage(SlidesApp.AlignmentPosition.CENTER);
}
```

In this script:

1. We first fetch the chart from the Google Sheet using **`SpreadsheetApp`** with the **`getCharts()`** method. This method retrieves the first chart instance from the "**`Stats`**" sheet.
2. We then use **`SlidesApp`'s `insertSheetsChart()`** method to insert the chart into a new slide in the Google Slides presentation.
3. The chart is centered on the page using the **`alignOnPage()`** method with the **`AlignmentPosition.CENTER`** enum.

After running this function, your last slide should look like this:

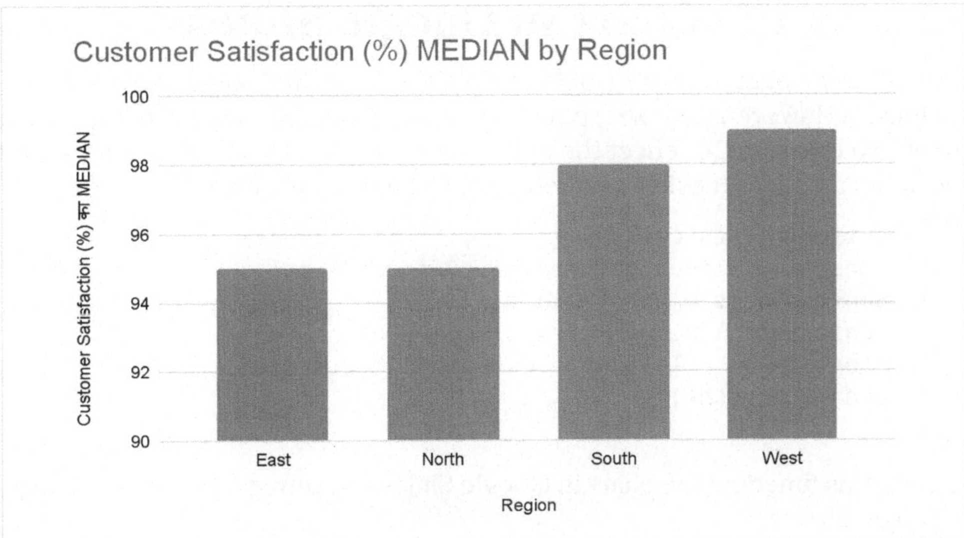

***Figure 8.13**: A slide with a Google Sheets Chart*

Retrieving a Sheets Chart from Google Slides

If your slide deck already contains a Sheets chart, you can retrieve it directly from Google Slides. Here is how you can do that:

```
function getChartFromSlides() {
  const p = SlidesApp.getActivePresentation();
  const slides = p.getSlides();
  const lastSlide = slides[slides.length - 1];
  const chart = lastSlide.getSheetsCharts()[0];
  Logger.log(chart.getSpreadsheetId());
  Logger.log(chart.getChartId());
}
```

This function:

- Retrieves the last slide in the presentation.
- Fetches the first **SheetsChart** object from the slide using **getSheetsCharts()**.
- Logs the **SpreadsheetId** and **ChartId** to the console.

If your last slide contains a chart, running this function will produce an output similar to the following:

```
1:20:49 PM   Notice Execution started
1:20:50 PM   Info   <PRESENTATION_ID>
1:20:50 PM   Info   3.11442584E8
1:20:50 PM   Notice Execution completed
```

Updating the Chart in Google Slides

If you modify the data in your Google Sheets, the chart in Google Sheets will update automatically. However, the corresponding chart in Google Slides will not update, even if you refresh the page. To reflect the updated data in your Google Slides presentation, you need to call the **refresh()** method on the **SheetsChart** object:

```
function refreshChart() {
  const p = SlidesApp.getActivePresentation();
  const slides = p.getSlides();
  const lastSlide = slides[slides.length - 1];
  const chart = lastSlide.getSheetsCharts()[0];
  chart.refresh();
}
```

By running this function, the chart in Google Slides will refresh, pulling the latest data from Google Sheets.

SheetsChart elements are perfect for dynamically linking charts to data stored in Sheets, ensuring that your presentations always display the most up-to-date information. However, there are times when you might want to include tabular data directly in your slides. Let us move on to examine the **Table** element and how it can be utilized in your presentations.

Table Element

The **Table** element in Google Slides allows you to present data in a structured, grid-like format directly within your slides. This is particularly useful when you want to display tabular data without having to rely on images or external tools. Let us explore how to create and manipulate tables using Google Apps Script.

Creating a Table on a New Slide

To start, let us create a new table in a slide using the following function:

```
function insertTable() {
  const p = SlidesApp.getActivePresentation();
  const newSlide = p.appendSlide(SlidesApp.PredefinedLayout.TITLE_
ONLY);
  newSlide.getShapes()[0].getText().setText('Apps Script-Generat-
ed Table');

  const tableData = [
    ['Header 1', 'Header 2', 'Header 3', 'Header 4'],
    ['Row 1 Col 1', 'Row 1 Col 2', 'Row 1 Col 3', 'Row 1 Col 4'],
    ['Row 2 Col 1', 'Row 2 Col 2', 'Row 2 Col 3', 'Row 2 Col 4'],
    ['Row 3 Col 1', 'Row 3 Col 2', 'Row 3 Col 3', 'Row 3 Col 4'],
    ['Row 4 Col 1', 'Row 4 Col 2', 'Row 4 Col 3', 'Row 4 Col 4'],
    ['Row 5 Col 1', 'Row 5 Col 2', 'Row 5 Col 3', 'Row 5 Col 4'],
  ];


  // Create a table in the slide with the specified number of rows
and columns
  const table = newSlide.insertTable(tableData.length, tableDa-
ta[0].length);


  // Loop through the 2D array and set the text for each cell in
the table
  tableData.forEach((row, rowIndex) => {
    row.forEach((cellText, colIndex) => {
      const cell = table.getCell(rowIndex, colIndex);
      cell.getText().setText(cellText);
```

```
        if (rowIndex === 0) cell.getText().getTextStyle().set-
Bold(true);
      });
    });
}
```

In this function:

1. A new slide is created with a **TITLE_ONLY** layout.
2. We use a two-dimensional array (**tableData**) to store the data that will populate the table.
3. **insertTable(numRows, numColumns)** creates a table with the specified number of rows and columns.
4. A nested loop iterates over each row and cell in the **tableData** array to set the text in each corresponding cell of the table.
5. The **getText()** method retrieves a **TextRange** object, which allows for both content and style manipulation. Here, we make the text in the first row bold.

The resulting table looks like this:

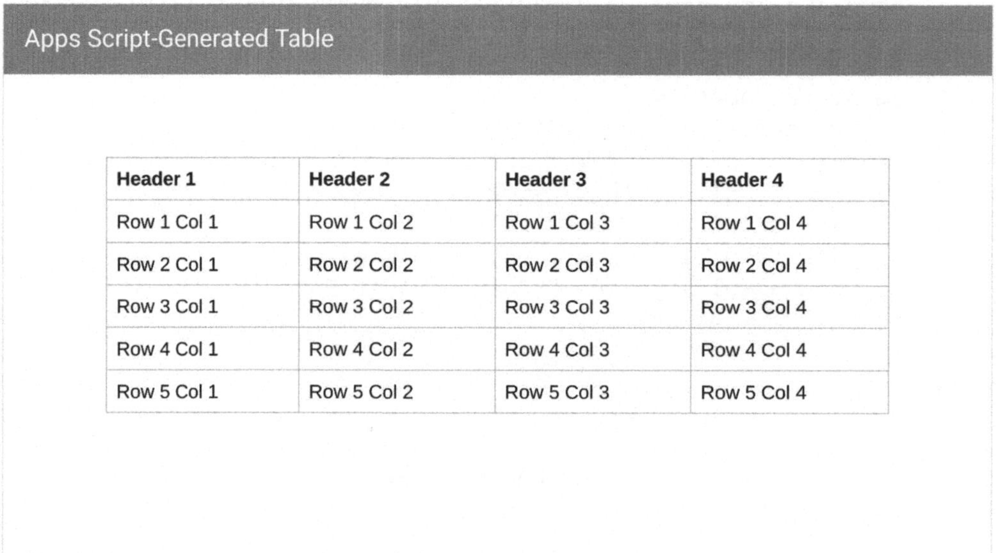

***Figure 8.14**: A table page element*

Modifying the Table

Next, let us manipulate the table by adding a new row and a new column:

```
function insertColumnsRows() {
  const p = SlidesApp.getActivePresentation();
  const slides = p.getSlides();
  const lastSlide = slides[slides.length - 1];
  const table = lastSlide.getTables()[0];

  let numCols = table.getNumColumns();
  let numRows = table.getNumRows();

  table.insertColumn(numCols);
  numCols++;

  const col = table.getColumn(numCols - 1);
  for (let i = 0; i < numRows; i++) {
    const textRange = col.getCell(i).getText();
    if (i === 0) {
      textRange.setText(`Header ${numCols}`);
      continue;
    }
    textRange.setText(`Row ${i} Col ${numCols}`);
  }


  table.insertRow(numRows);
  numRows++;

  const row = table.getRow(numRows - 1);
  for (let i = 0; i < numCols; i++) {
    const textRange = row.getCell(i).getText();
    textRange.setText(`Row ${numRows - 1} Col ${i + 1}`);
  }
}
```

This function:

1. Accesses the table on the last slide using **`getTables()[0]`**.
2. Tracks the current number of columns and rows using **`let`** variables to update these counts dynamically.
3. Uses **`insertColumn()`** and **`insertRow()`** to add a new column and row, respectively.

4. Utilizes loops to iterate over the new column and row, setting text values accordingly.
5. The **`getCell(index)`** method on both **`TableColumn`** and **`TableRow`** instances allows access to specific cells to manipulate their contents.

The modified table will look like this:

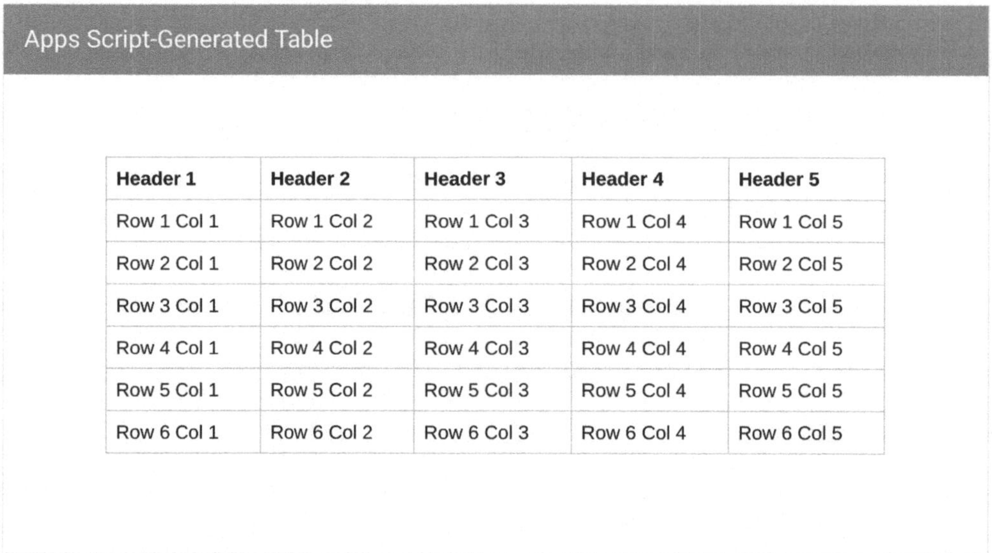

Header 1	Header 2	Header 3	Header 4	Header 5
Row 1 Col 1	Row 1 Col 2	Row 1 Col 3	Row 1 Col 4	Row 1 Col 5
Row 2 Col 1	Row 2 Col 2	Row 2 Col 3	Row 2 Col 4	Row 2 Col 5
Row 3 Col 1	Row 3 Col 2	Row 3 Col 3	Row 3 Col 4	Row 3 Col 5
Row 4 Col 1	Row 4 Col 2	Row 4 Col 3	Row 4 Col 4	Row 4 Col 5
Row 5 Col 1	Row 5 Col 2	Row 5 Col 3	Row 5 Col 4	Row 5 Col 5
Row 6 Col 1	Row 6 Col 2	Row 6 Col 3	Row 6 Col 4	Row 6 Col 5

Figure 8.15: *A table page element with a new row and a new column*

Removing Rows or Columns

To remove a row or column, you can call the **`remove()`** method on the respective **`TableRow`** or **`TableColumn`** instance. This flexibility allows for dynamic table adjustments as needed. For more information on manipulating tables, refer to the full documentation here: (https://developers.google.com/apps-script/reference/slides/table)

We have now explored various elements in Google Slides, but what if you need to manipulate multiple elements together as a single unit? Google Slides offers a grouping feature that allows you to group elements together for easier manipulation. Let us look into how to work with grouped elements next.

Group Element

The **`Group`** element in Google Slides is a way to combine multiple elements—such as shapes, images, and lines—into a single entity. Unlike other elements, a **`Group`** is not a stand-alone object but rather a collection of other elements that can be manipulated together. This feature is particularly useful when you want to move, resize, or apply transformations to multiple elements at once.

Creating a Group in Google Slides

In the Google Slides UI, you can create a group by selecting multiple elements while holding down the Ctrl or Shift key, then right-clicking and selecting "**`Group elements`**" from the context menu.

Figure 8.16: *Grouping elements on a slide*

Once grouped, these elements can be moved or resized together, maintaining their relative positions and sizes. Let us see how to create a group programmatically using Google Apps Script.

Creating a Group Programmatically

To group elements together programmatically, use the **`group()`** method available on the **`Slide`** class. Here is a simple example:

```
function createGroup() {
  const p = SlidesApp.getActivePresentation();
  const slide = p.getSlides()[3];
  const images = slide.getImages();
  slide.group(images);
}
```

In this function:

1. We retrieve the active presentation and select the slide at index 3.
2. We get all the images on the slide using **`getImages()`**.
3. The **`group()`** method is then called with the images as arguments to group them together.

Running the **createGroup()** function will group the selected images together, allowing you to manipulate them as a single unit.

Ungrouping Elements

If you need to ungroup previously grouped elements, you can use the **ungroup()** method. Here is how:

```
function ungroup() {
  const p = SlidesApp.getActivePresentation();
  const slide = p.getSlides()[3];
  slide.getGroups().forEach(g => g.ungroup());
}
```

This function:

1. Retrieves the active presentation and selects the slide at index 3.
2. Uses **getGroups()** to get all groups on the slide.
3. Calls **ungroup()** on each group to separate the elements back to their original state.

Grouping Specific Elements

You do not have to group only elements of the same type. For instance, you can group an image with a shape if they share some common attribute, like matching text descriptions. Here is a function that demonstrates this:

```
function groupImageAndShape() {
  const p = SlidesApp.getActivePresentation();
  const slide = p.getSlides()[3];
  const elements = [];


  slide.getPageElements().forEach(e => {
    const type = e.getPageElementType().toString();
    let text = '';
    if ('SHAPE' === type) text = e.asShape().getText().asString().
trim();
    if ('IMAGE' === type) text = e.asImage().getDescription().
trim();
    if (!!text && !text.startsWith('Lorem')) elements.push({ el: e,
text });
  });
```

```
  const uniqueText = [...new Set(elements.map(e => e.text))];
  uniqueText.forEach(text => {
    const els = elements.filter(e => e.text === text).map(e =>
e.el);
    if (els.length > 1) {
      try {
        console.log(`Grouping ${els.length} elements belonging to
${text}`);
        slide.group(els);
      } catch(err) {
        console.error(`Could not group elements: ${err}`);
      }
    }
  });
```

This function:

1. Retrieves all elements on a slide and checks their type.
2. Extracts text from shapes and descriptions from images.
3. Groups images and shapes together if their text matches.

The resulting group looks like this in the UI:

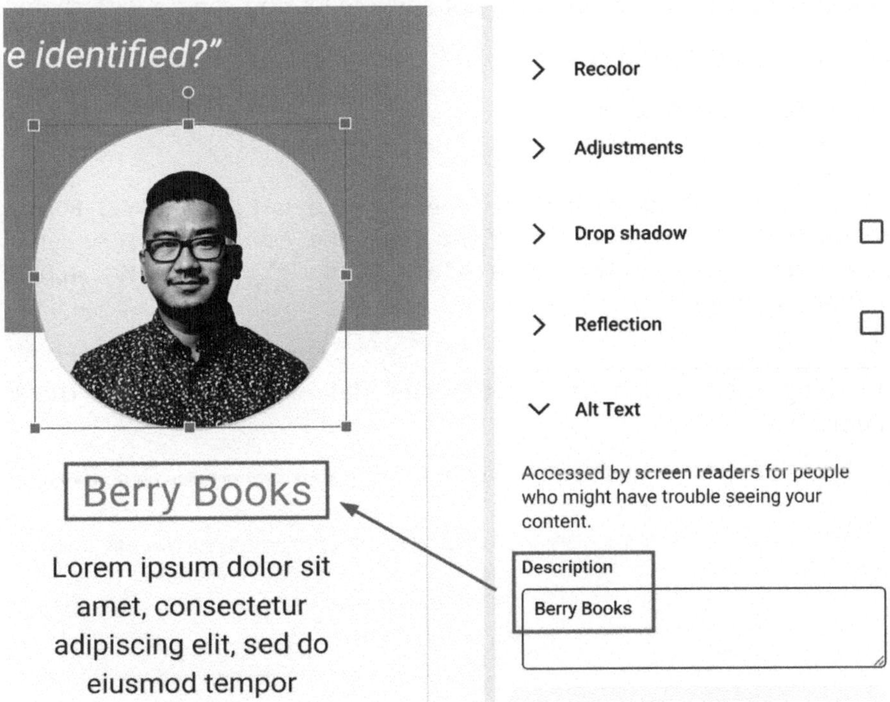

***Figure 8.17**: Matching text box value and image description*

Error Handling and Limitations

The **`try...catch`** block is used to handle any errors that may occur during grouping. Not all elements can be grouped—only shapes, images, and lines are eligible. Elements such as tables, videos, charts, word art, and diagrams cannot be grouped, which is why error handling is crucial.

Running this function will produce output similar to:

```
10:44:00 AM  Notice Execution started
10:44:00 AM  Info   Grouping 2 elements belonging to Wendy Writer
10:44:00 AM  Info   Grouping 2 elements belonging to Ronny Reader
10:44:00 AM  Info   Grouping 2 elements belonging to Abby Author
10:44:00 AM  Info   Grouping 2 elements belonging to Berry Books
10:44:02 AM  Notice Execution completed
```

Now that we have explored how to group elements in Google Slides, let us move on to another type of element that cannot be grouped: videos. Let us examine how to work with video elements in the next section.

Video Element

Google Slides supports videos. There is not a whole lot you can do with them.

Let us see how we would add one:

```
function insertVideo() {
  const p = SlidesApp.getActivePresentation();
  const slide =
    p.appendSlide(SlidesApp.PredefinedLayout.TITLE_AND_BODY);
  const videoUrl = 'https://www.youtube.com/watch?v=7vSnesQDLBE';
  const video = slide.insertVideo(videoUrl, 100, 100, 400, 300);
  return video;
}
```

1. Running this function will create a new slide with the video at the specified coordinates:

Figure 8.18: *A YouTube video inserted into slides with Apps Script*

2. Some other functions you can use with videos are: **`getVideos()`**, **`getUrl()`**, **`getVideoId()`**, **`getThumbnailUrl()`**; feel free to explore the documentation for more details.

3. And now let us look at the last element: lines.

`Line` Element

Lines in Google Slides are versatile elements that can be used for a variety of purposes, such as connecting shapes, creating diagrams, or adding visual elements to your presentation. The **`Line`** class provides several methods for creating and manipulating lines, and it can interact dynamically with other elements on the slide.

Versatility of Lines

Lines in Google Slides are quite versatile. They can vary in format, thickness, curvature, and pattern. Additionally, lines can connect to specific points on elements called "**`connection sites`**." When an element connected to a line is moved, the line maintains its connection, making lines particularly useful for creating interactive and dynamic diagrams.

Creating a Line and Connecting Elements

To demonstrate the use of lines, let us start by manually creating a new blank slide with two shapes on it, like this:

***Figure 8.19**: A slide with two shapes*

Now, let us execute the following function to add a line that connects these two shapes:

```
function insertLine() {
  const p = SlidesApp.getActivePresentation();
  const lastSlide = p.getSlides()[p.getSlides().length - 1];
  const shapes = lastSlide.getShapes();
  lastSlide
    .insertLine(
      SlidesApp.LineCategory.CURVED,
      shapes[0].getConnectionSites()[0],
      shapes[1].getConnectionSites()[1]
    )
    .setEndArrow(SlidesApp.ArrowStyle.FILL_ARROW);
}
```

This function performs the following actions:

1. Retrieves the last slide in the presentation.
2. Gets both shapes on the slide using **`getShapes()`**.
3. Inserts a curved line using **`insertLine()`**, connecting the first connection site of the first shape to the second connection site of the second shape.
4. Sets an arrow style (**`FILL_ARROW`**) at the end of the line for a more polished look.

The result will look like this:

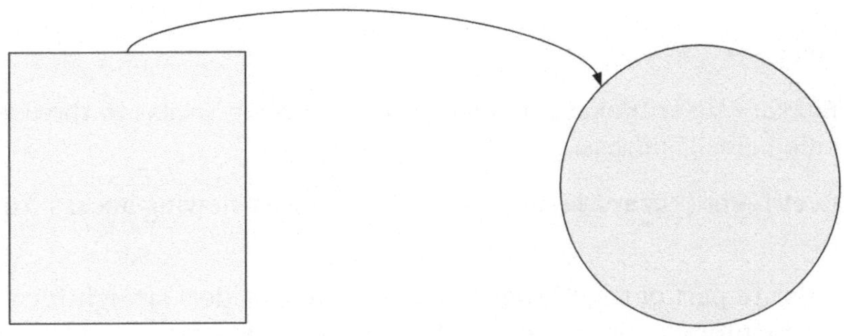

Figure 8.20: *A slide with two shapes joined by a line*

Additional Line Manipulations

You can further manipulate lines by setting their connections explicitly using **`setStartConnection()`** and **`setEndConnection()`** methods. This allows for more precise control over how and where lines connect to elements on your slides.

Lines can add significant value to your presentation by visually connecting related elements, guiding the viewer's eye, and creating structured diagrams. By leveraging the **`Line`** class's capabilities, you can enhance the visual coherence and impact of your slides.

With lines covered, we have now explored a wide range of elements available in Google Slides. Let us conclude by discussing how these elements can be effectively combined and manipulated to create dynamic, engaging presentations.

Managing Access to Presentations

Just like other Google Workspace services, **`SlidesApp`** provides methods to manage access to your presentations. This is especially useful in collaborative environments where you need to control who can view or edit a presentation. Using Google Apps Script, you can programmatically add or remove editors and viewers, streamlining the management process.

Here is a basic example of how to manage access to a presentation:

```
function sharePresentation() {
  const p = SlidesApp.getActivePresentation();
  p.addEditor('user1@example.com');
  p.removeViewer('user2@example.com');
}
```

In this example:

1. **addEditor('user1@example.com')** grants editing access to the user with the specified email address.
2. **removeViewer('user2@example.com')** removes viewing access from another user.

These methods are part of the **SlidesApp** class and provide a straightforward way to manage who can interact with your Google Slides presentations.

By utilizing these functions, you can ensure that only authorized users have the necessary access to your presentations, enhancing both collaboration and security.

Conclusion

In this chapter, we have explored the powerful capabilities of the **SlidesApp** class in Google Apps Script, which provides a robust set of tools for automating and enhancing your Google Slides presentations. From understanding the foundational architecture of Google Slides, including the role of masters, layouts, and individual slides, to manipulating various elements such as shapes, images, videos, and tables, you have learned how to programmatically create and modify presentations to suit your specific needs.

We also delved into more advanced features such as embedding dynamic content from Google Sheets using the **SheetsChart** element and managing access to presentations to facilitate collaboration. Whether you are creating a simple presentation or a complex, data-driven report, Google Apps Script enables you to automate repetitive tasks, maintain consistency, and reduce errors, all while saving valuable time.

By leveraging these tools and techniques, you can take full control of your presentations, making them not only more effective but also easier to manage and update. With a solid understanding of the **SlidesApp** class, you are well-equipped to push the boundaries of what's possible with Google Slides and bring your presentations to the next level.

As you continue to explore Google Apps Script, consider integrating these skills with other Google Workspace services to build more comprehensive and dynamic workflows that can automate and streamline your daily tasks. In the next chapter, we will dive into Google Docs.

Key Terms

- **SlidesApp:** A Google Apps Script service that enables programmatic interaction with Google Slides, allowing you to create, edit, and manage presentations.
- **Presentation:** Represents a Google Slides presentation, allowing you to access, modify, and manage the entire presentation or specific slides within it.
- **Slide:** A single page within a Google Slides presentation that can contain various elements such as text, images, shapes, and videos.
- **Master:** Also known as a theme, it defines the default styles for a presentation, including fonts, colors, and layouts. Masters control the overall appearance and consistency of slides.
- **Layout:** A predefined template within a master that determines the arrangement and style of elements on a slide, such as title slides, content slides, and custom layouts.
- **PageElement:** A generic class for any object that can be placed on a slide, including shapes, images, text boxes, videos, tables, and more. Provides common methods for manipulating elements.
- **Shape:** A type of page element that represents a text box or graphical shape, such as a rectangle, circle, or star. Shapes can contain text and be styled with colors and borders.
- **Image:** A type of page element that represents a graphic or photo added to a slide. Images can be inserted from a URL or Google Drive and manipulated within the slide.
- **SheetsChart:** A type of page element that represents a chart linked from a Google Sheets spreadsheet, allowing dynamic updates and integration of data visualization in slides.
- **Table:** A type of page element that represents a structured grid for displaying data in rows and columns, similar to tables in spreadsheets.
- **Group:** A collection of multiple page elements combined into a single unit, allowing for unified manipulation, such as moving or resizing, while maintaining their relative positions.
- **Video:** A type of page element that represents an embedded video from a URL, such as a YouTube video, allowing multimedia content to be included in presentations.
- **Line:** A type of page element that represents a straight or curved line used to connect elements, create diagrams, or add visual structure to slides.
- **Connection Site:** Specific points on elements where lines can attach, maintaining the connection even when the element is moved.
- **ArrowStyle:** An enum used to define the style of an arrow at the end of a line, providing various options for visual customization.

CHAPTER 9
DocumentApp

Introduction

Google Docs is one of the most essential tools within Google Workspace, widely appreciated for its simplicity and collaborative capabilities. While the manual use of Docs is powerful, combining it with Google Apps Script opens up a whole new dimension of productivity. With the **`DocumentApp`** class, you can automate repetitive actions, build workflows that meet unique business needs, and customize document functionality in ways that are not possible with the standard interface.

The **`DocumentApp`** class enables you to control nearly every aspect of a Google Doc programmatically. Whether it is creating new documents, modifying existing content, or adding advanced features such as dynamic tables of contents or automated formatting, this class provides the tools to make it happen.

Structure

In this chapter, we will cover the following topics:

- Compatibility with Legacy Scripts
- Understanding Google Docs Architecture
- Getting Started
- Working with the **`Document`** Class
- The Basic Structural Elements: Tabs and Sections
- Header and Footer Sections
- Footnotes Array
- Elements
- Ranges, Named Ranges, and Selection
- Mini Project: Document Merge

Compatibility with Legacy Scripts

The introduction of tabs in 2024 expanded the potential of Google Docs, but it also introduced new complexities. Scripts written for older versions of Google Docs may need adjustments to work with the tab-based structure. For example, older scripts may assume all content resides within a single body element, whereas new scripts should account for multiple tabs, each with its own body sections. Understanding how to manage these tabs is critical for developing scripts that are both forward-compatible and functional with legacy systems.

In this chapter, we will dive deep into how to use the `DocumentApp` class. You will learn how to create documents, manipulate their content, and explore advanced features such as interacting with headers, tables, and the new tabs functionality. Let us get started!

Understanding Google Docs Architecture

Google Docs is structured with a hierarchy designed to support a variety of content types while maintaining organization and flexibility. Understanding this architecture is essential for leveraging the full power of the `DocumentApp` class. Let us break it down:

Tabs and Sections

Every Google Doc consists of one or more **tabs**, each containing distinct **sections**. These sections allow for a clear separation of content, enhancing both document organization and scripting possibilities. Here is a closer look at the main sections:

- **Body**: This is where the primary content of the document resides. Most text, images, tables, and lists are placed here, making it the core area for editing and formatting.
- **Header and Footer**: These optional sections appear at the top and bottom of each page. They are commonly used for repeating information such as titles, page numbers, and branding elements.
- **Footnotes**: Located at the bottom of a page, footnotes provide additional context or references linked to the main body content. They are especially useful in academic or professional documents.

Document Elements

Google Docs content is composed of **elements**, which are the individual components that make up the structure of a document. Key elements include:

- **Paragraphs**: The foundation of textual content, used for blocks of text.

- **Lists**: Numbered or bulleted items, ideal for organizing information.
- **Images and Drawings**: Visual elements that can be embedded directly into the document.
- **Tables**: Structures for organizing data into rows and columns.

Each element type has specific methods and properties that you can manipulate programmatically with Apps Script.

Element Properties

Every element in a Google Doc has associated `properties` that define its appearance and behavior. These include:

- **Styles**: Attributes such as font, size, color, and alignment.
- **Links**: Hyperlinks attached to text or images.
- **Text Formats**: Features such as bold, italics, underlining, and highlighting.

These properties allow for granular control over document customization. By modifying them through Apps Script, you can enforce consistent styling or create dynamic, context-aware formatting.

Meta Information

Google Docs also includes metadata that provides context about the document itself. This includes:

- `Name`: The title of the document.
- `ID`: A unique identifier used to reference the document programmatically.
- `URL`: The web address of the document, useful for sharing or linking.

With Apps Script, you can easily access and manipulate this metadata to manage documents programmatically. For instance, you can generate a list of document links for a project or rename files dynamically based on their content.

Adapting to Legacy Code

Before the introduction of `tabs`, older scripts worked under the assumption that a document had a single body element. As a result, you may encounter legacy code using `document.getBody()` to retrieve the document's main content. While this method works for single-tab documents, modern scripts should embrace the new tab-based architecture for clarity and compatibility.

For example:

```
// Legacy method
let body = document.getBody();

// Modern approach for multi-tab compatibility
let body = document.getTabs()[0].asDocumentTab().getBody();
```

By using **getTabs()**, you explicitly reference the desired tab, making the script more robust and easier to maintain. This is especially useful for documents with multiple tabs or complex structures.

Getting Started

As you begin exploring the syntax of Apps Script, let us examine a practical example that showcases how to create a new Google Doc, append a paragraph to it, and retrieve the paragraph's content programmatically. This exercise introduces key elements of the **DocumentApp** class and demonstrates how it can be used to interact with documents dynamically.

```
const PARA =
  'As the sun dipped below the horizon, the city streets began
to glow with the soft, amber hue of streetlights. The air car-
ried a gentle breeze, cool and refreshing after the heat of the
day. People moved about, lost in their thoughts or conversations,
while the sound of distant music mixed with the rhythm of foot-
steps on the pavement. In the midst of the bustling evening,
there was a sense of calm--a moment where time seemed to slow,
allowing everyone to savor the peaceful transition from day to
night.';

function createDocument() {
  return DocumentApp.create('My Apps Script Document');
}

function appendParagraph(document, p) {
  const tab = document
    .getTabs()[0]
    .asDocumentTab()
    .getBody()
    .appendParagraph(p);
}

function getParagraphText(document, index) {
  return document
    .getTabs()[0]
    .asDocumentTab()
```

```
    .getBody()
    .getParagraphs()[index]
    .getText();
}

function main() {
  const d = createDocument();
  Logger.log(d.getUrl());
  appendParagraph(d, PARA);
  const appendedParagraph = getParagraphText(d, 1);
  Logger.log(appendedParagraph);
}
```

The script begins with a global constant, **`PARA`**, which contains a sample paragraph describing a serene evening scene. The **`createDocument()`** function uses **`DocumentApp.create(name)`** to create a new Google Doc titled "**`My Apps Script Document`**." This function returns the document object, which will be used in subsequent operations. Once the document is created, its URL is logged using **`Logger.log()`**, providing an easy way to locate the newly generated file.

The **`appendParagraph()`** function takes the document and the paragraph text as arguments. It appends the paragraph to the body of the first tab of the document. To ensure compatibility with multi-tab documents, the code explicitly references the first tab and asserts its type as a document tab with **`.asDocumentTab()`**. This makes the script both forward-compatible and clear.

Retrieving the text of the appended paragraph is handled by the **`getParagraphText()`** function. The function accesses the body of the first tab and retrieves the paragraph at a specific index. Because all new Google Docs include an empty paragraph by default, the appended paragraph is located at index **`1`** rather than **`0`**. This distinction is crucial to avoid unintentionally working with the default empty paragraph.

When you run the **`main()`** function, it creates a new document, appends the paragraph, and retrieves the text of the appended content. During execution, the URL of the created document and the text of the appended paragraph are logged for verification. The execution log shows the URL for accessing the document and confirms that the appended paragraph has been successfully added.

9:24:12 AM	Notice	Execution started
9:24:12 AM	Info	https://docs.google.com/open?id=1Bv_EUxpd6NZYobHx3aAbrPYHyn1cmh-cK8torXUE65A
9:24:13 AM	Info	As the sun dipped below the horizon, the city streets began to glow with the soft, amber hue of streetlights. The air carried a gentle breeze, cool and refreshing after the heat of the day. People moved about, lost in their thoughts or conversations, while the sound of distant music mixed with the rhythm of footsteps on the pavement. In the midst of the bustling evening, there was a sense of calm—a moment where time seemed to slow, allowing everyone to savor the peaceful transition from day to night.
9:24:13 AM	Notice	Execution completed

Figure 9.1: *Logging out the contents of an appended paragraph*

By following the URL in the log, you will find the new document titled "**`My Apps Script Document.`**" Its body contains two paragraphs: the default empty paragraph and the appended text. Each paragraph is separated by a single newline character, as is standard in Google Docs. The appended paragraph, formatted as per the global **`PARA`** variable, will reflect the serene description provided in the script.

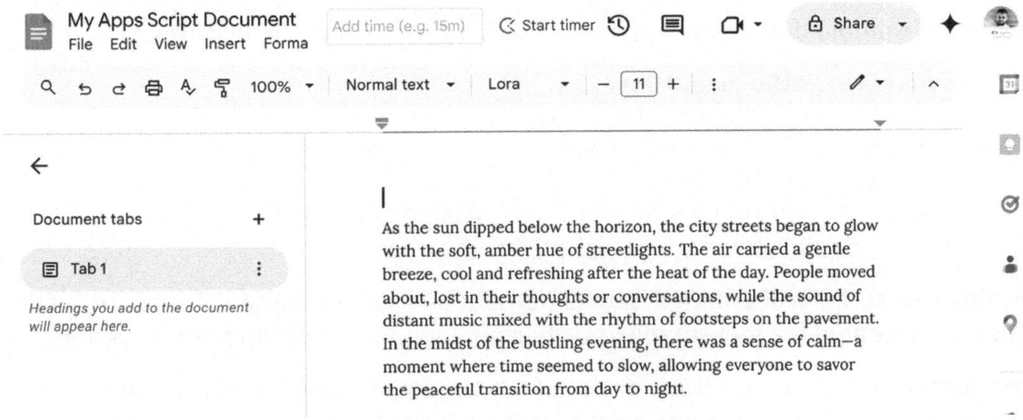

Figure 9.2: *A dynamically created Google Doc*

This example demonstrates the foundational aspects of working with the **`DocumentApp`** class, including document creation, content manipulation, and text retrieval. With these basics covered, you are ready to explore more advanced operations using the **`Document`** class in the next section.

Working With the `Document` Class

The **`Document`** class serves as your primary interface when interacting with a Google Doc through Apps Script. It allows you to perform high-level operations, such as retrieving document metadata, managing access rights, and working with the document's structural elements. Let us break down some of its key features and capabilities.

Every Google Doc has a set of **access rights** that determine what users can do with the document. These rights include editors, commenters, and viewers, which are managed outside the script but can also be referenced programmatically. For instance, you might retrieve a document to confirm if a particular user has editing privileges before making changes.

Each document has a unique `ID` that allows Apps Script to identify and interact with it. The ID is part of the document's URL and can be retrieved programmatically. Similarly, the **name** of the document, often displayed as the title, can also be accessed and modified using the `Document` class. These features enable dynamic workflows, such as renaming documents or fetching specific files based on their identifiers.

The **URL** of the document provides a direct link for sharing or viewing. Apps Script makes it easy to retrieve and log this information, which is particularly useful for automating document sharing or linking in other tools. While the `Document` class supports **named ranges** for working with sections of a document, this guide will not cover named ranges in detail.

Here is an example demonstrating how to access some of these features:

```
function getDocumentDetails() {
  const doc = DocumentApp.create('Example Document');
  Logger.log('Document Name: ' + doc.getName());
  Logger.log('Document ID: ' + doc.getId());
  Logger.log('Document URL: ' + doc.getUrl());
}
```

Running this script will create a new document and log its name, ID, and URL. These values are essential for identifying and sharing documents within your workflow.

Now that we have explored some basics of the `Document` class, let us turn our attention to its structural elements: `tabs` and `sections`. These features allow you to interact with specific parts of a document, such as the body, headers, and footers, enabling precise modifications and content organization.

The Basic Structural Elements: Tabs and Sections

Every Google Doc is divided into **tabs**, with each tab containing a **body** section as its main content area. Optionally, tabs may also include headers, footers, and footnotes. Understanding and interacting with these structural elements is key to effective document manipulation using Apps Script.

Tabs

Tabs represent separate sections of a Google Doc, similar to sheets in a Google Spreadsheet. Every document starts with one default tab, but additional tabs can be added for more complex workflows. To interact with tabs, you use **getTabs()** to retrieve an array of all tabs in a document. For operations, you must specify the type of tab you are working with by calling **.asDocumentTab()** on each tab. This ensures clarity when working with multi-tab documents.

For example, to log the body content of the first tab, you can use the following:

```
const body = document.getTabs()[0].asDocumentTab().getBody();
Logger.log(body.getText());
```

Each tab has a unique **ID**, which is part of the document's URL. This ID can be used to open a specific tab programmatically. For instance, in a URL like **https://docs.google.com/document/d/<DOCUMENT_ID>/edit?tab=t.mfdo8qp6d7in**, the **tab=** query string specifies the tab ID. You can also retrieve tab IDs programmatically:

```
function getTabs() {
  DocumentApp.getActiveDocument()
    .getTabs()
    .forEach(tab => {
      Logger.log(`Tab ID: {tab.getId()}, tab title:
{tab.getTitle()}`);
    });
}
```

Executing this function will produce a result similar to the following:

```
11:14:05 AM  Info  Tab ID: t.0, tab title: Tab 1
11:14:05 AM  Info  Tab ID: t.mfdo8qp6d7in, tab title: Tab 2
```

This script logs the ID and title of each tab. By default, the first tab always has the ID **t.0**. To work with a specific tab, you can retrieve it using its ID:

```
function getTabById() {
  const tab = DocumentApp.getActiveDocument()
    .getTab('t.mfdo8qp6d7in');
  Logger.log({ tabTitle: tab.getTitle() });
}
```

Body Section

The **body** is the primary content area of each tab in a Google Doc. It contains paragraphs, lists, tables, images, and other elements. Every tab includes a body section by default, and while you cannot delete or change it, you can retrieve it using **getBody()** on a **DocumentTab** instance:

```
function getBody() {
  const body = DocumentApp.getActiveDocument()
    .getActiveTab()
    .asDocumentTab()
    .getBody();
  return body;
}
```

Once you have the body, you can perform various operations such as appending content, clearing the body, or finding and replacing text.

Basic Operations

To append content to the body, use methods such as **appendParagraph()**, **appendTable()**, or **appendImage()**. These methods allow you to add text, tables, and images directly into the body. For instance, appending a paragraph can be done as follows:

```
const paragraph = body.appendParagraph('Lorem ipsum');
```

To modify or search for content, you can use methods such as **replaceText()** to find and replace text or **clear()** to remove all body content.

The following table lists some of the most useful methods for interacting with the body:

Method	Description
`clear()`	Removes the contents of the body.
`copy()`	Creates a copy of the body.
`findElement(elementType, [from])`	Searches for a child element by type.
`findText(text, [from])`	Searches for a specific text string.
`replaceText(searchPattern, replacement)`	Replaces text using regular expressions.
`getText()`	Retrieves the text from the body.

Table 9.1: *Useful methods for the Body class*

Consider a CV template document containing various list items.

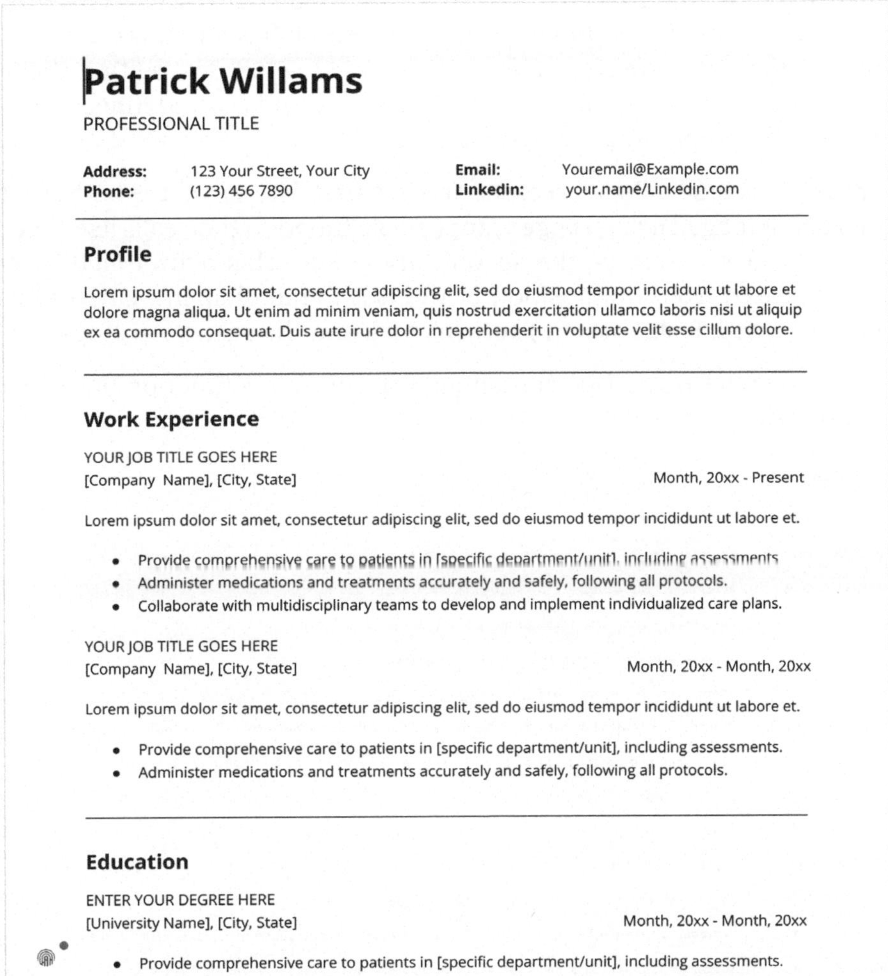

Patrick Willams

PROFESSIONAL TITLE

Address: 123 Your Street, Your City
Phone: (123) 456 7890
Email: Youremail@Example.com
Linkedin: your.name/Linkedin.com

Profile

Lorem ipsum dolor sit amet, consectetur adipiscing elit, sed do eiusmod tempor incididunt ut labore et dolore magna aliqua. Ut enim ad minim veniam, quis nostrud exercitation ullamco laboris nisi ut aliquip ex ea commodo consequat. Duis aute irure dolor in reprehenderit in voluptate velit esse cillum dolore.

Work Experience

YOUR JOB TITLE GOES HERE
[Company Name], [City, State] Month, 20xx - Present

Lorem ipsum dolor sit amet, consectetur adipiscing elit, sed do eiusmod tempor incididunt ut labore et.

- Provide comprehensive care to patients in [specific department/unit], including assessments
- Administer medications and treatments accurately and safely, following all protocols.
- Collaborate with multidisciplinary teams to develop and implement individualized care plans.

YOUR JOB TITLE GOES HERE
[Company Name], [City, State] Month, 20xx - Month, 20xx

Lorem ipsum dolor sit amet, consectetur adipiscing elit, sed do eiusmod tempor incididunt ut labore et.

- Provide comprehensive care to patients in [specific department/unit], including assessments.
- Administer medications and treatments accurately and safely, following all protocols.

Education

ENTER YOUR DEGREE HERE
[University Name], [City, State] Month, 20xx - Month, 20xx

- Provide comprehensive care to patients in [specific department/unit], including assessments.

Figure 9.3: *A sample Google Document with a CV template*

The following function demonstrates how to find and log the text of all list items in a Google Doc programmatically:

```
function findList(element) {
  const li = DocumentApp.getActiveDocument()
    .getActiveTab()
    .asDocumentTab()
    .getBody()
    .findElement(DocumentApp.ElementType.LIST_ITEM, element);
  if (null === li) return;
  Logger.log(li.getElement().asListItem().editAsText().get-
Text());
  findList(li);
}
```

The **findElement()** method is key to this function. It takes two arguments: the type of element to search for and an optional element to search from. In this example, the first argument specifies **DocumentApp.ElementType.LIST_ITEM**, instructing the script to look for list items. The second argument, **element**, is initially undefined, meaning the search starts at the beginning of the document.

When **findList()** is first called, it searches for the first list item in the body. If a list item is found, its text is logged using **Logger.log()**. The function then calls itself recursively, passing the found list item as the second argument. This allows **findElement()** to continue the search from the position of the last found element. Once all list items have been processed, **findElement()** returns null, and the recursion stops.

When executed on a Google Doc containing list items, this function produces output similar to the following:

Execution log

11:40:55 AM	Notice	Execution started
11:40:55 AM	Info	Provide comprehensive care to patients in [specific department/unit], including assessments.
11:40:55 AM	Info	Administer medications and treatments accurately and safely, following all protocols.
11:40:55 AM	Info	Collaborate with multidisciplinary teams to develop and implement individualized care plans.
11:40:55 AM	Info	Provide comprehensive care to patients in [specific department/unit], including assessments.
11:40:55 AM	Info	Administer medications and treatments accurately and safely, following all protocols.
11:40:55 AM	Info	Provide comprehensive care to patients in [specific department/unit], including assessments.
11:40:55 AM	Info	Administer medications and treatments accurately and safely, following all protocols.
11:40:55 AM	Info	Provide comprehensive care to patients in [specific department/unit], including assessments.
11:40:55 AM	Info	Administer medications and treatments accurately and safely, following all protocols.
11:40:55 AM	Info	Provide comprehensive care to patients in [specific department/unit], including assessments.
11:40:55 AM	Info	Administer medications and treatments accurately and safely, following all protocols.
11:40:55 AM	Info	Provide comprehensive care to patients in [specific department/unit], including assessments.
11:40:55 AM	Info	Administer medications and treatments accurately and safely, following all protocols.
11:40:55 AM	Notice	Execution completed

Figure 9.4: *Logging out the list item elements in a Google Doc*

In the example output, the list items contain placeholder values such as [specific department/unit]. These placeholders are often used in templates or drafts to represent fields that need to be replaced later.

This approach showcases how to programmatically traverse and interact with specific document elements, making it a versatile method for processing structured content in Google Docs.

Example: Replacing Placeholder Text

If the document contains placeholder values such as **[specific department/unit]**, you can replace them programmatically. For example, to replace **`[specific department/unit]`** with **`Emergency Department`**, use this function:

```
function replacePlaceholder() {
  const placeholder = '\\[.*department.*\\]';
  const value = 'Emergency Department';
  const body = DocumentApp.getActiveDocument()
    .getActiveTab()
    .asDocumentTab()
    .getBody();
  body.replaceText(placeholder, value);
}
```

Here, **`replaceText()`** takes a string-based regular expression as its first argument. Special characters must be double-escaped.

Clearing or Replacing Content

The **`DocumentApp`** class provides straightforward methods to clear or replace content in the body of a Google Doc. These operations are essential for automating tasks such as resetting document content or making batch edits.

The **`clear()`** method removes all content from the body. This is useful when you need to start fresh or prepare the document for new data. For example:

```
body.clear();
```

To find and replace specific text within the body, use the **`replaceText(searchPattern, replacement)`** method. This method supports regular expressions, allowing you to search for patterns and make precise replacements. For instance, the following code snippet replaces the word "**`Document`**" with "**`Scripted Document`**":

```
body.replaceText('Document', 'Scripted Document');
```

These methods enable efficient manipulation of document content, whether you are making targeted edits or clearing the slate for new content. Their simplicity and power make them invaluable tools for document automation.

Navigating Child Elements

The body contains child elements such as paragraphs, tables, and lists. You can navigate these elements using **`getChild(index)`**. For instance, the following function identifies all unique element types in a document:

```
function printElementTypes() {
  const body = DocumentApp.getActiveDocument()
    .getActiveTab()
    .asDocumentTab()
```

```
    .getBody();
  const numChildren = body.getNumChildren();
  const types = new Set();
  for (let i = 0; i < numChildren; i++) {
    types.add(body.getChild(i).getType());
  }
  types.forEach(Logger.log);
}
```

Running this script outputs the unique element types in the document, such as **PARAGRAPH**, **TABLE**, or **LIST_ITEM**.

```
2:12:19 PM  Notice  Execution started
2:12:20 PM  Info  PARAGRAPH
2:12:20 PM  Info  TABLE
2:12:20 PM  Info  LIST_ITEM
2:12:20 PM  Notice  Execution completed
```

These examples demonstrate how to interact with the structural elements of Google Docs, laying the groundwork for more advanced operations in upcoming sections.

Combining with Other Services

Google Apps Script allows seamless integration with other services to enhance the capabilities of your document automation. One such service is **LanguageApp**, which provides tools for language detection and translation. Using **LanguageApp.translate()**, you can programmatically translate the text content of a document's body into different languages, making your documents more accessible to a diverse audience.

Here is an example of how to translate the entire body content of a Google Doc from English to Spanish:

```
const translatedText = LanguageApp.translate(body.getText(),
'en', 'es');
body.clear().appendParagraph(translatedText);
```

In this script:

1. **body.getText()** retrieves all the text content from the body of the document.

2. **LanguageApp.translate()** translates the retrieved text from English (**'en'**) to Spanish (**'es'**).

3. **body.clear()** removes the original content of the body, ensuring only the translated text remains.

4. **appendParagraph(translatedText)** inserts the translated content back into the body as a single paragraph.

This method can be used for various translation tasks, making it easy to adapt and share documents in multiple languages without manual effort. Integrating **LanguageApp** into your Apps Script workflows unlocks powerful features for multilingual communication and document customization.

Header and Footer Sections

Headers and footers are optional sections in Google Docs that provide spaces for consistent information at the top and bottom of each page, respectively. These sections are particularly useful for adding content such as titles, page numbers, or logos that should appear across all pages of a document.

Headers

A **header** appears at the top of each page and is unique to its tab. To work with a header, use the **getHeader()** method on a **DocumentTab** instance. This method retrieves the header section, allowing you to add or modify its content. For example, to append a paragraph to the header of the first tab, you can use the following code:

```
const header = document.getTabs()[0].asDocumentTab().getHeader();
header.appendParagraph('This is the document header.');
```

This snippet retrieves the header of the first tab and adds a paragraph with the specified text. Headers, like other sections, can contain various elements such as text, tables, images, and lists.

Footers

A **footer** functions similarly to a header but appears at the bottom of each page. To interact with a footer, use the **getFooter()** method on a **DocumentTab** instance. You can append content to the footer in the same way as the header. For example:

```
const footer = document.getTabs()[0].asDocumentTab().getFooter();
footer.appendParagraph('This is the document footer.');
```

This code appends a paragraph to the footer of the first tab.

Working with Headers and Footers

Headers and footers share many capabilities with the body section. They can include paragraphs, tables, and other elements, making them versatile for document customization. However, this overlap also means you need to be explicit in your code about which section (header, footer, or body) you are working with to avoid confusion. By clearly specifying the target section, you ensure your scripts interact with the correct part of the document.

These features make headers and footers essential tools for creating professional, consistent documents that adhere to specific formatting requirements.

Footnotes Array

Footnotes are annotations in Google Docs that appear at the bottom of a page, linked to specific points within the document's body. These are commonly used for citations, references, or additional notes. While Google Apps Script allows you to **`retrieve`**, **`modify`**, and **`delete`** footnotes, it does not support creating footnotes directly with the **`DocumentApp`** service. Footnote creation requires the Advanced Document Service.

Modifying Footnotes

You can programmatically update the contents of existing footnotes to customize their text or make bulk changes. This capability is useful for tasks such as adding prefixes or labels, renumbering footnotes, or standardizing formatting.

For example, the following function modifies all footnotes in the first tab of a document by prepending a numbered label:

```
function modifyFootnote() {
  const footnotes = DocumentApp.getActiveDocument()
    .getTabs()[0]
    .asDocumentTab()
    .getFootnotes();

  footnotes.forEach((note, i) =>
    note
      .asFootnote()
      .getFootnoteContents()
      .setText(
        `Note {i + 1}: {note.asFootnote().getFootnoteContents().
getText()}`
      )
  );
}
```

In this function:

1. **`getFootnotes()`** retrieves all footnotes in the first tab.
2. Each footnote's content is updated by adding a numbered label (**`Note 1:`**, **`Note 2:`**, etc.) using **`setText()`**.

Deleting Footnotes

To clean up a document, you can remove footnotes using the **removeFromParent()** method. This operation deletes the footnote from the document entirely.

Here is an example of a function that removes all footnotes in the first tab:

```
function removeAllFootNotes() {
  const footnotes = DocumentApp.getActiveDocument()
    .getTabs()[0]
    .asDocumentTab()
    .getFootnotes();
  footnotes.forEach(note => note.removeFromParent());
}
```

Retrieving Footnotes

You can retrieve all footnotes in a document or target specific footnotes based on their parent elements, such as paragraphs or list items. Once retrieved, you can log or process their content.

The following example logs the content of all footnotes in the first tab:

```
const footnotes = DocumentApp.getActiveDocument()
  .getTabs()[0]
  .asDocumentTab()
  .getFootnotes();
footnotes.forEach(footnote => Logger.log(footnote.getFootnote
Contents().getText()));
```

This script loops through the footnotes and logs their text content using **getFootnoteContents().getText()**.

Footnote Limitations

While powerful, working with footnotes in Apps Script has some important restrictions:

1. **Creation**: Footnotes cannot be created using **DocumentApp**. To create new footnotes, you must use the Advanced Document Service.
2. **Modification**: You can update the text of existing footnotes, but you cannot change their parent elements or relocate them within the document.
3. **Element Restrictions**: Footnotes are tied to text elements such as paragraphs and list items. They cannot be added to non-text elements such as tables or images.

These limitations mean that while you can manage and modify footnotes effectively, their creation and placement require more advanced tools. By understanding these constraints, you can better incorporate footnote operations into your Apps Script workflows.

Elements

We have explored how to access and manipulate elements within a section. Google Docs uses elements extensively to structure content, and much like the **`Slides`** service, these elements implement the **`Element`** interface. This interface defines shared behaviors and methods for all document elements.

Elements in Google Docs must often be converted to their specific types using methods such as **`asParagraph() or asTable()`**. This type of conversion is required unless you use a dedicated method that already returns a list of specific element types. For example, calling **`getChild(index)`** on a body or other section retrieves a general **`Element`** object, which needs to be converted before performing actions specific to its type.

Because elements implement the **`Element`** interface, they share several common methods. These methods enable actions such as copying, removing, merging, or modifying elements. The following table summarizes the most useful methods provided by the **`Element`** interface:

Method	**Description**	**Return type**
`getType()`	Gets the element type	**`Element`**
`copy()`	Creates a copy of the element	**`Element`**
`getAttributes()`	Gets style attributes	**`Object`**
`setAttributes(attr)`	Sets style attributes	**`Element`**
`removeFromParent()`	Deletes the element	**`Element`**
`merge()`	Merges the element with the previous sibling of the same **`ElementType`**	**`Element`**

Table 9.2: *Methods of the Element Interface*

These shared methods are powerful for managing document content. For example, you can clone elements with **`copy()`**, remove unwanted elements with **`removeFromParent()`**, or adjust formatting using **`getAttributes()`** and **`setAttributes(attr)`**.

Paragraphs are one of the most commonly used elements in Google Docs. Let us dive deeper into their functionality and learn how to manipulate them programmatically.

Paragraphs

Paragraphs are the foundational elements of most Google Docs content. Defined as blocks of text separated by a new line, they are versatile and widely used for structuring document content. Even table cells or headings contain paragraphs, making them integral to the document's organization.

Manipulating Paragraphs

Apps Script provides several methods to create and manage paragraphs:

- **`appendParagraph(text)`**: Adds a new paragraph at the end of the body or another section.
- **`insertParagraph(index, text)`**: Inserts a paragraph at a specified position in the document.
- **`getParagraphs()`**: Retrieves all paragraphs in a section as an array.
- **`paragraph.appendText(text)`**: Appends additional text to an existing paragraph.
- **`paragraph.copy()`**: Creates a copy of a paragraph, which can be inserted elsewhere.

Example: Inserting a Heading

You can insert a heading as a paragraph and set its style using the **`setHeading()`** method. Here is an example of inserting a title at the beginning of the document:

```
body.insertParagraph(0, 'Document Title').setHeading(DocumentApp.
ParagraphHeading.HEADING1);
```

This code inserts a paragraph at position **`0`** and applies the **Heading 1** style.

To insert a paragraph into the body of a document:

```
body.insertParagraph(0, 'This is the first paragraph.');
```

Working with Styles

Paragraph styles, such as font size, color, and weight, can be adjusted programmatically. Apps Script provides methods such as **`setFontSize()`**, **`setBold()`**, and **`setForegroundColor()`** to make these changes.

This example appends a paragraph with specific styling:

```
const para = body.appendParagraph('Styled paragraph');
para.setFontSize(14).setBold(true).setForegroundColor('#0000FF');
// Blue, bold text
```

To modify the color of text within a paragraph, use **editAsText()** to access and manipulate the text content:

```
const para = body.appendParagraph('Styled Text');
const text = para.editAsText();
text.setForegroundColor(0, text.getText().length - 1, '#FF0000');
// Red text
```

Alternatively, you can apply multiple style attributes at once using **setAttributes()**. This method will be explored in more detail later.

Advanced Example: Simulating Typing

The following function demonstrates how to simulate typing a paragraph, character by character, into a document. This uses recursive calls with a slight delay to mimic real-time typing:

```
const MSG = "Lorem ipsum dolor sit amet, consectetur adipiscing
elit, sed do eiusmod tempor incididunt ut labore et dolore magna
aliqua. Ut enim ad minim veniam, quis nostrud exercitation ulla-
mco laboris nisi ut aliquip ex ea commodo consequat. Duis aute
irure dolor in reprehenderit in voluptate velit esse cillum do-
lore eu fugiat nulla pariatur. Excepteur sint occaecat cupidatat
non proident, sunt in culpa qui officia deserunt mollit anim id est
laborum.";

function type(char = 0) {
  const doc = DocumentApp.getActiveDocument();
  const b = doc.getBody();
  const p = b.getParagraphs()[0];
  p.appendText(MSG[char]);
  doc.saveAndClose();
  if (char >= MSG.length - 1) return;
  Utilities.sleep(30);
  type(char + 1);
}
```

In this function:

1. The first paragraph of the document body is selected.
2. A character from **MSG** is appended to the paragraph.
3. The document is saved and closed after each character to simulate typing.
4. A 30-millisecond delay is added between characters using **Utilities.sleep()**.

This creates a visual effect of typing text dynamically into the document.

Next, let us look at tables.

Tables

Tables are a structured way to organize and display data in rows and columns within a Google Doc. They are versatile elements used for creating content such as schedules, data comparisons, and forms.

Creating Tables

The simplest and most convenient way to create a table in Apps Script is by using a two-dimensional array, similar to how data is organized in Google Sheets. Each inner array represents a row, and the elements within the inner array represent the cells in that row.

Here is an example function to create a new table in a Google Doc:

```
function newTable() {
  const indianAnimals = [
    ["Animal", "Scientific Name", "Habitat", "Conservation Status"],
    ["Bengal Tiger", "Panthera tigris", "Tropical forests,
Grasslands", "Endangered"],
    ["Indian Elephant", "Elephas maximus indicus", "Forests,
Grasslands", "Endangered"],
    ["Indian Peacock", "Pavo cristatus", "Forest edges,
Farmlands", "Least Concern"],
    ["Indian Cobra", "Naja naja", "Forests, Wetlands, Urban
areas", "Least Concern"],
    ["Asiatic Lion", "Panthera leo persica", "Dry forests,
Grasslands", "Endangered"]
  ];

  const body = DocumentApp
    .getActiveDocument()
    .getActiveTab()
    .asDocumentTab()
    .getBody();

  const table = body.appendTable(indianAnimals);

  const firstRow = table.getChild(0).asTableRow();
  firstRow.setAttributes({
    [DocumentApp.Attribute.BOLD]: true,
  });
}
```

In this script:

1. A two-dimensional array **indianAnimals** is defined, with the first row representing table headers.
2. **body.appendTable(indianAnimals)** creates a new table in the document body with the provided data.
3. The first row of the table, retrieved using **getChild(0).asTableRow()**, is styled with bold text using **setAttributes()**.

Modifying Tables

While creating tables is straightforward, modifying them requires working with the specific classes associated with table elements, such as **TableRow** and **TableCell**.

The following function demonstrates how to append new rows to an existing table:

```
function addRowsToTable() {
  const dummyData = [
    ['John', 'Doe', 'Unknown'],
    ['Michael', 'Scott', 'Manager, thinker']
  ];

  const table = DocumentApp
    .getActiveDocument()
    .getActiveTab()
    .asDocumentTab()
    .getBody()
    .getTables()[0];

  dummyData.forEach(row => {
    const r = table.appendTableRow();
    row.forEach(value => r.appendTableCell(value));
  });
}
```

In this script:

1. **dummyData** defines the data to be appended as new rows.
2. **getTables()[0]** retrieves the first table in the document body.
3. For each row in **dummyData**, a new **TableRow** is appended to the table using **appendTableRow()**.
4. Each cell in the row is populated with **appendTableCell(value)**.

Key Notes on Table Manipulation

- Tables in Google Docs are not as dynamic as in Google Sheets, so operations such as resizing columns or complex formatting require manual adjustments or advanced scripting.
- When creating or modifying tables programmatically, always ensure data consistency to prevent errors in table structure or content.

Now that we have covered tables, let us explore how to add and manipulate images in a Google Doc.

Images

Images in Google Docs can either be of type **InlineImage** or **PositionedImage**. Understanding the differences between these types and their manipulation methods is key to effectively handling images programmatically.

InlineImage is embedded within a document's content and can be part of a paragraph or a list item. Some useful methods for interacting with **InlineImage** include:

Method	Description	Return type
`getAltTitle()`, `getAltDescription()`	Returns the alternate title/ description	`String`
`setAltTitle(title)`, `setAltDescription(desc)`	Sets the alternate title/ description	`InlineImage`
`getAs(contentType)`	Returns a blob that can be converted	`Blob`
`getHeight()`, `getWidth()`	Returns height/width	`Integer`
`setHeight(height)`, `setWidth(width)`	Sets height/width	`InlineImage`

Table 9.3: *Image class methods*

PositionedImage, on the other hand, is anchored to an element such as a paragraph or list item but is not itself an **Element**. It is positioned relative to its anchor using specified offsets. Here is how to add and position such an image:

```
function addPositionedImage() {
  const body = DocumentApp.getActiveDocument()
    .getActiveTab()
    .asDocumentTab()
    .getBody();

  const text = "Sometimes it's the first moment of the day that
catches you off guard. That's what Wendy was thinking. She opened
```

```
her window to see fire engines screeching down the street. While
this wasn't something completely unheard of, it also wasn't nor-
mal. It was a sure sign of what was going to happen that day. She
could feel it in her bones and it wasn't the way she wanted the
day to begin.";
  const para = body.appendParagraph(text);

  const image = DriveApp
    .getFileById('1KXSQvFUmruwyiHJbKf00_gfYXNm23WsQ')
    .getBlob();

  para.addPositionedImage(image)
    .setWidth(50)
    .setHeight(75)
    .setLeftOffset(50)
    .setTopOffset(20);
}
```

Running this function adds a paragraph of text and positions an image relative to it. The image's width and height are set, and it is offset from the left and top of the paragraph. The output is a cleanly integrated positioned image within the text layout.

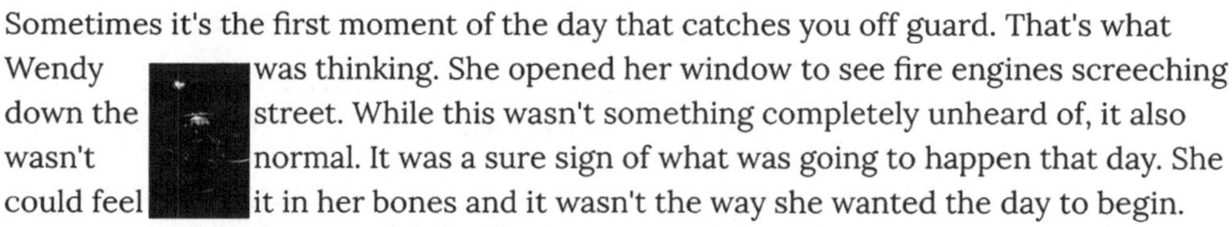

Sometimes it's the first moment of the day that catches you off guard. That's what Wendy was thinking. She opened her window to see fire engines screeching down the street. While this wasn't something completely unheard of, it also wasn't normal. It was a sure sign of what was going to happen that day. She could feel it in her bones and it wasn't the way she wanted the day to begin.

Figure 9.5: *A paragraph with a positioned image*

Next, let us look at lists.

Lists

Lists in Google Docs consist of **`ListItem`** elements, which are essentially specialized paragraphs. These items can include additional elements, such as inline images or horizontal rules, providing flexibility in content organization. Lists are grouped by a shared list ID, allowing for consistent formatting and structure. Lists can be either numbered or bulleted, and their appearance can be customized using different glyph types.

Here is an example of how to create and customize lists:

```
function addList(items = [], type = DocumentApp.GlyphType.BULLET) {
  const body = DocumentApp.getActiveDocument()
    .getActiveTab()
    .asDocumentTab()
```

```
    .getBody();

  let listId = null;
  items.forEach((listItem, i) => {
    const item = body.appendListItem(listItem).setGlyphType
(type);
    if (null !== listId) item.setListId(item);
    if (0 === i) listId = item;
  });
}

const SHOPPING_LIST = [
  'Fruit: bananas, berries, or mangoes',
  'Vegetable to eat raw: avocados, mixed greens, or cucumber',
  'Vegetable to cook: Brussels sprouts, sweet potatoes, or
cauliflower',
  'Protein: chicken, fish, tofu, or eggs',
  'Starch: pasta, quinoa, or rice',
  'Legume: chickpeas, black beans, or lentils',
  'Breakfast item: oats, cereal, or granola',
  'Pantry staple: jarred sauce, spices, or herbs',
  'Wildcard: tortillas, bread, or chicken stock',
];

function addBulletedList() {
  addList(SHOPPING_LIST);
}

function addNumberedList() {
  addList(SHOPPING_LIST, DocumentApp.GlyphType.NUMBER);
}
```

In this script:

1. The **addList()** function creates a list from an array of items. By default, it uses **DocumentApp.GlyphType.BULLET** for a bulleted list.
2. For each item in the array, a new **ListItem** is added to the document body, and the glyph type is set.
3. The first item in the list is assigned a list ID, which is reused for subsequent items to ensure they are grouped as part of the same list.
4. **addBulletedList()** and **addNumberedList()** call **addList()** with different glyph types (**BULLET** and **NUMBER**, respectively).

The result is two lists: one bulleted and one numbered, created with minimal changes to the function arguments. The list ID ensures consistent formatting and grouping of list items.

The output of the function is as follows:

- Fruit: bananas, berries, or mangoes
- Vegetable to eat raw: avocados, mixed greens, or cucumber
- Vegetable to cook: Brussels sprouts, sweet potatoes, or cauliflower
- Protein: chicken, fish, tofu, or eggs
- Starch: pasta, quinoa, or rice
- Legume: chickpeas, black beans, or lentils
- Breakfast item: oats, cereal, or granola
- Pantry staple: jarred sauce, spices, or herbs
- Wildcard: tortillas, bread, or chicken stock

1. Fruit: bananas, berries, or mangoes
2. Vegetable to eat raw: avocados, mixed greens, or cucumber
3. Vegetable to cook: Brussels sprouts, sweet potatoes, or cauliflower
4. Protein: chicken, fish, tofu, or eggs
5. Starch: pasta, quinoa, or rice
6. Legume: chickpeas, black beans, or lentils
7. Breakfast item: oats, cereal, or granola
8. Pantry staple: jarred sauce, spices, or herbs
9. Wildcard: tortillas, bread, or chicken stock

Figure 9.6: *Lists with different glyph types*

Next, let us look at horizontal rules.

Horizontal Rules

Horizontal rules are simple elements used to create a visual separation between sections of a document. They consist of a horizontal line that spans the width of the page. Although they can be part of a list item or a paragraph, horizontal rules cannot contain any child elements of their own.

To demonstrate the use of horizontal rules, let us modify the previous example by adding a horizontal rule between two lists:

```
function addLists() {
  const body = DocumentApp.getActiveDocument()
    .getActiveTab()
    .asDocumentTab()
    .getBody();

  addBulletedList();
  body.appendHorizontalRule();
  addNumberedList();
}
```

This function first calls **addBulletedList()** to append a bulleted list to the document body. It then inserts a horizontal rule using **appendHorizontalRule()**, which adds the rule directly after the bulleted list. Finally, **addNumberedList()** is called to append a numbered list, creating a clear separation between the two sections.

The resulting output is as follows:

- Fruit: bananas, berries, or mangoes
- Vegetable to eat raw: avocados, mixed greens, or cucumber
- Vegetable to cook: Brussels sprouts, sweet potatoes, or cauliflower
- Protein: chicken, beef, fish, tofu, or eggs
- Starch: pasta, quinoa, or rice
- Legume: chickpeas, black beans, or lentils
- Dairy product: milk, yogurt, or cheese
- Breakfast item: oats, cereal, or granola
- Pantry staple: jarred sauce, spices, or herbs
- Wildcard: tortillas, bread, or chicken stock

---

1. Fruit: bananas, berries, or mangoes
2. Vegetable to eat raw: avocados, mixed greens, or cucumber
3. Vegetable to cook: Brussels sprouts, sweet potatoes, or cauliflower
4. Protein: chicken, beef, fish, tofu, or eggs
5. Starch: pasta, quinoa, or rice
6. Legume: chickpeas, black beans, or lentils
7. Dairy product: milk, yogurt, or cheese
8. Breakfast item: oats, cereal, or granola
9. Pantry staple: jarred sauce, spices, or herbs
10. Wildcard: tortillas, bread, or chicken stock

Figure 9.7: *Lists separated by a horizontal rule*

Next, let us look at page breaks.

Page Breaks

Page breaks are straightforward elements that start all subsequent content on a new page. They are useful for structuring long documents, ensuring that sections or chapters begin on fresh pages.

To insert a page break, use the **`appendPageBreak()`** method on the document body. For example:

```
body.appendPageBreak();
```

This adds a page break at the current end of the document content.

To remove an existing page break, you can call **`removeFromParent()`** on the page break element. This deletes the page break from the document, allowing content to flow continuously.

Page breaks are an essential tool for document organization, especially in reports, books, or any structured documents requiring precise pagination.

Ranges, Named Ranges, and Selection

A **range** is a collection of elements in a Google Document, such as paragraphs, tables, or lists. For instance, when a user selects multiple elements with their mouse, they create a range. Ranges can also include partial selections, such as part of a paragraph, which Apps Script can detect and process.

Consider the CV document example where a user makes a selection:

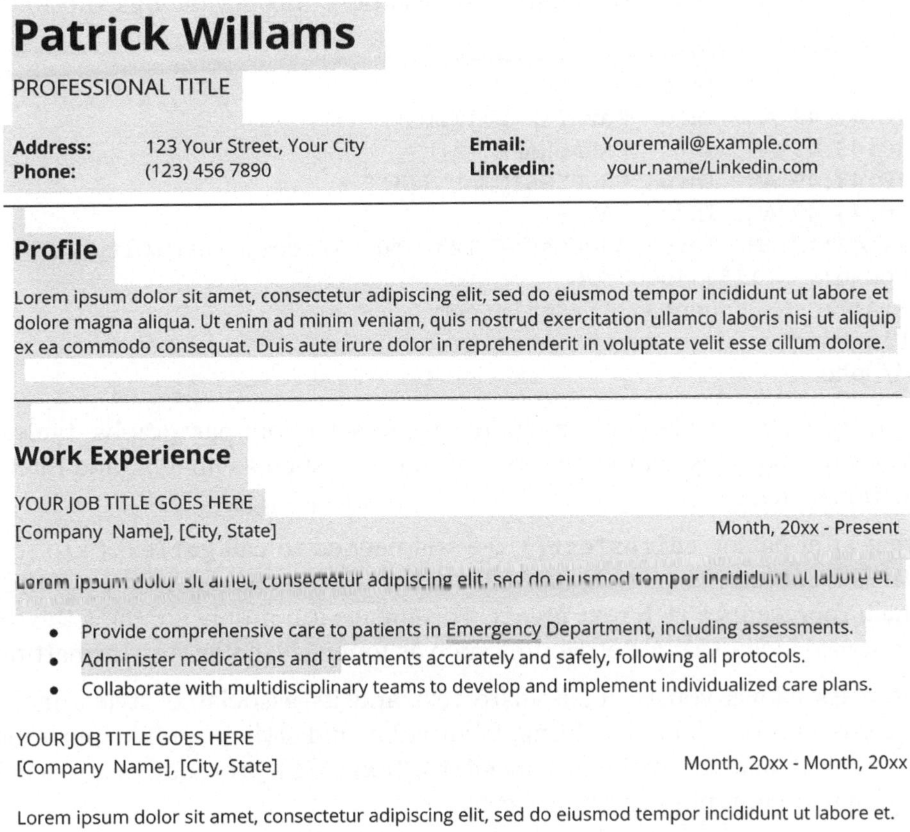

Patrick Willams

PROFESSIONAL TITLE

Address:	123 Your Street, Your City	**Email:**	Youremail@Example.com
Phone:	(123) 456 7890	**Linkedin:**	your.name/Linkedin.com

Profile

Lorem ipsum dolor sit amet, consectetur adipiscing elit, sed do eiusmod tempor incididunt ut labore et dolore magna aliqua. Ut enim ad minim veniam, quis nostrud exercitation ullamco laboris nisi ut aliquip ex ea commodo consequat. Duis aute irure dolor in reprehenderit in voluptate velit esse cillum dolore.

Work Experience

YOUR JOB TITLE GOES HERE

[Company Name], [City, State] Month, 20xx - Present

Lorem ipsum dolor sit amet, consectetur adipiscing elit, sed do eiusmod tempor incididunt ut labore et.

- Provide comprehensive care to patients in Emergency Department, including assessments.
- Administer medications and treatments accurately and safely, following all protocols.
- Collaborate with multidisciplinary teams to develop and implement individualized care plans.

YOUR JOB TITLE GOES HERE

[Company Name], [City, State] Month, 20xx - Month, 20xx

Lorem ipsum dolor sit amet, consectetur adipiscing elit, sed do eiusmod tempor incididunt ut labore et.

***Figure 9.8**: A selection inside a Google Doc*

To process this selection, use the following script:

```
function processSelection() {
  const sel = DocumentApp.getActiveDocument()
    .getSelection();

  if (!sel) return;

  sel.getRangeElements().forEach(rangeEl => {
    const el = rangeEl.getElement();
    Logger.log(el.getType());

    if (!el?.editAsText()) return;

    const txt = el.editAsText();
    Logger.log(txt.getText());
  });
}
```

If you work with the same document and selection, this script logs the following output:

```
10:43:49 AM  Info  PARAGRAPH
10:43:49 AM  Info  Patrick Willams
10:43:49 AM  Info  PARAGRAPH
10:43:49 AM  Info  PROFESSIONAL TITLE
10:43:49 AM  Info  TABLE
10:43:49 AM  Info  Address:  123 Your Street, Your City
Phone:   (123) 456 7890
Email:     Youremail@Example.com
Linkedin:   your.name/Linkedin.com
// etc.
```

This output reflects the elements included in the selection: paragraphs, tables, and lists. The script also skips over elements without text, such as images, and interrupts if no selection is made.

Notice that after calling **`editAsText()`**, we still needed to call **`getText()`** to retrieve the actual text content. This is because **`editAsText()`** returns an instance of the **`Text`** class, which represents a **rich text object**. This means it not only contains the textual content but also includes style attributes such as font, size, color, and formatting.

The **`Text`** class allows you to manipulate text and its associated styles, making it versatile for operations such as editing, formatting, and styling specific portions of a document. This dual functionality is why **`editAsText()`** is a prerequisite for accessing or modifying text content programmatically.

Working with Text

When dealing with text elements, **`editAsText()`** is used to convert the element to a **`Text`** object, which contains both the text and its style attributes. Additional methods of the **`Text`** class include:

Method	Description	Return type
`appendText()`	Appends text to the end of the element	**`Text`**
`deleteText(startOffset, endOffset)`	Deletes a portion of the text	**`Text`**
`findText(pattern, [from])`	Searches for text within element	**`RangeElement`**
`getFontFamily([offset])`	Returns font family at a specified character or the whole element	**`String`**
`setFontFamily(startOffset, endOffset, fontFamilyName)`	Sets font family for the given range	**`Text`**

***Table 9.4**: Methods of the Text class*

Handling Partial Selections

To identify and process partial selections, the **`isPartial()`** method is used on the **`RangeElement`** instance. Here is an updated version of the function:

```
function processSelection() {
  const sel = DocumentApp.getActiveDocument()
    .getSelection();

  if (!sel) return;

  sel.getRangeElements().forEach(rangeEl => {
    const el = rangeEl.getElement();
    Logger.log(el.getType());

    if (!el?.editAsText()) return;

    const txt = el.editAsText();
    const isPartial = rangeEl.isPartial();

    const textValue = txt.getText();
    if (!isPartial) Logger.log(textValue);

    const [startOffset, endOffset] = [
      rangeEl.getStartOffset(),
      rangeEl.getEndOffsetInclusive()
    ];
    Logger.log(textValue.substring(startOffset, endOffset + 1));
  });
}
```

If the selection contains a partial paragraph like this:

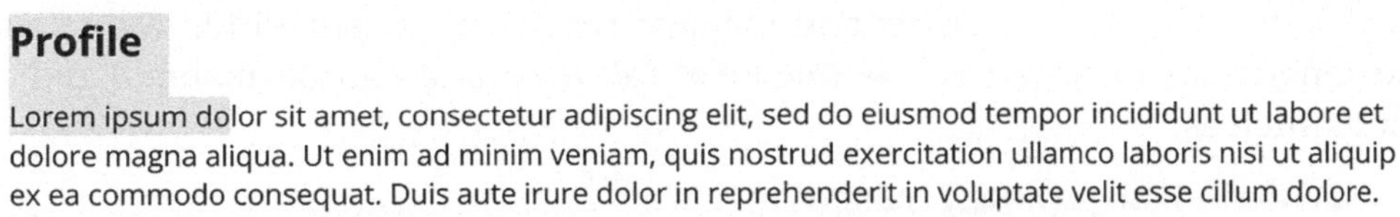

Figure 9.9: *A partial selection inside a Google Document*

The output will be:

```
11:16:10 AM  Info  PARAGRAPH
11:16:10 AM  Info  Profile
11:16:10 AM  Info
11:16:10 AM  Info  TEXT
11:16:10 AM  Info  Lorem ipsum do
```

The title is identified as a **Paragraph**, while the partial selection within the paragraph is identified as a **Text** object. Using **isPartial()** helps detect if only a portion of the element is selected, allowing for precise substring extraction.

Working with Cursor and Selection

You can use the **getCursor()** or **getSelection()** methods to interact with the user's current cursor position or selected text. For example, inserting text at the cursor position can be achieved with:

```
const cursor = document.getCursor();
if (cursor) {
  cursor.insertText('Inserted text at cursor.');
}
```

You can also programmatically move the cursor by creating a new position using **Document.newPosition()**:

```
function moveCursor(from, count = 1) {
  const doc = DocumentApp.getActiveDocument();
  const body = doc.getActiveTab().asDocumentTab().getBody();
  const re = body.findText('Emergency Department', from);
  if (null === re) return;
  const pos = doc.newPosition(re.getElement(), re.getStartOffset());
  doc.setCursor(pos);
  Logger.log(`Moved cursor ${count} times`);
  doc.saveAndClose();
  Utilities.sleep(1000);
  moveCursor(re, count + 1);
}
```

Named Ranges

Named ranges allow you to label and manage recurring ranges within a document. These ranges are managed at the **DocumentTab** level and can be manipulated with methods such as:

- **addNamedRange(name, range)**
- **getNamedRangeById(id)**
- **getNamedRanges()**
- **getNamedRanges(name)**

Named ranges simplify the process of working with specific parts of a document, making it easier to create reusable workflows. For more details, consult the official Apps Script documentation.

Mini Project: Document Merge

This project builds on skills covered in previous chapters to create personalized Google Docs, convert them to PDFs, and send them as email attachments. You will use **DocumentApp**, **DriveApp**, and **GmailApp** to automate the process while ensuring temporary files are removed after use.

To start, prepare your Google Doc template. This document should include placeholders for dynamic content, such as **{{name}}** or **{{email}}**. Use a notation that is unique and unlikely to appear in normal text. Populate the template with all the fields you intend to personalize, such as names, addresses, or custom messages.

Next, set up a Google Spreadsheet that holds the data to be merged. The first row of the spreadsheet should contain headers that match the placeholders in your template. For example, if your template contains **{{name}}**, the spreadsheet should have a column titled **name**. Below the headers, add rows of data with personalized values for each recipient.

Compose a draft email in Gmail for the personalized messages. In the draft, use placeholders for dynamic content, just as you did in the template. Be sure to use a clear and identifiable subject line for the draft, as this will make it easier to fetch the correct draft programmatically. Leave the recipient field blank, as the script will populate this dynamically.

When implementing the script, the workflow begins by reading data from the Google Spreadsheet. The script should use the first row of the spreadsheet to map placeholders to data fields. For each record, the script will create a copy of the template Google Doc, replacing placeholders with the corresponding values from the spreadsheet. Once the placeholders are replaced, the script will convert the modified Google Doc into a PDF.

To send the email, the script will retrieve the Gmail draft by its subject and attach the personalized PDF. The draft's body can also be updated with personalized content if needed. Once the email is sent, the script will delete the temporary Google Doc and PDF files to ensure your Google Drive remains organized.

When preparing your workflow, ensure the template's placeholders match the spreadsheet headers exactly to avoid errors. Additionally, test the script with a small dataset before scaling up to ensure everything is functioning correctly. This project showcases how various Google Workspace services can be integrated to automate repetitive tasks and improve efficiency in document workflows.

Conclusion

The Google Apps Script **DocumentApp** service is a powerful tool for automating and enhancing your workflows in Google Docs. Throughout this chapter, we explored the foundational elements of the `DocumentApp` service, including how to create and manipulate sections, work with paragraphs, lists, tables, and images, and handle specialized elements such as headers, footers, and footnotes. We also delved into advanced functionalities, such as processing user selections and working with ranges, enabling precise document interactions.

These capabilities not only streamline repetitive tasks but also unlock opportunities for building customized solutions, such as the Document Merge mini-project. By integrating `DocumentApp` with other Google Workspace services such as Gmail and Drive, you can create seamless, end-to-end workflows that save time and increase productivity.

As you continue exploring Apps Script, think of the `DocumentApp` service as your toolbox for transforming static documents into dynamic, interactive resources. Whether you are automating template generation, integrating data from external sources, or collaborating on shared documents, the skills you have gained here will serve as a solid foundation for more complex and creative projects.

Until now, we have only covered Apps Script functions that we could only run manually. In the next chapter, we will cover triggers, a construct that allows us to run Apps Script functions automatically in response to certain events or at certain times.

Key Terms

- `DocumentApp`: A Google Apps Script service that allows for programmatic interaction with Google Docs, enabling the creation, modification, and automation of documents.
- `Body`: The primary content area of a Google Doc where elements such as paragraphs, tables, and images reside. Each tab contains its own body.
- `Tabs`: Separate sections of a document, introduced in August 2024, allowing for multi-part documents. Each tab can include a body, header, footer, and footnotes.
- `Header`: An optional section at the top of a page that can contain elements such as text, images, or tables, typically used for titles, logos, or page numbers.
- `Footer`: An optional section at the bottom of a page that can contain similar elements to the header, often used for footnotes, page numbers, or additional references.
- `Footnotes`: Annotations or supplementary information tied to specific points in the document, appearing at the bottom of the page.
- `Element`: The base class representing any content in a document, such as paragraphs, lists, tables, or images.

- `Children`: Elements that reside within another element, such as table cells within a table or paragraphs within the body.
- `Paragraph`: A block of text terminated by a newline. It serves as a versatile element for headings, text content, or even table cell content.
- `ListItem`: A paragraph that is part of a numbered or bulleted list.
- **Horizontal Rule**: A simple horizontal line used to visually separate sections of a document.
- `Range`: A selection of one or more elements within a document, which can include paragraphs, tables, lists, or specific portions of text.
- `Selection`: The content currently selected by the user can be retrieved and processed programmatically.
- `Text`: A rich text object representing text within a document, which includes style attributes such as font, color, and size.
- `InlineImage`: An image embedded directly within the content of a document, often as part of a paragraph or list item.
- `PositionedImage`: An image anchored to an element and positioned relative to its anchor using offsets.
- **Named Range**: A labeled range within a document that can be reused or manipulated programmatically.
- **Attributes**: Style properties associated with elements, such as font size, boldness, or text color.
- `Table`: A structured element consisting of rows and columns, used to organize data.
- `TableRow`: A single row within a table, which can contain one or more cells.
- `TableCell`: An individual cell within a table, which itself contains elements such as paragraphs or images.
- `Cursor`: The current position of the user's cursor in the document, which can be used to insert text or elements programmatically.

CHAPTER 10
Triggers

Introduction

Triggers are a cornerstone of automation in Google Apps Script. They allow your scripts to execute automatically in response to events or at scheduled times, freeing you from the need to run scripts manually. Whether you want to respond to user actions, such as opening a document or editing a spreadsheet, or schedule tasks to run periodically, triggers make it possible to build powerful, hands-off workflows.

There are two main categories of triggers: **event-driven triggers** and **time-driven triggers**.

- **Event-driven triggers** react to user actions, such as opening a file, editing a cell, or submitting a form. They are perfect for automating tasks based on specific interactions.
- **Time-driven triggers** operate on a schedule, running scripts at regular intervals or predefined times. These are ideal for recurring tasks such as sending reports, performing maintenance, or enabling and disabling forms.

Additionally, triggers come in two flavors: **simple triggers** and **installable triggers**. Simple triggers are easier to set up but come with restrictions, whereas installable triggers require more configuration but offer expanded capabilities, such as access to additional services and extended runtimes.

This chapter will guide you through each type of trigger, starting with simple triggers and gradually progressing to more advanced examples. Along the way, you will learn how to:

- Set up simple and installable triggers.
- Automate tasks using event-driven and time-driven triggers.
- Manage triggers programmatically to enhance your workflows.

By the end of this chapter, you will have a solid understanding of how triggers work and how to leverage them to automate Google Workspace applications effectively.

Structure

In this chapter, we will cover the following topics:

- Simple versus Installable Triggers
- Event-Driven versus Time-Driven Triggers
- Web App and Chat Triggers

Simple versus Installable Triggers

When working with triggers in Google Apps Script, you have two fundamental types to choose from: **simple triggers** and **installable triggers**. The key difference lies in their ease of use versus their power and flexibility. Simple triggers are easier to set up but come with limitations, whereas installable triggers require additional configuration and authorization but offer more capabilities.

Let us begin with simple triggers. These are a great starting point for automating tasks because they do not require complex setup or permissions.

Simple Triggers

Simple triggers are special functions with **reserved names** in Google Apps Script. When you use these reserved names, Apps Script automatically recognizes and executes the function in response to specific events. They are quick to implement and perfect for lightweight automations.

Here are some commonly used simple triggers:

- **`onOpen`**: Executes when a user opens a file.
- **`onInstall`**: Fires when an add-on is installed. (We will cover add-ons in detail in Volume 2.)
- **`onEdit`**: Responds when a user edits a cell in Google Sheets.
- **`onSelectionChange`**: Reacts when a user changes their cell selection in Google Sheets.

Restrictions of Simple Triggers

While simple triggers are convenient, they come with notable restrictions:

- **Container-bound**: Simple triggers only work within a specific container file (Docs, Sheets, Slides, or Forms).
- **Limited Services**: They cannot prompt for authorization, so they have restricted access to certain Google services, such as Gmail.

- **Time Limit**: They are limited to 30 seconds of execution time.
- **File Scope**: Simple triggers can only modify the file they are bound to.

Despite these limitations, they are ideal for many scenarios. Let us explore a few of them with examples.

onOpen

The **onOpen** trigger fires whenever a user opens a Google Sheet, Document, Slide, or Form. To demonstrate, let us start with a simple example:

```
function onOpen() { // onOpen is a reserved function name for
declaring a trigger
  Logger.log('Someone opened our Google Sheet');
}
```

Save the script, refresh your Google Sheet, and check the **Execution Log**:

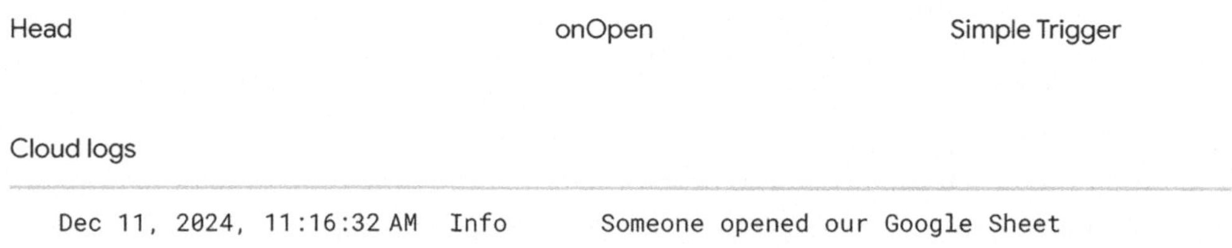

***Figure 10.1:** Output of an **onOpen** trigger*

Neat, right? But logging when someone opens the file is not very practical. A more common use case for **onOpen** is adding a custom menu.

Adding a Custom Menu

Let us update the **onOpen** function to add a menu item that runs another script:

```
function onOpen() { // onOpen is a reserved word for declaring a
trigger
  Logger.log('Someone opened our Google Sheet');

  SpreadsheetApp.getUi()
    .createMenu('My Apps Script Menu')
    .addItem('Randomize colors', 'randomizeCellColors')
    .addToUi();
}

function randomizeCellColors() {
  const sheet = SpreadsheetApp.getActiveSpreadsheet().get
ActiveSheet();
```

```
  const range = sheet.getRange('A1:E20');

  const colors = generateRandomHexColors(
    range.getNumRows(),
    range.getNumColumns()
  );

  range.setBackgrounds(colors);
}

function generateRandomHexColors(numRows, numCols) {
  return Array.from({ length: numRows }, () =>
    Array.from({ length: numCols }, getRandomColor)
  );
}

function getRandomColor() {
  const letters = '0123456789ABCDEF';
  let color = '#';
  for (let i = 0; i < 6; i++) {
    color += letters[Math.floor(Math.random() * 16)];
  }
  return color;
}
```

Here is what happens:

1. **`SpreadsheetApp.getUi()`** gives access to the user interface.
2. The **`createMenu()`** method creates a custom menu named "**`My Apps Script Menu`**".
3. **`addItem()`** adds an option to the menu that calls the **`randomizeCellColors()`** function.
4. **`addToUi()`** finalizes and displays the menu.

Refresh the Google Sheet, and you will see the menu appear:

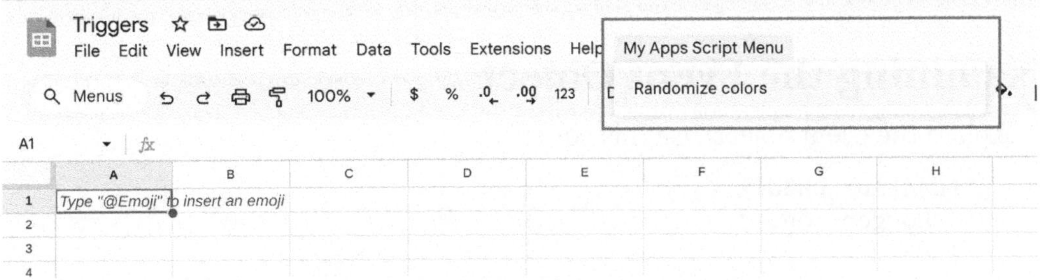

Figure 10.2: *A custom menu in a Google Sheet*

Clicking "**Randomize colors**" generates random colors in the sheet:

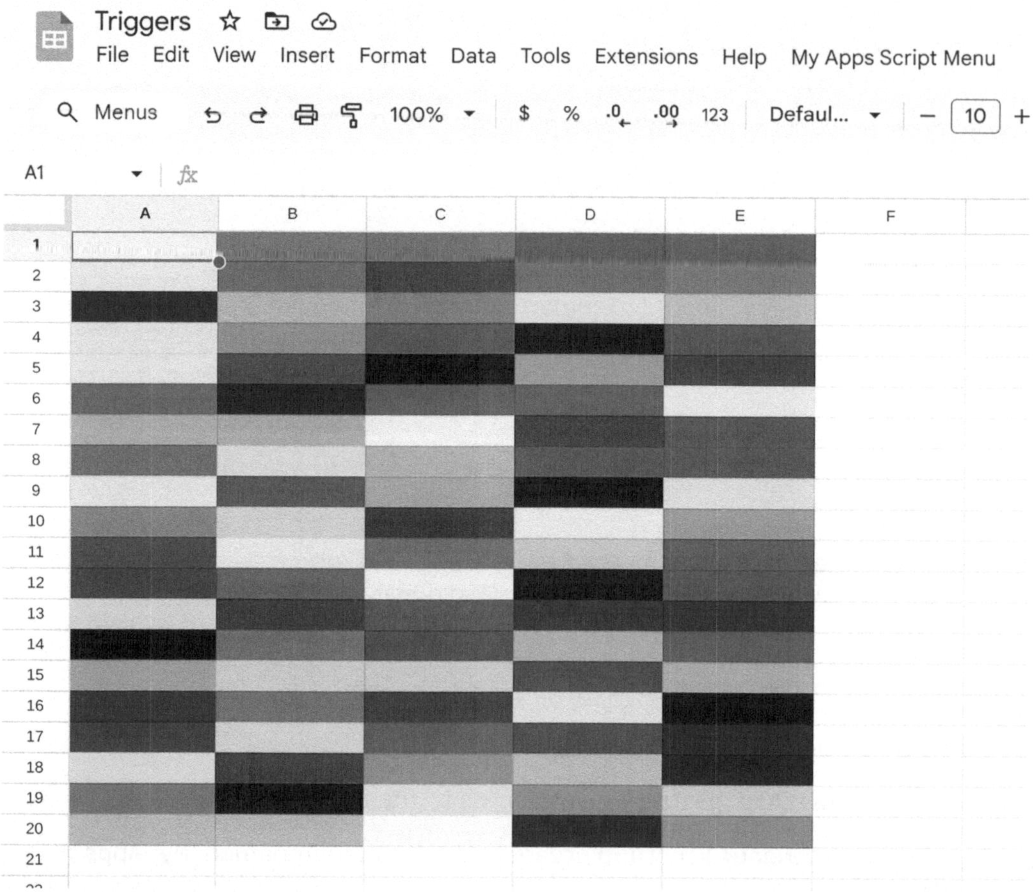

Figure 10.3: *The result of running randomizeCellColors() from the custom menu*

onEdit

The **onEdit** trigger fires when a user edits a cell in a Google Sheet. It is slightly more advanced because it receives an event object that provides useful details about the edit.

Examining the Event Object

To explore the event object, use this code:

```
function onEdit(e) {
  Logger.log(e);
}
```

Save it, change a value in the spreadsheet, and inspect the execution log:

```
{
  oldValue=false,
  range=Range,
  source=Spreadsheet,
  value=TRUE,
  authMode=LIMITED,
  user=dmitry@wurkspaces.dev
}
```

The event object provides details like:

- **`oldValue`** and value: The cell's previous and new values.
- **`range`**: The range that was edited.
- **`source`**: The spreadsheet where the change occurred.

Automating a Task List

Let us automate a to-do list. When a checkbox in column `A` is checked, we will add the current date to column `C`.

```
function onEdit(e) {
  const { range, value } = e;
  const ws = range.getSheet();
  const sheetName = ws.getName();
  if ('Task List' !== sheetName || 1 !== range.columnStart) return;
  const newValue = 'TRUE' === value ? new Date().toISOString() :
'';
  ws.getRange(range.rowStart, 3).setValue(newValue);
}
```

How it works:

1. Extracts the range and value from the event object.
2. Validates that the edit happened in column `A` of the "**`Task List`**" sheet.
3. Inserts the current date if the checkbox is checked **`("TRUE")`**. If unchecked, clears the value.

Here is what the result looks like:

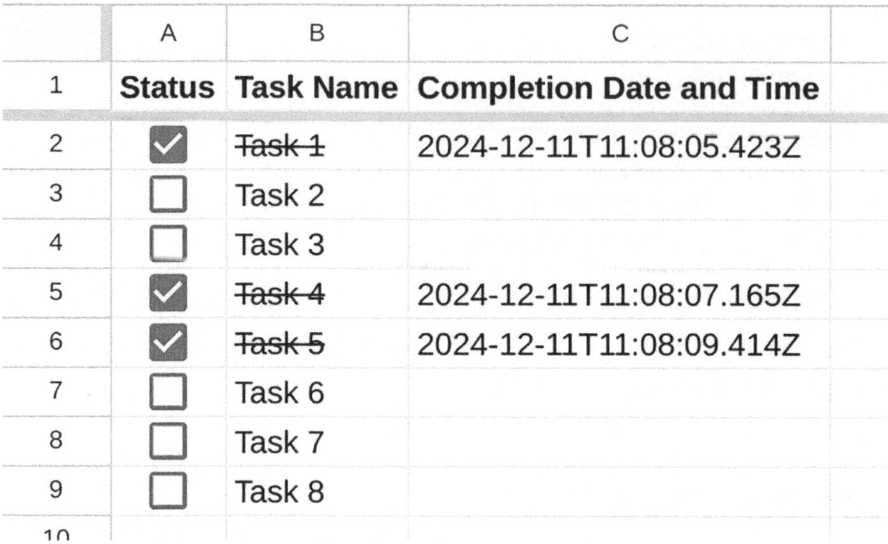

Figure 10.4: *A task list that records completion dates and times when status checkboxes are clicked*

onSelectionChange

The **onSelectionChange** trigger fires when a user selects a new cell or range. Like **onEdit**, it also receives an event object.

Tracking Cell Selection

Here is a simple example that logs the user's current selection in a sheet named "**Selection**":

```
function onSelectionChange(e) {
  const { range } = e;
  const wsName = range.getSheet().getName();
  const addr = range.getA1Notation();
  SpreadsheetApp.getActive()
    .getSheetByName('Selection')
    .getRange('A2')
    .setValue(`{wsName}!{addr}`);
}
```

How it works:

1. Extracts the current range from the event object.
2. Writes the A1 notation of the selection into the "**Selection**" sheet.

Create a sheet named "**`Selection`**" and see the result:

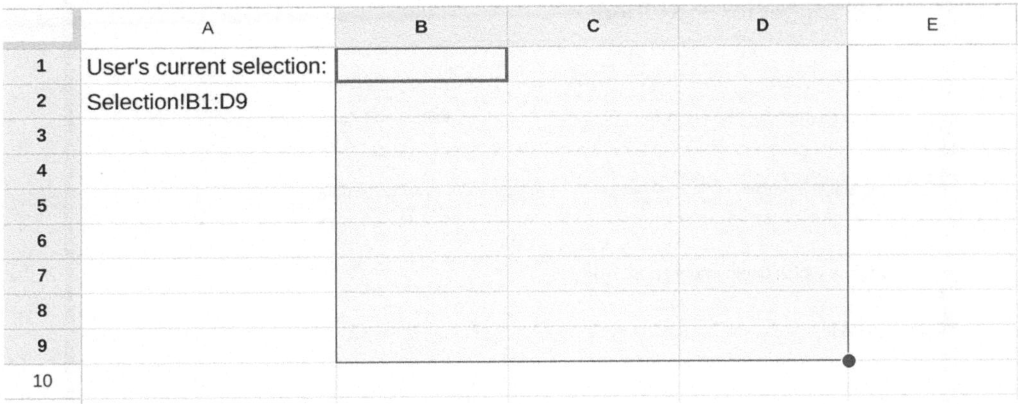

Figure 10.5: *The user's selection is detected with the onSelectionChange trigger*

Simple triggers such as **`onOpen`**, **`onEdit`**, and **`onSelectionChange`** are a great starting point for automating tasks in Google Sheets. While they have limitations, they are lightweight, easy to implement, and perfect for quick automations.

Installable Triggers

Installable triggers expand on the functionality of simple triggers, allowing for more powerful automations. Unlike simple triggers, they require explicit activation, either through the UI or programmatically. While they involve more setup, they unlock additional capabilities such as calling more services, running longer scripts, and performing complex tasks.

Installable triggers have several key advantages:

- They can access additional services (e.g., Gmail) and operate under the script owner's account.
- They can be managed programmatically using the **`ScriptApp`** class.
- They support features such as access to user information and trigger metadata, such as the trigger ID.
- However, they are **not fired by programmatic events**; they only respond to user actions.

Compare a Simple and Installable `onEdit`

Let us compare the behavior of a simple **`onEdit`** trigger with its installable version. First, install the trigger through the UI:

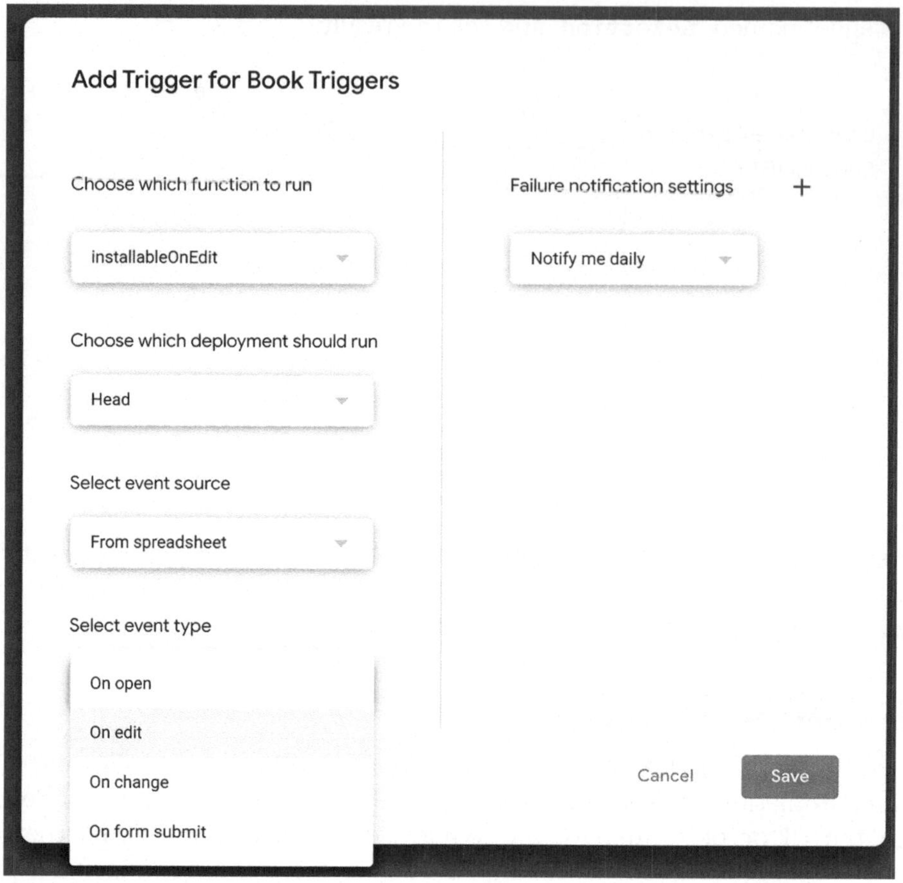

Figure 10.6: *The UI in the online IDE for managing installable triggers*

Then consider the following code:

```
function installableOnEdit(e) {
  Logger.log('Installable `onEdit` event object:');
  Logger.log(JSON.stringify(e));
}
```

When the trigger fires, inspect the log output:

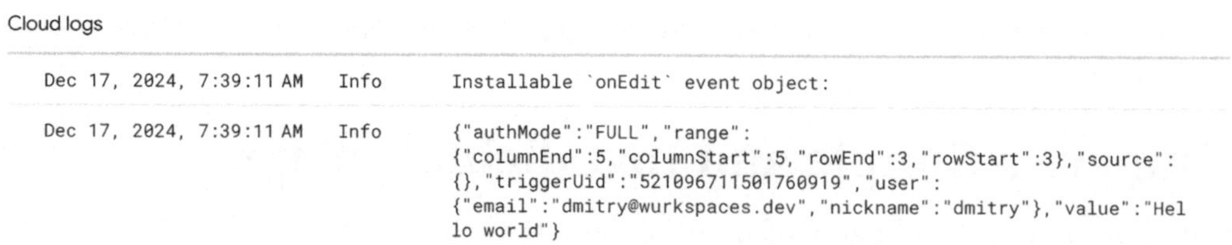

Figure 10.7: *Inspecting the event object of the installable onEdit trigger*

The key differences include:

- **`authMode`**: For installable triggers, this is set to **`FULL`**, allowing access to more services.
- Installable triggers provide a more detailed User object
- Additional property **`triggerUid`** is available for tracking.

Programmatically Creating Installable Triggers

You can also install triggers programmatically. Here is an example:

```
function installNewTrigger() {
  ScriptApp.newTrigger('installableOnEdit')
    .forSpreadsheet(SpreadsheetApp.getActive())
    .onEdit()
    .create();
}
```

After running this function, you will need to authorize the trigger:

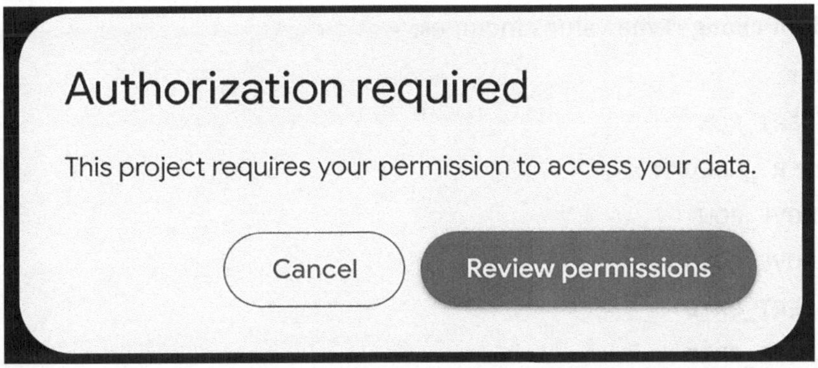

Figure 10.8: *Installing a trigger programmatically triggers an authorization request*

You can then inspect your installed triggers to see both the simple and installable versions:

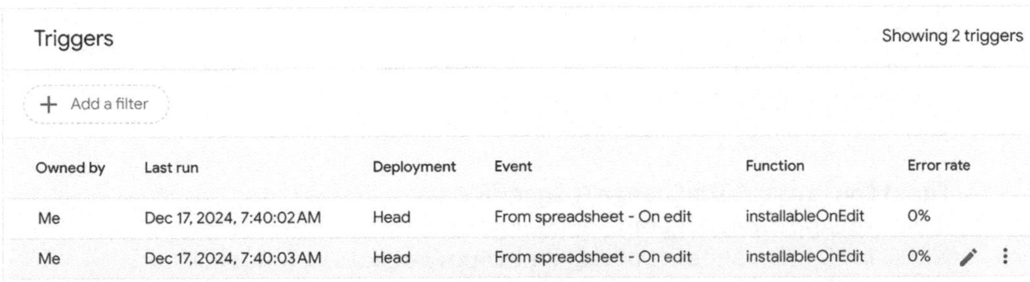

Figure 10.9: *Programmatically installed triggers are also visible in the online IDE*

Removing Installable Triggers

To clean up your triggers and keep only the simple ones, you can programmatically delete all installable triggers using the following script:

```
function cleanUpTriggers() {
  ScriptApp.getProjectTriggers()
    .forEach(trigger => ScriptApp.deleteTrigger(trigger));
}
```

Run this script, and your installable triggers will be removed.

onChange

The **onChange** trigger differs from **onEdit** in that it reacts to **structural changes** in a spreadsheet, not edits to cell values. Structural changes include:

- Inserting or deleting rows/columns.
- Adding or deleting sheets (tabs).

The full list of **changeType** values includes:

- **EDIT**
- **INSERT_ROW**
- **INSERT_COLUMN**
- **REMOVE_ROW**
- **REMOVE_COLUMN**
- **INSERT_GRID**
- **REMOVE_GRID**
- **FORMAT**
- **OTHER**

Here is how to set up and inspect the **onChange** event object:

```
function onChange(e) {
  Logger.log(e);
  Logger.log(JSON.stringify(e));
}

function installOnChangeTrigger() {
  ScriptApp.newTrigger('onChange')
    .forSpreadsheet(SpreadsheetApp.getActive())
    .onChange()
    .create();
}
```

After installing the trigger and, for example, inserting a row, the output will look like this:

```
{
  "authMode": "FULL",
  "changeType": "INSERT_ROW",
  "source": {},
  "triggerUid": "491961496",
  "user": {
    "email": "name@domain.com",
    "nickname": "dmitry"
  }
}
```

onFormSubmit

The **onFormSubmit** trigger works differently depending on the source:

1. **Google Forms trigger**: Fires when a Google Form is submitted.
2. **Google Sheets trigger**: Fires when a linked Google Form submits data to a Sheet.

Event Objects

- The **Google Forms** version includes a **response** object corresponding to the **FormResponse** class.
- The **Google Sheets** version includes:
  - A **Range object** indicating the affected cells.
  - A **values array** with form responses.
  - A **namedValues object** with question-response pairs.

For detailed descriptions of the event objects, refer to the official documentation: https://developers.google.com/apps-script/guides/triggers/events

Event-Driven versus Time-Driven Triggers

Until now, we have focused on event-driven triggers—triggers that respond to user actions, such as opening a file, editing a cell, or inserting a row. Event-driven triggers depend on specific events to fire, making them great for interactive automations.

There is, however, another type of trigger: time-driven triggers. These triggers are scheduled to execute at pre-determined time slots, either once or recurring. Time-driven triggers operate independently of user actions, making them ideal for periodic or background tasks.

All time-driven triggers are installable, meaning they need to be explicitly created and authorized.

Time-Driven Triggers

Time-driven triggers are scheduled to run at regular intervals or specific times. They can be configured to trigger:

- **Hourly** (for example, every hour, or a specific hour each day)
- **Daily** (for example, every morning at 8 a.m.)
- **Weekly** (for example, every Monday at 9 a.m.)
- **Monthly** (for example, on the 1st of each month)
- **Once** (at a specific date and time)

Use Cases

Time-driven triggers are perfect for tasks that need automation on a schedule, such as:

- Sending weekly reports via email.
- Performing automated maintenance (for example, clearing old data).
- Enabling/disabling Google Form submissions during office hours.
- Sending birthday reminders or regular meeting notifications.
- Fetching calendar events and sending reminders to attendees.
- Automating delayed tasks by pausing and resuming scripts.

Example: Controlling Google Form Office Hours

Let us use time-driven triggers to enable or disable form submissions for a Google Form based on office hours. In this example:

- Submissions are allowed during weekdays from 8 a.m. to 7 p.m.
- Submissions are disabled on weekends and after office hours.

Here is the script:

```
function getForm() {
  return FormApp.openById('form-id-here');
}

function isWeekEnd() {
  return [0, 6].includes(new Date().getDay());
}
```

```
function openFormIfWeekday() {
  if (!isWeekEnd()) return getForm().setAcceptingResponses(true);
  return getForm().setAcceptingResponses(false);
}

function closeForm() {
  return getForm().setAcceptingResponses(false);
}

function createOpenFormTrigger() {
  ScriptApp.newTrigger('openFormIfWeekday')
    .timeBased()
    .atHour(8)
    .everyDays(1)
    .create();
}

function createCloseFormTrigger() {
  ScriptApp.newTrigger('closeForm')
    .timeBased()
    .atHour(19)
    .everyDays(1)
    .create();
}
```

Script Breakdown

1. **`getForm()`**: Opens the target Google Form using its ID.
2. **`isWeekEnd()`**: Returns true if the current day is Saturday (6) or Sunday (0).
3. **`openFormIfWeekday()`**: Enables form submissions during weekdays.
    a. On weekends, it explicitly disallows submissions.
4. **`closeForm()`**: Disables form submissions daily at 7 p.m.
5. **`createOpenFormTrigger()`**: Creates a time-driven trigger that runs **`openFormIfWeekday`** at 8 a.m. every day.
6. **`createCloseFormTrigger()`**: Creates a time-driven trigger that runs **`closeForm`** at 7 p.m. every day.

Important Notes About Hourly Triggers

Hourly triggers in Apps Script operate within a **1-hour window**. For example, if you set a trigger at 8 a.m., the function will run **sometime between 8 a.m. and 9 a.m.**. However, once the script runs at a specific time (for example, 8:17 a.m.), it will **consistently run at that time** every day.

1. **Morning Trigger**: Runs `openFormIfWeekday()` between 8 a.m. and 9 a.m.
   a. Enables form responses **only on weekdays**.
2. **Evening Trigger**: Runs `closeForm()` between 7 p.m. and 8 p.m.
   b. Disables form responses every evening, regardless of the day.

Result

With these time-driven triggers in place, the Google Form will:

- Accept responses during office hours (8 a.m.–7 p.m.) on weekdays.
- Automatically close for submissions outside office hours and on weekends.

This type of automation is especially useful for schools, offices, or event managers who need to control when users can access and submit forms.

Web App Triggers (`doGet` and `doPost`) and Chat Triggers

Web app triggers use **`doGet`** and **`doPost`** functions as **entry points** for web applications built with Google Apps Script. These triggers allow you to:

- Build web apps that interact with users through **HTML-based interfaces** created using the **`HTMLService`**.

We will cover web app triggers and the **`HTMLService`** in detail in a later chapter.

Chat triggers allow scripts to interact with Google Chat, responding to messages or commands. This functionality will be explored in **Volume 2** of this book.

Conclusion

Triggers are a powerful tool in Google Apps Script, enabling you to automate workflows and respond to events seamlessly. By understanding the differences between **simple** and **installable triggers**, as well as **event-driven** and **time-driven** triggers, you can choose the right approach for your specific use case.

Simple triggers are quick to set up and perfect for lightweight automations, but they come with limitations. Installable triggers, on the other hand, provide extended capabilities, such as access to more Google services and the ability to run scripts for longer durations. Time-driven triggers allow you to schedule tasks at regular intervals, making them ideal for recurring processes such as report generation, maintenance, or managing form availability.

Additionally, triggers can be managed programmatically, giving you full control over their creation, execution, and cleanup. This flexibility allows you to build robust automations that scale with your needs.

As you progress in your Apps Script journey, you will find that triggers form the backbone of many automated workflows. Whether you are responding to user interactions, scheduling periodic tasks, or building interactive applications, mastering triggers will unlock a new level of productivity and efficiency.

In the next chapter, we will explore how to extend these capabilities even further, diving into advanced techniques that enhance user interaction and streamline your scripts.

Key Terms

- **Triggers**: Mechanisms in Google Apps Script that automatically execute a function in response to an event or at a scheduled time.
- **Simple Triggers**: Lightweight triggers with reserved function names (e.g., `onOpen`, `onEdit`) that execute automatically for specific user actions but come with restrictions on runtime and service access.
- **Installable Triggers**: Advanced triggers that require explicit setup but offer expanded capabilities, such as accessing additional Google services, running longer scripts, and managing triggers programmatically.
- **`onOpen`**: A simple trigger that runs when a user opens a Google Doc, Sheet, Slide, or Form, often used to create custom menus.
- **`onEdit`**: A simple trigger that executes when a user edits a cell in Google Sheets. It cannot be triggered programmatically.
- **`onSelectionChange`**: A simple trigger that fires when a user selects a new cell or range in Google Sheets.
- **`onChange`**: An installable trigger that responds to structural changes in a Google Sheet, such as inserting or deleting rows, columns, or tabs.
- **`onFormSubmit`**: An installable trigger that runs when a Google Form submission is recorded. The event object differs between Form and Sheet contexts.
- **Time-Driven Trigger**: An installable trigger that executes functions on a pre-determined schedule, such as hourly, daily, weekly, or monthly.
- **`ScriptApp`**: A Google Apps Script service that allows for managing installable triggers programmatically, including creating, deleting, and listing triggers.

- **Event Object**: An object passed to trigger functions that contains contextual information about the event, such as edited ranges, form responses, or change types.
- **`HTMLService`**: A Google Apps Script service used to build and serve HTML-based interfaces, often for web apps or custom dialogs.
- **`doGet/doPost`**: Entry-point functions for Apps Script web apps, allowing HTTP **`GET`** and **`POST`** requests to interact with scripts.
- **Time-Based Scheduling**: The process of configuring time-driven triggers to run at specific times or intervals, enabling automated background tasks such as sending reports or performing maintenance.

CHAPTER 11
User Interfaces

Introduction

When working with Google Apps Script, you have likely encountered two straightforward ways to execute your functions: by running them directly from the online integrated development environment's (IDE) graphical user interface (GUI) or by setting up triggers. While these methods are convenient for developers, they fall short when creating apps intended for end-users.

For most apps, you will need to enable users to interact with your script in a way that feels intuitive and seamless. This might mean offering buttons, forms, or menus that let users initiate functions without diving into code. Importantly, this applies regardless of how your script is deployed: whether as an add-on, a standalone app, or embedded within Google Workspace tools such as Docs, Sheets, or Slides.

In this chapter, we will explore three core approaches to building user interfaces in Google Apps Script: custom menus, HTML Service, and Card Service.

Custom Menus provide a simple way to enhance Google Workspace apps such as Sheets or Docs by adding your own commands to their existing menu bars. HTML Service allows for creating more complex UIs, such as modal dialogs and sidebars, using custom HTML, CSS, and JavaScript. Card Service are tailored for Google Workspace add-ons, this approach lets you build structured UIs optimized for Workspace apps.

We will start with the basics, **custom menus**, as they are an excellent entry point for adding user interactivity to your Apps Script projects.

Structure

In this chapter, we will cover the following topics:

- Custom Menus and Simple User Interfaces
- HTML Service
- Card Service

Custom Menus and Simple User Interfaces

Google Apps Script includes built-in tools for creating user interfaces, making it easy to build simple User Interfaces (UIs) without a lot of effort. If your application does not require complex interactions, you can quickly create menus and basic UI elements to allow users to interact with your script.

In this section, we will explore custom menus and interactive elements such as alerts, prompts, and toasts. Let us start with **custom menus**.

Custom Menus

Custom menus provide an intuitive way to allow users to interact with your script directly within Google Workspace applications such as Sheets or Docs. They are easy to implement and are a great first step toward building user-friendly interfaces.

We briefly touched on creating simple menus when discussing triggers in previous chapters. Let us expand on that by adding new functionality to our task list example: toggling all tasks as done or undone. Consider the following code:

```
function markAllTasks_(asDone = true) {
  const ws = SpreadsheetApp.getActive().getSheetByName('Task
List');
  const lastRow = ws.getLastRow();
  const date = new Date().toISOString();
  const checkboxes = new Array(lastRow - 1).fill(asDone ? ['TRUE']
: ['FALSE']);
  ws.getRange(2, 1, checkboxes.length, checkboxes[0].length).
setValues(
    checkboxes
  );
  const datesRange = ws.getRange(2, 3, lastRow - 1, 1);
  const datesValues = asDone
    ? datesRange.getValues().map(row => ('' === row[0] ? [date] :
row))
    : new Array(lastRow - 1).fill(['']);

  datesRange.setValues(datesValues);
}

function markAllAsDone() {
  markAllTasks_(true);
}
```

```
function markAllAsUndone() {
  markAllTasks_(false);
}
```

Here is what is happening:

- The **markAllTasks_()** function takes a boolean parameter **asDone**.
- It checks or unchecks all checkboxes and updates the corresponding completion dates based on the parameter.
- The leading underscore _ in the function name indicates it is private. In Apps Script, private functions are not listed in the IDE's execution menu and can only be called by other functions.
- Two additional public functions, **markAllAsDone()** and **markAllAsUndone()**, call the private function with the appropriate parameters.

Note that **markAllTasks_** does not appear in the list of functions in the IDE:

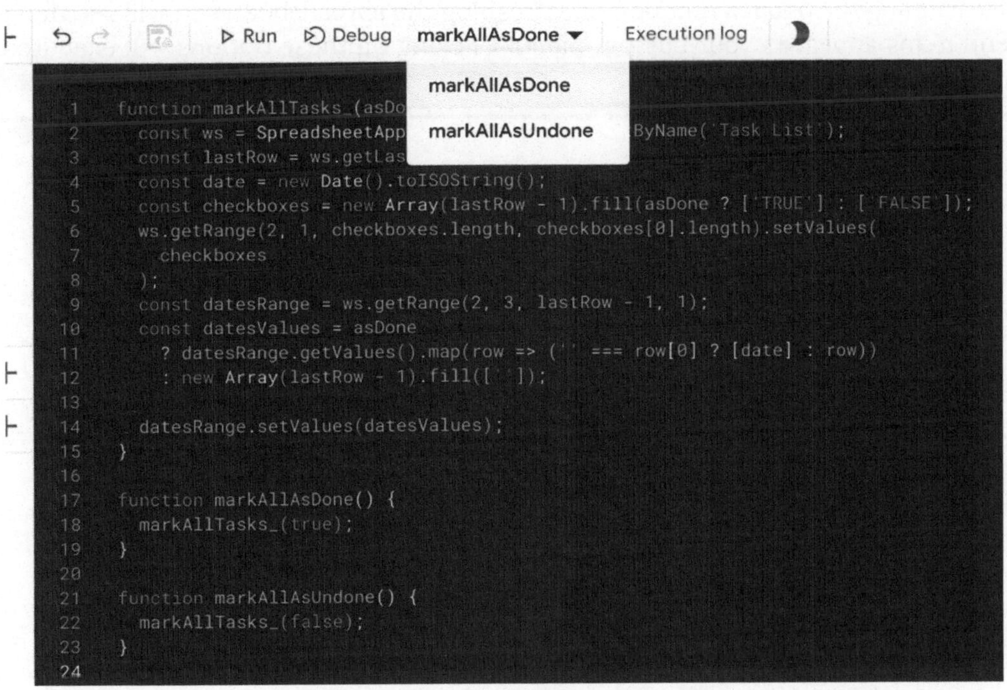

Figure 11.1: *Private functions can only be executed by other functions*

Adding Menu Items

To allow users to execute these functions from the UI, we add them to a custom menu created using the **onOpen** trigger:

```
function onOpen() { // onOpen is a reserved function name for
declaring a trigger
  Logger.log('Someone opened our Google Sheet');

  SpreadsheetApp.getUi()
    .createMenu('My Apps Script Menu')
    .addItem('Randomize colors', 'randomizeCellColors')
    .addItem('Mark all tasks as done', 'markAllAsDone')
    .addItem('Mark all tasks as undone', 'markAllAsUndone')
    .addToUi();
}
```

After running the **onOpen** function or refreshing the spreadsheet, you will see the new menu items appear in your custom menu. Clicking on these options will execute the corresponding functions.

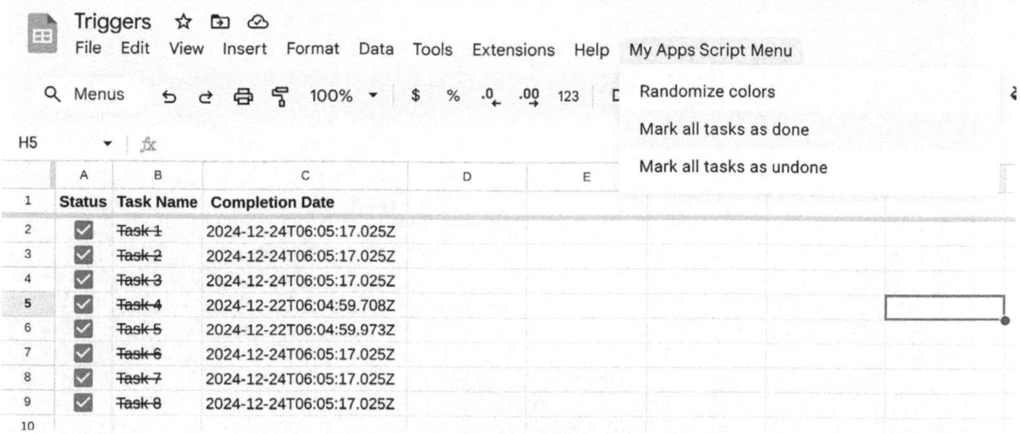

Figure 11.2: *Custom menu built with Apps Script*

Improving Menu Organization

If your menu contains unrelated items, the user experience can become confusing. To improve organization:

1. Add a **separator** to group similar items visually:

```
function onOpen() { // onOpen is a reserved word for declaring a
trigger
  Logger.log('Someone opened our Google Sheet');
```

```
  SpreadsheetApp.getUi()
    .createMenu('My Apps Script Menu')
    .addItem('Randomize colors', 'randomizeCellColors')
+     .addSeparator()
    .addItem('Mark all tasks as done', 'markAllAsDone')
    .addItem('Mark all tasks as undone', 'markAllAsUndone')
    .addToUi();
}
```

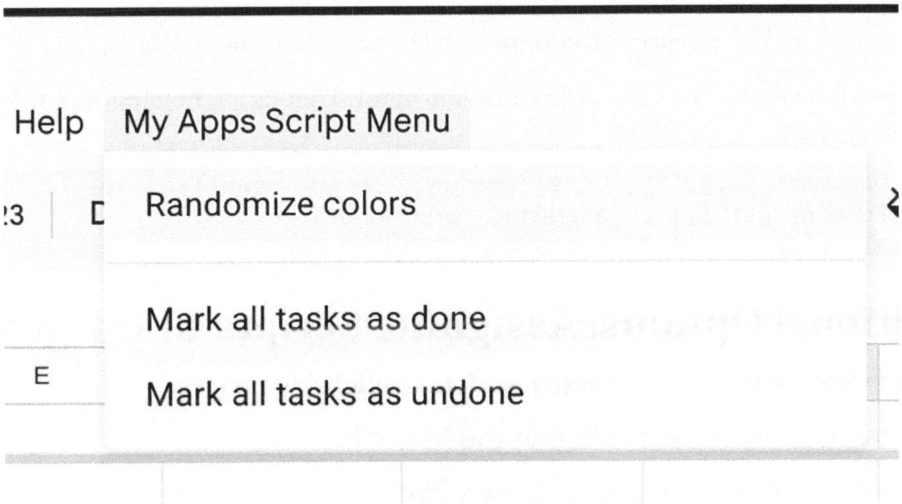

Figure 11.3: *Add-on installation confirmation message*

2. Use **submenus** to nest related commands:

```
function onOpen() {
  Logger.log('Someone opened our Google Sheet');

  SpreadsheetApp.getUi()
    .createMenu('My Apps Script Menu')
    .addSubMenu(
      SpreadsheetApp.getUi()
        .createMenu('Task List')
        .addItem('Mark all tasks as done', 'markAllAsDone')
        .addItem('Mark all tasks as undone', 'markAllAsUndone')
    )
    .addSubMenu(
      SpreadsheetApp.getUi()
        .createMenu('Other')
        .addItem('Randomize colors', 'randomizeCellColors')
    )
    .addToUi();
}
```

The **addSubMenu()** method nests menus into logical groupings for better organization.

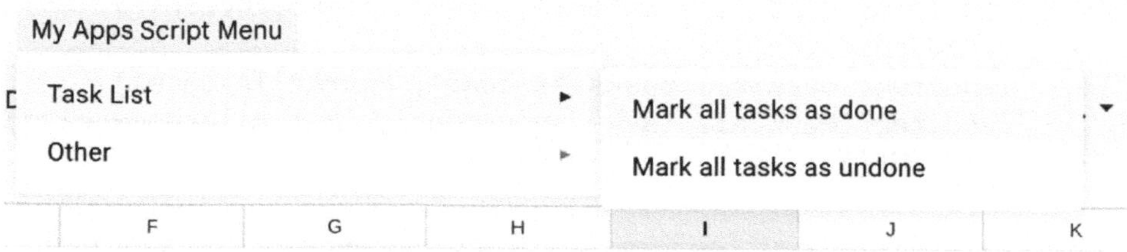

Figure 11.4: *A custom menu with submenus*

This approach also works in Google Docs, Forms and Slides as they follow a practically identical syntax:

```
DocumentApp.getUi().createMenu('Document menu');
FormApp.getUi().createMenu('Form menu');
SlidesApp.getUi().createMenu('Slides menu');
```

Additional Options: Assigning Scripts to Images

In Google Sheets, you can also assign scripts to **clickable images**:

1. Insert an image over cells (not within a cell).
2. Use the image's menu to assign a script.

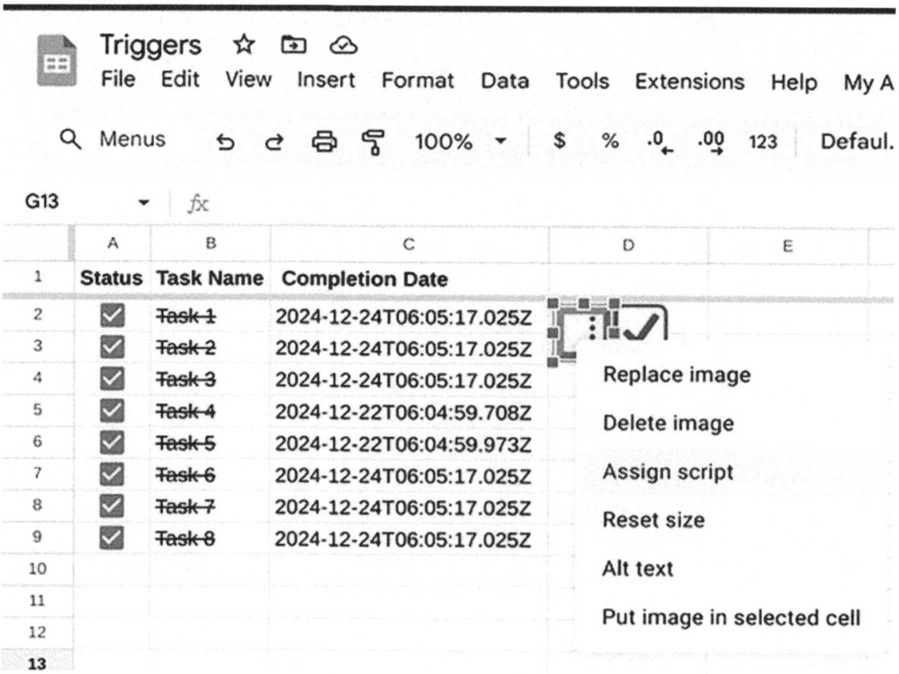

Figure 11.5: *Assigning scripts to images*

This method provides a visual alternative to menus, but it can be less robust for complex interfaces. Users might accidentally unassign scripts or delete the images. Make choices that make sense in your specific context.

If you want to go beyond menus and images, you can enhance user engagement with additional interactive elements such as alerts, prompts, and toasts. Let us explore those next.

Alerts, Prompts, and Toasts

Alerts, prompts, and toasts are effective tools for adding interactivity to Google Apps Script. They allow scripts to give feedback to users and collect their input in a structured way. Let us explore how to use these elements, and apply them to our task list example.

Alerts and Toasts

First, we will add confirmation messages to our task list workflow. Start by including the following functions in your code base:

```
function alert(title, message) {
  const ui = SpreadsheetApp.getUi();
  const buttonSet =  ui.ButtonSet.YES_NO_CANCEL;
  const userResponse = ui.alert(title, message, buttonSet);
  return userResponse;
}

function toast(title, message) {
  SpreadsheetApp.getActive().toast(message, title);
}
```

The **alert** function uses the built-in **alert()** method of the **UI** class. This method requires three arguments: a title, a message, and a button set. It returns the user's response, representing the button they clicked.

The **toast** function, on the other hand, works differently. Toasts display notifications in the bottom-right corner of the spreadsheet. Unlike **alert**, **toast** is a method of the **Spreadsheet** class rather than the **UI** object.

Using Alerts and Toasts in the onEdit Trigger

Let us integrate these functions into the previously built **onEdit** trigger to confirm task changes and notify users of the outcome:

```
function onEdit(e) {
-  const { range, value } = e;
+  const { range, value, oldValue } = e;
```

```
const ws = range.getSheet();
const sheetName = ws.getName();
if ('Task List' !== sheetName || 1 !== range.columnStart) return;
const newValue = 'TRUE' === value ? new Date().toISOString() :
'';
+  const userResponse = alert('Are you sure?', `You are about to
update a task`);
+  const ui = SpreadsheetApp.getUi();
+  if (ui.Button.YES === userResponse) {
+   toast('Task List', 'The task has been updated');
-   ws.getRange(range.rowStart, 3).setValue(newValue);
+   return ws.getRange(range.rowStart, 3).setValue(newValue);
+  }
+  toast('Task List', 'The task has been reverted');
-  ws.getRange(range.rowStart, 1).setValue(oldValue);
+  return ws.getRange(range.rowStart, 1).setValue(oldValue);
}
```

Now, when a task is checked or unchecked, the following workflow occurs:

1. An alert asks for confirmation:

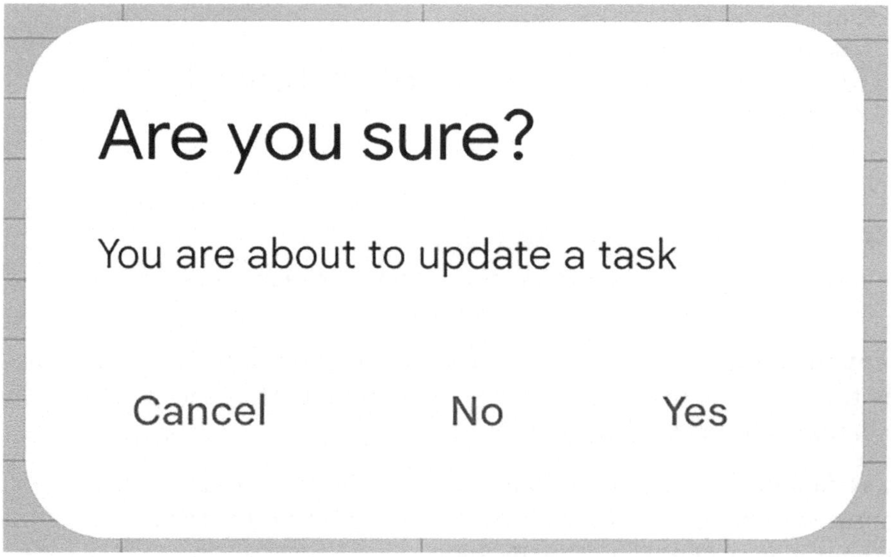

Figure 11.6: *An Apps Script alert*

2. If the user clicks **Yes**, the task is updated, and a toast confirms the change.

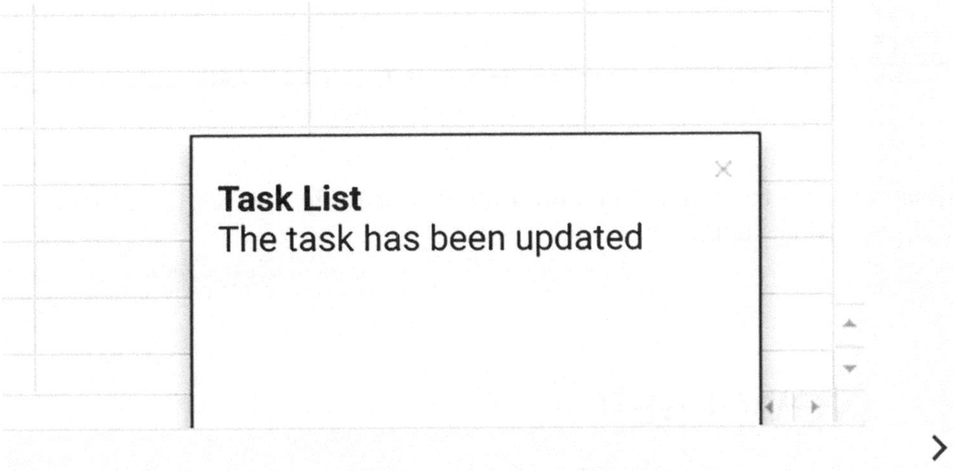

Figure 11.7: *An Apps Script Toast*

3. If the user declines, the change is reverted, and another toast notifies the user.

Prompts

Prompts are slightly more interactive because they allow users to input text. Consider the following function that wraps the **prompt()** method:

```
function prompt(title, message) {
  const ui = SpreadsheetApp.getUi();
  const buttonSet =  ui.ButtonSet.YES_NO_CANCEL;
  const userResponse = ui.prompt(title, message, buttonSet);
  if (userResponse.getSelectedButton() === ui.Button.YES)
    return userResponse.getResponseText();
  return null;
}
```

The **prompt** function provides a dialog where users can input data. It returns the user's text response if they click **Yes**; otherwise, it returns **null**. This is achieved by working with the **PromptResponse** object, which contains both the selected button and the entered text.

Using Prompts to Add a Task

Here is how you can use the **prompt** function to create a task-adding feature:

```
function addTask() {
  const ws = SpreadsheetApp.getActive().getSheetByName('Task
List');
  const lastRow = ws.getLastRow();
  const userResponse = prompt('New task', 'Enter the task
```

```
name:');
    if (null === userResponse) return;
    ws.appendRow(['', userResponse, '']);
    ws.getRange(lastRow + 1, 1).insertCheckboxes();
}
```

Assign this function to an image, menu item, or button in an HTML interface. When triggered, the prompt appears:

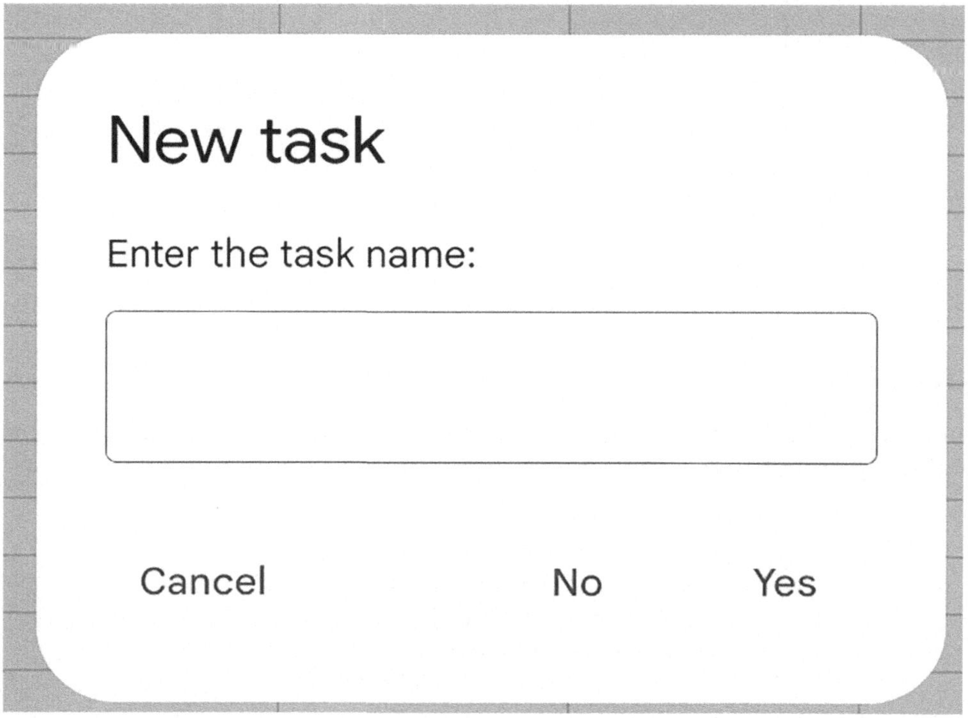

Figure 11.8: *An Apps Script prompt*

If the user enters a task name and clicks **Yes**, the task is added to the bottom of the task list, complete with a checkbox.

Menus, alerts, prompts, and toasts are excellent for lightweight interactions. But if you need a fully functional user interface, the HTML Service provides the tools to create custom GUIs using HTML, CSS, and JavaScript. Let us dive into how to build advanced UIs with the HTML Service.

HTML Service

The HTML Service in Google Apps Script provides the tools to create fully customized graphical user interfaces (GUIs) using HTML, CSS, and JavaScript. With this service, you can design interfaces as simple or as complex as needed, complete with buttons, cards, drop-down menus, carousels, or any other HTML components. By integrating CSS and JavaScript frameworks, you can achieve precise control over the UI and state management.

Let us create an HTML interface for our task list. We will start by building a **sidebar**.

Sidebars

Sidebars appear on the right side of your editor. They have a fixed width of 300 pixels and stretch to occupy the maximum vertical space available in the editor. Importantly, sidebars must be explicitly opened by the user; they cannot open automatically. To enable the sidebar in your script, follow these steps:

Step 1: Add a New HTML File

a. Go to the Apps Script IDE and create a new file, selecting "`HTML`" as the file type.

b. Add the following HTML code:

```
<!DOCTYPE html>
<html lang="en">
<head>
  <meta charset="UTF-8">
  <meta name="viewport" content="width=device-width, initial
-scale=1.0">
  <title>Apps Script Task List</title>
  <style>
    body {
      margin: 0;
      font-family: Arial, sans-serif;
      background-color: #f4f4f9;
      display: flex;
      justify-content: center;
      align-items: flex-start; /* Aligns the sidebar vertically to
the top */
      padding: 20px; /* Adds a small margin around the content */
    }

    .sidebar {
      width: 300px;
      background-color: #ffffff;
      box-shadow: 0 4px 6px rgba(0, 0, 0, 0.1);
      border-radius: 8px;
      padding: 20px;
      box-sizing: border-box;
    }
```

```
      .sidebar h1 {
        font-size: 1.5rem;
        margin: 0;
        color: #333333;
        text-align: center;
        margin-bottom: 20px;
      }

      .button-container {
        display: flex;
        flex-direction: column;
        gap: 10px;
      }

      button {
        padding: 10px 20px;
        font-size: 1rem;
        font-weight: bold;
        border: none;
        border-radius: 5px;
        cursor: pointer;
        transition: background-color 0.3s ease;
      }

      button.mark-done {
        background-color: #28a745;
        color: white;
      }

      button.mark-done:hover {
        background-color: #218838;
      }

      button.mark-undone {
        background-color: #ffc107;
        color: white;
      }

      button.mark-undone:hover {
        background-color: #e0a800;
      }
    </style>
  </head>
  <body>
```

```
  <div class="sidebar">
    <h1>Apps Script Task List</h1>
    <div class="button-container">
      <button class="mark-done" onclick="markAllAsDone()">Mark
all as done</button>
      <button class="mark-undone" onclick="markAllAs
Undone()">Mark all as undone</button>
    </div>
  </div>

  <script>
    function markAllAsDone() {
      console.log('Mark all as done clicked');
    }

    function markAllAsUndone() {
      console.log('Mark all as undone clicked');
    }
  </script>
</body>
</html>
```

Step 2: Create a Function to Open the Sidebar

Next, create a function in your script to open the sidebar:

```
function openSidebar() {
  SpreadsheetApp.getUi()
    .showSidebar(
      HtmlService.createHtmlOutputFromFile('sidebar')
    );
}
```

In this function:

a. The **SpreadsheetApp.getUi()** method is used to get the UI of the active spreadsheet.

b. The **showSidebar()** method displays the sidebar.

c. You use **HtmlService.createHtmlOutputFromFile('sidebar')** to load the HTML code from the file named **sidebar**. Alternatively, you could use **HtmlService.createHtmlOutput(htmlString)** to directly pass an HTML string, but separating HTML files from scripts is recommended for better maintainability.

Step 3: Add the Function to the Menu

Modify the **onOpen** function to add the new sidebar option to the custom menu:

```
function onOpen() {
  Logger.log('Someone opened our Google Sheet');

  SpreadsheetApp.getUi()
    .createMenu('My Apps Script Menu')
    .addSubMenu(
      SpreadsheetApp.getUi()
        .createMenu('Task List')
        .addItem('Mark all tasks as done', 'markAllAsDone')
        .addItem('Mark all tasks as undone', 'markAllAsUndone')
    )
+     .addSubMenu(
+       SpreadsheetApp.getUi()
+         .createMenu('HTML Service')
+         .addItem('Open sidebar', 'openSidebar')
+     )
    .addSubMenu(
      SpreadsheetApp.getUi()
        .createMenu('Other')
        .addItem('Randomize colors', 'randomizeCellColors')
    )

    .addToUi();
}
```

After this change, you will see a new menu item under the "**HTML Service**" submenu: **Open sidebar**.

Step 4: Open the Sidebar

Clicking the new menu option will open the sidebar. The interface will look like this:

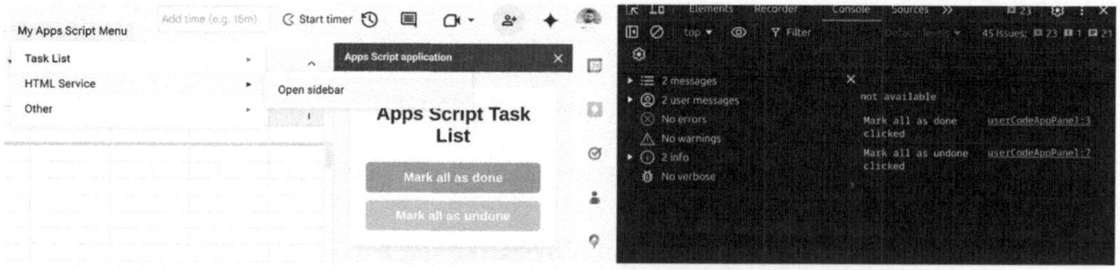

Figure 11.9: *Sidebar and the developer console*

The sidebar contains two buttons: **Mark all as done** and **Mark all as undone**. Clicking these buttons currently does not perform any action beyond logging a message to the developer console.

In the next section, we will attach meaningful functionality to these buttons, enabling them to interact with the spreadsheet data. This will complete the process of building a working sidebar for managing tasks.

Calling Apps Script Functions from HTML Service

To make your buttons functional, you need to call Apps Script functions from the HTML Service. Here is how to set up the communication between the client-side JavaScript in your HTML file and your Apps Script functions.

Step 1: Add Client-Side JavaScript

Include the following JavaScript code in your HTML file:

```
<script>
  function markAllAsDone() {
    const button = document.querySelector('.mark-done');
    button.disabled = true;
    google.script.run
      .withSuccessHandler(() => {
        button.disabled = false;
      })
      .withFailureHandler((error) => {
        button.disabled = false;
        alert(`Error: ${error}`);
      })
      .markAllAsDone();
  }

  function markAllAsUndone() {
    const button = document.querySelector('.mark-undone');
    button.disabled = true;
    google.script.run
      .withSuccessHandler(() => {
        button.disabled = false;
      })
      .withFailureHandler((error) => {
        button.disabled = false;
        alert(`Error: ${error}`);
      })
      .markAllAsUndone();
  }
</script>
```

Step 2: Add CSS for Disabled Buttons

Enhance your CSS to visually indicate when a button is disabled:

```
button:disabled {
  background-color: #cccccc;
  color: #666666;
  cursor: not-allowed;
}
```

How it works:

`google.script.run` Object:

a. The HTML Service provides the built-in **`google.script.run`** object, which allows you to call all non-private Apps Script functions bound to the container document.

b. For example, calling **`google.script.run.markAllAsDone()`** executes the **`markAllAsDone`** function in your Apps Script project.

Callback Functions:

- **`withSuccessHandler`**: Executes the specified callback when the function call succeeds.
- **`withFailureHandler`**: Executes the specified callback if the function call fails.

Disabling and Re-Enabling Buttons: Buttons are disabled to prevent multiple clicks while the Apps Script function is processing. After the call completes, the buttons are re-enabled in both success and failure handlers.

Error Handling: If the Apps Script function fails, the failure handler displays an error message to the user using **`alert`**.

Now, both buttons in your sidebar will call their respective Apps Script functions when clicked and handle state transitions gracefully.

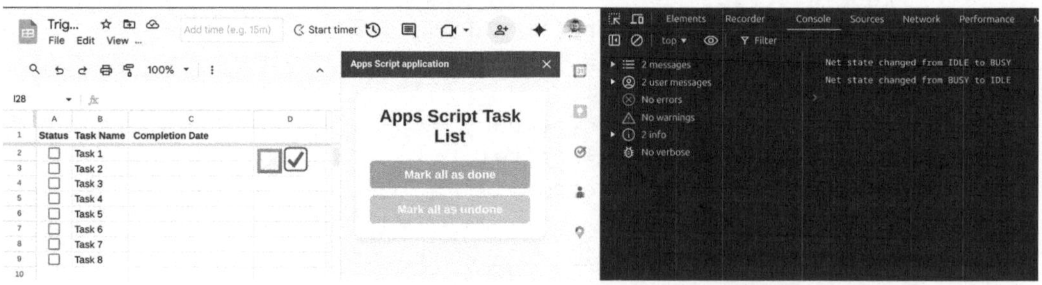

Figure 11.10: *A sidebar built with HTML Service*

Developer Console Messages

You will notice the following messages in the developer console during function execution:

- **"Net state changed from IDLE to BUSY"**: Indicates the start of the Apps Script function call.
- **"Net state changed from BUSY to IDLE"**: Indicates the end of the call.

These messages are helpful for debugging and tracking the state of your application.

Passing Arguments and Receiving Return Values

You can pass arguments to Apps Script functions using **`google.script.run`** and retrieve the return values in the success handler. For more details, refer to the Apps Script HTML Service communication documentation at https://developers.google.com/apps-script/guides/html/communication.

With a simple interface like this, managing code in a single file is straightforward. However, as your project grows, you may want to break the HTML into multiple files or dynamically generate portions of it with Apps Script. This is where **HTML templates** come in. Let us explore how they can simplify your workflow.

HTML Templates

Apps Script supports built-in templating functionality, similar to many server-side scripting languages. This feature allows you to separate concerns by breaking your interface into multiple files for HTML, CSS, and JavaScript. It also enables dynamic content rendering.

Breaking Down the Sidebar

We will break the sidebar into three separate files:

1. **`style.html`**: Contains CSS in a **`<style>`** tag.

```
<style>
    body {
      margin: 0;
      font-family: Arial, sans-serif;
      background-color: #f4f4f9;
      display: flex;
      justify-content: center;
      align-items: flex-start;
      /* Aligns the sidebar vertically to the top */
      padding: 20px;
      /* Adds a small margin around the content */
```

```
}

.sidebar {
  width: 300px;
  background-color: #ffffff;
  box-shadow: 0 4px 6px rgba(0, 0, 0, 0.1);
  border-radius: 8px;
  padding: 20px;
  box-sizing: border-box;
}

.sidebar h1 {
  font-size: 1.5rem;
  margin: 0;
  color: #333333;
  text-align: center;
  margin-bottom: 20px;
}

.button-container {
  display: flex;
  flex-direction: column;
  gap: 10px;
}

button {
  padding: 10px 20px;
  font-size: 1rem;
  font-weight: bold;
  border: none;
  border-radius: 5px;
  cursor: pointer;
  transition: background-color 0.3s ease;
}

button.mark-done {
  background-color: #28a745;
  color: white;
}

button.mark-done:hover {
  background-color: #218838;
}

button.mark-undone {
  background-color: #ffc107;
  color: white;
```

```
    }

    button.mark-undone:hover {
      background-color: #e0a800;
    }

    button:disabled {
      background-color: #cccccc;
      color: #666666;
      cursor: not-allowed;
    }
  </style>
```

2. **`javascript.html`**: Contains JavaScript in a **`<script>`** tag.

```
<script>
  function markAllAsDone() {
    const button = document.querySelector('.mark-done');
    button.disabled = true;
    google.script.run
      .withSuccessHandler(() => {
        button.disabled = false;
      })
      .withFailureHandler((error) => {
        button.disabled = false;
        alert(`Error: ${error}`);
      })
      .markAllAsDone();
  }

  function markAllAsUndone() {
    const button = document.querySelector('.mark-undone');
    button.disabled = true;
    google.script.run
      .withSuccessHandler(() => {
        button.disabled = false;
      })
      .withFailureHandler((error) => {
        button.disabled = false;
        alert(`Error: ${error}`);
      })
      .markAllAsUndone();
  }
</script>
```

3. **sidebar.html**: The main HTML file, referencing the CSS and JavaScript files.

```
<!DOCTYPE html>
<html lang="en">

<head>
  <meta charset="UTF-8">
  <meta name="viewport" content="width=device-width, initial-
scale=1.0">
  <title>Apps Script Task List</title>
  <?!= include('style') ?>
</head>

<body>
  <div class="sidebar">
    <h1>Apps Script Task List</h1>
    <div class="button-container">
      <button class="mark-done" onclick="markAllAsDone()">Mark
all as done</button>
      <button class="mark-undone"
onclick="markAllAsUndone()">Mark all as undone</button>
    </div>
  </div>

<?!= include('javascript') ?>

</body>

</html>
```

How Templates Work

Templates allow Apps Script code to be embedded directly into HTML files using special tags:

a. **<? ... ?>**: Executes JavaScript code

b. **<?= ... ?>**: Prints the result of the expression, escaping HTML characters to prevent XSS attacks.

c. **<?!= ... ?>**: Prints the result of the expression without escaping HTML characters. Use this only when embedding safe HTML or content you fully control.

The **sidebar.html** file includes these template tags to reference **style.html** and **javascript.html**:

```
<?!= include('style') ?>
<?!= include('javascript') ?>
```

Apps Script Code for Templates

To render the templates, Apps Script provides **createTemplateFromFile**. The **openSidebar** function now uses this method:

```
function openSidebar() {
  SpreadsheetApp.getUi()
    .showSidebar(
      HtmlService.createTemplateFromFile('sidebar')
        .evaluate()
    );
}

function include(filename) {
  return HtmlService.createHtmlOutputFromFile(filename).get
Content();
}
```

Here is what happens:

a. **HtmlService.createTemplateFromFile('sidebar')** creates a template object from the **sidebar.html** file.

b. The **include** function fetches the source code of the referenced files, which the **<?!= include('filename') ?>** tags then embed into the output.

c. Calling **evaluate()** on the template renders the HTML with the embedded code.

Dynamic Content with Templates

Templates allow loops, conditionals, and other logic within HTML. For instance, let us display a list of incomplete tasks dynamically in the sidebar.

1. **Modify sidebar.html by adding the following code**:

```
<div class="task-list-container">
  <ul class="task-list">
    <? const tasks = getUndoneTasks(); ?>
    <? for(let i = 0; i < tasks.length; i++) { ?>
    <li class="task-item">
      <?= tasks[i] ?>
    </li>
    <? } ?>
  </ul>
</div>
```

   a. The **getUndoneTasks()** function is called to retrieve tasks.

   b. A **for** loop iterates through the tasks, generating **<li>** elements for each.

2. **Add getUndoneTasks() function**:

```
function getUndoneTasks() {
  const ws = SpreadsheetApp.getActive().getSheetByName('Task
List');
  const lastRow = ws.getLastRow();
  const tasks = ws.getRange(2, 1, lastRow - 1, 3)
    .getValues()
    .filter(row => !row[0])
    .map(row => row[1]);
  return tasks;
}
```

This function retrieves task data from the spreadsheet, filtering for tasks that are not marked as done.

3. **Add CSS for the task list to style.html**.

```
.task-list-container {
  margin-top: 20px;
  padding: 10px;
  background-color: #f9f9f9;
  border: 1px solid #ddd;
  border-radius: 8px;
}

.task-list {
  list-style: none;
  padding: 0;
  margin: 0;
}

.task-item {
  padding: 8px;
  margin-bottom: 6px;
  background-color: #ffffff;
  border: 1px solid #ddd;
  border-radius: 5px;
  color: #333333;
  font-size: 1rem;
}

.task-item:last-child {
  margin-bottom: 0;
```

```
    }

    .task-item:hover {
      background-color: #f0f0f0;
      cursor: pointer;
    }
```

Output

When you open the sidebar, it will display a list of incomplete tasks styled using the provided CSS:

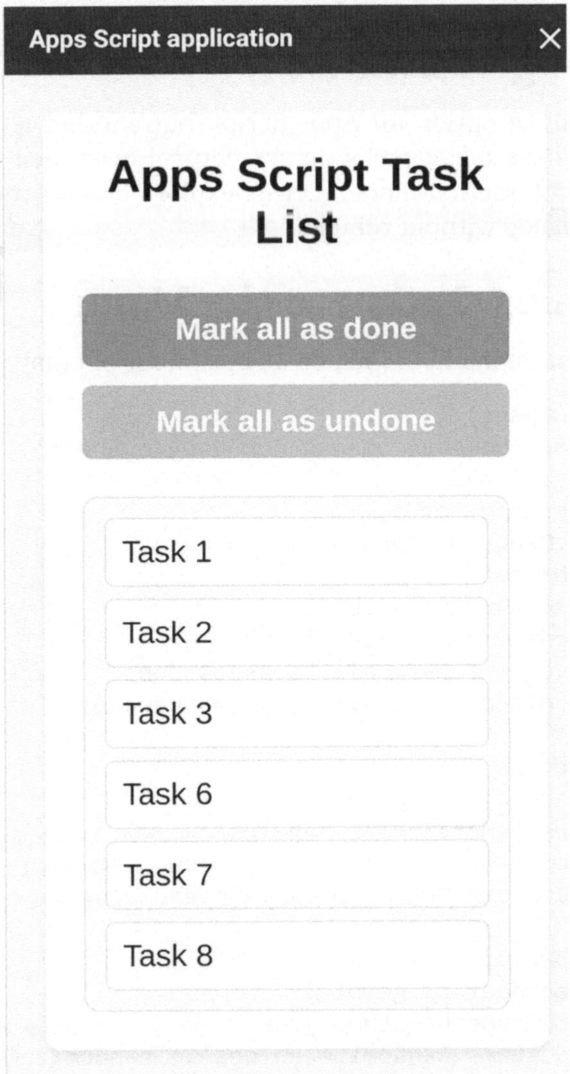

Figure 11.11: *A sidebar built with Apps Script templates*

Benefits of Templates:

- **Separation of Concerns**: By splitting the interface into separate files, the HTML, CSS, and JavaScript are easier to manage.
- **Dynamic Content**: Templates allow you to render dynamic data within the interface.
- **Reusability**: Components such as the **`include`** function simplify code reuse across multiple templates.

HTML Service is not limited to sidebars, however. We can also open dialog windows. Let us adapt our task list to open in one.

Modal Dialog Windows

Sidebars are a useful UI option for Apps Script, but another alternative is modal or modeless dialogs. These dialogs allow more control over their dimensions and can provide a different interaction model. Let us explore how to repurpose the existing HTML for a modal dialog without rebuilding it.

Adding a Dialog Option to the Menu

First, update the custom menu to include an option for opening the modal dialog:

```
function onOpen() {
  Logger.log('Someone opened our Google Sheet');

  SpreadsheetApp.getUi()
    .createMenu('My Apps Script Menu')
    .addSubMenu(
      SpreadsheetApp.getUi()
        .createMenu('Task List')
        .addItem('Mark all tasks as done', 'markAllAsDone')
        .addItem('Mark all tasks as undone', 'markAllAsUndone')
    )
    .addSubMenu(
      SpreadsheetApp.getUi()
        .createMenu('HTML Service')
        .addItem('Open sidebar', 'openSidebar')
+       .addItem('Open dialog', 'openDialog')
    )
    .addSubMenu(
      SpreadsheetApp.getUi()
        .createMenu('Other')
        .addItem('Randomize colors', 'randomizeCellColors')
```

```
    )

    .addToUi();
}
```

Creating the `openDialog` Function

Add the following function to your script file to handle opening the dialog:

```
function openDialog() {
  SpreadsheetApp.getUi()
    .showModalDialog(
      HtmlService.createTemplateFromFile('sidebar')
        .evaluate()
        .setWidth(350)
        .setHeight(600),
        'My Apps Script Task List'
    );
}
```

Key Differences from `openSidebar`:

- **`showModalDialog`**: Instead of **`showSidebar`**, we call **`showModalDialog`** to open a dialog.
- **Custom Dimensions:** Unlike sidebars, dialogs can have any dimensions. We set the size with **`.setWidth(350)`** and **`.setHeight(600)`**.
- **Title:** A dialog requires a title, which we specify as the second parameter in **`showModalDialog`**.

Client-Side Dimension Control

You can also adjust the dialog dimensions programmatically from the client side using the **`google.script.host`** object. For example:

- **Change Width**: `google.script.host.setWidth(width)`
- **Change Height**: `google.script.host.setHeight(height)`
- **Close Dialog**: `google.script.host.closeDialog()`

These methods allow dynamic control over the dialog's behavior and appearance.

Modal versus Modeless Dialogs

Apps Script provides two types of dialogs:

- **Modal Dialog** (**`showModalDialog`**): Prevents interaction with the spreadsheet while open.

- **Modeless Dialog** (`showModelessDialog`): Allows users to continue interacting with the spreadsheet while the dialog is open.

Choose the dialog type based on your app's requirements.

Using CSS and JavaScript Frameworks

So far, we have used plain CSS and JavaScript, but integrating frameworks such as **Bootstrap** or **Alpine.js** is straightforward. You can include their CDN links directly in your HTML file. For example:

- **Bootstrap**: Add the `<link>` and `<script>` tags from the Bootstrap CDN.
- **Alpine.js**: Include the script tag for Alpine.js.

However, frameworks such as **Tailwind CSS** or **React**, which require a build step, involve more complexity. While possible, these setups require additional configuration and will be covered in Volume 2 of this book.

Next, we will explore the **Card Service**, which is particularly useful for creating sidebars and interfaces for Google Workspace add-ons, such as Gmail and Drive.

Card Service

The Card Service is another powerful option for building UIs in Google Apps Script. Similar to the HTML Service, it lets you create sidebars and extend Google Workspace, but instead of relying on HTML and CSS, the Card Service provides a built-in library of pre-designed components. This makes it easier to create functional interfaces without requiring advanced web development skills.

Unlike the HTML Service, the Card Service:

- Is proprietary to Apps Script and cannot be used outside of its ecosystem.
- Works with both **editor add-ons** (such as Google Sheets) and **Workspace add-ons** (such as Gmail and Drive).

In this example, we will build a Gmail add-on that translates the currently open email to Hindi. The translation will display in the sidebar whenever the add-on is launched and a message is open.

Publishing Considerations

The Card Service requires more setup compared to the HTML Service, as it involves publishing your script as an add-on. This includes:

1. Setting up a Google Cloud Project
2. Configuring the OAuth consent screen

3. Adding appropriate scopes to the manifest
4. Configuring the Google Workspace Marketplace SDK

Let us start by creating a Google Cloud Project.

Connecting to Google Cloud

Step 1: Create a Google Cloud Project

a. Navigate to Google Cloud Project Creation at https://console.cloud.google.com/projectcreate.

b. Fill in the required details, including selecting a billing project (note: for testing purposes, you will stay within the free tier).

Step 2: Configure the OAuth Consent Screen

a. Open the hamburger menu in Google Cloud Console, go to **`APIs & Services`**, and select the **`OAuth consent screen`**.

b. Set the app type to **`Internal`** (since we are not publishing this add-on to external users).

c. Provide an **`App name`** and **`User support email`**.

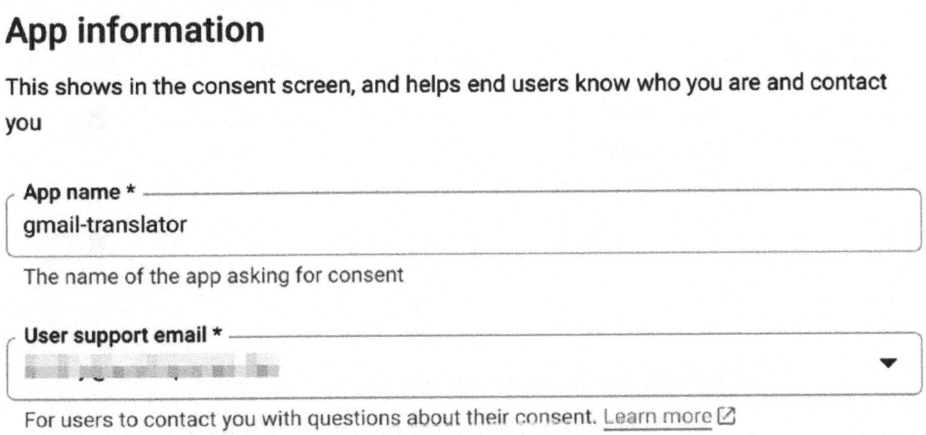

Figure 11.12: *Setting up the OAuth consent screen*

Step 3: Add the following scopes to the project

a. `https://www.googleapis.com/auth/gmail.addons.current.message.readonly`

b. `https://www.googleapis.com/auth/gmail.addons.execute`

These scopes allow the add-on to:

- Access the content of the currently open email.
- Execute the add-on's functions.

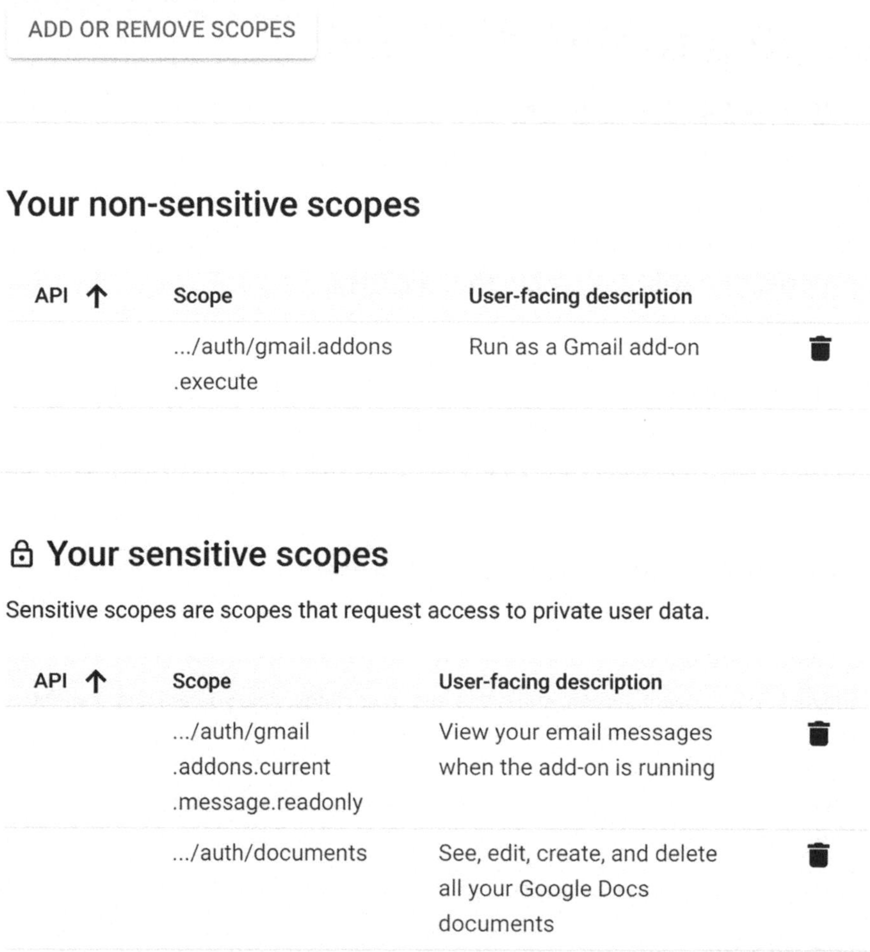

Figure 11.13: *Adding scopes to the consent screen*

Reference for scopes: https://developers.google.com/identity/protocols/oauth2/scopes

The Apps Script Project and Manifest

Every Apps Script project contains a hidden **`appsscript.json`** file known as the **manifest**. This file controls the behavior and configuration of your script.

Step 1: Make the Manifest Visible

a. Click the gear icon in the Apps Script editor.

b. Check **`Show "appsscript.json" manifest file in editor`**.

c. Update the Google Cloud Platform (GCP) project number (found in your Google Cloud dashboard).

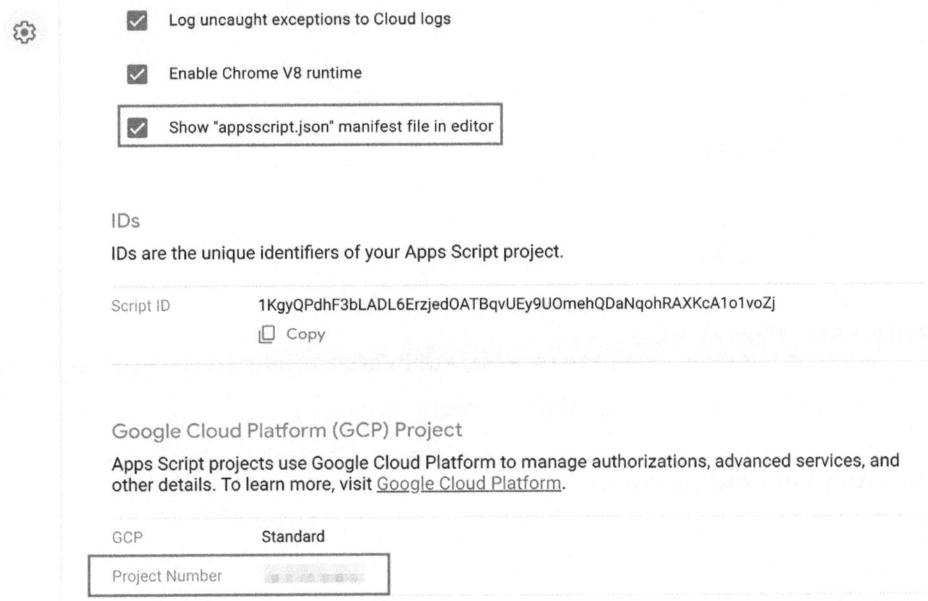

Figure 11.14: *Modifying Apps Script settings to show the manifest and link to the GCP project*

After enabling the manifest, it will appear in the file list:

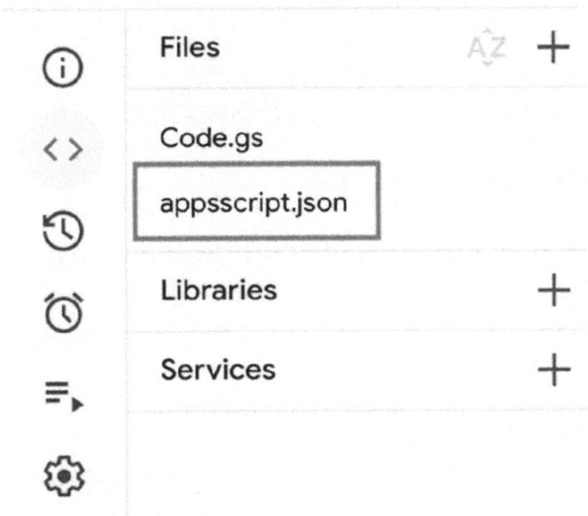

Figure 11.15: *Locating the appsscript.json file (the manifest) in the online IDE*

Step 2: Update the Manifest

The default manifest contains minimal configuration:

```
{
  "timeZone": "Europe/Paris",
  "dependencies": {},
  "exceptionLogging": "STACKDRIVER",
  "runtimeVersion": "V8"
}
```

For the Gmail add-on, update the manifest as follows:

a. **Add OAuth Scopes**:

```
{
// ...
  "oauthScopes": [
    "https://www.googleapis.com/auth/gmail.addons.current.mes-
sage.readonly",
    "https://www.googleapis.com/auth/gmail.addons.execute"
  ]
}
```

b. **Add Add-On Configuration**:

```
{
// ...
  "addOns": {
    "common": {
      "name": "Email Translator",
      "logoUrl": "https://<your logo url here>"
    },
    "gmail": {
      "homepageTrigger": {
        "runFunction": "onGmailHomepage"
      },
      "contextualTriggers": [
        {
          "unconditional": {},
          "onTriggerFunction": "onGmailMessageOpen"
        }
      ]
    }
  }
}
```

addOns object: Contains settings specific to the add-on.

- **common**: Includes global app information, such as the name and logo URL.
- **gmail**: Configures the add-on's behavior in Gmail.
  - **homepageTrigger**: Specifies the function to run when the add-on is opened without context.
  - **contextualTriggers**: Specifies the function to run when an email is opened.
- Both the **onGmailHomepage** and **onGmailMessageOpen** functions must return instances of the **Card** class from the Card Service. These cards define the layout and functionality of the add-on's UI. Let us explore how to build these cards next.

Explanation of Cards Architecture

The Card Service uses a modular approach to build UIs with pre-defined components. These components, known as cards, group related content into visually consistent layouts. Cards are reusable, and their widgets (such as buttons, text fields, or paragraphs) provide interactivity.

Card Structure

- **Header**: Every card has a header that can include a title, subtitle, and optional icon.
- **Sections**: Cards are composed of one or more sections, which organize widgets into logical groupings.
- **Widgets**: Pre-built elements such as text paragraphs, buttons, or input fields added to sections. Widgets:
  - Are styled automatically to match the host application.
  - Cannot be manipulated after being added to a section.

Interactivity

Actions, such as **setOnClickAction()** or **setOpenLink()**, can be linked to widgets for user interaction. While we will not dive deeply into actions here, the official documentation provides detailed explanations:

https://developers.google.com/workspace/add-ons/how-tos/building-workspace-addons

Types of Cards

There are two types of cards you need to be aware of:

- **Contextual Cards**: Adapt to the user's context, such as displaying information about the currently open email.
- **Non-Contextual Cards**: Serve as a home page or general interface when no specific context exists.

Card Service can become complex quickly, so let us focus on creating two basic cards: a non-contextual card and a contextual card.

Defining Non-Contextual Card

In the manifest, we configured the homepage trigger as follows:

```
"homepageTrigger": {
  "runFunction": "onGmailHomepage"
},
```

This requires defining the **onGmailHomepage** function to return a **Card** object. The following is an example implementation:

```
function onGmailHomepage() {
  const introText = CardService.newTextParagraph()
    .setText(
      'Select an email to see translation options or use the
toolbar above to start translating.'
    )

  const footerText = CardService.newTextParagraph()
    .setText('Powered by Google Translate API')

  const header = homepageHeader()
  const section = homepageSection(introText, footerText);
  return homepageCard(header, section);
}

function homepageHeader() {
  return CardService.newCardHeader()
    .setTitle('Gmail Translator')
    .setSubtitle('Translate your emails effortlessly');
}

function homepageSection(...widgets) {
  const section = CardService.newCardSection();
  widgets.forEach(widget => section.addWidget(widget));
```

```
  return section;
}

function homepageCard(header, section) {
  return CardService.newCardBuilder()
    .setHeader(header)
    .addSection(section)
    .build()
}
```

Explanation:

a. **Helper Functions**:
   i. **homepageHeader()**: Creates the card's header with a title and subtitle.
   ii. **homepageSection()**: Creates a single section containing widgets.
   iii. **homepageCard()**: Assembles the card by combining the header and section.

b. **Widgets**: Two text paragraphs are added to the card: one with instructions and another with a footer message.

c. **Builder Pattern**: Like other Apps Script services, the Card Service uses a builder pattern. The **build()** method is called to finalize the card creation.

This creates a simple non-contextual card to serve as a landing page for the add-on.

Defining Contextual Card

The contextual card is triggered by the following manifest configuration:

```
"contextualTriggers": [
  {
    "unconditional": {},
    "onTriggerFunction": "onGmailMessageOpen"
  }
]
```

The **onGmailMessageOpen** function must return a **Card** object. Here is an example implementation:

```
function onGmailMessageOpen(e) {
  const { messageId, accessToken } = e.gmail;

  GmailApp.setCurrentMessageAccessToken(accessToken);
  const message = GmailApp.getMessageById(messageId);

  const body = message.getPlainBody();
  const translated = LanguageApp.translate(body, '', 'hi');
```

```
  const para = CardService.newTextParagraph()
    .setText(
      `${translated}`
    )

  const header = messageHeader();
  const section = messageSection(para)
  return messageCard(header, section);
}

function messageHeader() {
  return CardService.newCardHeader()
    .setTitle('Gmail Translator - Message')
    .setSubtitle("Here's the translated message: ");
}

function messageSection(text) {
  return CardService.newCardSection()
    .addWidget(text)
}

function messageCard(header, section) {
  return CardService.newCardBuilder()
    .setHeader(header)
    .addSection(section)
    .build()
}
```

Explanation:

1. **Event Object**: The event object contains the **`message ID`** and **`access token`**. These are extracted from the **`gmail`** property:
    - **`` `messageId`: ``** Identifies the currently open email.
    - **`` `accessToken`: ``** Grants temporary access to the email content.
2. **Token Handling**: The **`GmailApp.setCurrentMessageAccessToken(token)`** method ensures the script has permission to access the email.
3. **Gmail Service**: The message body is retrieved using **`GmailApp.getMessageById(messageId).getPlainBody()`**.
4. **Translation**: The email body is translated to Hindi using **`LanguageApp.translate()`**. The source language is left as an empty string (**`''`**) to enable automatic language detection.
5. **Card Construction**: A similar pattern is used in the non-contextual card:
    - **`messageHeader()`** creates the header.

- **messageSection()** creates the section with a single widget displaying the translated text.
- **messageCard()** assembles the card.

Event Object Structure

The event object passed to **onGmailMessageOpen** looks like this:

```
{
  "hostApp": "gmail",
  "gmail": {
    "messageId": "msg-a:r<numeric_id>",
    "accessToken": "<message_token>",
    "threadId": "thread-f:<numeric_id>"
  },
  "clientPlatform": "web",
  "commonEventObject": {
    "platform": "WEB",
    "hostApp": "GMAIL"
  }
}
```

More details on event objects can be found in the official documentation.

With both the non-contextual and contextual cards defined, the next step is to test the functionality to ensure everything works as expected. This process involves configuring the development environment and verifying that the add-on behaves correctly in Gmail.

Configuring the Add-on for Testing

To test the Gmail add-on you created, follow these steps to deploy it in test mode.

Steps to Deploy the Add-on for Testing:

1. In the Apps Script online IDE, locate the "**Deploy**" button in the top-right corner of the interface.
2. Click the button, and from the dropdown menu, select "**Test deployments**".
3. A modal dialog will appear. Under "**Select type**", choose "**Google Workspace Add-on**".
4. Under "**Deployments**", select "**Test latest code**".
5. At the bottom of the dialog, find the "**Install**" button and click it. This will install the add-on in test mode.

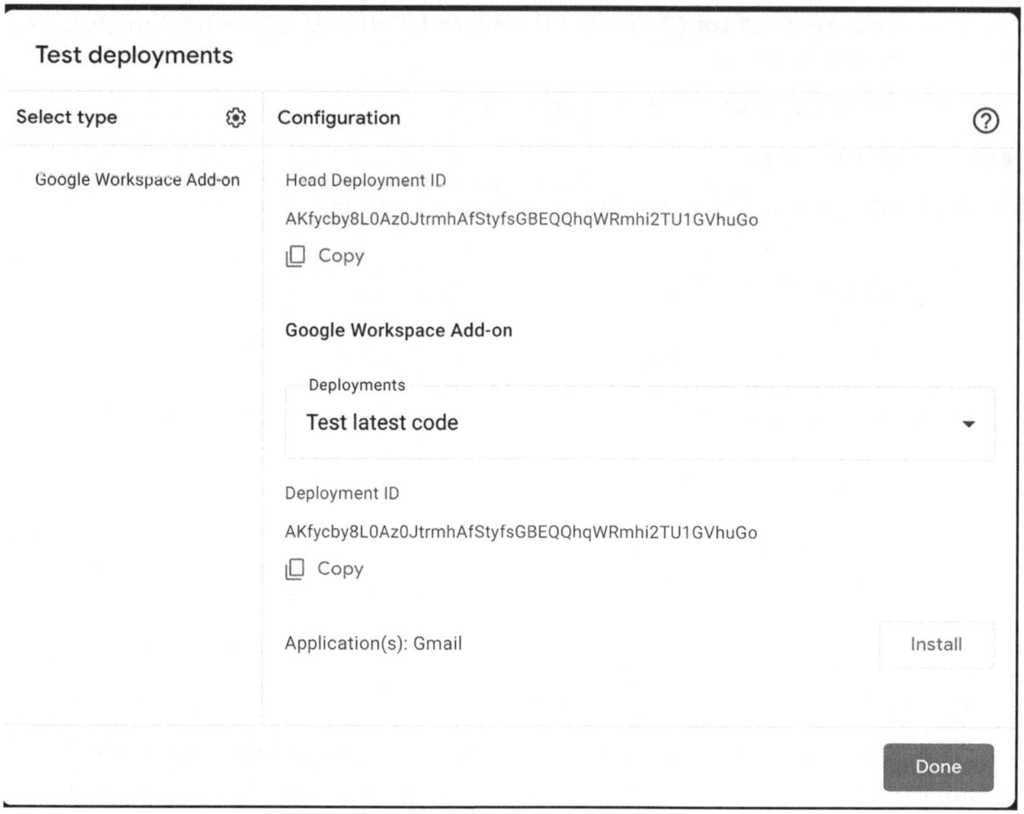

Figure 11.16: *Testing the Card Service-based add-on*

Testing in Gmail:

1. Refresh your Gmail account, and you will notice the add-on icon in the right-hand pane. This icon corresponds to the logo URL provided in your manifest.
2. The first time you click on the add-on, Gmail will request authorization to access your account:

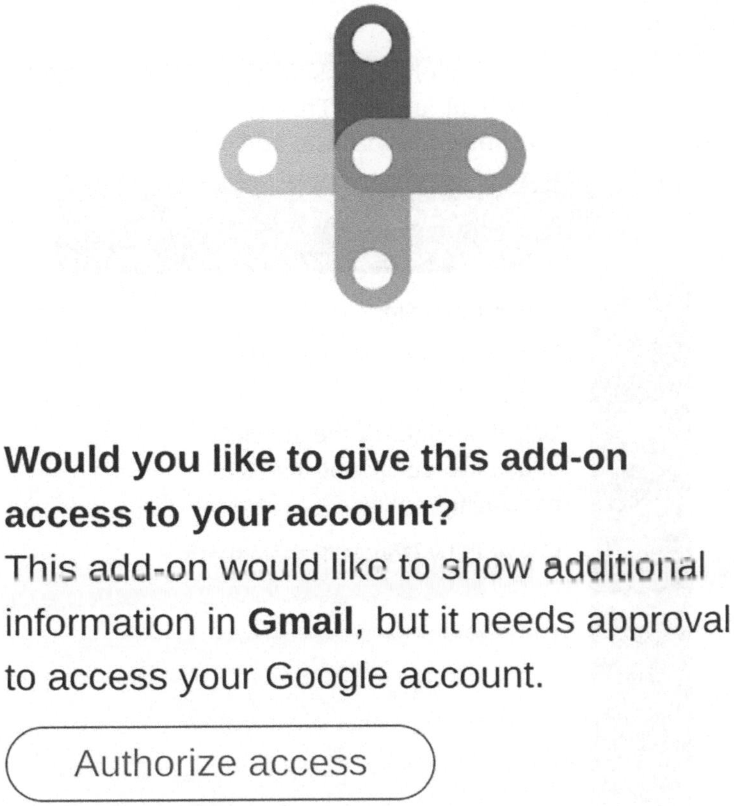

Figure 11.17: *Authorizing the add-on*

3. Clicking "`Authorize access`" will display the consent screen you configured earlier:

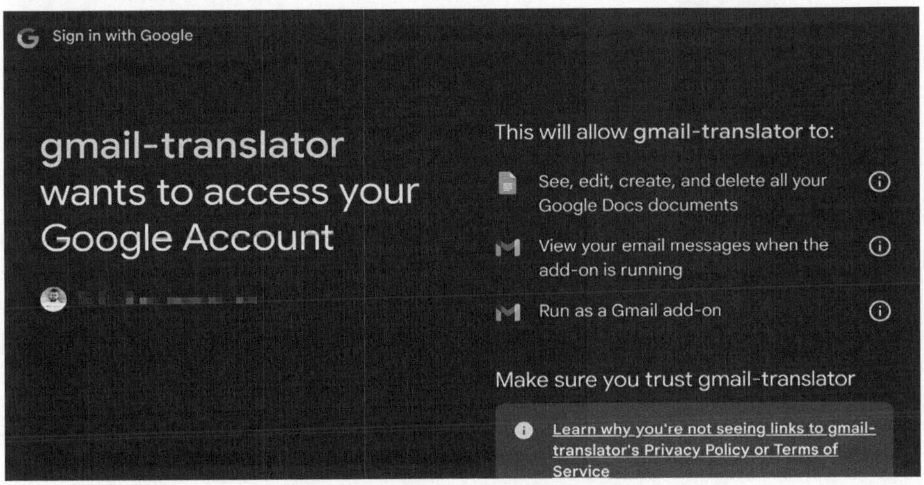

Figure 11.18: *The consent screen*

Testing the Cards

- **Non-Contextual Card:** If no email is selected when the add-on is opened, the non-contextual card will appear. This serves as the add-on's homepage, guiding users on how to interact with the add-on:

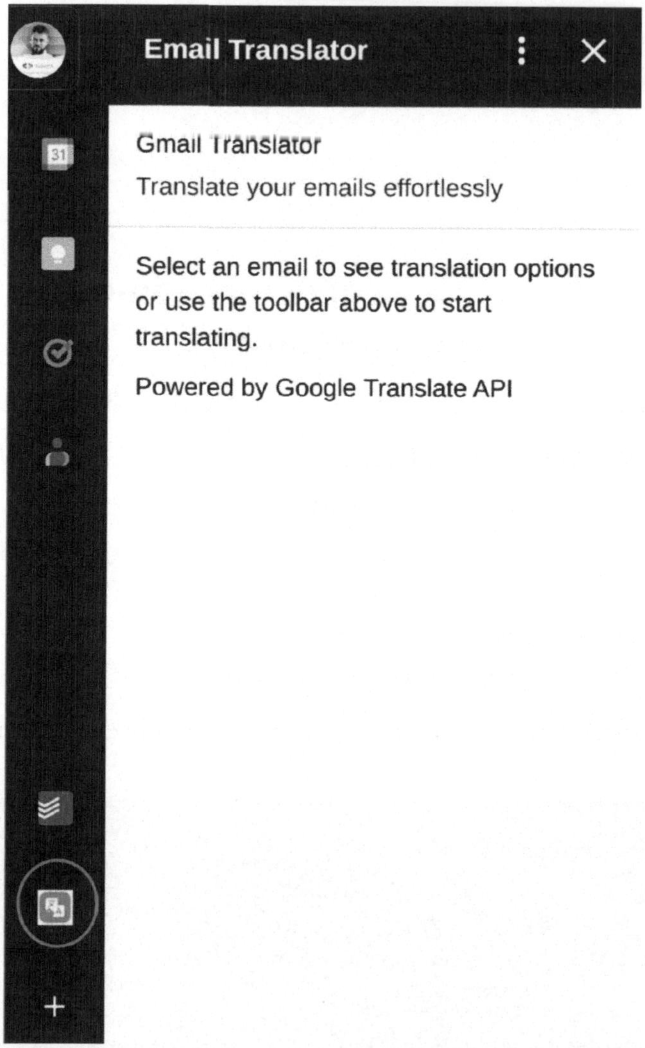

Figure 11.19: *A sidebar containing a non-contextual card*

- **Contextual Card:** When an email is selected, the contextual card will appear, displaying the translated content of the selected email in Hindi:

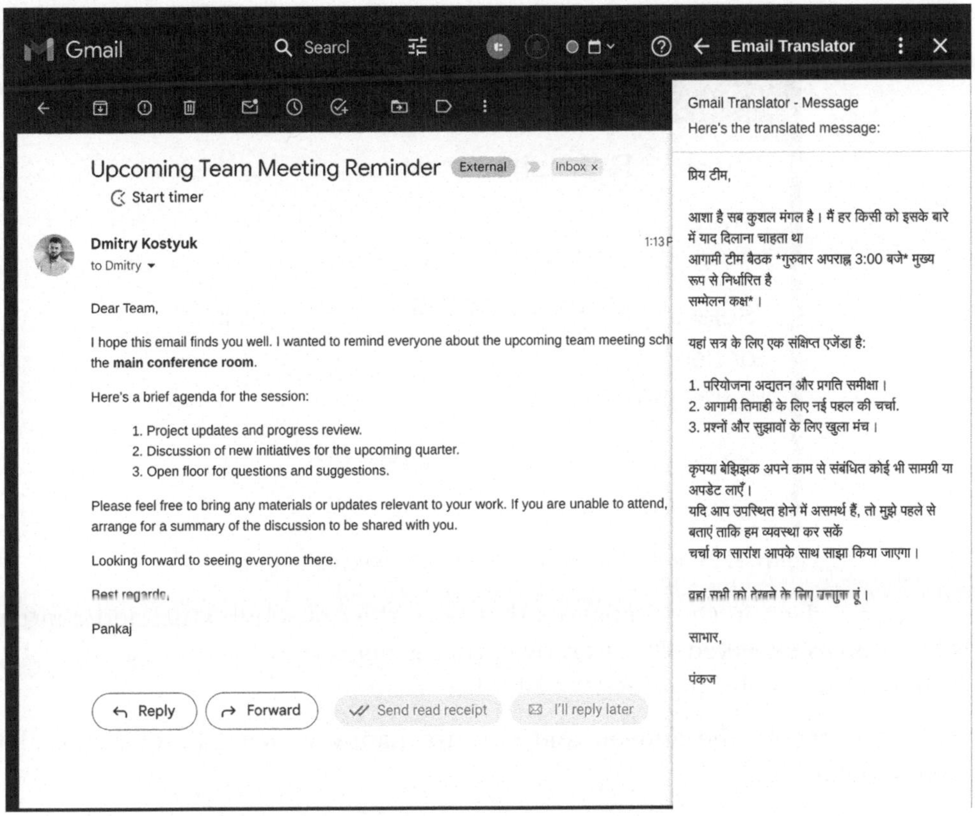

Figure 11.20: A sidebar containing a contextual card

Refreshing During Development

As you update the source code for the add-on, you don't need to refresh your entire Gmail tab to see the changes. Instead:

1. Click the three-dot menu in the **`add-on`** sidebar.
2. Select "**`Refresh`**" to reload the **`add-on`** with the latest code changes.

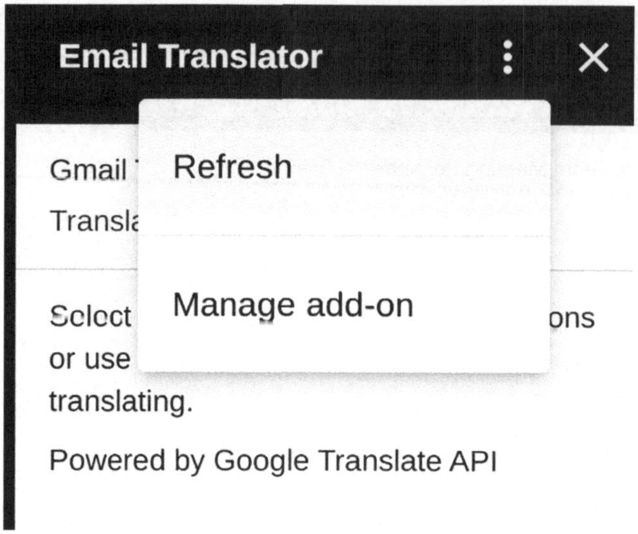

Figure 11.21: *Refreshing the add-on for development purposes*

Testing your add-on in Gmail ensures that both the non-contextual and contextual cards function as expected. This iterative process helps refine your add-on's behavior and layout before publishing it for broader use.

Assuming you tested the add-on and you are happy with its functionality, let us proceed to publish it.

Publishing

So far, we have been running the Gmail add-on in test mode, which means it is only available to the developer. To make the add-on accessible to others, it needs to be published. There are two types of publications:

- **Internal**: Allows access only to users within the same Google Workspace domain.
- **External**: Makes the add-on publicly available, but requires a review by Google.

In this section, we will focus on publishing an **internal add-on**. Note: this process requires a Google Workspace account. Free Gmail accounts cannot publish internal add-ons.

Linking the Google Cloud Project:

1. Open your Google Cloud project dashboard and copy the **`Project Number`**.
2. In the Apps Script IDE, go to **`Settings`** and paste the project number into the appropriate field. If you already linked the project while configuring the manifest, you can skip this step.

Creating a New Deployment:

1. Click the **`Deploy`** button in the top-right corner of the IDE and select **`New deployment`**.

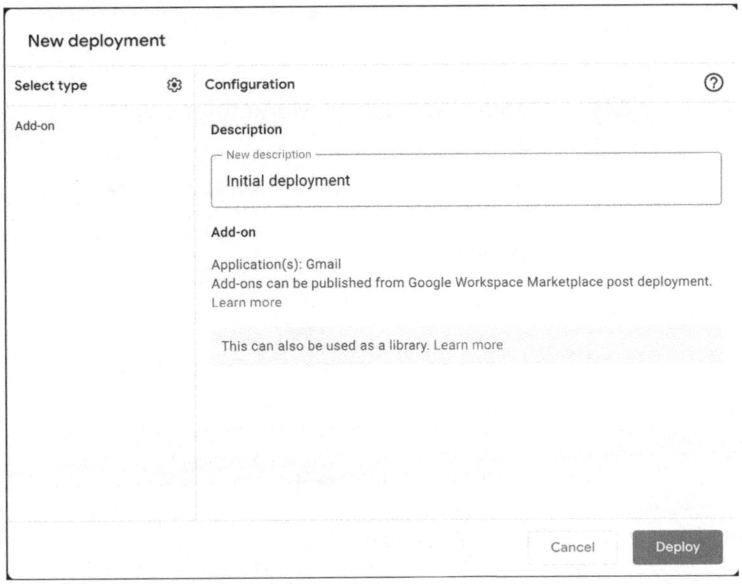

Figure 11.22: *Initiating a new deployment*

2. Complete the deployment process. A **`Version Number`** and an **`ID`** will be generated. Copy the deployment ID; you will need it later.

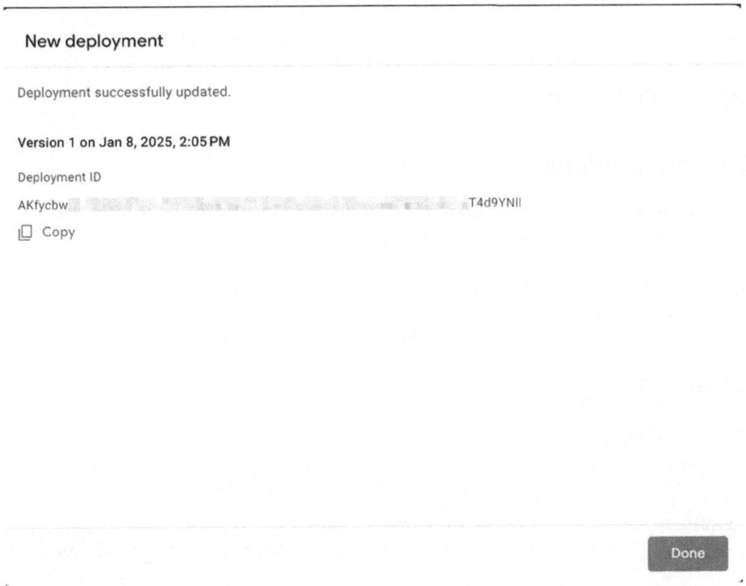

Figure 11.23: *A new deployment with a version number and an ID*

Enabling the Google Workspace Marketplace SDK:

1. In your Google Cloud project, search for **`Google Workspace Marketplace SDK`** and enable it.

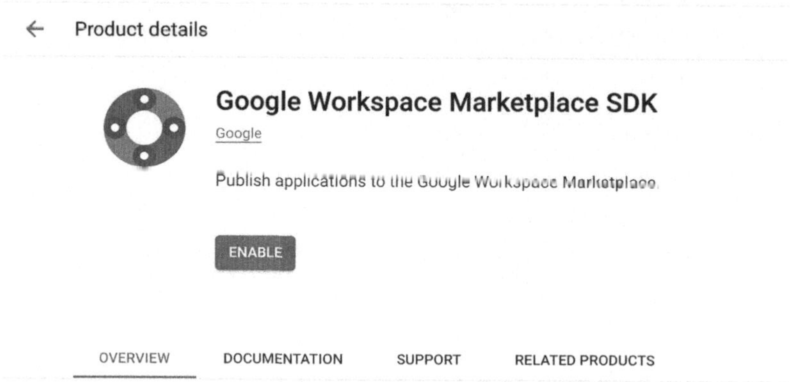

Figure 11.24: *Enabling the Google Workspace Marketplace SDK*

2. Go to the **`App Configuration`** section and:
    a. Set the app visibility to **`Private`**.
    b. Check **`Google Workspace Add-on`** and **`Apps Script`** in **`App Integrations`**.
    c. Paste the deployment ID into the provided field.
    d. Fill out any other required fields.

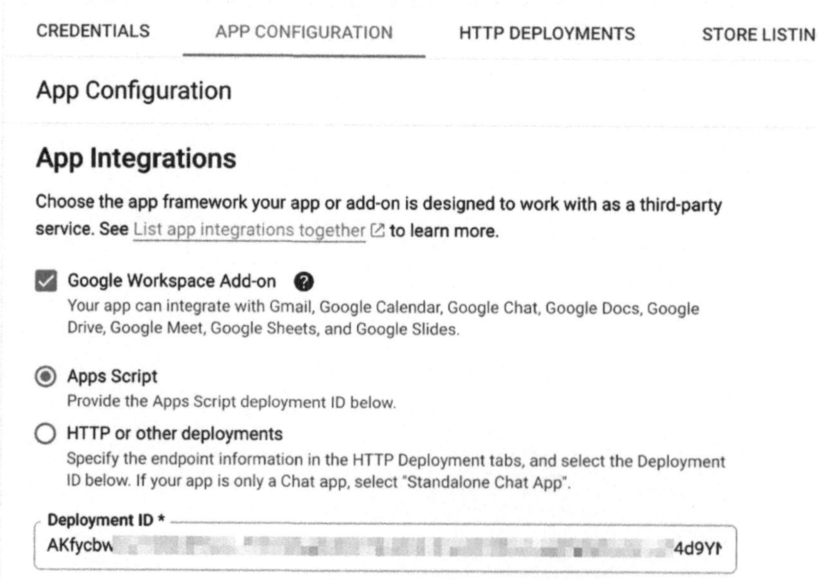

Figure 11.25: *Configuring the add-on*

Setting Up the Store Listing:

1. Navigate to the **`Store Listing`** section in the Google Workspace Marketplace SDK.
2. Fill out all required details:
    a. Provide app icons (32×32 and 128×128 pixels).
    b. Upload a banner (220×140 pixels).
    c. Include at least one screenshot (1200×800 pixels).

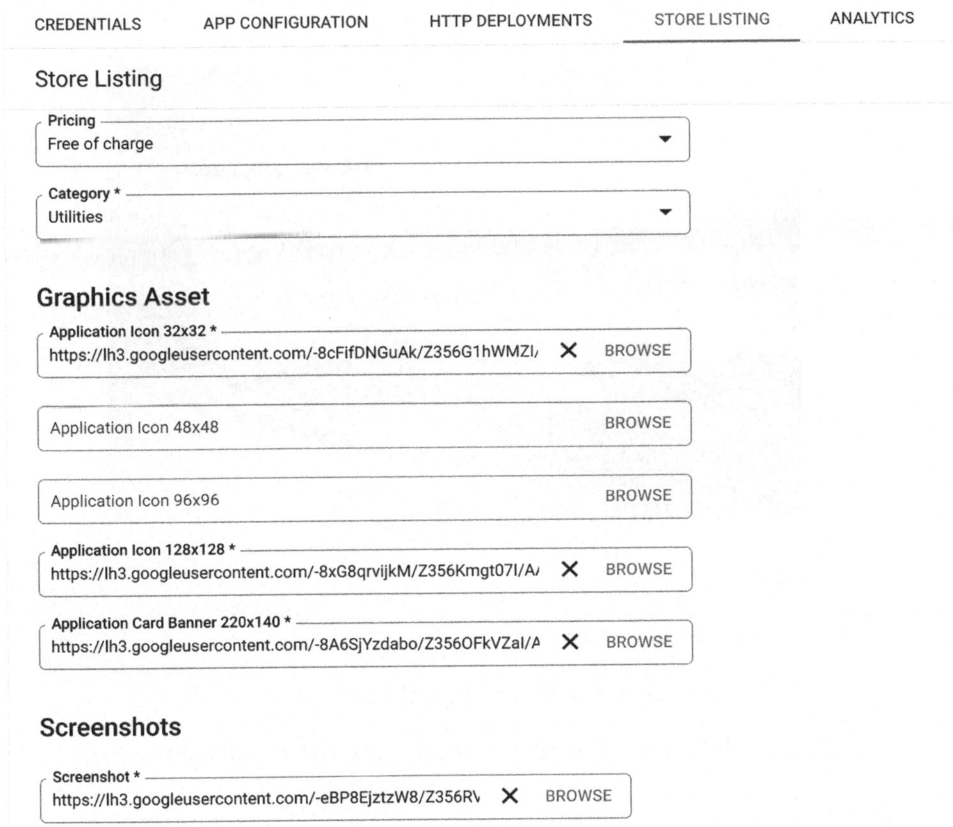

Figure 11.26: *Configuring the store listing*

3. Save the draft and click **`Publish`**.

Installing the Published Add-On

The published add-ons appear in the Google Workspace Marketplace at https://workspace.google.com/marketplace. Click **`Internal Apps`**, find your published add-on, and select **`Individual install`**.

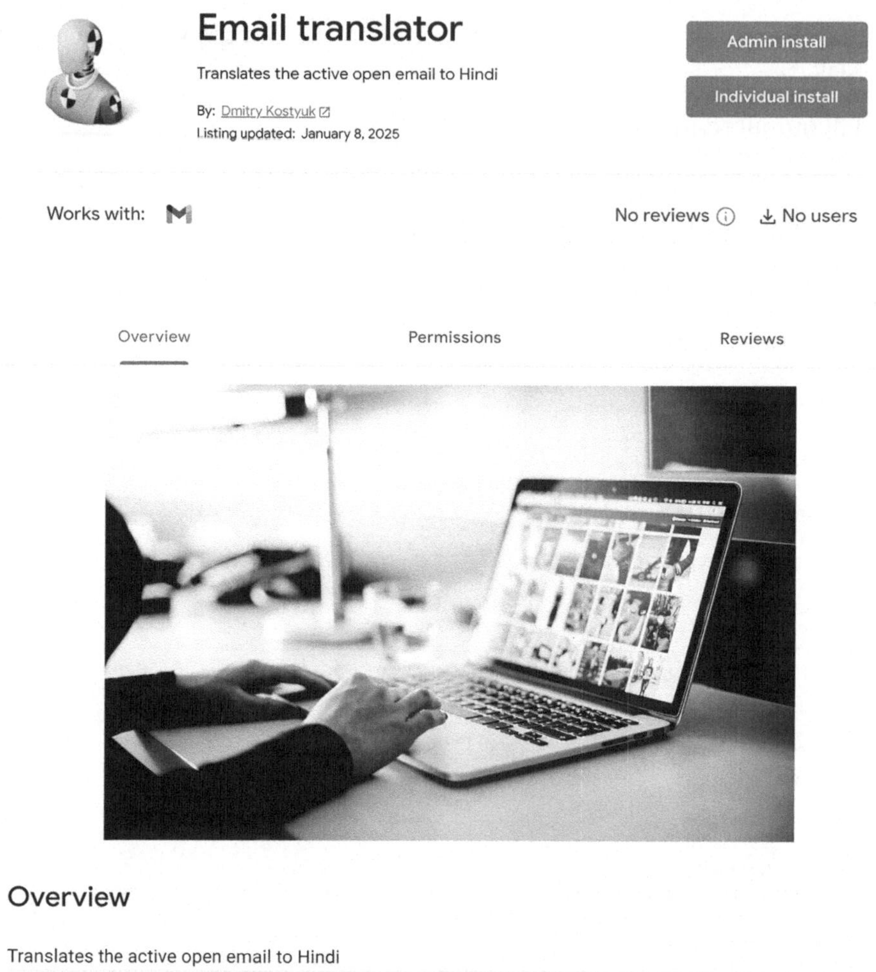

Figure 11.27: *Installing the add-on*

Accept the scopes on the consent screen to complete the installation.

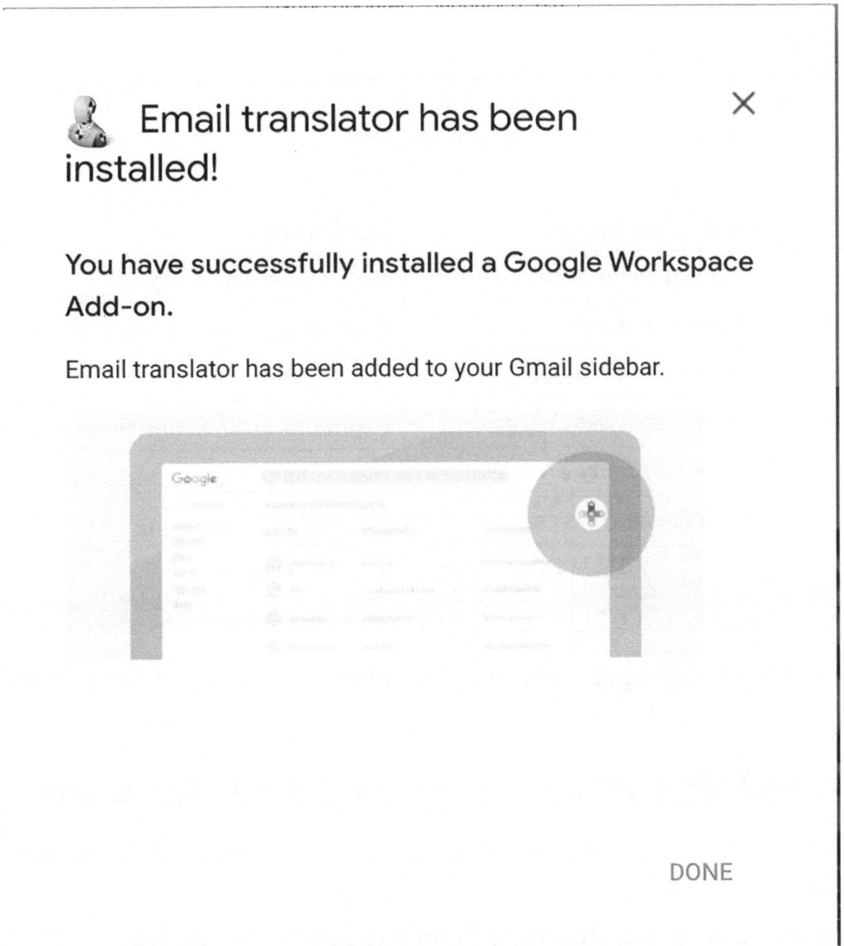

***Figure 11.28:** Add-on installation confirmation message*

Testing the Published Add-On

After installation, refresh Gmail. You will notice two icons for the add-on:

- The first icon represents the installed version.
- The second icon represents the test version, which can still be used for development.

Triggers

Beyond the contextual and non-contextual triggers we have used in Gmail, other Google Workspace apps support unique triggers for specific actions. Here are some examples:

App	Contextual Trigger	Fired when
Gmail	`onTriggerFunction`	User opens a message
Gmail	`composeTrigger`	User starts composing a message
Calendar	`eventUpdateTrigger`	User updates an event
Calendar	`eventAttachmentTrigger`	User adds an attachment to an event
Drive	`onItemsSelectedTrigger`	User selects files or folders in Drive
Docs	`linkPreviewTrigger`	User hovers over a link

Table 11.1: *A list of contextual triggers*

For a full list of supported triggers, refer to the documentation:

https://developers.google.com/workspace/add-ons/concepts/workspace-manifests

Advanced Functionality in Card Service

There is more to the Card Service than what we have covered. Here are some features worth exploring:

- **Actions and Action Builders**: Enable dynamic interactivity by responding to user actions.
- **Navigating Between Cards**: Manage a stack of cards to guide users through complex workflows.
- **Smart Chips**: Build custom link previews with the **`linkPreviewTrigger`**, allowing cards to appear when users hover over links.

These features allow for building more powerful and user-friendly add-ons.

Conclusion

In this chapter, we have only scratched the surface of building UIs in Google Apps Script. While we explored the basics of Custom Menus, HTML Service, and Card Service, truly mastering these tools will require you to build multiple projects and dive deep into the documentation. Unfortunately, there isn't a shortcut—practice and exploration are key.

Mastering these UI capabilities transforms your Google Apps Script projects from simple automation scripts into full-fledged applications. With robust UIs, you can offer your users a seamless experience, enabling sophisticated input handling and dynamic feedback.

As you continue your journey, focus on experimenting with the techniques and services covered here, and expand your knowledge by exploring advanced functionality and best practices. The possibilities are vast and limited only by your creativity and persistence.

Key Terms

- **Triggers:** Mechanisms in Google Apps Script that automatically execute a function in response to an event or at a scheduled time.
- **Custom Menus:** User-defined menu items that can be added to Google Workspace applications such as Sheets or Docs to execute Apps Script functions.
- **HTML Service:** A Google Apps Script service that allows developers to create custom UIs using HTML, CSS, and JavaScript.
- **Card Service:** A Google Apps Script service that provides pre-designed components for building structured, consistent UIs in Google Workspace add-ons.
- **Widgets:** Pre-built elements in Card Service, such as buttons, text fields, and paragraphs, that allow user interaction and display information.
- **Non-Contextual Cards:** Cards that serve as a homepage or general interface without being tied to a specific user action or context.
- **Contextual Cards:** Cards that adapt to the user's context, such as displaying information about the currently open Gmail message.
- **OAuth Scopes:** Permissions requested by an Apps Script project to access specific resources or perform certain actions on behalf of the user.
- **Google Cloud Project:** A configuration space in Google Cloud Console that manages API access, OAuth credentials, and other settings for Apps Script projects.
- **Manifest (`appsscript.json`):** A configuration file in Apps Script projects that define project metadata, OAuth scopes, triggers, and other settings.
- **Smart Chips:** Custom link previews or contextual UIs that appear when users interact with specific elements, such as links in Google Docs.

CHAPTER 12
Web Apps

Introduction

So far, we have worked with Apps Script user interfaces that run inside Google Workspace apps such as Google Sheets, Docs, and Forms. These UIs, while useful, are limited to the Google environment. But Apps Script is not just for extending Workspace apps, it can also be used to build full-fledged web apps.

With Apps Script, you can create web applications that anyone can access through a URL, just like any other website. These apps can collect user input, display dynamic content, and even interact with Google services such as Sheets, Drive, and Gmail. If you have worked with HTML Service before, you are already familiar with some of the tools we will be using.

In this chapter, we will take things further. Beyond web apps, we will also explore how to build webhooks and APIs using Apps Script. These can be useful for integrating with third-party services or automating workflows that go beyond a traditional user interface.

Before diving into the details, let us take a moment to understand what web apps are and how Apps Script makes them work.

Structure

In this chapter, we will cover:

- Understanding Web App
- Core Concepts
- User Authentication
- Leave Requests Web App

Understanding Web App

A web app is a program that runs in a web browser and is built using web technologies such as HTML, CSS, and JavaScript and runs in a browser. Unlike Apps Script interfaces that run inside Google Workspace apps, a web app can be accessed independently through a URL.

An Apps Script web app still has full access to Apps Script services, meaning it can interact with Google Sheets, Drive, Gmail, and other services. This makes it a powerful tool for creating internal applications that extend the functionality of Google Workspace while providing a custom user experience.

To put these ideas into practice, we will build a web app in this chapter: a leave request and approval system. Employees will submit leave requests through the web app based on their available quota. Their manager will receive an email with buttons to approve or reject the request.

Before we start building, let us go over the core concepts behind a web app.

Core Concepts

A Google Apps Script web app relies on the HTML Service to generate and serve web pages. This is the same service used for creating editor add-ons, but in this case, it allows the app to run independently in a web browser. Another option is the Content Service, which we will discuss later.

To make the web app accessible, Apps Script provides special triggers:

- **`doGet(e)`**: Handles HTTP GET requests, which are typically used to serve web pages.
- **`doPost(e)`**: Handles HTTP POST requests, which are often used for APIs and webhooks.

While these triggers allow Apps Script to function as a basic web server, there are limitations. Apps Script does not support HTTP methods such as **`PUT`**, **`DELETE`**, or **`PATCH`**, which are common in more advanced API solutions. If you need full REST API functionality, you may want to explore professional development options beyond Apps Script.

Everything covered about the HTML Service in editor add-ons applies to web apps as well. Now, let us look at the **`doGet()`** trigger and how to deploy a web app.

Triggers

To create a web app with Apps Script, you need to use the **`doGet()`** function. This is a reserved function name, meaning Apps Script automatically detects and runs it when the web app receives an HTTP **`GET`** request.

Here is a simple example of **`doGet()`** in action:

```
const htmlResponse = /* html */ `<!DOCTYPE html>
<html lang="en">
  <head>
    <meta charset="UTF-8">
    <meta name="viewport" content="width=device-width,
initial-scale=1.0">
    <meta http-equiv="X-UA-Compatible" content="ie=edge">
    <title>My Apps Script Web App</title>
    <link rel="stylesheet" href="./style.css">
    <link rel="icon" href="./favicon.ico" type="image/x-icon">
  </head>
  <body>
    <main>
        <h1>Welcome to my Apps Script Web App!</h1>
        <p>Hello world!</p>
    </main>
    <script src="index.js"></script>
  </body>
</html>`;

function doGet() {
  // Reserved function name
  return HtmlService.createHtmlOutput(htmlResponse);
}
```

This function returns an HTML page using **`HtmlService.createHtmlOutput()`**, allowing the web app to display content in the browser.

Using an External HTML File

Instead of embedding HTML directly in the script file, you can place it in a separate HTML file, such as **`index.html`**. This makes the code easier to manage, especially for larger projects.

If the HTML content is moved to **`index.html`**, the **`doGet()`** function needs a small adjustment:

```
function doGet() { // Reserved function name
- return HtmlService.createHtmlOutput(htmlResponse);
+ return HtmlService.createHtmlOutputFromFile('index');
}
```

This approach keeps your Apps Script code clean and allows for better separation between logic and presentation.

Deployment

Now that we have our `doGet()` function ready, the next step is to deploy the web app. Unlike Apps Script projects that run inside a container document (such as a Google Sheet or Doc), a web app needs to be deployed manually.

To begin, click the "**`Deploy`**" button in the Apps Script editor and select "**`New deployment`**".

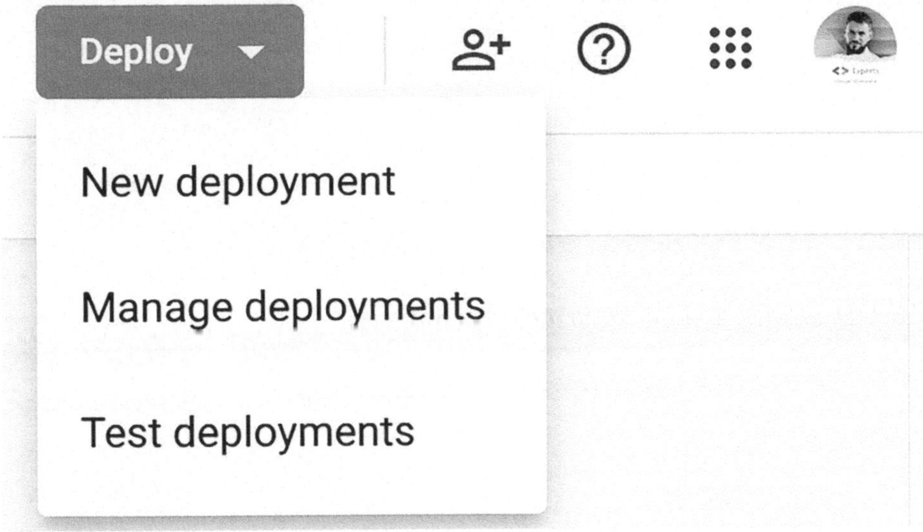

Figure 12.1: *Initiate web app deployment by clicking the "Deploy" button"*

Configuring Deployment Settings

After selecting "**`New deployment`**," you will see a few options to configure:

1. **Deployment type**: Select "**`Web app`**" from the dropdown list.
2. **Description**: You can enter an optional description. While not required, it is a good habit to add one so you can track changes over time.
3. **Execute as**:
    - "**`Me`**": The app runs under your Google account and can access your files, emails, and calendar.
    - "**`User accessing the web app`**": The app runs with the permissions of the person using it.
4. **Who has access**:
    - Options include "**`Only me`**," "**`Anyone within your organization`**," or "**`Anyone with a Google account`**."

For our leave request web app, we want it to execute **`as me`** and be available **`only within our organization`**. Once these options are selected, click "**`Deploy`**."

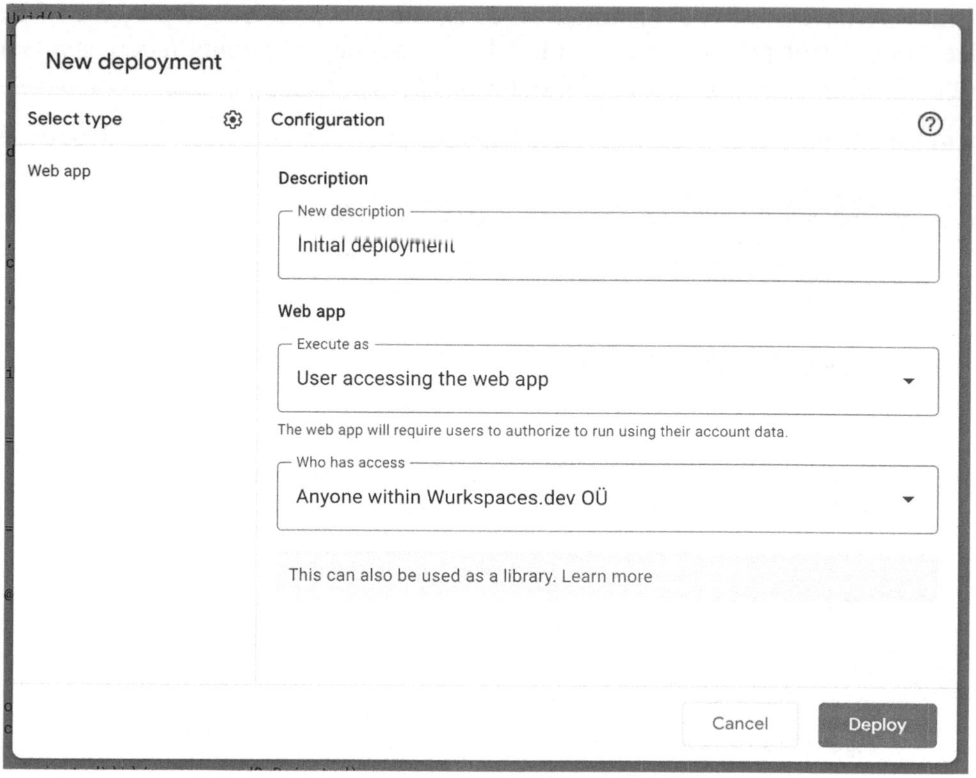

Figure 12.2: *Web app deployment options*

Deployment Confirmation

After clicking "**`Deploy`**," you will receive a confirmation with the following details:

- **Version number**: Starts at 1 and increments with each new deployment.
- **Deployment ID**: A unique identifier for this deployment.
- **Web app URL**: The link to access the web app.

The web app URL is the key piece of information here. Every new deployment generates a new URL, but if you want to maintain the same URL, you need to use "**`Manage deployments`**" instead of "**`New deployment`**." Since this is our first deployment, we do not need to worry about that yet.

Testing versus Production

The URL provided after deployment is the production URL, meaning it serves the current deployed version of the web app. However, making direct changes to a live web app can be risky, especially if users are actively using it.

For safer testing, follow these steps:

1. Close the deployment dialog.
2. Click "`Deploy`" > "`Test deployments`."
3. Ensure "`Web app`" is selected as the type.
4. Copy the **`test URL`**, which is different from the production URL.

The key difference is how updates are handled:

- **Production URL**: Only updates when you create a new deployment.
- **Test URL**: Always runs the latest saved version of your script, making it easy to test changes without affecting users.

With this setup, you can make changes, refresh the test URL, and see the results immediately. Once everything is working as expected, you can deploy the updated version to production.

Before we move forward, let us look at the types of responses a web app can return using the **HTML Service** and **Content Service**.

HTML Service and Content Service

We have already covered the HTML Service in the previous chapter, so we will not go over it again in detail. Instead, we will focus on a more advanced approach to handling data in our web app. Rather than using the `<? ?>` templating tags to insert Apps Script data into HTML, we will use a promisified version of **`google.script.run`**. We will explain what that means soon, but for now, keep in mind that HTML Service is responsible for serving HTML, CSS, and JavaScript, making web apps possible.

Content Service

In addition to the HTML Service, Apps Script provides the Content Service, which can be used to return raw text in various formats. One of the most useful formats is JSON, which is ideal for building APIs and webhooks. Unlike HTML Service, which is designed for rendering user interfaces, Content Service is meant for app-to-app communication.

We will not go deep into Content Service in this chapter, but if you are interested, you can check out the documentation: Content Service Documentation (https://developers.google.com/apps-script/reference/content)

Here is a simple example of a **doGet()** function that returns a JSON response using Content Service:

```
function doGet() {
  const returnValue = {
    result: 'OK',
    message: 'Hello world',
  };
  return ContentService.createTextOutput(
    JSON.stringify(returnValue)
  ).setMimeType(ContentService.MimeType.JSON);
}
```

Choosing Between HTML Service and Content Service

- **Use HTML Service** when your web app needs to present a user interface to a human user. It allows you to build pages with HTML, CSS, and JavaScript.
- **Use Content Service** when your web app needs to provide data to another application, such as an API or a webhook. JSON responses work well in these cases because they are lightweight and easy to process.

For our leave request web app, we will primarily use HTML Service, but keep Content Service in mind for situations where you need structured data responses instead of a full UI.

User Authentication

When building a web app, it is often necessary to identify the user interacting with it. Apps Script provides two ways to determine user identity:

- **Active user**: The person currently using the web app.
- **Effective user**: The account under which the script is executing.

Understanding Active versus Effective User

If a web app is set to execute **as the user accessing the app**, then the active user and the effective user will be the same. However, in our case, we chose to execute the web app **as the script owner**. This means:

- The **effective user** is the account that deployed the script (our account).
- The **active user** is the person currently using the app.

Why did we choose this approach? Because the web app will interact with a Google Sheet that end users do not have direct access to. By running the script under our account, we ensure that the necessary read/write operations work smoothly while still detecting which employee is making the request. This distinction will become more apparent as we build the app.

Handling User Access

Apps Script does not provide built-in role-based access control, so if you need granular user management, you must implement it yourself. A few options include:

- Maintaining a list of authorized users in a Google Sheet.
- Using a Google Group to manage access more efficiently.

Now that we have covered the core concepts behind our leave request app, let us start building it!

Leave Requests Web App

Like most web applications, our leave request app will have two main components:

- **Client-side**: The front end that handles user interaction. This will be built using HTML, CSS, and JavaScript.
- **Server-side**: The backend logic written in Apps Script. This part will handle business rules, interact with the spreadsheet, and send email notifications.

To get started, we need a structured way to store leave requests. Let us set up our database in a Google Sheet.

Preparing the Database in a Spreadsheet

Let us prepare the database:

1. Create a new Google Sheet.
2. Add the following column headers:
   - `request_id`
   - `user_email`
   - `start_date`
   - `end_date`
   - `duration`
   - `status`

A quick way to populate test data is to generate it in CSV format using an AI tool, save it as a file, and import it into Google Sheets. This saves time, especially when setting up a realistic dataset.

Make sure some of the rows contain your email so you can view, submit, and cancel requests during testing. Your spreadsheet should look like this:

	A	B	C	D	E	F
1	request_id	user_email	start_da	end_dat	durati	status
2	d84549f4-9e79-4d08-b71e-e164c5378361	dmitry@[illegible]	2025-12-18	2025-12-25	8	Approved
3	02192d2d-475c-4cf4-b2a2-cc9cbf4f0328	dave@example.com	2025-12-06	2025-12-10	5	Pending
4	05aa1574-92f3-4003-9691-41ead2047f5c	carol@example.com	2025-08-08	2025-08-18	11	Approved
5	1e0d4856-775c-4742-821a-a2a1cd4fe886	carol@example.com	2026-01-10	2026-01-15	6	Approved
6	bf06291d-41e9-4c9e-8b7b-4956dd5b91be	carol@example.com	2025-11-17	2025-11-23	7	Rejected
7	76e8b724-aa6d-4cd8-9db7-fd4068013857	bob@example.com	2025-08-27	2025-09-06	11	Rejected
8	bb426dd2-0c05-4a09-a5b4-348355fb2687	carol@example.com	2025-02-12	2025-02-16	5	Rejected
9	6ff2dfca-b710-473e-8648-5b0a38fc763a	dave@example.com	2025-07-23	2025-07-27	5	Rejected
10	87767bd0-f813-45b1-b3f9-52ab011f000a	carol@example.com	2025-11-30	2025-12-06	7	Approved
11	38d58412-edaf-4dc2-aeee-a6e3d83a7d44	dmitry@[illegible]	2025-11-10	2025-11-15	6	Rejected
12	[illegible]	[illegible]	[illegible]	[illegible]	[illegible]	[illegible]

Figure 12.3: *The structure of our database in a Google Sheet*

At this point, we do not need to do anything else with the spreadsheet. Just copy the spreadsheet ID, and let us move on to writing some Apps Script code.

The Apps Script Code

Start by creating a stand-alone Apps Script project. This project will handle all the server-side logic, including interacting with the spreadsheet, managing leave requests, and sending notifications.

Global Variables

First, define some global variables that we will use throughout the script:

```
const DATABASE_ID = '<SPREADSHEET_ID>';
const FULL_QUOTA = 30;
const WEB_APP_URL =
  'https://script.google.com/macros/s/<TEST_URL_ID>/dev';
```

- **`DATABASE_ID`**: Stores the ID of the Google Sheet acting as our database.
- **`FULL_QUOTA`**: Defines the total number of leave days available to each employee.
- **`WEB_APP_URL`**: The test deployment URL of the web app. We will use this initially, and later switch to the production URL.

Backend Responsibilities

The backend will handle several key tasks:

1. Retrieve user information (email).
2. Fetch user's leave requests from the spreadsheet.

3. Calculate remaining leave quota based on approved leave days.
4. Perform CRUD operations (Create, Read, Update, Cancel, Reject) on leave requests.
5. Send email notifications to managers and employees when requests are submitted or updated.
6. Render the web app interface using HTML Service.

Obtaining the User's Email and Data

As mentioned earlier, the active user is the person currently using the app. We can retrieve their email using:

```
function getUserEmail() {
  return Session.getActiveUser().getEmail();
}
```

This email will allow us to filter leave requests and determine the remaining quota for each employee.

Retrieving All Leave Requests

Before filtering requests by user, we need a function to retrieve all leave requests from the spreadsheet. To make processing easier, we will convert the raw spreadsheet data into an array of objects, where each object represents a row. This follows the same approach we used in the Sheets chapter.

```
function getAllRequests() {
  const ws = SpreadsheetApp.openById(DATABASE_ID).getSheets()[0];
  const data = ws.getDataRange().getValues();
  const headers = data.shift(); // Extract column headers
  const objAr = data.map(row =>
    row.reduce((acc, cell, i) => {
      return { ...acc, [headers[i]]: cell };
    }, {})
  );
  return { headers, objAr };
}
```

This function does the following:

1. Opens the spreadsheet using **DATABASE_ID**.
2. Reads all data, extracting headers from the first row.
3. Maps each row into an object where column names serve as keys.

4. Returns both the headers and the array of objects.

Filtering Requests for the Logged-in User

Now that we have all requests, we can filter them based on the active user's email:

```
function getRequests() {
  const userEmail = getUserEmail();
  const userData = getAllRequests().objAr.filter(
    obj => userEmail === obj.user_email
  );
  console.log(userData);
  return JSON.stringify(userData);
}
```

Here, **`getRequests()`** does the following:

1. Retrieves the current user's email.
2. Calls **`getAllRequests()`** and filters the data based on the **`user_email`** field.
3. Logs the result for debugging purposes.
4. Returns the data as a JSON string for easier server-to-client communication.

Calculating Remaining Leave Quota

Since we now have user-specific data, we can compute how many leave days they have left.

```
function getRemainingQuota() {
  const usedQuota = JSON.parse(getRequests()).reduce
((acc, request) => {
    if (['Approved', 'Pending'].includes(request.status))
      return acc + request.duration;
    return acc;
  }, 0);
  return FULL_QUOTA - usedQuota;
}
```

This function works as follows:

1. Calls **`getRequests()`** to retrieve the user's leave requests.
2. Converts the JSON string back into an array of objects.
3. Iterates through the requests and sums up only "**`Approved`**" and "**`Pending`**" requests.
4. Subtracts the total used leave from **`FULL_QUOTA`**.

Rejected or canceled requests do not count against the quota, as those leave days remain available.

Now that we can retrieve user-specific data, the next step is processing leave requests.

Processing Leave Requests

Now that we can retrieve user data, the next step is allowing users to submit, update, and cancel leave requests.

Submitting a Leave Request

To add a new request, we will define a function that inserts a row into our spreadsheet:

```
function saveRequest(start, end, status = 'Pending') {
  const MS_IN_DAY = 1000 * 60 * 60 * 24;
  const durationDays = Math.ceil((new Date(end) - new
Date(start)) / MS_IN_DAY + 1);
  const uuid = Utilities.getUuid();

  SpreadsheetApp.openById(DATABASE_ID)
    .getSheets()[0]
    .appendRow([uuid, getUserEmail(), start, end, durationDays,
status]);


  SpreadsheetApp.flush();
  notifyManager(start, end, durationDays, uuid);
  return true;
}
```

How it works:

1. **Calculates leave duration**:
    - Converts dates to timestamps and calculates the difference in days.
    - Adds 1 to ensure leave days are inclusive.
2. **Generates a unique ID**:
    - Uses **`Utilities.getUuid()`** to generate a UUID (Universally Unique Identifier).
    - This ensures every request has a distinct, unchanging identifier.
3. **Writes data to the spreadsheet**:
    - Inserts a new row containing the request details.

4. **Sends an email notification**:
    - Calls **`notifyManager()`**, which we will cover in the next section.

Updating a Leave Request

Pending requests can be approved, rejected, or canceled. To modify a request, we will identify it by its unique ID and update its status in the spreadsheet:

```
function updateRequestById(requestId, status) {
  const allRequests = getAllRequests();
  const requestIndex = allRequests.objAr.findIndex(
    request => requestId === request.request_id
  );
  if (requestIndex === -1) return false;

  const request = allRequests.objAr[requestIndex];
  if (request.status === status) return null; // Avoid
unnecessary updates


  SpreadsheetApp.openById(DATABASE_ID)
    .getSheets()[0]
    .getRange(requestIndex + 2, 6) // +2 accounts for zero-based
index and headers
    .setValue(status);


  SpreadsheetApp.flush();
  return request;
}
```

How it works:

1. **Finds the request index**:
    a. Uses **`findIndex()`** to locate the row matching the **`requestId`**.
2. **Prevents unnecessary updates**:
    a. If the request is already in the desired status, the function exits early.
3. **Updates the spreadsheet**:
    a. Uses **`.getRange(row, column)`** to target the **status column (6th column)**.
    b. Adds **2** to the index to adjust for the zero-based array and skipped headers.
4. **Commits changes with `flush()`**.

Shorthand Functions for Common Status Changes

For convenience, we will create **three helper functions** to modify request status:

```
function cancelRequest(requestId) {
  return !!updateRequestById(requestId, 'Cancelled');
}


function approveRequest(requestId) {
  console.log('🆗 Approving request');
  return updateRequestById(requestId, 'Approved');
}


function rejectRequest(requestId) {
  console.log('⚠️ Rejecting request');
  return updateRequestById(requestId, 'Rejected');
}
```

1. These functions call **`updateRequestById()`** with a predefined status.
2. The **`cancelRequest()`** function returns **`true`** or **`false`**, ensuring a boolean response.

With the ability to create and modify requests, the next step is sending email notifications to managers when requests are submitted or updated.

Sending Email Notifications

The **`saveRequest()`** function includes a call to **`notifyManager()`**, which sends an email notification when a new leave request is submitted. Let us take a closer look at how this works.

```
function notifyManager(start, end, duration, uuid) {
  const htmlBody = HtmlService.createHtmlOutputFromFile('email_
template')
    .getContent()
    .replace('{{start_date}}', start)
    .replace('{{end_date}}', end)
    .replace('{{duration}}', duration)
    .replace('{{employee_email}}', getUserEmail())
    .replace(
      '{{approve_url}}',
      `${WEB_APP_URL}?action=approve&requestId=${uuid}`
    )
    .replace(
```

```
      '{{reject_url}}',
      `${WEB_APP_URL}?action=reject&requestId=${uuid}`
    );


  GmailApp.sendEmail('manager@example.com', 'New leave request',
'', {
    htmlBody,
  });
}
```

This function does the following:

1. Reads the email template from an external HTML file (**`email_template`**).
2. Replaces placeholders (merge fields) with real values using **`.replace()`**.
3. Constructs approval and rejection URLs by appending query parameters (**`action=approve`** and **`action=reject`**) to the web app URL.
4. Sends an HTML email to the manager.

To test this function, replace **`'manager@example.com'`** with a real email address.

Email Template for Manager Notifications

Here is what the email template (**`email_template.html`**) looks like:

```
<!DOCTYPE html>
<html>
<head>
  <meta charset="utf-8"><meta name="viewport" content="width=
device-width, initial-scale=1.0">
  <title>Leave Request Approval</title>
</head>
<body style="margin: 0; padding: 0; font-family: Arial, sans-
serif; background-color: #f4f4f4;">
  <div style="max-width: 600px; margin: 0 auto; padding: 20px;">
    <div style="background-color: #ffffff; padding: 30px; border-
radius: 5px; box-shadow: 0 2px 4px rgba(0,0,0,0.1);">
      <h1 style="color: #333333; margin-top: 0; font-size:
24px;">Leave Request Approval</h1>
      <p>{{employee_email}} has submitted a leave request for
your approval.</p>
      <div style="background-color: #f8f9fa; padding: 20px;
border-radius: 5px;">
        <p><strong>Start Date:</strong> {{start_date}}</p>
        <p><strong>End Date:</strong> {{end_date}}</p>
        <p><strong>Duration:</strong> {{duration}} days</p>
```

```
      </div>
      <div style="text-align: center;">
        <a href="{{approve_url}}" style="background-color:
#28a745; color: #ffffff; text-decoration: none; padding: 12px 25px;
border-radius: 4px;">Approve</a>
        <a href="{{reject_url}}" style="background-color:
#dc3545; color: #ffffff; text-decoration: none; padding: 12px 25px;
border-radius: 4px;">Reject</a>
      </div>
      <p style="color: #999999; font-size: 12px; text-align:
center;">This is an automated message. Please do not reply.</p>
    </div>
  </div>
</body>
</html>
```

A few key points:

1. Merge fields are placed in double curly braces (**{{ }}**). These are replaced dynamically before sending the email.
2. **Approval and rejection buttons** contain unique links for processing requests.
3. **Inline styles** are used instead of external stylesheets for better email client compatibility.

Sending Confirmation Emails to Employees

Once a leave request is approved or rejected, the employee should be notified. The **`notifyEmployee()`** function handles this:

```
function notifyEmployee(approvedOrRejected, userEmail, start,
end, duration) {
  const htmlBody = HtmlService.createHtmlOutputFromFile
('confirmation_email')
    .getContent()
    .replace(/\{\{approved_or_rejected\}\}/g, approvedOrRejected)
    .replace('{{start_date}}', start)
    .replace('{{end_date}}', end)
    .replace('{{duration}}', duration);


  GmailApp.sendEmail(userEmail, 'Re: your leave request', '', {
    htmlBody,
  });
}
```

1. Reads the **confirmation email template** (**`confirmation_email.html`**).
2. Replaces placeholders with actual values.
3. Uses a **regular expression** (**`/\{\{approved_or_rejected\}\}/g`**) to replace multiple occurrences of **`{{approved_or_rejected}}`**.
4. Sends the email to the **employee**.

Email Template for Employee Notifications

```
<html>
<head>
  <meta charset="utf-8" /><meta name="viewport"
content="width=device-width, initial-scale=1.0" />
  <title>Leave Request {{approved_or_rejected}}</title>
</head>
<body style="margin: 0; padding: 0; font-family: Arial, sans-
serif; background-color: #f4f4f4;">
  <div style="max-width: 600px; margin: 0 auto; padding: 20px">
    <div style="background-color: #ffffff; padding: 30px; border-
radius: 5px;">
      <h1>Leave Request {{approved_or_rejected}}</h1>
      <p>Your leave request has been <strong>{{approved_or_
rejected}}</strong> by your manager.</p>
      <div style="background-color: #f8f9fa; padding: 20px;
border-radius: 5px;">
        <p><strong>Start Date:</strong> {{start_date}}</p>
        <p><strong>End Date:</strong> {{end_date}}</p>
        <p><strong>Duration:</strong> {{duration}} days</p>
      </div>
      <p style="color: #999999; font-size: 12px; text-align:
center;">This is an automated message. Please do not reply.</p>
    </div>
  </div>
</body>
</html>
```

Key differences from the manager's email:

- **No buttons**, as there is no further action required.
- **Merge field `{{approved_or_rejected}}` appears multiple times**, hence the use of a regular expression in **`notifyEmployee()`**.

Now that email notifications are set up, the last step is to render the **web app UI** with the **`doGet()`** trigger. Let us dive into that next.

Rendering the Front End

The `doGet()` trigger is responsible for serving different user interfaces based on the request parameters. Specifically, it handles three cases:

1. **Employee UI:** The main web app interface for submitting and managing leave requests.
2. **Manager UI:** A confirmation page for approving or rejecting requests.
3. **Error UI:** A message for managers if an invalid action is detected.

Here is the source code:

```
function doGet(e) {
  // Return default page if no parameters
  if (!e?.parameter?.action || !e?.parameter?.requestId) {
    return HtmlService.createHtmlOutputFromFile('index');
  }

  const { action, requestId } = e.parameter;

  // Return error for invalid action
  if (!['approve', 'reject'].includes(action)) {
    return HtmlService.createHtmlOutput(
      HtmlService.createHtmlOutputFromFile('unrecognized')
        .getContent()
        .replace('{{action}}', action)
    );
  }


  // Process approval or rejection
  const request =
    'approve' === action ? approveRequest(requestId) : rejectRe-
quest(requestId);
  const actionText = 'approve' === action ? 'Approved' :
'Rejected';


  // Notify the employee if the request was processed
  if (null !== request) {
    notifyEmployee(
      actionText,
      request.user_email,
      request.start_date.toISOString().split('T')[0],
      request.end_date.toISOString().split('T')[0],
```

```
        request.duration
      );
    }


    // Return confirmation page
    return HtmlService.createHtmlOutput(
      HtmlService.createHtmlOutputFromFile('success')
        .getContent()
        .replace(/\{\{approved_or_rejected\}\}/g, actionText)
    );
  }
```

How it works:

1. **Checks for URL parameters**:
   - If **`action`** and **`requestId`** are **not** in the query string, it loads the **employee UI** (**`index.html`**).
   - If they are present, it assumes the request comes from a **manager's email notification**.
2. **Handles invalid actions**:
   - If **`action`** is not "**`approve`**" or "**`reject`**", it loads an **error page** (**`unrecognized.html`**) with a message.
3. **Processes approvals or rejections**:
   - Calls **`approveRequest(requestId)`** or **`rejectRequest(requestId)`**.
   - Sends a **`notification email`** to the employee if the request was processed.
4. **Returns a confirmation page**:
   - Loads **`success.html`** and replaces **`{{approved_or_rejected}}`** with "**`Approved`**" or "**`Rejected`**".

Using Query Parameters in doGet()

Apps Script provides an **`Event`** object (**`e`**) to web apps, allowing us to access query string parameters.

For example, if a manager clicks this URL: `https://script.google.com/macros/s/.../exec?action=approve&requestId=12345`

Then:

```
console.log(e.parameter.action);    // "approve"
console.log(e.parameter.requestId); // "12345"
```

The full documentation for handling query parameters in **doGet()** is here: https://developers.google.com/apps-script/guides/web

Rendering HTML Pages Dynamically

The confirmation and error messages use the same approach as notification emails:

1. Load an HTML file (**success.html** or **unrecognized.html**).
2. Replace merge fields (**{{approved_or_rejected}}** or **{{action}}**).
3. Serve it as an Apps Script HTML output.

Now that the backend logic is complete, let us build the main user interface for employees.

The Client-Side Code

To keep the front-end simple and maintainable, we will focus mainly on JavaScript while minimizing the need for custom CSS. Instead of writing CSS from scratch, we will use a CSS framework to style our web app.

Using Bulma for Styling

We will use Bulma, a free and lightweight CSS framework that requires no installation, just a single CDN link. This makes it a perfect fit for Apps Script web apps, which do not have a traditional build process.

You can check out the Bulma documentation here: https://bulma.io/

In the next volume of this book, we will explore more advanced front-end frameworks (both CSS and JavaScript) that require a build step. For now, let us keep things straightforward and focus on getting our UI up and running.

Now, let us dive into the HTML markup for our web app.

HTML Markup

Here is the starting HTML structure for our leave request web app:

```
<!doctype html>
<html lang="en" theme="light" class="theme-light">
<head>
  <meta charset="UTF-8" /><meta name="viewport"
content="width=device-width, initial-scale=1.0" />
  <title>Leave Request Manager</title>
  <link rel="stylesheet" href="https://cdn.jsdelivr.net/npm/
bulma/css/bulma.min.css" />
```

```
  <link rel="shortcut icon" href="https://www.freepik.com/icon/
code_7784482" />
</head>
<body>
  <section class="section"><div class="container">
    <h1 class="title">Leave Request Manager</h1>
    <p class="subtitle">Manage your leaves with ease!</p>


    <div class="box is-flex is-align-items-center">
      <p><strong>Logged in as:</strong></p>
      <span id="user-email" class="ml-3"><progress
class="progress is-small is-primary" max="100" style="width:
200px"></progress></span>
    </div>


    <div class="box">
      <p class="is-flex is-align-items-center">
        <strong>Days Left in Quota:</strong>
        <span id="days-left" class="ml-2"><progress
class="progress is-small is-primary" max="100" style="width:
50px"></progress></span>
        <span class="ml-2">days</span>
      </p>
    </div>


    <div class="box">
      <h2 class="subtitle">Your Leave Requests</h2>
      <table class="table is-striped is-hoverable is-fullwidth">
        <thead><tr><th>Start Date</th><th>End Date</th><th>Total
Days</th><th>Status</th><th>Actions</th></tr></thead>
        <template id="cancel-button-template"><button class=
"button is-small is-danger is-light">Cancel</button></template>
        <tbody id="leave-requests">
          <tr><td colspan="5"><div class="skeleton-lines"><div></
div><div></div><div></div><div></div><div></div></div></td></tr>
        </tbody>
      </table>
    </div>


    <div class="box">
      <h2 class="subtitle">Request a New Leave</h2>
      <div class="field"><label class="label">Start Date</la-
bel><input class="input" type="date" id="start-date" /></div>
```

```
      <div class="field"><label class="label">End Date</label>
<input class="input" type="date" id="end-date" /></div>
    </div>


    <div class="is-flex is-align-items-center">
      <button class="button is-primary" onclick="submitLeave
Request(this)">Submit Leave Request</button>
      <div id="leave-error" class="ml-4 has-text-danger
is-hidden"></div>
    </div>
  </div></div></section>
</body>
</html>
```

Key Features

1. **Bulma for Styling**
   - There is **no custom CSS**—everything is styled using **Bulma classes**.
   - Bulma's grid and flex utilities make layout management easy.
2. **Four Main UI Sections**
   - **`User Info`**: Displays the logged-in user's email.
   - **`Leave Quota`**: Shows the number of leave days remaining.
   - **`Leave Requests Table`**: Displays past requests and their statuses.
   - **`Leave Request Form`**: Allows users to submit new requests.
3. **Loading Indicators**
   - The **`email`** and **`remaining days`** sections display progress bars while loading.
   - The **`leave requests table`** shows a skeleton loader instead of empty space.

Preview and Testing

If you open this file locally using a tool like live-server (https://www.npmjs.com/package/live-server), you will see a static page with placeholder loaders.

At this stage, no real data is loaded because we have not written any JavaScript yet. The next step is to fetch user data from Apps Script and update the UI dynamically.

Let us start writing the client-side JavaScript to connect the front-end with our Apps Script backend.

Figure 12.4: *The web app interface with loaders and a skeleton, awaiting to load user data*

Client-Side JavaScript

To connect our front-end UI with the Apps Script backend, we will use **`google.script.run`**, which allows us to call server-side functions from the client.

Instead of using traditional callback functions, we will promisify **`google.script.run`** to enable cleaner, **`async/await`**-based code.

Promisifying `google.script.run`

```
async function runGas(functionName, args = []) {
  return new Promise((resolve, reject) => {
    google.script.run
      .withSuccessHandler(resolve)
      .withFailureHandler(reject)
      [functionName](...args);
  });
}
```

This function takes an Apps Script function name and an array of arguments. It returns a Promise, which resolves on success and rejects on failure. This allows us to use **`async/await`** instead of nested callbacks.

Fetching Data from Apps Script

Now, let us load user data from the back-end.

```
async function loadData() {
  console.log('⏳ Loading data...');
  const [userEmail, requests, remainingQuota] = await Promise.
all([
    runGas('getUserEmail'),
    runGas('getRequests'),
    runGas('getRemainingQuota'),
  ]);

  storage.set('userEmail', userEmail);
  storage.set('remainingQuota', remainingQuota);
  storage.set('requests', JSON.parse(requests));

  ['#start-date', '#end-date'].forEach(input => (qs(input).value
= ''));

  window.dispatchEvent(new Event('data-loaded'));
}

window.onload = loadData;
```

1. Calls **`getUserEmail()`**, **`getRequests()`**, and **`getRemainingQuota()`** in parallel using **`Promise.all()`**.
2. Stores the fetched data in the **`Storage`** class (defined below).
3. Clears the start date and end date inputs.
4. Dispatches a custom event (**`data-loaded`**), which will trigger UI updates.

Storing Data Locally

To ensure a separation of concerns, we store data in **`localStorage`** using a wrapper class, and we separate it from the function that renders this data in the UI.

```
class Storage {
  constructor(prefix = 'leaves_') {
    this.prefix = prefix;
  }


  set(key, value) {
    localStorage.setItem(this.prefix + key, JSON.stringify(value));
  }
```

```
  get(key, defaultValue = null) {
    const value = localStorage.getItem(this.prefix + key);
    return value ? JSON.parse(value) : defaultValue;
  }


  remove(key) {
    localStorage.removeItem(this.prefix + key);
  }


  clear() {
    Object.keys(localStorage)
      .filter(key => key.startsWith(this.prefix))
      .forEach(key => localStorage.removeItem(key));
  }
}

const storage = new Storage();
```

1. **Stores, retrieves,** and **removes data** from **`localStorage`**.
2. Uses a **prefix (`leaves_`)** to avoid conflicts with other web apps.

Displaying Data in the UI

Once data is loaded, we trigger **`displayData()`** by listening to the **`data-load`** event.

```
window.addEventListener('data-loaded', displayData);

function displayData() {
  qs('#user-email').innerText = storage.get('userEmail');
  qs('#days-left').innerText = storage.get('remainingQuota');
  qs('#leave-requests').innerHTML = storage
    .get('requests')
    .map(req => {
      const btn =
        'Pending' === req.status ? cloneCancelButton(req.request_
id) : ' ';
      return `
        <tr>
          <td>${formatDate(req.start_date)}</td>
          <td>${formatDate(req.end_date)}</td>
          <td>${req.duration}</td>
          <td>${req.status}</td>
          <td>${btn}</td>
        </tr>
```

```
            `;
        })
        .join('\n');
    }


    function qs(selector) {
      return document.querySelector(selector);
    }
```

How it works:

1. **Updates placeholders (`#user-email`, `#days-left`)** with user data.
2. **Generates a table** dynamically, adding a **`Cancel` button** for pending requests.
3. Uses **`qs()`** as a shortcut for **`document.querySelector()`**.

Generating Cancel Buttons

The **`cancel` button** is only displayed for `Pending` requests.

```
function cloneCancelButton(requestId) {
  const button = qs('#cancel-button-template')
    .content.cloneNode(true)
    .querySelector('button');
  button.dataset.requestId = requestId;
  button.setAttribute('onclick', `cancelRequest(this,
'${requestId}');`);
  return button.outerHTML;
}
```

This function:

1. Clones the **HTML template**:

```
<template id="cancel-button-template">
  <button class="button is-small is-danger is-light">Cancel</
button>
</template>
```

2. Attaches the **`request ID`** to **`data-requestId`**.
3. Sets an **`onclick`** handler that calls **`cancelRequest()`**.

Canceling a Leave Request

```
async function cancelRequest(self, requestId) {
  self.disabled = true;
  self.textContent = 'Cancelling...';
  const r = await runGas('cancelRequest', [requestId]);
  console.log({ r });
  window.dispatchEvent(new Event('reload-data'));
}
```

1. **Disables the button** while processing.
2. Calls **`cancelRequest()`** in **Apps Script**.
3. If successful, **reloads data** by dispatching **`reload-data`**.

```
window.addEventListener('reload-data', loadData);
```

Since **`loadData()`** already updates the UI, the user sees the latest leave requests without refreshing the page.

Submitting a Leave Request

```
<button class="button is-primary" onclick="submitLeaveRequest
(this)">
  Submit Leave Request
</button>

async function submitLeaveRequest(self) {
  const start = new Date(qs('#start-date').value);
  const end = new Date(qs('#end-date').value);
  console.log({ start, end });
  checkDuration(start, end);
  try {
    self.disabled = true;
    self.innerText = 'Submitting...';
    await runGas('saveRequest', [
      start.toISOString().split('T')[0],
      end.toISOString().split('T')[0],
    ]);
    dispatchEvent(new Event('reload-data'));
  } catch (err) {
    return showLeaveError(err);
  } finally {
    self.disabled = false;
    self.innerText = 'Submit Leave Request';
  }
}
```

1. **Validates input** (**`checkDuration`**).
2. **Calls `saveRequest()`** in Apps Script.
3. If successful, triggers **`reload-data`** to refresh the UI.
4. **Handles errors gracefully** with **`showLeaveError()`**.

Validating Input

```
function checkDuration(start, end) {
  if ('Invalid Date' == start) return showLeaveError('Invalid start date');
  if ('Invalid Date' == end) return showLeaveError('Invalid end date');
  if (end <= start)
    return showLeaveError('End date cannot be earlier than start date');
  if (start <= Date.now())
    return showLeaveError('Leave request cannot start before tomorrow');
  const MS_IN_DAY = 1000 * 60 * 60 * 24;
  if (Math.ceil((end - start) / MS_IN_DAY) > storage.get('remainingQuota'))
    return showLeaveError(
      `Leave duration exceeds remaining quota of ${storage.get('remainingQuota')} days`
    );
}
```

Displaying Errors

```
function showLeaveError(msg) {
  const errorDiv = qs('#leave-error');
  errorDiv.textContent = msg;
  errorDiv.classList.remove('is-hidden');
  setTimeout(() => {
    errorDiv.classList.add('is-hidden');
    errorDiv.textContent = '';
  }, 3000);
  throw new Error(msg);
}
```

1. Displays error messages in the UI.
2. Automatically hides errors after 3 seconds.
3. Throws an error to stop execution.

Final Result

Once everything is connected, the web app dynamically loads and updates data from the Apps Script backend without requiring a full page refresh.

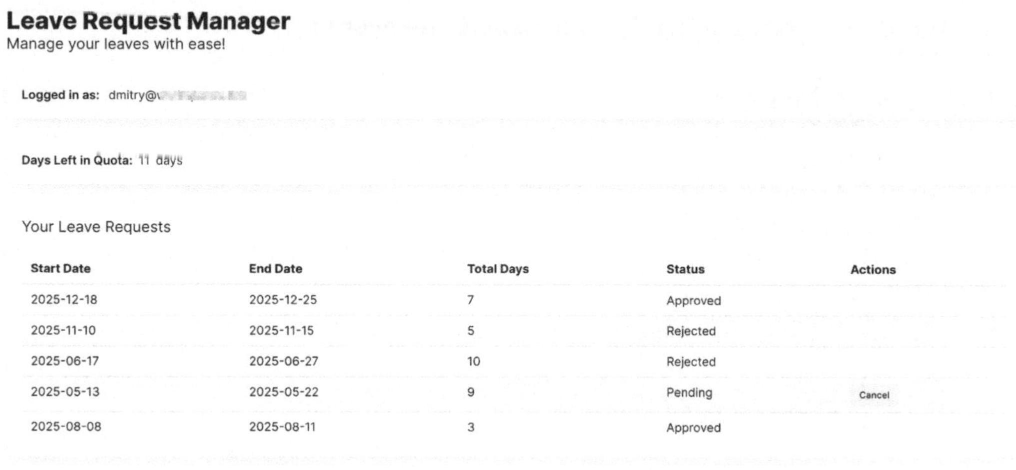

***Figure 12.5:** The web app with data from the spreadsheet*

This completes the Leave Request Web App!

Putting It All Into Action

Now that we have built the leave request web app, it is time to test its functionality. We will go through submitting, canceling, approving, and rejecting requests to ensure everything works as expected.

Submitting a New Leave Request

1. Open the web app and enter start and end dates.
2. Click "**`Submit Leave Request`**".

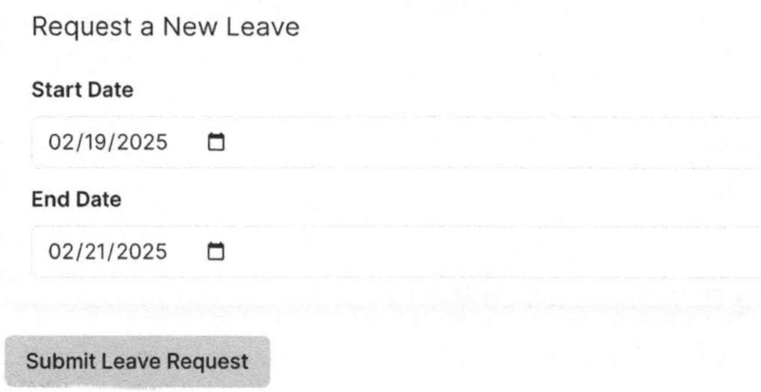

***Figure 12.6:** Submitting a new leave request on the UI*

After submission:

1. The UI refreshes with the new request appearing in Pending status.
2. The quota updates to reflect the deducted leave days.

Your Leave Requests

Start Date	End Date	Total Days	Status	Actions
2025-12-17	2025-12-24	8	Approved	
2025-11-09	2025-11-14	6	Rejected	
2025-06-16	2025-06-26	11	Rejected	
2025-06-30	2025-07-06	7	Pending	Cancel
2025-05-09	2025-05-13	5	Approved	
2025-02-11	2025-02-17	7	Rejected	
2025-02-18	2025-02-20	3	Pending	Cancel

Figure 12.7: *The new request appears in the UI*

3. **Verify the spreadsheet**: A new row should be added with the request details.
4. **Check the manager's inbox**: They should receive an email notification.

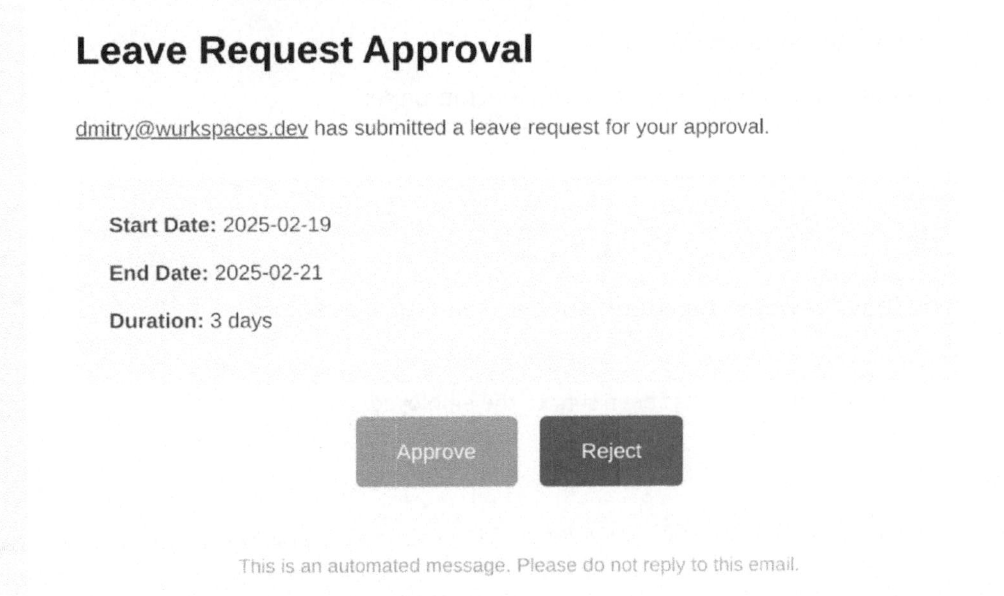

Figure 12.8: *The email received by the manager*

Canceling a Leave Request

1. **Ignore the approval email for now** (you can delete it).
2. **Click "`Cancel`"** next to the request in the UI.

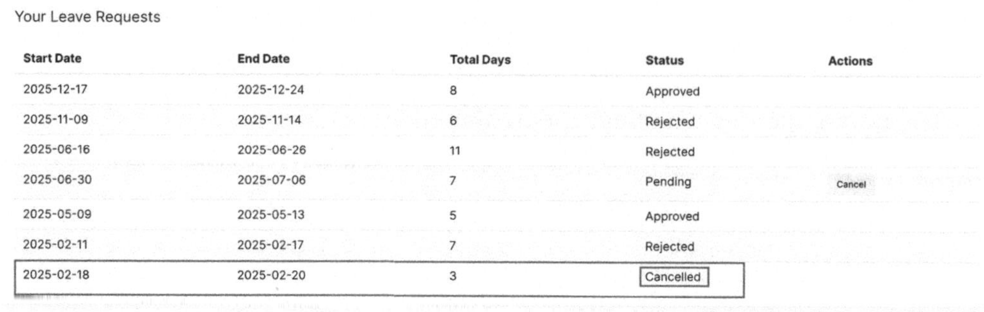

Your Leave Requests

Start Date	End Date	Total Days	Status	Actions
2025-12-17	2025-12-24	8	Approved	
2025-11-09	2025-11-14	6	Rejected	
2025-06-16	2025-06-26	11	Rejected	
2025-06-30	2025-07-06	7	Pending	Cancel
2025-05-09	2025-05-13	5	Approved	
2025-02-11	2025-02-17	7	Rejected	
2025-02-18	2025-02-20	3	Cancelled	

Figure 12.9: *The request switched to the "Cancelled" status*

After canceling:

1. The UI updates, and the request status changes to "**`Cancelled`**".
2. The leave quota is restored.

Approving a Leave Request

1. Submit a new request and check the manager's inbox.
2. Click "**`Approve`**" in the email.

After clicking, the manager sees a confirmation page:

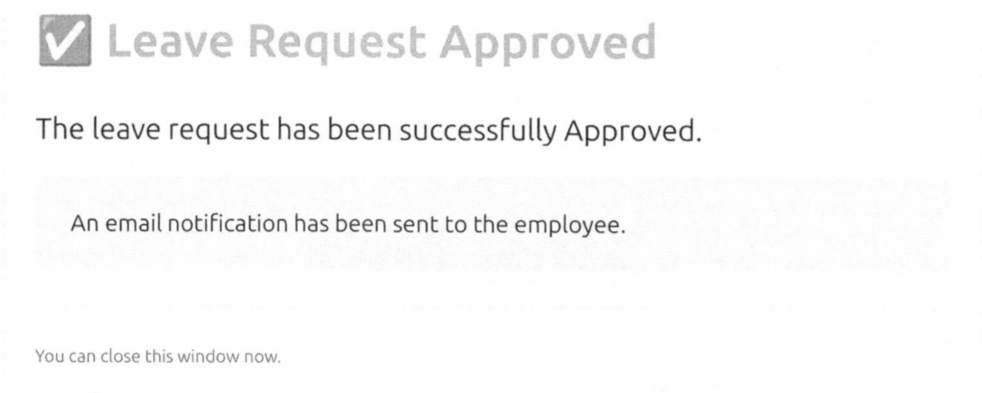

Figure 12.10: *Leave request approval confirmation*

3. The employee receives a confirmation email:

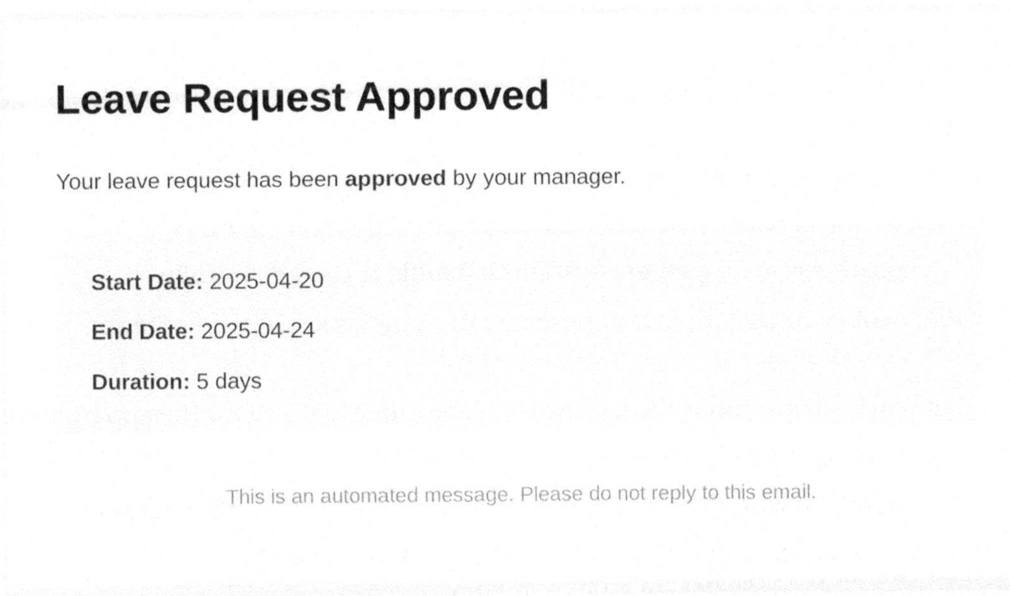

Figure 12.11: *The employee confirmation email*

4. When the employee refreshes the web app, the status updates to **Approved**.

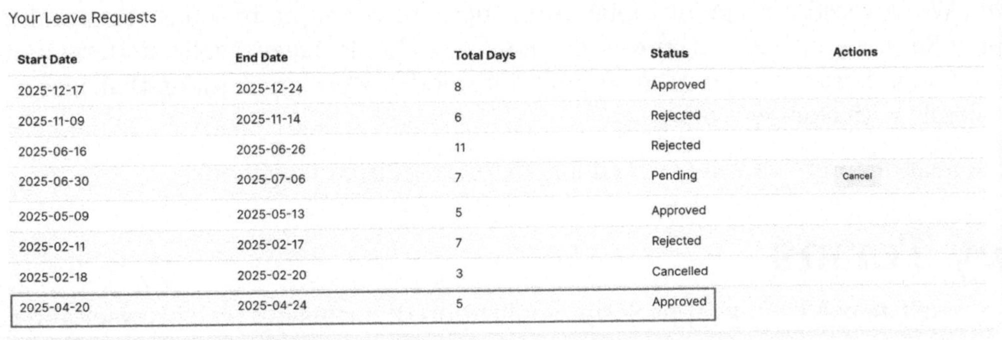

Your Leave Requests

Start Date	End Date	Total Days	Status	Actions
2025-12-17	2025-12-24	8	Approved	
2025-11-09	2025-11-14	6	Rejected	
2025-06-16	2025-06-26	11	Rejected	
2025-06-30	2025-07-06	7	Pending	Cancel
2025-05-09	2025-05-13	5	Approved	
2025-02-11	2025-02-17	7	Rejected	
2025-02-18	2025-02-20	3	Cancelled	
2025-04-20	2025-04-24	5	Approved	

Figure 12.12: *The request switched to approved status*

Congratulations!

If you followed along, well done! You have successfully built a functional web app using Google Apps Script. This app:

- Manages leave requests with an intuitive UI.
- Interacts with Google Sheets as a database.
- Sends email notifications to employees and managers.
- Implements client-server communication using `google.script.run`.

Next Steps

Although this web app works, it is not production-ready. A real-world deployment would require:

- More robust error handling.
- Improved security measures, such as authentication checks.
- A better user management system to handle roles dynamically.

To further explore Apps Script web apps, check out the official documentation: https://developers.google.com/apps-script/guides/web

Now that you have mastered the basics, try experimenting! Extend the app by adding:

- A dashboard for managers to see all requests in one place.
- An approval workflow that supports multiple levels of authorization.
- A calendar integration to block leave days automatically.

Conclusion

In this chapter, we explored how to build a Google Apps Script web app from start to finish. We covered a range of topics from the core concepts to integrating multiple Google Services in our workflows. By now, you should have a solid understanding of how Apps Script can be used to build interactive web applications that integrate seamlessly with Google Workspace.

In the next chapter, we will cover calling external APIs and webhooks.

Key Terms

- **`Web App`**: A Google Apps Script application that runs in a web browser and can be accessed via a unique URL.
- **`doGet(e)`**: A reserved function in Apps Script that handles **`HTTP GET`** requests and is used to serve web app interfaces.
- **`doPost(e)`**: A reserved function in Apps Script that handles **`HTTP POST`** requests, commonly used for APIs and webhooks.
- **`HTML Service`**: An Apps Script service that allows developers to build and serve web pages using HTML, CSS, and JavaScript.
- **`Content Service`**: A service that returns plain text or JSON responses instead of an HTML UI, useful for building APIs.
- **`Session.getActiveUser()`**: A method that retrieves the email address of the currently logged-in user.

- **`google.script.run`**: A client-side object that allows JavaScript in an HTML file to call Apps Script functions asynchronously.
- **`Promise`**: A JavaScript object that represents the eventual completion (or failure) of an asynchronous operation, enabling **`async/await`** syntax.
- **`localStorage`**: A browser storage API used to store key-value pairs persistently on the client-side.
- **Universally Unique Identifier `(UUID)`**: A randomly generated string used to uniquely identify records, such as leave requests in the database.
- **`Email Notification`**: An automated email sent from Apps Script, often used to inform users of status updates.
- **`Bulma`**: A lightweight CSS framework used to style web apps without requiring custom CSS.

CHAPTER 13
APIs and Web Hooks

Introduction

In the previous chapter, we explored web apps, where users interacted with Apps Script functions through a graphical interface. But sometimes, our applications need to interact with other applications directly, without human input. This is where **Application Programming Interfaces (APIs)** and **web hooks** come into play.

APIs allow applications to send requests to other applications and receive responses. For example, when you use Google Maps to check for available ride-hailing drivers nearby, Google Maps communicates with the ride-hailing service's API to fetch and display real-time locations.

Web hooks work differently. Instead of actively requesting information, a web hook listens for an event from another application and reacts when that event occurs. For example, a web hook can notify an application when a new commit is pushed to a GitHub repository, allowing the application to take action automatically.

In this chapter, we will build a Google Apps Script project that interacts with the **GitHub API** in both ways:

- We will **query all commits** for a given repository using the GitHub API.
- We will set up a **web hook** that listens for commit events and updates a Google Sheet automatically.

This means that instead of manually refreshing or updating our spreadsheet, GitHub will push updates to us whenever a new commit is made.

To follow along, you should already be familiar with **git** and **GitHub**. Every developer should be comfortable with these tools, as they are fundamental to modern software development. If you are not, take a couple of days to learn them, it is one of the most valuable skills you can acquire.

If you are ready, let us start by looking into the **GitHub API documentation** to understand how we can interact with it.

Structure

In this chapter we will cover:

- Making API calls to the GitHub API using **`UrlFetchAppp`**
- Setting up a web hook to listen to GitHub events

Making API Calls to the GitHub API Using `UrlFetchApp`

Before we start coding, let us take a moment to understand how the GitHub API works. Whenever you integrate a new service, **always start with the documentation**. This helps you understand what the API expects, how to authenticate, and what kind of responses you will receive.

GitHub provides detailed documentation on its REST API, which you can find here: https://docs.github.com/en/rest/quickstart

For this project, we will focus on the **`/commits`** endpoint, which allows us to retrieve commit history from a repository. Before diving into the API calls, let us first set up the spreadsheet where we will store the commit data.

Creating a New Spreadsheet

The spreadsheet setup is straightforward. All we need is a blank Google Sheet where the commit data will be displayed. However, make sure to create a **bound script** because that is where we will write all the automation logic.

To create a bound script:

1. Open a new Google Sheet.
2. Click on **`Extensions`** > **`Apps Script`**.
3. This will open the script editor, where we will write our code.

Now that we have our spreadsheet ready, let us move on to authentication.

Generating a GitHub API Token

GitHub requires authentication to access private data and some rate-limited endpoints. We need to generate a **Personal Access Token (classic)** to make authorized API requests.

Steps to Create a GitHub Token:

1. Go to your GitHub profile.
2. Navigate to **Settings** > **Developer Settings**.
3. Click **Tokens (classic)** under **Personal access tokens** in the left sidebar.
4. Click **Generate new token**, then select **Generate new token (classic)**.
5. Under "**Select scopes**," choose **repo** to allow access to repository commits.
6. Click **Generate token**.
7. **Copy the token immediately**—you will not be able to see it again.

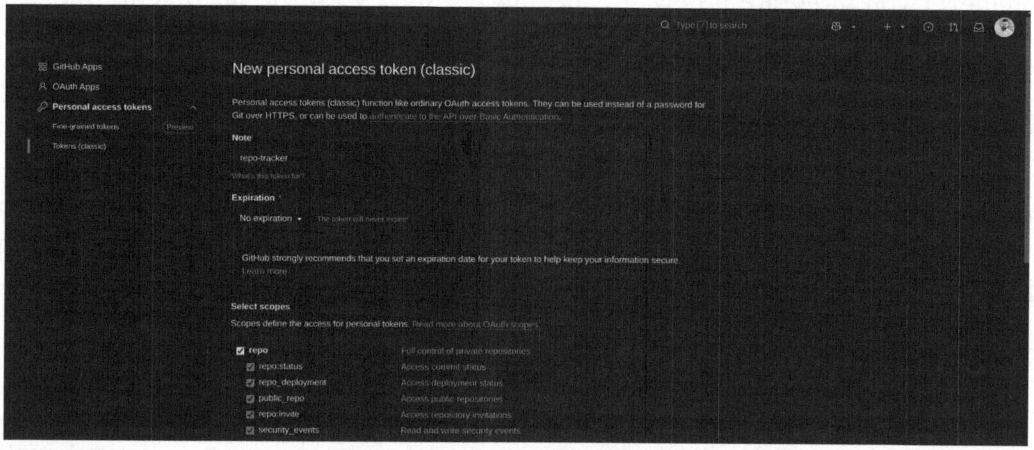

Figure 13.1: *Granting **repo** permissions to our key*

To store this token in our script, add the following line at the top of your Apps Script project:

```
const GITHUB_TOKEN = 'YOUR_GITHUB_TOKEN';
```

Important: *In production, storing sensitive tokens directly in the script is not secure. A better approach is to use the* **Properties Service** *to store credentials safely. You can refer to earlier chapters on how to do this. For now, we will keep things simple and focus on working with the API.*

Calling the `/commits` Endpoint

To retrieve commit history, we need to break down the API documentation and translate it into an Apps Script function.

Understanding the API Request

According to the GitHub API documentation, here is what we need:

- **Method:** `GET`
- **Base URL:** `https://api.github.com`
- **Endpoint:** `/repos/<REPO_OWNER>/<REPO_NAME>/commits`
- **Headers:**
    - `"Accept": "application/vnd.github+json"`
    - `"X-GitHub-Api-Version": "2022-11-28"`

These elements define the request that we need to send.

Translating the API Request to Apps Script

First, define the repository details in the script:

```
const REPO_OWNER = '<YOUR_GITHUB_NAME>';
const REPO_NAME = '<YOUR_REPO_NAME>';
```

Now, create a function to fetch commit data from GitHub:

```
function getGitHubCommits() {
  const options = {
    method: 'GET',
    headers: {
      Accept: 'application/vnd.github+json',
      'X-GitHub-Api-Version': '2022-11-28',
      Authorization: `Bearer ${GITHUB_TOKEN}`,
    },
    muteHttpExceptions: true,
  };

  const url = `https://api.github.com/repos/${REPO_OWNER}/$
{REPO_NAME}/commits`;
  const response = UrlFetchApp.fetch(url, options);

  if (response.getResponseCode() === 200) {
    const commits = JSON.parse(response.getContentText());
    PubSub.init().publish('commits-load', commits);
    return commits;
  } else {
    console.error('Error fetching commits:', response.getContent-
Text());
    return null;
  }
}
```

How it works:

1. The **`options`** object defines the HTTP request method and headers.
2. The **`Authorization`** header includes our GitHub token using the **`Bearer`** scheme.
3. The **`muteHttpExceptions: true`** option prevents errors from stopping script execution. If the request fails, we can handle it manually.
4. We send the request using **`UrlFetchApp.fetch(url, options)`**.
5. If the response is successful (**`200 OK`**), we parse the JSON response and **`publish`** an event with the commit data.
6. If the request fails, we log the error.

Using Event-Based Architecture

Instead of calling functions directly, we use an event-based system. This makes our script **more modular** and **easier to extend**.

The PubSub Class

Apps Script does not have built-in event listeners, so we create our own **publish-subscribe system**:

```
class PubSub {
  constructor() {
    if (PubSub.instance) return PubSub.instance;
    this.subscriptions = [];
    PubSub.instance = this;
    return PubSub.instance;
  }
  static init() {
    return new PubSub();
  }
  static get instance() {
    return PubSub.__instance;
  }
  static set instance(pubsub) {
    PubSub.__instance = pubsub;
  }
  subscribe(eventName, callback) {
    this.subscriptions.push({ eventName, callback });
  }
  publish(eventName, data) {
```

```
    this.subscriptions.forEach(
      subscription =>
        subscription.eventName === eventName && subscription.
callback(data)
    );
  }
}
```

How it works:

1. The class is a **Singleton**, ensuring only one instance exists.
2. The **subscribe(event, callback)** method registers event listeners.
3. The **publish(event, data)** method triggers all subscribed functions.

Now, let us subscribe to the **commits-load** event and process the commit data.

Displaying Commits in Google Sheets

Create the following functions:

```
function main() {
  PubSub.init().subscribe('commits-load', printCommits);
  getGitHubCommits();
}


function printCommits(commits) {
  const data = commits.map(item => ({
    avatar: item.committer.avatar_url,
    name: item.commit.author.name,
    date: item.commit.committer.date,
    message: item.commit.message,
    sha: item.sha,
    url: item.url,
  }));
  const ws = SpreadsheetApp.getActive().getSheets()[0];
  ws.clearContents();
  const twoDimAr = [['Avatar', 'Committer', 'Date', 'Message',
'SHA']];
  const ssData = data.reduce(
    (acc, row) => [
      ...acc,
      [
        `=image("${row.avatar}")`,
        row.name,
        row.date,
```

```
          row.message,
          `=hyperlink("${row.url}", "${row.sha}")`,
        ],
      ],
      twoDimAr
    );
    ws.getRange(1, 1, ssData.length, ssData[0].length).setVal-
ues(ssData);
}
```

How it works:

1. **`main()`**:
    a. Subscribes to the **`commits-load`** event.
    b. Calls **`getGitHubCommits()`**.
2. **`printCommits()`**:
    a. Transforms API data into a **2D array**.
    b. Uses **`=IMAGE()`** to show author avatars.
    c. Uses **`=HYPERLINK()`** to make commit SHA clickable.
    d. Clears the sheet and inserts new commit data.

Now, let us add a simple menu to trigger **`main()`**.

Adding a Custom Menu

To add a custom menu, the code is as follows:

```
function onOpen() {
  SpreadsheetApp.getUi()
    .createMenu('• GitHub Tracker')
    .addToUi();
}
```

When you open the spreadsheet, you will see a **`GitHub Tracker`** menu that lets you fetch commits with one click.

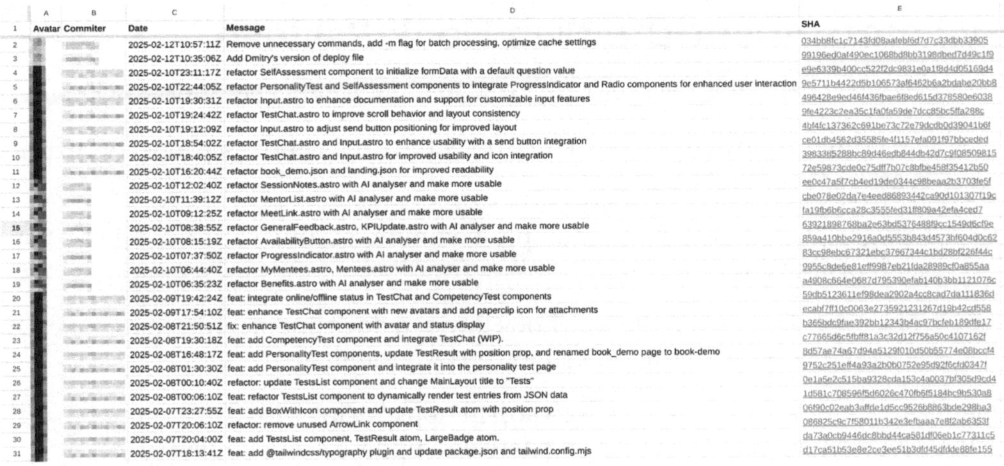

	A	B	C	D	E
1	Avatar	Commiter	Date	Message	SHA
2			2025-02-12T10:57:11Z	Remove unnecessary commands, add -m flag for batch processing, optimize cache settings	034bb8fc1c7143fd08aafebf6d7d7c33dbb33905
3			2025-02-12T10:35:06Z	Add Dmitry's version of deploy file	99196ed0af490ec1068bd8bb3198dbed7d49c1f9
4			2025-02-10T23:11:17Z	refactor SelfAssessment component to initialize formData with a default question value	e9e6339b400cc522f2dc9831e0a1f8d4d05169d4
5			2025-02-10T22:44:05Z	refactor PersonalityTest and SelfAssessment components to integrate ProgressIndicator and Radio components for enhanced user interaction	9e5711b4422d5b106573af6462b6a2bdabe20bb8
6			2025-02-10T19:30:31Z	refactor Input.astro to enhance documentation and support for customizable input features	496428e9ed46f436fbae6f8ed615d378580e6038
7			2025-02-10T19:24:42Z	refactor TestChat.astro to improve scroll behavior and layout consistency	9fe4223c2ea35c1fa0fa59de7dcc85bc5ffa288c
8			2025-02-10T19:12:09Z	refactor Input.astro to adjust send button positioning for improved layout	4bf4fc137362c691be73c72e79dcdb0d39041b6f
9			2025-02-10T18:54:02Z	refactor TestChat.astro and Input.astro to enhance usability with a send button integration	ce01db4562d35585fe4f1157efa091f97bbceded
10			2025-02-10T18:40:05Z	refactor TestChat.astro and Input.astro for improved usability and icon integration	3983385288bc89d46edb844db42d7c9f08509815
11			2025-02-10T16:20:44Z	refactor book_demo.json and landing.json for improved readability	72e59873cde0c75dff7b07c8bfbe458f35412b50
12			2025-02-10T12:02:40Z	refactor SessionNotes.astro with AI analyser and make more usable	ee0c47a5f7cb4ed19de0344c98beaa2b3703fe5f
13			2025-02-10T11:39:12Z	refactor MentorList.astro with AI analyser and make more usable	cbe078e02da7e4eed86893442ca90d101307f19c
14			2025-02-10T09:12:25Z	refactor MeetLink.astro with AI analyser and make more usable	fa19fb6b6cca28c3555fed31ff809a42efa4ced7
15			2025-02-10T08:38:55Z	refactor GeneralFeedback.astro, KPIUpdate.astro with AI analyser and make more usable	63921898768ba2e63bd5376488f9cc1549d6cf9e
16			2025-02-10T08:15:19Z	refactor AvailabilityButton.astro with AI analyser and make more usable	859a410bbe2916a0d5553b843d4573bf604d0c62
17			2025-02-10T07:37:50Z	refactor ProgressIndicator.astro with AI analyser and make more usable	83cc98ebc67321ebc37667344c1bd28bf226f44c
18			2025-02-10T06:44:40Z	refactor MyMentees.astro, Mentees.astro with AI analyser and make more usable	9955c8de6e81eff9987eb21fda28989cf0a855aa
19			2025-02-10T06:35:23Z	refactor Benefits.astro with AI analyser and make more usable	a4908c664e0687d795390efab140b3bb1121076c
20			2025-02-09T19:42:24Z	feat: integrate online/offline status in TestChat and CompetencyTest components	59db5123611ef98dea2902a4cc8cad7da111836d
21			2025-02-09T17:54:10Z	feat: enhance TestChat component with new avatars and add paperclip icon for attachments	ecabf7ff10c0063e2735921231267d19b42cd558
22			2025-02-08T21:50:51Z	fix: enhance TestChat component with avatar and status display	b365bdc9fae392bb12343b4ac97bcfeb189dfe17
23			2025-02-08T19:30:18Z	feat: add CompetencyTest component and integrate TestChat (WIP).	c77665d6c5fbff81a3c32d12f756a50c4107162f
24			2025-02-08T16:48:17Z	feat: add PersonalityTest components, update TestResult with position prop, and renamed book_demo page to book-demo	8d57ae74a67d94a5129f010d50b55774e08bccf4
25			2025-02-08T01:30:30Z	feat: add PersonalityTest component and integrate it into the personality test page	9752c251eff4a93a2b0b0752e95d92f6cfd0347f
26			2025-02-08T00:10:40Z	refactor: update TestsList component and change MainLayout title to "Tests"	0e1a5e2c515ba9328cda153c4a0037bf305d9cd4
27			2025-02-08T00:06:10Z	feat: refactor TestsList component to dynamically render test entries from JSON data	1d581c708596f5d6026c470fb6f5184bc9b530a8
28			2025-02-07T23:27:55Z	feat: add BoxWithIcon component and update TestResult atom with position prop	06f90c02eab3affde1d5cc9526b8863bde298ba3
29			2025-02-07T20:06:10Z	refactor: remove unused ArrowLink component	086825c9c7f58011b342e3efbaaa7e8f2ab6353f
30			2025-02-07T20:04:00Z	feat: add TestsList component, TestResult atom, LargeBadge atom.	da73a0cb9446dc8bbd44ca581df06eb1c77311c5
31			2025-02-07T18:13:41Z	feat: add @tailwindcss/typography plugin and update package.json and tailwind.config.mjs	d17ca51b53e8e2ce3ee51b3dfd45dfdde88fe155

Figure 13.2: *The commits downloaded from the API to the spreadsheet*

Now that we can fetch GitHub commits, let us move on to setting up a web hook that updates the spreadsheet automatically when a new commit is made!

Setting Up a Web Hook to Listen to GitHub Events

To complete our integration with GitHub, we need to set up a **web hook**. This will allow GitHub to send **real-time updates** to our Apps Script whenever new commits are pushed to the repository.

The official GitHub documentation on web hooks can be found here: https://docs.github.com/en/rest/repos/webhooks

This page covers various operations such as creating, updating, deleting, and listing web hooks. While we will not go into all of these, it is worth reviewing them on your own. Our focus will be on **setting up a web hook in Apps Script** and registering it with GitHub.

Processing the Web Hook's Payload

Before writing code, we need to understand the payload structure that GitHub will send to our web hook.

For a `push` event (which is triggered when commits are pushed to a repository), the payload format is documented here: https://docs.github.com/en/webhooks/webhook-events-and-payloads#push

Key Points About the Web Hook Payload

1. GitHub sends a **POST** request to our web hook when a commit is pushed.
2. The request body contains a JSON object, with a **commits** property that holds an array of commit objects.
3. A single push can include multiple commits, so our script needs to handle batch processing.
4. Unlike the GitHub API, the web hook payload does not include commit avatars—we would need an extra API call to retrieve them.

To handle this, we need to deploy a web app in Apps Script with a **doPost(e)** function. This function will process the incoming data and update our Google Sheet.

Writing the Web Hook Handler

Here is our **doPost(e)** function:

```
function doPost(e) {
  const { contents } = e.postData;
  const { commits } = JSON.parse(contents);
  const data = commits.map(item => ({
    name: item.author.name,
    date: item.timestamp,
    message: item.message,
    sha: item.id,
    url: item.url,
  }));
  const ssData = data.reduce(
    (acc, row) => [
      ...acc,
      [
        '',
        row.name,
        row.date,
        row.message,
        `=hyperlink("${row.url}", "${row.sha}")`,
      ],
    ],
    []
  );
  const ws = SpreadsheetApp.getActive().getSheets()[0];
  ws.insertRows(2, ssData.length);
```

```
  ws.getRange(2, 1, ssData.length, ssData[0].length).
setValues(ssData);
  SpreadsheetApp.flush();
}
```

How it works:

1. Extracts JSON data from the incoming **`POST`** request using **`e.postData.contents`**.
2. Parses the JSON and extracts the **`b`** array.
3. Transforms each commit object into a simpler structure containing:
   - **`name`**: Commit author's name
   - **`date`**: Commit timestamp
   - **`message`**: Commit message
   - **`sha`**: Commit SHA (unique commit ID)
   - **`url`**: Link to the commit on GitHub
4. Formats the data as a 2D array for Google Sheets.
5. Inserts new rows at the top of the sheet (row **`2`**), so that new commits appear at the top.
6. Uses the **`=HYPERLINK()`** formula to make commit SHAs clickable.
7. Calls **`SpreadsheetApp.flush()`** to ensure the update is applied immediately.

The GitHub web hook **does not include the `avatar_url` field**. If you want to display avatars, you would need to make an **extra API call** to fetch them. This is a good exercise to try on your own!

Deploying the Web Hook

To allow GitHub to send requests to our script, we need to **deploy it as a web app**.

1. Open the **`Apps Script editor`** (**`Extensions`** > **`Apps Script`**).
2. Click **`Deploy`** > **`New Deployment`**.
3. Under **`Select type`**, choose **`Web app`**.
4. Set **`Who has access`** to **`Anyone`** (this is required for GitHub to send data).
5. Click **`Deploy`**, then copy the **`Web App URL`**.

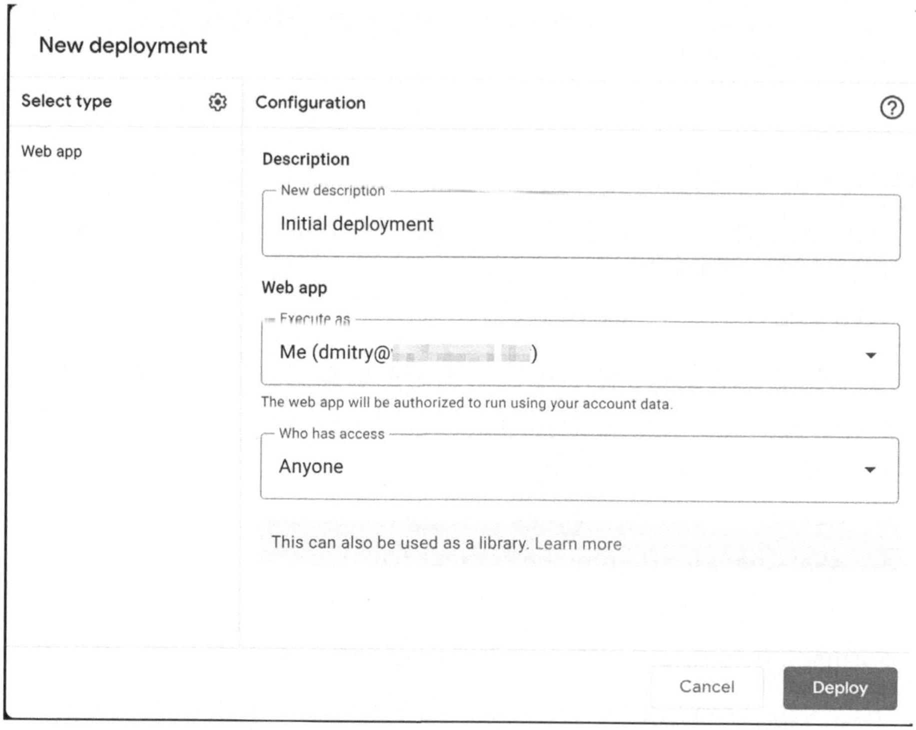

Figure 13.3: *Deploying the web hook with the* ***`doPost()`*** *trigger*

Now that we have the deployment URL, we can proceed to registering the web hook on GitHub!

Registering the Web Hook

At this stage, our Apps Script web hook is ready, but GitHub does not know about it yet. We need to register it with the GitHub API, so that GitHub knows where to send commit events.

To do this, we will make an API call to GitHub to create a web hook for our repository. Let us build a function in Apps Script to handle this.

Creating the Web Hook via API

The following function **sends a `POST` request** to GitHub's API to register our web hook:

```
function createWebhook_(webhookUrl, events = ['push',
'pull_request']) {
 const options = {
    method: 'POST',
    headers: {
      Accept: 'application/vnd.github+json',
```

```
      'X-GitHub-Api-Version': '2022-11-28',
      Authorization: `Bearer ${GITHUB_TOKEN}`,
      'Content-Type': 'application/json',
    },
    payload: JSON.stringify({
      name: 'web',
      active: true,
      events,
      config: {
        url: webhookUrl,
        content_type: 'json',
        insecure_ssl: '0',
      },
    }),
    muteHttpExceptions: true,
  };

  const url = `https://api.github.com/repos/${REPO_OWNER}/$
{REPO_NAME}/hooks`;
  const response = UrlFetchApp.fetch(url, options);

  if (response.getResponseCode() === 201) {
    const webhook = JSON.parse(response.getContentText());
    console.log('Webhook created successfully:', webhook);
    return webhook;
  } else {
    console.error('Error creating webhook:', response.getContent-
Text());
    return null;
  }
}
```

How it works:

1. Defines a **POST** request with required headers.
2. Specifies the web hook configuration:
    a. **url**: The URL of our Apps Script web app (this is where GitHub will send **POST** requests).
    b. **events**: Listens for **push** and **pull_request** events.
    c. **content_type**: **json** ensures the payload is JSON.
    d. **insecure_ssl**: Set to **'0'** to enforce HTTPS.

3. Sends the request to GitHub's API.
4. Checks the response:
   a. If successful (**201**), logs the created web hook.
   b. If there is an error, logs the response.

Adding a Simple UI to Register the Web Hook

To make this process easier, let us add a **prompt** that lets us **enter the web hook URL** instead of hardcoding it.

```
function newWebHook() {
  const ui = SpreadsheetApp.getUi();
  const userResp = ui.prompt(
    'Please paste the web hook URL',
    ui.ButtonSet.OK_CANCEL
  );
  const [button, url] = [
    userResp.getSelectedButton(),
    userResp.getResponseText(),
  ];
  if (button === ui.Button.CANCEL) return;

  const re = /(https:\/\/www\.|http:\/\/www\.|https:\/\/|http:\
/\/)?[a-zA-Z]{2,}(\.[a-zA-Z]{2,})(\.[a-zA-Z]{2,})?\/[a-zA-Z0-9]
{2,}|((https:\/\/www\.|http:\/\/www\.|https:\/\/|http:\/\/)
?[a-zA-Z]{2,}(\.[a-zA-Z]{2,})(\.[a-zA-Z]{2,})?)|(https:\/\/
www\.|http:\/\/www\.|https:\/\/|http:\/\/)?[a-zA-Z0-9]{2,}\.
[a-zA-Z0-9]{2,}\.[a-zA-Z0-9]{2,}(\.[a-zA-Z0-9]{2,})?/g;

  if (!re.test(url)) throw new Error('Invalid URL syntax');

  const ws = SpreadsheetApp.getActive();
  ws.toast(`Creating a repo webhook at this URL: ${url}`);
  const result = createWebhook_(url, ['push']);
  if (null === result)
    throw new Error(
      'Could not create web hook; see execution log for details.'
    );
  ws.toast(`Repo web hook created at this URL: ${url}`);
}
```

How it works:

1. **Displays a prompt** asking the user to paste the web hook URL.

2. **Handles user input:**
    a. If the user clicks "**Cancel**," the function exits.
    b. Otherwise, it checks if the input matches a **valid URL pattern**.
3. **Calls `createWebhook_()`** to register the web hook.
4. **Displays a toast message** showing whether the web hook was successfully created.

Updating the Menu

Now, let us **modify** the **`onOpen()` function** so we can easily register a new web hook from the menu.

```
function onOpen() {
  SpreadsheetApp.getUi()
    .createMenu(' GitHub Tracker')
    .addItem('⬇ Download commits', 'main')
    .addItem(' Create web hook', 'newWebHook')
    .addToUi();
}
```

After reloading the menu, you will now see the option to create a **GitHub web hook**:

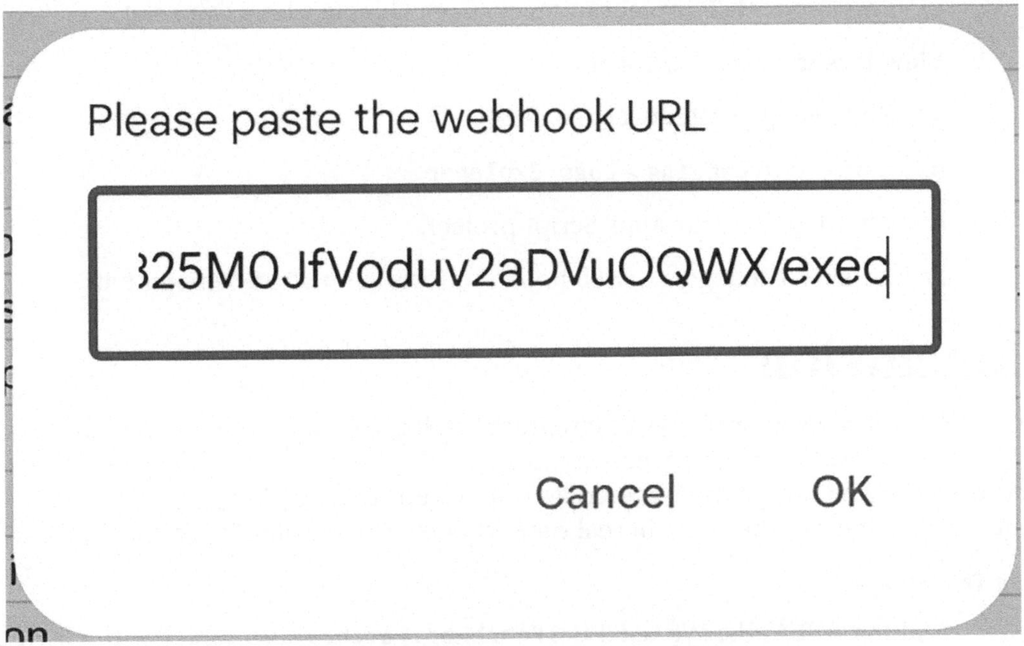

***Figure 13.4:** Submitting the web hook URL*

Testing the Web Hook

Now that the web hook is registered, let us test it:

1. Make sure your Apps Script is deployed as a web app.
2. Register the web hook using the menu.
3. Push a new commit to the GitHub repository.
4. Watch the spreadsheet update in real-time!

If everything is set up correctly, new commits will automatically appear at the top of the sheet whenever a push is made to the repository.

Viewing Logs in a Deployed Web App

Apps Script logs (`console.log()`) **do not appear** in the online IDE when running as a deployed web app. To view logs, you need to:

1. **Enable logging in Google Cloud Platform (GCP):**
    a. Go to the **`Apps Script IDE`**.
    b. Click on **`Project Settings`**.
    c. Enter your **GCP project number** (from Google Cloud Console).
2. **View logs in "`Logs Explorer`":**
    a. Go to **`Google Cloud Console`**.
    b. Navigate to **`Logging`** > **`Logs Explorer`**.
    c. Filter logs by your Apps Script project.

This will allow you to debug your web hook requests **even after deployment**.

Conclusion

In this chapter, we explored how to integrate GitHub's API and web hooks with Google Apps Script to track repository activity in a Google Sheet. By combining API requests and event-driven automation, we created a system that fetches commit history on demand and updates the sheet in real time whenever new commits are pushed.

Key Takeaways:

- **Making API Calls:** We used `UrlFetchApp.fetch()` to interact with GitHub's REST API, fetching commit data and displaying it in a Google Sheet.

- **Event-Driven Updates:** We implemented a **PubSub** system to handle API responses asynchronously and improve modularity.
- **Web Hooks:** Instead of polling GitHub for updates, we set up a **web hook listener** (`doPost(e)`) that automatically updates the spreadsheet when new commits are made.
- **Registering the Web Hook:** We created an Apps Script function to register the web hook with GitHub, ensuring seamless integration.
- **Deploying and Debugging:** We learned how to deploy Apps Script as a **web app** and view logs in **Google Cloud Logging** to troubleshoot issues.

Next Step

This setup can be expanded in many ways:

- Fetch additional data like commit author avatars by making extra API calls.
- Track multiple repositories by allowing users to input different repo names.
- Improve security by storing API tokens securely using Properties Service instead of hardcoding them.
- Handle more GitHub events such as issue creation, pull requests, or repository changes.

By mastering APIs and web hooks, you can automate workflows, sync data in real time, and build powerful integrations between Google Workspace and external services.

Key Terms

- **Application Programming Interface (`API`)**: A set of rules that allows applications to communicate with each other, typically via HTTP requests and responses.
- **Web Hook**: A mechanism that enables one application to send real-time data to another application when a specific event occurs.
- **`UrlFetchApp`**: An Apps Script service that allows scripts to make HTTP requests to external APIs.
- **`doPost(e)`**: A reserved function in Apps Script that handles HTTP **`POST`** requests, commonly used for processing web hook payloads.
- **`GitHub API`**: A RESTful web service provided by GitHub that allows users to interact with repositories, commits, issues, and other GitHub resources programmatically.
- **Personal Access Token (`PAT`)**: A secret authentication token used to make API requests on behalf of a GitHub user.

- **`Bearer Token`**: A type of authentication token sent in the **`Authorization`** header of an HTTP request to verify access to an API.
- **`Event-Driven Architecture`**: A programming model where actions are triggered by specific events, such as a web hook receiving new commit data.
- **Publish-Subscribe (`PubSub`)**: A design pattern where publishers send messages (events), and subscribers listen for those messages to react accordingly.
- **`muteHttpExceptions`**: A property in Apps Script's **`UrlFetchApp.fetch()`** method that prevents errors from stopping script execution, allowing error handling through code.
- **`Google Cloud Logging`**: A service that collects and displays logs from Apps Script executions, useful for debugging deployed web apps.
- **`SpreadsheetApp.flush()`**: A method that forces pending spreadsheet changes to be applied immediately.

CHAPTER 14
Exercises and Solutions

Introduction

Congratulations on reaching the final chapter of this book! By now, you should have a solid understanding of the core services and concepts that underpin modern Google Apps Script development. We have journeyed through the fundamentals of JavaScript within the online editor, explored the nuances of bound versus stand-alone scripts, and delved into the specifics of manipulating various Google Workspace applications such as Sheets, Gmail, Drive, Forms, Calendar, Slides, and Docs. We have also touched upon the power of user interfaces, web apps, and integrations with external APIs and webhooks.

This concluding chapter serves as an opportunity to solidify your learning through a series of comprehensive practical exercises. These exercises are designed to challenge you to apply the knowledge gained throughout the book in integrated scenarios, mimicking real-world automation tasks. By working through these problems, you will not only reinforce your understanding of individual services but also learn how to combine them effectively to build more complex and powerful solutions.

This chapter is structured to guide you through a learning process that involves actively problem-solving and reflecting on the concepts you have encountered. We will start with an outline of the chapter, followed by the exercises themselves, detailed answers to help you understand the solutions, and finally, a concluding summary to encourage your continued exploration of Google Apps Script.

Structure

In this chapter, we will cover:

- **Practical Exercises:** A Series of Hands-on Coding Challenges Divided into Sections Based on the Key Areas Covered in the Book. These Exercises will Require you to:

  - Utilize Core JavaScript Concepts within the Apps Script Environment
  - Decide Between Bound and Stand-Alone Scripts for Specific Tasks
  - Interact with Google Sheets to Read and Write Data
  - Send and Manage Emails Using GmailApp
  - Manage Files and Folders in Google Drive
  - Create and Process Google Forms
  - Automate Calendar Events and Guest Management
  - Manipulate Google Slides Presentations
  - Work with Google Docs Content and Structure
  - Implement Simple and Installable Triggers for Automation
  - Build Basic User Interfaces Using Custom Menus and the HTML Service
  - Understand the Fundamental Structure of Web Apps Using `doGet()`
  - Conceptualize Interactions with External APIs Using `UrlFetchApp`
- **Answers to Exercises:** Detailed Explanations and Code Solutions for Each of the Practical Exercises

Practical Exercises

The following exercises are designed to test your understanding of the concepts and services covered in this book. Try to solve them independently before referring to the answers provided in the next section.

Section 1: JavaScript Fundamentals and Script Types

JavaScript Refresher: Write a Google Apps Script function that takes an array of numbers as input and returns the sum of all even numbers in the array.

Bound versus Stand-Alone: Describe a scenario where using a **bound script** would be more appropriate than a stand-alone script, and explain why. Provide a specific example of the Google Workspace application and the task.

Bound versus Stand-Alone: Describe a scenario where using a **stand-alone script** would be more appropriate than a bound script, and explain why. Provide a specific example of the task and the Google Workspace application(s) it might interact with.

Section 2: Google Sheets Automation (`SpreadsheetApp`)

Reading and Writing Data: Write a function that opens the currently active Google Sheet, reads the values from the range "`A1:B5`", and writes these values into the range "`D1:E5`" of the same sheet.

Formatting: Modify the function from the previous `D1:E5` exercise to also apply bold formatting to the header row (row 1) of the destination range "`D1:E5`".

Creating and Deleting Sheets: Write a function that creates a new sheet named "`Summary`" in the active spreadsheet and then deletes it.

Section 3: Gmail Integration (`GmailApp`)

Sending Emails: Write a function that sends an email with the subject "`Automated Report`" to a specified email address. The body of the email should be "`This is an automated report generated by Google Apps Script.`"

Creating Drafts: Modify the previous function to create a draft email instead of sending it directly.

Reading Email Information: Write a function that logs the subjects of the 10 most recent emails in your Gmail inbox.

Section 4: Google Drive Management (`DriveApp`)

Creating Folders: Write a function that creates a new folder named "`Automated Backups`" in your Google Drive root.

Listing Files: Write a function that logs the names of all Google Sheets files present in a specific folder (you will need the folder ID).

Changing Permissions: Write a function that finds a file in your Google Drive (you will need the file ID) and adds a specific email address as a viewer.

Section 5: Google Forms Automation (`FormApp`)

Creating a Basic Form: Write a function that creates a new Google Form with the title "`Feedback Form`" and adds a single short text question titled "`Your Name`".

Getting Form Responses: Write a function that opens the currently active Google Form and logs the email of each respondent and their answer to the first question.

Section 6: Google Calendar Automation (`CalendarApp`)

Creating Calendar Events: Write a function that creates a new calendar event titled "`Meeting with Team`" for the next day at 10:00 AM for one hour in your primary Google Calendar.

Inviting Guests: Modify the previous function to invite a specified email address as a guest to the event.

Section 7: Google Slides Automation (`SlidesApp`)

Creating a Presentation: Write a function that creates a new Google Slides presentation with the title "`Project Update`".

Adding Slides and Text: Modify the previous function to add a new slide to the presentation with the title "`Introduction`" and a text box containing the text "`This presentation provides an update on the project.`"

Section 8: Google Docs Automation (`DocumentApp`)

Creating a Document: Write a function that creates a new Google Doc with the title "`Meeting Notes`".

Adding Text and Formatting: Modify the previous function to add a paragraph to the document with the text "`Attendees: [List of Attendees]`" and apply bold formatting to the word "`Attendees`".

Section 9: Triggers

Simple Trigger: Describe a scenario where a simple `onEdit` trigger could be used to automate a task in Google Sheets. What are the limitations of this type of trigger?

Installable Trigger: Describe a scenario where an installable time-driven trigger would be necessary, highlighting the benefits over a simple trigger.

Programmatic Trigger Management: Outline the steps involved in creating an installable `onFormSubmit` trigger programmatically.

Section 10: User Interfaces (UIs)

Custom Menu: Write a function that creates a custom menu in the active Google Sheet named "`Automation Tools`" with a single item "`Run Script`" that, when clicked, executes a function named `myAutomatedFunction`.

HTML Service - Basic Dialog: Create two files in your Apps Script project: `Code.gs` and **dialog.html**. In **Code.gs**, write a function that displays a simple modal dialog with the title "**Information**" containing the text "**This is a message from a dialog**." The content of the dialog should be in **dialog.html**.

Section 11: Web Apps

Basic Web App: Write a simple **doGet()** function that returns an HTML output displaying the text "**Welcome to my basic web app!**". Deploy this script as a web app and describe how you would access it.

Section 12: APIs and Web Hooks (Conceptual)

Using UrlFetchApp: Describe the basic steps involved in making an HTTP GET request to an external API using the **UrlFetchApp** service in Google Apps Script. What is the purpose of handling the response?

Web Hooks: Explain the concept of a web hook and provide a potential use case for integrating a web hook with Google Apps Script. What Apps Script function is typically used to handle incoming web hook requests?

Answers to Exercises

This section provides detailed answers and code solutions for each of the exercises presented above.

Section 1: JavaScript Fundamentals and Script Types

JavaScript Refresher:

```
// The classic version
function sumOfEvenNumbers(numbers) {
  let sum = 0;
  for (let i = 0; i < numbers.length; i++) {
    if (numbers[i] % 2 === 0) {
      sum += numbers[i];
    }
  }
  return sum;
}

// A more concise version
function sumOfEvenNumbers2(numbers) {
  return numbers.reduce(
```

```
    (sum, number) => (number % 2 === 0 ? sum + number : sum),
    0
  );
}

// Example usage:
const data = [1, 2, 3, 4, 5, 6, 7, 8, 9, 10];
const evenSum = sumOfEvenNumbers(data);
const evenSum2 = sumOfEvenNumbers2(data);
console.log(`The sums of even numbers: ${evenSum} | 
${evenSum2}`);
```

Explanation: This function iterates through the input array **`numbers`**. For each number, it checks if it is even using the modulo operator (**%**). If the remainder when divided by 2 is 0, the number is even and is added to the **`sum`**. Finally, the function returns the total **`sum`** of the even numbers.

Bound versus Stand-Alone (Bound Script): A scenario where a **bound script** is appropriate is when you need to automate tasks that directly interact with the content or structure of a specific Google Workspace document. For example, in a **Google Sheet**, you might have a bound script that automatically formats new rows of data entered by users or creates a summary chart based on the data in the sheet.

Why Bound Script? Bound scripts have direct and easy access to their container document (the Sheet in this case) using built-in methods such as **`SpreadsheetApp.getActiveSpreadsheet()`** or **`SpreadsheetApp.getActiveSheet()`**. They are saved within the document and are automatically available when the document is opened by users with editing permissions. Custom menus and UI elements created by bound scripts are also integrated directly into the host application's interface.

Bound versus Stand-Alone (Stand-Alone Script): A scenario where a **stand-alone script** is appropriate is when you need to automate tasks that are not tied to a specific Google Workspace document or that interact with multiple different documents or services. For example, a stand-alone script could be used to periodically check a Google Sheet for new entries and then send personalized emails using GmailApp to the email addresses listed in the sheet. This script might also update a master tracking sheet in a different Google Sheet or create summary reports in Google Docs.

Why Stand-Alone Script? Stand-alone scripts exist independently in Google Drive and can be scheduled to run at specific times using installable triggers, regardless of whether a specific document is open. They are ideal for utility-type scripts that perform broader automation tasks across multiple applications or that operate in the background. To interact with specific documents, stand-alone scripts need to explicitly open them using their IDs or URLs (e.g., **`SpreadsheetApp.openById('your_spreadsheet_id')`**).

Section 2: Google Sheets Automation (SpreadsheetApp)

Reading and Writing Data:

```
function copyData() {
   const ss = SpreadsheetApp.getActiveSpreadsheet();
   const sourceRange = ss.getActiveSheet().getRange("A1:B5");
   const values = sourceRange.getValues();
   const destinationRange = ss.getActiveSheet().get-
Range("D1:E5");
   destinationRange.setValues(values);
 }
```

Explanation: This function first gets a reference to the active spreadsheet. Then, it gets the range "**A1:B5**" from the active sheet and retrieves its values into a 2D array called **values**. Finally, it gets the destination range "**D1:E5**" and writes the **values** into it.

Formatting:

```
function copyDataAndFormat() {
  const ss = SpreadsheetApp.getActiveSpreadsheet();
  const ws = ss.getActiveSheet();
  const sourceRange = ws.getRange('A1:B5');
  const values = sourceRange.getValues();
  const destinationRange = ws.getRange('D1:E5');
  destinationRange.setValues(values);
  const headerRange = ws.getRange('D1:D5');
  headerRange.setFontWeight('bold');
}
```

Explanation: This function builds upon the previous one. After setting the values in the destination range, it gets the first row of the destination range and applies bold formatting to the font using **setFontWeight("bold")**.

Creating and Deleting Sheets:

```
function createAndDeleteSheet() {
  const ss = SpreadsheetApp.getActiveSpreadsheet();
  const newSheet = ss.insertSheet("Summary");
  ss.deleteSheet(newSheet);
  Logger.log("Created and deleted a sheet named 'Summary'.");
}
```

Explanation: This function gets the active spreadsheet and uses **insertSheet**

("Summary") to create a new sheet named "**Summary**". The **deleteSheet(newSheet)** method then immediately deletes the newly created sheet.

Section 3: Gmail Integration (GmailApp)

Sending Emails:

```
function sendAutomatedReport() {
  const recipientEmail = "your_email@example.com"; // Replace
with a valid email address
  const subject = "Automated Report";
  const body = "This is an automated report generated by Google
Apps Script.";
  GmailApp.sendEmail(recipientEmail, subject, body);
  Logger.log(`Email sent to ${recipientEmail} with subject
'${subject}'.`);
}
```

Explanation: This function uses the **GmailApp.sendEmail()** method, which takes the recipient's email address, the email subject, and the email body as arguments.

Remember to replace "your_email@example.com" with an actual email address for testing.

Creating Drafts:

```
function createAutomatedDraft() {
  const recipientEmail = "your_email@example.com"; // Replace
with a valid email address
  const subject = "Automated Report";
  const body = "This is an automated report generated by Google
Apps Script.";
  GmailApp.createDraft(recipientEmail, subject, body);
  Logger.log(`Draft email created for ${recipientEmail} with
subject '${subject}'.`);
}
```

Explanation: Instead of **sendEmail()**, this function uses **GmailApp.createDraft()**, which creates a new draft email in the user's Gmail account with the specified recipient, subject, and body.

Reading Email Information:

```
function logRecentEmailSubjects() {
  const threads = GmailApp.getInboxThreads(0, 10); // Get the
first 10 inbox threads (most recent)
  for (let i = 0; i < threads.length; i++) {
    const messages = threads[i].getMessages();
    if (messages.length > 0) {
```

```
    Logger.log(`Subject of recent email ${i + 1}: ${messages.
getSubject()}`);
      }
    }
}
```

Explanation: This function uses **`GmailApp.getInboxThreads(0, 10)`** to retrieve the 10 most recent threads in the inbox (starting from index 0, getting 10 threads). It then iterates through these threads and, for each thread, gets the messages within it. It logs the subject of the first message in each thread (which is usually the original email).

Section 4: Google Drive Management (`DriveApp`)

Creating Folders:

```
function createAutomatedBackupsFolder() {
  const folderName = "Automated Backups";
  const newFolder = DriveApp.createFolder(folderName);
  Logger.log(`Folder '${folderName}' created with ID: ${new
Folder.getId()}`);
}
```

Explanation: This function uses **`DriveApp.createFolder("Automated Backups")`** to create a new folder in the root of the user's Google Drive with the specified name. It then logs the ID of the newly created folder.

Listing Files:

```
function listSheetsInFolder(folderId) {
  const folder = DriveApp.getFolderById(folderId);
  const files = folder.getFilesByType(MimeType.GOOGLE_SHEETS);
  Logger.log(`Google Sheets files in folder with ID
'${folderId}':`);
  while (files.hasNext()) {
    const file = files.next();
    Logger.log(file.getName());
  }
}
```

Explanation: This function takes a **`folderId`** as input. It uses **`DriveApp.getFolderById(folderId)`** to get the specified folder. Then, it uses **`folder.getFilesByType(MimeType.GOOGLE_SHEETS)`** to get an iterator of all Google Sheets files within that folder. The **`while (files.hasNext())`** loop iterates through these files, and **`file.getName()`** logs the name of each file.

Remember to replace "your_folder_id_here" with the actual ID of a folder in your Drive.

Changing Permissions:

```
function addViewerPermissionToFile(fileId, viewerEmail) {
   const file = DriveApp.getFileById(fileId);
   file.addViewer(viewerEmail);
   Logger.log(`Added ${viewerEmail} as a viewer to file with ID
'${fileId}'.`);
 }
```

Explanation: This function takes a **fileId** and a **viewerEmail** as input. It uses **DriveApp.getFileById(fileId)** to get the specified file. Then, **file.addViewer(viewerEmail)** adds the given email address as a viewer of the file.

Remember to replace "your_file_id_here" and "viewer_email@example.com" with actual values.

Section 5: Google Forms Automation (FormApp)

Creating a Basic Form:

```
function createBasicFeedbackForm() {
  const formTitle = "Feedback Form";
  const form = FormApp.create(formTitle);
  form.addTextItem().setTitle("Your Name");
  Logger.log(`Form '${formTitle}' created with URL: ${form.get-
PublishedUrl()}`);
}
```

Explanation: This function uses **FormApp.create("Feedback Form")** to create a new Google Form with the specified title. Then, **form.addTextItem().setTitle("Your Name")** adds a short text question to the form with the title "**Your Name**". Finally, it logs the published URL of the created form.

Getting Form Responses:

```
function logFormResponses() {
  const form = FormApp.getActiveForm();
  const responses = form.getResponses();
  Logger.log(`Number of responses: ${responses.length}`);
  responses.forEach(response => {
    const respondentEmail = response.getRespondentEmail();
    Logger.log(`Respondent Email: ${respondentEmail}`);
    const itemResponses = response.getItemResponses();
    if (itemResponses.length > 0) {
```

```
      Logger.log(`Answer to first question: ${itemResponses.
getResponse()}`);
    }
  });
}
```

Explanation: This function first gets the currently active Google Form. It then retrieves all the responses to the form using **`form.getResponses()`**. It iterates through each **`response`**, gets the respondent's email using **`response.getRespondentEmail()`**, and then gets the individual item responses using **`response.getItemResponses()`**. It logs the answer to the first question (**`itemResponses.getResponse()`**).

Section 6: Google Calendar Automation (CalendarApp)

Creating Calendar Events:

```
function createTeamMeetingEvent() {
  const calendar = CalendarApp.getDefaultCalendar();
  const tomorrow = new Date();
  tomorrow.setDate(tomorrow.getDate() + 1);
  tomorrow.setHours(10, 0, 0, 0); // Set to 10:00 AM

  const endTime = new Date(tomorrow);
  endTime.setHours(endTime.getHours() + 1); // Set end time to
11:00 AM

  const eventTitle = "Meeting with Team";
  const event = calendar.createEvent(eventTitle, tomorrow,
endTime);
  Logger.log(`Event '${eventTitle}' created with ID: ${event.
getId()}`);
}
```

Explanation: This function gets the user's default Google Calendar. It creates a **`Date`** object for tomorrow at 10:00 AM and another **`Date`** object for one hour later. It then uses **`calendar.createEvent()`** to create a new event with the specified title, start time, and end time.

Inviting Guests:

```
function createTeamMeetingWithGuest(guestEmail) {
  const calendar = CalendarApp.getDefaultCalendar();
  const tomorrow = new Date();
  tomorrow.setDate(tomorrow.getDate() + 1);
  tomorrow.setHours(10, 0, 0, 0);
```

```
  const endTime = new Date(tomorrow);
  endTime.setHours(endTime.getHours() + 1);

  const eventTitle = "Meeting with Team";
  const event = calendar.createEvent(eventTitle, tomorrow,
endTime, {
    guests: guestEmail
  });
  Logger.log(`Event '${eventTitle}' created with guest
${guestEmail}, ID: ${event.getId()}`);
}
```

Explanation: This function is similar to the previous one, but it includes an optional **`options`** object as the fourth argument to **`calendar.createEvent()`**. This object has a **`guests`** property, which is set to the **`guestEmail`** provided as input. **Remember to replace "`guest@example.com`" with an actual email address for testing.**

Section 7: Google Slides Automation (`SlidesApp`)

Creating a Presentation:

```
function createProjectUpdatePresentation() {
  const presentationTitle = "Project Update";
  const presentation = SlidesApp.create(presentationTitle);
  Logger.log(`Presentation '${presentationTitle}' created with
ID: ${presentation.getId()}`);
}
```

Explanation: This function uses **`SlidesApp.create("Project Update")`** to create a new Google Slides presentation with the specified title. It then logs the ID of the newly created presentation.

Adding slides and text:

```
function addSlideWithTitleAndText() {
  const presentation = SlidesApp.getActivePresentation();
  const slide = presentation.insertSlide(1); // Insert at the
second position (index 1)
  const titleShape = slide.insertTextBox("Introduction");
  titleShape.setLeft(100).setTop(50).setWidth(600).setHeight(50);
// Example positioning

  const bodyShape = slide.insertTextBox("This presentation
provides an update on the project.");
  bodyShape.setLeft(100).setTop(150).setWidth(600).
setHeight(100); // Example positioning
}
```

Explanation: This function gets the currently active presentation. It inserts a new slide at index 1 (the second slide) using **`presentation.insertSlide(1)`**. It then inserts two text boxes using **`slide.insertTextBox()`**, setting their text content and example positioning using methods such as **`setLeft()`**, **`setTop()`**, **`setWidth()`**, and **`setHeight()`**.

Section 8: Google Docs Automation (DocumentApp)

Creating a Document:

```
function createMeetingNotesDocument() {
  const documentTitle = "Meeting Notes";
  const document = DocumentApp.create(documentTitle);
  Logger.log(`Document '${documentTitle}' created with ID:
${document.getId()}`);
}
```

Explanation: This function uses **`DocumentApp.create("Meeting Notes")`** to create a new Google Doc with the specified title. It then logs the ID of the newly created document.

Adding Text and Formatting:

```
function addAttendeesParagraph() {
  const doc = DocumentApp.getActiveDocument();
  const body = doc.getBody();
  const attendeesText = "Attendees: [List of Attendees]";
  const paragraph = body.appendParagraph(attendeesText);
  const start = attendeesText.indexOf("Attendees:");
  const end = start + "Attendees:".length;
  paragraph.editAsText().setBold(start, end, true);
}
```

Explanation: This function gets the active Google Doc and its body. It appends a new paragraph with the text "**`Attendees: [List of Attendees]`**". It then uses **`editAsText().setBold(start, end, true)`** to apply bold formatting to the substring "**`Attendees:`**" within the paragraph. It calculates the **`start`** and **`end`** indices of the word "**`Attendees:`**" to apply the formatting correctly.

Section 9: Triggers

Simple Trigger:

A simple **`onEdit`** trigger could be used in Google Sheets to automatically format a cell when a specific value is entered. For example, if a user enters the word "**`Completed`**" in column C, the **`onEdit`** trigger could automatically change the background color of that cell to green.

Limitations of Simple Triggers:

- **Limited Scope:** They are limited to the document they are bound to.
- **Specific Events:** They can only respond to certain simple events such as **`onOpen`**, **`onEdit`**, and **`onFormSubmit`** (for bound forms).
- **User Restrictions:** They run under the authorization of the user who triggered the event.
- **Runtime Limits:** They have shorter execution time limits compared to installable triggers.
- **Service Restrictions:** They cannot access services that require authorization unless the user explicitly authorizes the script through a custom menu or by running a function directly. For example, they cannot typically send emails using GmailApp without prior authorization.

Installable Trigger: An installable time-driven trigger would be necessary if you need to run a script at a specific time each day to perform a task that requires authorization or has a longer runtime. For example, a script that automatically generates a daily summary report from a Google Sheet and emails it to a distribution list using GmailApp would require an installable time-driven trigger.

Benefits over Simple Triggers:

- **Authorization:** Installable triggers run under the authorization of the user who set them up, even if another user opens or edits the document. This allows them to access services requiring authorization (for example, GmailApp) without each user needing to authorize the script.
- **Flexibility:** They can be set up for various time-driven schedules (for example, daily at a specific time, hourly, weekly, monthly) and for a wider range of event-driven triggers (for example, **`onChange`** in Sheets, **`onFormSubmit`** for stand-alone forms, calendar event updates).
- **Longer Runtime:** They generally have longer allowed execution times compared to simple triggers, making them suitable for more complex tasks.
- **Programmatic Management:** Installable triggers can be created, deleted, and managed programmatically using the **`ScriptApp`** service.

Programmatic Trigger Management: To create an installable **`onFormSubmit`** trigger programmatically:

a. **Get the Form Object:** Obtain a reference to the Google Form using **`FormApp.getActiveForm()`** (if the script is bound) or **`FormApp.openById('your_form_id')`** (if stand-alone).

b. **Use `ScriptApp.newTrigger()`:** Use the **`ScriptApp.newTrigger('yourFunctionName')`** method to start building a new trigger, where

'yourFunctionName' is the name of the Apps Script function you want to run when the form is submitted.

c. **Specify the Event Source:** Use the **forForm(form)** method, passing in the form object obtained in step 1, to associate the trigger with the specific form.

d. **Specify the Event Type:** Use the **onFormSubmit()** method to specify that the trigger should fire when a form submission occurs.

e. **Create the Trigger:** Finally, use the **create()** method to create and save the installable trigger.

```
function createFormSubmitTrigger() {
  const form = FormApp.getActiveForm();
  ScriptApp.newTrigger('processFormSubmission') // Function to
run on submit
      .forForm(form)
      .onFormSubmit()
      .create();
  Logger.log('Form submit trigger created for function process-
FormSubmission');
}

    // You would also need to define the function 'processForm
Submission'
function processFormSubmission(e) {
  // Your code to process the form submission data (in the 'e'
event object)
  Logger.log('Form submitted!');
}
```

Section 10: User Interfaces (UIs)

Custom Menu:

```
function onOpen() {
  SpreadsheetApp.getUi()
      .createMenu('Automation Tools')
      .addItem('Run Script', 'myAutomatedFunction')
      .addToUi();
}

function myAutomatedFunction() {
  const ui = SpreadsheetApp.getUi();
  ui.alert('Your automated function has been executed.');
  Logger.log('myAutomatedFunction executed.');
}
```

Explanation: The **onOpen()** function is a simple trigger that automatically runs when the Google Sheet is opened. It uses **SpreadsheetApp.getUi()** to get the user interface environment for the spreadsheet. It then creates a new menu named "**Automation Tools**" using **createMenu()** and adds a menu item named "**Run Script**" that will execute the function **myAutomatedFunction** when clicked using **addItem()**. Finally, **addToUi()** adds the menu to the spreadsheet's user interface. The **myAutomatedFunction()** is a placeholder function that simply displays a message box.

HTML Service: Basic Dialog

Code.gs:

```
function showInformationDialog() {
  const html = HtmlService.createHtmlOutputFromFile('dialog')
      .setWidth(300)
      .setHeight(150);
  SpreadsheetApp.getUi().showModalDialog(html, 'Information');
}
```

Dialog.html:

```
<!DOCTYPE html>
<html>
<head>
  <title>Information</title>
</head>
<body>
  <p>This is a message from a dialog.</p>
</body>
</html>
```

Explanation: In **Code.gs**, the **showInformationDialog()** function uses **HtmlService.createHtmlOutputFromFile('dialog')** to load the content of the **dialog.html** file. **setWidth(300)** and **setHeight(150)** set the dimensions of the dialog. Finally, **SpreadsheetApp.getUi().showModalDialog(html, 'Information')** displays the HTML content as a modal dialog with the title "**Information**" in the Google Sheet.

Section 11: Web Apps

Basic Web App:

```
function doGet(e) {
  return HtmlService.createHtmlOutput('<h1>Welcome to my basic
web app!</h1>');
}
```

Explanation: The **doGet(e)** function is a reserved function name in Google Apps Script that is executed when the web app receives an HTTP GET request. This function uses

HtmlService.createHtmlOutput() to generate an HTML output containing a simple **<h1>** heading with the text "**Welcome to my basic web app!**".

Accessing the Web App: To access this web app, you would need to deploy the Google Apps Script project as a web app. You would do this by: Clicking on "**Deploy**" in the script editor. Selecting "**New deployment**". Under "**Select type**", choose "**Web app**". Configure the "**Execute as**" and "**Who has access**" settings appropriately (e.g., "**Me (your_email@example.com)**" and "**Anyone with the link**"). Click "**Deploy**". Google Apps Script will provide you with a unique URL for your web app. You can access the web app by opening this URL in a web browser.

Section 12: APIs and Web Hooks (Conceptual)

Using `UrlFetchApp`:

The basic steps involved in making an HTTP GET request to an external API using **UrlFetchApp** are:

1. **Specify the API Endpoint URL:** Determine the URL of the API endpoint you want to access.
2. **Use `UrlFetchApp.fetch()`:** Call the **UrlFetchApp.fetch(url)** method, passing in the API endpoint URL as the argument. This will send an HTTP GET request to the specified URL.
3. **Get the Response:** The **fetch()** method returns a **HTTPResponse** object containing the API's response.
4. **Handle the Response:** You typically need to process the **HTTPResponse** object to extract the data sent back by the API. Common steps include:
   a. Getting the content as a string using **response.getContentText()**.
   b. Parsing the content if it is in a structured format like JSON using **JSON.parse(response.getContentText())**.
   c. Checking the HTTP status code of the response using **response.getResponseCode()** to ensure the request was successful (e.g., a 200 OK status).
   d. Handling potential errors or different status codes as needed.

The purpose of handling the response is to extract the useful data provided by the API and use it within your Google Apps Script for further processing or automation tasks.

Web Hooks: A **web hook** is a mechanism that allows one application to send real-time information to another application whenever a specific event occurs. Instead of the receiving application constantly polling the sending application for updates, the sending application pushes the data to a pre-configured URL (the web hook URL) when the event happens.

A potential use case for integrating a web hook with Google Apps Script could be to automatically update a Google Sheet whenever a new customer order is placed in an e-commerce platform. The e-commerce platform could be configured to send a web hook request containing the order details to a Google Apps Script web app URL every time a new order is created. The Google Apps Script would then parse the incoming data and add a new row to the Google Sheet with the order information.

The Google Apps Script function typically used to handle incoming web hook requests is **`doPost(e)`**. When an application sends data to a web hook URL using an HTTP POST request, the **`doPost(e)`** function in the deployed Google Apps Script web app is executed, and the event object **`e`** contains the data sent in the request (e.g., in **`e.postData.contents`**).

Conclusion

You have now completed the practical exercises in this concluding chapter. Working through these challenges should have provided you with a valuable opportunity to apply and integrate the various Google Apps Script concepts and services discussed throughout this book. Remember that the key to mastering Google Apps Script lies in consistent practice and experimentation.

The possibilities with Google Apps Script are vast and continue to evolve. As you move forward, we encourage you to:

- **Continue Experimenting:** Do not hesitate to try out new ideas and explore the capabilities of the different Apps Script services.
- **Consult the Documentation:** The official Google Apps Script documentation (https://developers.google.com/apps-script) is an invaluable resource for detailed information and advanced features.
- **Engage with the Community:** Online forums and communities can be great places to ask questions, share your projects, and learn from other developers.
- **Build Real-World Solutions:** The best way to solidify your skills is by working on projects that solve real problems or automate tasks that you or others perform regularly.

We hope this book has provided you with a strong foundation in modern Google Apps Script development and has inspired you to leverage its power to enhance your productivity and create innovative solutions within the Google Workspace ecosystem.

Happy scripting!

Key Terms

- **Hypertext Markup Language (HTML):** Implements the **structure** of web pages.
- **Cascading Style Sheets (CSS):** Styles web pages with **layouts, fonts, colors**, and so on.
- **JavaScript:** Makes the web pages **interactive** for the end user. In Google Apps Script, JavaScript can also **manipulate spreadsheets, documents, forms, emails, Google Drive files, and all other Google Workspace applications.**
- **Integrated Development Environment (IDE):** A **text editor for code packed with valuable tools**. Google Apps Script comes with a free IDE accessible by navigating to https://script.google.com and clicking "`New Project`". The IDE includes features such as **code highlighting, autocomplete, a powerful search tool, a debugger, access to libraries, event-driven triggers, an execution log, and customizable settings**.
- **Function:** A **block of code** that performs a specific task. When you start a new project in Google Apps Script, the IDE greets you with an empty function named `myFunction`.
- **Execution Log:** A tool that permits developers to **print messages visible exclusively to them** and helps monitor the state of the application.
- **Comments: Blocks of text within your code that are not executed** but are purely descriptive annotations designed to provide clarity to human readers.
- **Object:** Robust **collections of data comprising properties and methods. Properties are akin to variables, and methods are akin to functions** but encompassed in their own structure with a slightly different syntax.
- **Dot Notation:** The method used to **interact with the properties and methods of an object**. The `Logger.log()` syntax is an example of dot notation, where `Logger` is an object and `log()` is its method.
- **Array:** A **special variable type designed to hold a list of values**. These values, known as **elements**, each have an assigned **index starting from 0**. Elements within a JavaScript array can be of **different types**, including strings, numbers, booleans, null values, undefined, symbols, and even other arrays or objects.
- **Scope:** Determines **where in your script a variable is accessible**. There are primarily three types of scope in JavaScript: **Global Scope** (variables declared outside a function), **Function Scope** (variables declared within a function), and **Block Scope** (a scope defined within curly braces).

Index

Symbols

A

B

C

D

E

F

G

H

I

R

S